THE LABOUR OF READING

THE SOCIETY OF BIBLICAL LITERATURE
SEMEIA STUDIES

Series Editors
Danna Nolan Fewell
Fred W. Burnett

Number 36
THE LABOUR OF READING
Desire, Alienation, and
Biblical Interpretation

edited by
Fiona C. Black
Roland Boer
Erin Runions

THE LABOUR OF READING
Desire, Alienation, and Biblical Interpretation

edited by
Fiona C. Black
Roland Boer
Erin Runions

The essays in this volume are presented
in honour of
Robert C. Culley
at the time of his retirement.

Society of Biblical Literature
Atlanta, Georgia

THE LABOUR OF READING
Desire, Alienation, and
Biblical Interpretation

edited by
Fiona C. Black
Roland Boer
Erin Runions

Cover art by Shelagh Culley
Cover design by Mary Vachon

Library of Congress Cataloging-in-Publication Data

The labour of reading : desire, alienation, and biblical interpretation /
edited by Fiona C. Black, Roland Boer, Erin Runions.
    p. cm.— (The Society of Biblical Literature Semeia studies)
    Includes bibliographical references and indexes.
    ISBN 0-88414-011-3 (pbk. : alk. paper)
    1. Bible —Criticism, interpretation, etc. I. Title: Labour of reading.
II. Culley, Robert C. III. Black, Fiona C. IV. Boer, Roland, 1961–
V. Runions, Erin.

BS531 .L33 1999
220.6 21—dc21
                                    99-044174

08 07 06 05 04 03 02 01 00 99   5 4 3 2 1

Printed in the United States of America
on acid-free paper

∞

TABLE OF CONTENTS

PART 2: WRITERS, POWER AND THE ALIENATION OF LABOUR

ABBREVIATIONS

AB	Anchor Bible
AGJU	Arbeiten zur Geschichte des antiken Judentums und des Urchristentums
AnBib	Analecta Biblica
ATD	Das Alte Testament Deutsch
BA	*Biblical Archaeologist*
BET	Beiträge zur evangelischen Theologie
Bib	*Biblica*
BibInt	*Biblical Interpretation*
BJS	Brown Judaic Studies
BKAT	Biblischer Kommentar: Altes Testament
BN	*Biblische Notizen*
BT	*The Bible Translator*
BZ	*Biblische Zeitschrift*
EstBib	*Estudios bíblicos*
FOTL	Forms of the Old Testament Literature
HAR	*Hebrew Annual Review*
HKAT	Handkommentar zum alten Testament
HSM	Harvard Semitic Monographs
HTR	*Harvard Theological Review*
HUCA	*Hebrew Union College Annual*
ICC	International Critical Commentary
IOSOT	International Organization for the Study of the Old Testament
Int	*Interpretation*
JAAR	*Journal of the American Academy of Religion*
JAOS	*Journal of the American Oriental Society*
JBL	*Journal of Biblical Literature*

JFSR	*Journal of Feminist Studies in Religion*
JNES	*Journal of Near Eastern Studies*
JNSL	*Journal of Northwest Semitic Languages*
JSNT	*Journal for the Study of the New Testament*
JSNTSup	Journal for the Study of the New Testament Supplement Series
JSOT	*Journal for the Study of the Old Testament*
JSOTSup	Journal for the Study of the Old Testament Supplement Series
JTS	*Journal of Theological Studies*
NCBC	New Century Bible Commentary
NICOT	New International Commentary on the Old Testament
NovTSup	Novum Testamentum Supplements
NRT	*La nouvelle revue théologique*
OBT	Overtures to Biblical Theology
OTL	Old Testament Library
PTMS	Pittsburgh Theological Monograph Series
SBLDS	Society of Biblical Literature Dissertation Series
SBLEJL	Society of Biblical Literature Early Judaism and Its Literature
SBLRBS	Society of Biblical Literature Resources for Biblical Study
SBS	Stuttgarter Bibelstudien
SEÅ	*Svensk exegetisk årsbok*
SJSJ	Supplements to the Journal for the Study of Judaism
SR	*Studies in Religion/Sciences religieuses*
ST	*Studia Theologica*
TU	Texte und Untersuchungen
VT	*Vetus Testamentum*
VTSup	Vetus Testamentum Supplements
ZAH	*Zeitschrift für Althebraistik*
ZAW	*Zeitschrift für die alttestamentliche Wissenschaft*
ZBAT	Zürcher Bibelkommentare/Altes Tastament
ZNW	Zeitschrift für die neutestamentliche Wissenschaft

PREFACE

There is a very personal dimension to a volume like this, in which we want to register our thanks and appreciation for the work of Robert Culley as teacher, scholar, colleague and friend. That it has been possible to produce a volume whose theme—the labour of reading—expresses what we have found to be a fitting description of his life's work has been deeply satisfying. And it is entirely fitting that this collection of essays should appear in *Semeia Studies*, given the deep involvement that Robert has had with the journal *Semeia* and *Semeia Studies* itself.

It is some two and a half years since the first discussions were held amongst us about the possibilities of producing a collection of essays to celebrate Robert Culley's work upon his retirement as Professor from the Faculty of Religious Studies at McGill University. Each of us had been or was still working with Robert in some capacity or other. Since then we have worked together in various ways on this project, mostly through endless emails between Montreal (Erin), Sheffield (Fiona) and Sydney (Roland), but also by international telephone linkups and meetings at San Francisco, Orlando, and finally Montreal in the last northern summer of the millennium. The project was a mix of laughter, disagreements, beer, wine, endless bananas, the occasional cigarette, and of course, good friendship.

Along the way there have been some people who have lent the project their invaluable assistance. Chris Kelm was a most energetic participant who was instrumental in the early stages of the task. Sasha Culley, Robert's partner, discussed with us the volume as a whole, but especially the art work of their daughter, Shelagh, that is found on the front cover. We owe a particular debt to Shelagh herself, for allowing us to reproduce her work on a book that honours her father's work.

Danna Fewell and Fred Burnett, the editors of *Semeia Studies*, encouraged us throughout the process, ensuring the success of the volume at those stages beyond our control. Michael Bradley at Scholars Press was a most helpful editor at the press itself, seeing the volume through to its final printing. Other support was also crucial: the United Theological College in Sydney assisted with Roland's travel costs to Montreal for the last rush in July 1999, and the Faculty of Religious Studies at McGill provided administrative assistance. In particular, Samieun Khan, with her distinctive mastery and skillful application of the tasks of editing, type setting and production of Camera Ready Copy, eased the burden, especially of the last days, and ensured that we were on time with a calm expertise that kept us all sane. Finally, we thank Robert Culley, for the warm personality that has made this project a pleasurable labour for the three of us.

July 1999
Montreal

Fiona Black
Roland Boer
Erin Runions

INTRODUCTION

There is something arcane and esoteric, simultaneously contractual and deeply personal, about the relation between teacher and pupil, as there is about the web of interactions and associations of intellectuals. A segment of those relations rises to the surface in a volume such as this, whose essays cohere around the theme of the "labour of reading." That both the celebration of a person and the theme intersect with each other should come as no surprise for those who know Robert C. Culley, Professor Post-Retirement at the Faculty of Religious Studies, McGill University. Robert's work is marked by thinking through intersections: of biblical text and theory, of particular themes and larger structures, of hermeneutic and interpretative practices. Thus in this volume, honouring Robert's work and marking his retirement from McGill University, we find person, theme and biblical text woven together, much like the tapestry that adorns the cover of the book.

The Labour of Reading

With Robert's disciplined and rigorous reading of texts in mind, we gave contributors from across Canada and the world the theme, "the labour of reading," and asked them to produce readings in recognition and celebration of the important contribution that Robert has made to the discipline of biblical studies. The result is a collection of essays, intricately varied and inter-related, that read the biblical text (in good Culleian fashion) on a number of levels (theological, ideological, historical, psychoanalytical, political, poetic, feminist etc.). And while at times, as editors, we might have found ourselves perplexed, wondering how the pieces would all fit together, we have discovered that even the most diverse (perhaps even conflicting) interpretative methods and levels of reading are woven together by the threads of the biblical text and the theme of laborious reading.

Moreover, configured here together, these essays have drawn our editorial eye to "the labour of reading" on another level, by illuminating the complex relation between labour, pleasure, desire, alienation and action. Thus just as text and method are mutually informing in the Culleian style of reading, so too are the essays and the theme in this volume. We find that all of the papers fall, broadly speaking, into the subthematics of desire or pleasure and alienation, focusing either on the pleasure, longing and play produced by the biblical text, or on the alienation of the writers and readers of the biblical text. Not surprisingly these subthemes, quite apart from the intention of the contributors, reveal the logic of labour that is woven into the cultural fabric of late capitalist society within which this volume is produced. That is, the desire and pleasure inherent to the logic of labour and production, the yearning for that which is just beyond reach, often give way in the power relations that govern production, to alienation. Alienation ultimately provokes some kind of response, be this writing, or some other form of action that alleviates the alienating circumstances. Reading all of these relations together, labour can be understood as much more than simply hard work; it can also be seen as a complicated and driving force that moves readers through a range of emotions, responses, and practices.

We have therefore organized the volume in two sections. The first, Pleasurable Labour/Laborious Pleasure, groups texts that cele- brate the pleasure and desire described and provoked in readers by the poetics and structures of the biblical text. This is followed by a second section, Writers, Power and the Alienation of Labour, which groups texts that deal with alienated writers and readers of biblical texts, and the responses that this alienation prompts, whether that be made manifest in textual rhetoric or in readerly practice. The papers are by no means statically fixed within these groupings, since many of them explore both pleasure and alienation in some way or another. Rather, the interplay between these sides of labour is (yet again) mutually informing, and runs throughout the volume.

Pleasurable Labour/Laborious Pleasure

The volume's collective consideration of pleasure produced by the Culleian style of careful, laborious reading begins with papers by Landy and Black which celebrate the pleasure of the text. Landy's piece looks at the pleasure invoked by the poetics of the mystic and mystifying image of the Seraph in the Hebrew Bible; his own style, moving between a lyrical main text and detailed footnote, provides a distinct enjoyment. Black looks at what it is within the Song of Songs that arouses readers' sexual desire for the text itself, and how this desire both mirrors the desire between the lover and beloved in the text, and is reflected in commentators' fantasies about the text.

These reflections on textual pleasure are followed by papers which take up, in one way or another (as do Black and Landy), desire as a rhetorical strategy with which the text implicates readers and urges certain kinds of identifications. The grouping begins with Reinhartz, Exum and Robinson who all read the Song, by itself (Exum) or in conjunction with other texts (Reinhartz, Robinson). Reinhartz, reading the Song intertextually with John 20 to illumine the erotics of the Johannine text, writes of believers' desire for intimacy with the risen Christ, as urged by the desire of Mary Magdalene—herself a disciple—for Jesus in the garden. This kind of multileveled desire provoked by text is explored in an entirely different way in Exum's consideration of the structural formation of desire and consummation in the Song, and the subtle and multifarious ways in which sexual longing and consummation take place there. Such poetic and structural pleasures can also be, and indeed often are, understood on the theological level, and it is this relation—between theology and poetics—that is taken up in Robinson's exhortations to readers to hear and respond to the desire for God in Genesis, the Song, Hosea and Lamentations. Slater's paper rounds out this group of essays (and provides a transition into the next), considering the way in which Deuteronomy 1–3 positions the reader to desire the promised land, and (foreshadowing the alienating side of labour here) the discomfort of certain kinds of readers with respect to this identification.

The desire for bodies, God and land invoked by the biblical text becomes the twentieth-century desire for (holy) land, as shown in the papers by Gunn and Long. Both look at the continual desire and yearning for land, which fuels the need to stake out territory, or continually to make new territory; this is made doubly interesting in the authors' choices to read texts as they appear in media that "create" spaces: in the early twentieth century, stereoscopes (Long), and in the late twentieth century, the yet unstaked internet (Gunn). The biblical text, as Gunn points out, is powerful enough in its poetics to fuel the Zionist movement, both religiously and politically. But, as Long and Slater both indicate, this desire for tangible, grounded, governable holiness moves quickly to alienation (in the case of Slater, from points of identification urged by the text; in the case of Long, from the "real" land and its inhabitants). Long's paper as the last in the first section, then, traces the movement from desire through labour or production to alienation.

Writers, Power and the Alienation of Labour

Thus the second section begins with Boer's paper which fittingly takes up the movement from desire to alienation, in the figuration of the "theft of enjoyment," when the object of desire, or the fantasy object (the king) becomes the figure of alienating power relations, a drain on resources and a despised display of self-indulgence. The papers that follow are also concerned with the alienating Israelite power relations at play in the production of the text. Jobling's paper looks at the alienation of an autonomous and political woman in 2 Kings 4–8 as a signal of the forgetting of an egalitarian past, emergent class struggles and increasing alliance between prophets and kings. Niditch's paper looks at the complexities of power relations that are revealed by looking carefully at the variations in, and combinations of, the traditional material and formulas found in Judges 1. And Gottwald's paper brings all these themes together, looking through the lens of Icelandic political history and its relation to Icelandic literature onto the manifestations in ancient Israelite literature of the ongoing reaction to centralized politics and the oppression of hierarchy.

As the next three papers show, the specific alienation of the writer is manifested through rhetorical attempts to urge an identification of the reader with the alienated context in which the text was produced. Van Seters shows how alienation by northen Israelite religious practices manifests itself in a badly written piece of anti-

Samaritan propaganda in 1 Kings 13. Crossan's paper compares early Christian texts (the *Q Gospel*, *Didache*, and the *Shepherd of Hermas*), and finds that the correspondences there show how tense economic and class relations within the early Christian community manifests itself in textual imperatives to redistribute wealth.

But if these papers show the rhetorical expression of alienation, the next three papers show that perhaps sometimes the rhetoric of the text works a little too well, leaving readers alienated or even dead, as is aptly pointed out in Phillips's discussion of the genocidal impulses of Matthean rhetoric, and the continued influence of these impulses into twentieth-century entertainment and warfare. Milne's paper, too, takes up the debilitating long term effects of certain kinds of biblical reading, in her discussion of patriarchal alienation of women in late Hebrew texts, such as Judith and Ben Sira, and the reasons for which patriarchal reading has continued on into the contemporary period. Such readerly alienation is taken to its logical conclusion (if the logic is at all Marxist) in Runions's consideration of the possibility of oppression lurking behind the utopic world order presented in Micah and the movement toward a more militant political stance produced by this possibility.

Finally, Greenstein's paper brings us full circle to pleasure, not only because it is a pleasure to read with its two columned chiasmic structure, but because it offers a reading of Job that considers first Job's alienation (from God and from the reader) then resolves this alienation, not by humiliating Job through repentant capitulation, but by restoring Job's integrity and autonomy. Thus Greenstein's piece moves away from alienation and leads us back to the pleasure of the text, and the pleasure of reading.

In all of these papers we see the capacity of the biblical text to provoke pleasure and alienation, and equally, of readers both to respond to and resist these kinds of pleasures and alienations. We also see reading strategies that are laborious in another way: in resisting facile and habitual readerly identifications with various elements in the text, such strategies, through wary and thorough reading, find something both new and liberatory. Further, having thought through labour in this way, guided by this collection of papers, we are more aware of the ideological contours of labour, and are more able to recognize our own implication in its logic. This means that rigorous and detailed reading practice is able to illuminate presuppositions in readers themselves. Such an awareness of interpretive stance and presupposition can, in turn, only facilitate a new impulse to attentive, perceptive and creative reading of biblical texts. And this is precisely what Robert Culley himself carries out in his work.

The Work of Robert Culley

Academic Career

Robert Culley was born 1932, in Toronto, Canada, where he lived most of his life until he moved to Montreal. He did an honours Bachelor of Arts in oriental languages at the University of Toronto, in what is now the Department of Near Eastern Studies. He then went on to do a Master of Arts there, while at the same time completing a Bachelor of Divinity at Knox College, University of Toronto. A propensity for language and a liking for the Hebrew Bible led him to continue on to do doctoral studies at the University of Toronto, during which time he spent two years in Germany at the University at Bonn, working with Martin Noth. Upon completion of the Ph.D. in 1963, he was offered a position at McGill University, where he began teaching in the fall of 1964. He held the position as Professor of Old Testament there until his retirement in 1996.

During his career Robert has contributed greatly to the organizational development of biblical studies both in Canada and internationally, through work with the Canadian Society of Biblical Studies and the Society of Biblical Literature. His work in these societies has been consistent and diverse. Although it would be impossible to list all of his involvements on this level, some of his major contributions should be noted here. Robert was actively involved with the Canadian Society for Biblical Studies (CSBS) for most of his career. He served as Executive Secretary for six years near the beginning of his career (1969–1975), and for most of that time and a little beyond, he was a member of the Board of Directors of the Canadian Corporation for Studies in Religion (1970–1978). He also served as President of CSBS from 1981–1982. Concurrent with his involvement with the CSBS, he worked, for much of his career, in various capacities with the Society of Biblical Literature (SBL). Along with many shorter term commitments, he was member of the Council of the SBL from 1979–1982, a member of the Research and Publications Committee of the SBL from

1989–1992, and he is currently the chair of the Nominating Committee of the SBL.

Robert has also, through his editorial involvements, been a major influence on some of the newer directions that biblical scholarship is now taking. Most notably, his interest in theory and in reading prompted him to take the initiative, with others, to start a forum for new and more experimental kinds of biblical interpretation. The forum that Robert and his colleagues initiated, the journal *Semeia*, has been immensely successful and influential, especially for younger biblical scholars. Robert was a founding associate editor of *Semeia* from 1974–1979 and then general editor from 1986–1992. Over the last 25 years, he has also edited and co-edited a number of *Semeia* volumes, on several important methodological issues (see 1975a, 1976b, 1979, 1981a, 1993a, 1995). In addition, he has contributed to the development of the Semeia Studies Series, both through serving on the *Semeia* board, and through contributing to the high quality of the series with two books published there (1976a, 1992).

Teaching and Research

Robert's work as teacher and scholar, has been and is characterized by an emphasis on the importance of the continued labour of scholarship and interpretation. Whereas Robert's theoretical reflection is both subtle and concise, his interest is primarily in the task of interpretation, in how theory works in the reading of texts. The test of any theory or literary approach, for Robert, is in whether it assists in the production of plausible new angles on the biblical text in question. Thus, his continued interest in newer directions in biblical studies and his willingness to explore new kinds of interpretive strategies have always been subject to close reading of the text. Indeed, it is his insistence on the need to work with the text, as well as the important role of the text in influencing the critical theories and approaches that are used to interpret it, that has led us to choose the "labour of reading" as a cohesive theme for his work and this volume.

Robert's approach in teaching, especially with his graduate students, was similar, and the high standards he set for this sort of labour were those he imposed on himself. When teaching, Robert would always say to his students that what counts is working with the text. His model for teaching and research was Martin Noth, with whom he worked in Germany. Noth would lead his classes and seminars with nothing but the Hebrew Bible before him, reading the text closely, working hard at each word and phrase. Graduate seminars with Robert were always like this: an open text, be it biblical or theoretical, followed by careful discussion. Where students would want to rush through, Robert would ask the most exacting and perceptive questions. Likewise, his thesis supervision is marked, often exasperatingly, by meticulously thorough questioning of what students have written. What counts for Robert, in other words, is the labour of reading itself.

In his own research and writing, Robert has maintained an emphasis on careful reading of text, enhanced by consideration of various interpretative strategies. Though he has moved between poetry and prose, between the Psalms and Hebrew narrative, he has always engaged in careful examination of the patterns, structures and features of the text.

His interest in both text and method began with his Ph.D. dissertation (1967) on variations in the formulaic language in the Psalms as crucial signals about the way such traditional material was being adapted. Here he was influenced by work being done in folklore studies, particularly that of Vladimir Propp on the Russian Folktale and A. B. Lord on Homeric literature. His interest in folklore studies was the start of a continuing concern with the interweaving between oral and written literature, and the way oral literature leaves its marks in the written, particularly when the transition between the two is highly fluid.

After the publication of his dissertation, he moved to consider the patterns and structures of various narratives in the Hebrew Bible. Here again he used Propp and a structuralist approach to inform his work. This was not so much the "high" structuralism of Greimas or Levi-Strauss—although Robert remains keenly interested in their work—as much as an approach that allows the text to play a large role in establishing the structures, rather than imposing onto it a universal pattern of deep structures. He was not willing to go as far as Propp, for instance, in arguing for a single, uniform pattern for all the narratives of the Hebrew Bible. He preferred to isolate distinct story types, patterns and transitions and the variations that may be found in those patterns. Two monographs and a series of essays were devoted to these explorations (see 1972b, 1974, 1975b, 1976a, 1978a, 1980a, 1980b, 1985b, 1990, 1992).

More recently Robert has returned to the Psalms, seeking to develop a reading of the Psalms that is informed by his study of Hebrew narrative, but one which is, once again, sensitive to the features of the text, in this case Hebrew poetry. In this work he takes account of the various types of Psalms, the different uses of the pool of images, motifs and also narrative patterns—for instance those of suffering and rescue—that combined make up the poetics of the Psalms (see 1988, 1991, 1993b, 1994b, and his monograph, *The Figure of the Sufferer in the Complaint Psalms*, in progress).

The other dimension that has returned again and again in Robert's work is the mutual interaction between text and method. This appears in his deliberations on the different ways of reading biblical texts (see 1963, 1972a, 1972b, 1974, 1976b, 1976d, 1978b, 1981a, 1982, 1985b, 1992, 1993a, 1995). For Robert, texts can be read by adapting existing methods that have been used elsewhere before being applied to the study of biblical text, or by allowing the biblical text to critique or inform a theoretical method. The approaches which Robert tends to find most useful are those that are open to the determining role of the text in the way that it is read: the picking up of hints and guidelines for the reader, as it were, in the process of reading.

But there is also a more comprehensive schema to his deliberations on text and interpretation, and that is the whole notion of levels of reading that he continues to explore (see 1992). Thus, the structures of Hebrew narrative and poetry that he has examined over the years constitute but one level at which a text may be read. At another level are those questions and answers that lead to the formulations of source, form, history and redaction. On such a level the text is read as both composite and traditional, prompting a consideration of the many traditions, both oral and written, that feed into the final composite text. A further level is interested in the text as a unity, as something that should be read as an intricate unit whose meaning can only be explicated with regard for compositional intricacy and finesse. At yet another level may be found the readings of the Bible as problematic, provoking difficult questions of gender and sexuality (feminism and queer theory), emancipatory politics (Marxism and postcolonialism), the unitary subject and structures themselves (poststructuralism), loss of depth and an explosion of surfaces (postmodernism), economics and culture (cultural and ideological criticism) and so on. A final level may be located at the religious itself, for the Bible is read in various faith communities, as a text that has some form of sanction for the singular and collective religious life. These levels are by no means exhaustive, but they show the range of readings to which Robert is open, as well as the kinds of presuppositions to which he is attentive when interacting with other biblical scholars. What is interesting is that not only do these levels provide a theoretical framework for Robert's continual interest in the promise of the new, but that they also find themselves woven together by the text itself, forming a tapestry whose connection lies in the text they seek to interpret, no matter how conflictual such methods may be to one another.

What better way then, but to start the volume with a tapestry (cover art) by Robert's daughter Shelagh Culley. We have chosen this piece because it speaks to the artistic side of Robert—who is himself a fine painter, as any visitor to the Culleys' home will discover—doubtless one of the reasons he is constantly interested in the new and the creative in biblical studies. The tapestry is a figure for the kinds of diverse readings that are woven together in this volume. Moreover, this weaving represents for us the creative process of interpreting biblical texts, along with the attendant pleasures (and frustrations) of producing creative ideas and readings. For Shelagh this hanging was a daunting project, as it was the most ambitious she has done to date. She took a blank canvas and a box of coloured wools and began creating, filling in small bits of colour here, and large patches there, in a seemingly random fashion that perturbed her onlooking parents. Yet she brought all these colourful shapes into a beautifully intricate and integrated composition of form and colour. As former students of Robert, we the editors feel that the piece is analogous at some level to Robert's willingness, in supervising, to give his students a blank page and some texts, to ask exacting questions of seemingly formless work which, with perseverance, gives way to creative and thorough readings of biblical texts.

So, we offer this volume—with Robert's inspiration at its base —as a creative labour of reading, a tapestry of biblical text and interpretive strategy woven through the pleasure and alienation of careful and laborious reading. To Robert Culley, our mentor and model: a great reader of texts.

Bibliography
Robert C. Culley

Monographs

1967	*Oral Formulaic Language in the Biblical Psalms*. Near and Middle East Series 4. Toronto: University of Toronto Press.
1976a	*Studies in the Structure of Hebrew Narrative*. Semeia Supplements. Missoula: Scholars Press; Philadelphia: Fortress.
1992	*Themes and Variations: A Study of Action in Biblical Narrative*. Semeia Studies. Atlanta: Scholars Press.
In progress	*The Figure of the Sufferer in the Complaint Psalms*.

Volumes Edited and Co-edited

1975a	*Classical Hebrew Narrative. Semeia* 3.
1976b	*Oral Tradition and Old Testament Studies. Semeia* 5.
1979	*Perspectives on Old Testament Narrative. Semeia* 15.
1981a	Ed. with Thomas W. Overholt, *Anthropological Perspectives on Old Testament Prophecy. Semeia* 21.
1993a	Ed. with Robert B. Robinson. *Textual Determinacy, Part One. Semeia* 62.
1994a	Ed. with William Klempa. *The Three Loves: Philosophy, Theology, World Religions. Essays in Honour of Joseph C. McLelland*. McGill Studies in Religion. Atlanta: Scholars Press.
1995	Ed. with Robert B. Robinson. *Textual Determinacy, Part Two. Semeia* 71.

Articles and Chapters in Volumes

1963	"An Approach to the Problem of Oral Tradition." *VT* 13:113–25.
1970	"Metrical Analysis of Classical Hebrew Poetry." Pp. 12–28 in *Essays on the Ancient Semitic World*. Ed. J. W. Wevers and D. B. Redford. Toronto Semitic Texts and Studies. Toronto: University of Toronto Press.
1972a	"Oral Tradition and Historicity." Pp. 102–16 in *Studies on the Ancient Palestinian World*. Ed. J. W. Wevers and D. B. Redford. Toronto Semitic Texts and Studies. Toronto: University of Toronto Press.
1972b	"Some Comments on Structural Analysis and Biblical Studies." Pp. 129–42 in *Congress Volume: Uppsala 1971*. VTSup 22. Leiden: Brill.
1974	"Structural Analysis: Is It Done with Mirrors?" *Int* 28:165–81.
1975b	"Themes and Variations in Three Groups of Old Testament Narratives." *Semeia* 3:3–13.

1976c   "Oral Tradition and Old Testament Studies." *Semeia* 5:1–33.
1976d   "Response to Daniel Patte." Pp. 151–58 in *Semiology and Parables.* Ed. Daniel Patte. PTMS 9. Pittsburgh: Pickwick.
1978a   "Action Sequences in Gen 2–3." Pp. 51–60 in *Seminar Papers: Society of Biblical Literature, 1978.* Ed. Paul J. Achtemeier. Missoula: Scholars Press.
1978b   "Analyse altestamentlicher Erzählungen—Erträge der jüngsten Methodendiscussion." *BN* 6:27–39
1980a   "Punishment Stories in the Legends of the Prophets." Pp. 167–81 in *Orientation By Disorientation: Studies in Literary Criticism Presented in Honor of William A. Beardslee.* Ed. Richard A. Spencer. PTMS 35. Pittsburgh: Pickwick Press.
1980b   "Action Sequences in Gen 2–3." *Semeia* 18:25–33. (A revised version of 1978a.)
1981b   "Anthropology and Old Testament Studies: An Introductory Comment." *Semeia* 21:1–5.
1982   "'Nothing New Under the Sun' is Bad for Business: Biblical Studies Today." The Presidential Address to the Canadian Society of Biblical Studies/Société canadienne des études bibliques, Ottawa, June 1982. *Bulletin of the Canadian Society of Biblical Studies/Bulletin de la société canadienne des études bibliques* 42:1–30.
1985a   "Exploring New Directions." Pp. 167–200 in *The Old Testament and Its Modern Interpreters.* Ed. Douglas A. Knight and Gene M. Tucker. Philadelphia: Fortress Press; Chico: Scholars Press.
1985b   "Stories of the Conquest: Joshua 2, 6, 7, and 8." *Hebrew Annual Review* 8:25–44.
1986   "Oral Tradition and Biblical Studies." *Oral Tradition* 1:30–65.
1988   "Psalm 88 among the Complaints." Pp. 289–302 in *Ascribe to the Lord: Biblical and Other Studies in Memory of Peter C. Craigie.* JSOTSup 67. Ed. Lyle Eslinger and Glen Taylor. Sheffield: Sheffield Academic Press.
1990   "Five Tales of Punishment in the Book of Numbers." Pp. 25–34 in *Text and Tradition: The Hebrew Bible and Folklore.* Semeia Studies. Ed. Susan Niditch. Atlanta: Scholars Press.
1991   "Psalm 3: Content, Context, and Coherence." Pp. 29–39 in *Text, Methode, und Grammatik: Wolfgang Richter zum 65. Geburtstag.* Ed. Walter Gross, Hubert Irsigler, and Theodor Seidl. St. Ottilien: EOS Verlag.
1993b   "Psalm 102: A Complaint with a Difference." *Semeia* 62:19–35.
1994b   "The Temple in Psalms 84, 63, and 42–43." Pp. 187–97 in *Où demeures-tu? (Jn 1,38): La Maison depuis le monde biblique: En hommage au professeur Guy Couturier à l'occasion de ses soixante-cinq ans.* Ed. Jean-Claude Petit in collaboration with André Charron and André Myre. Montreal: Fides.

PART 1

PLEASURABLE LABOUR/
LABORIOUS PLEASURE

SERAPHIM AND POETIC PROCESS

Francis Landy

Samuel said to R. Hiyya b. Rab: . . . Every day ministering angels are created from
the river of fire, utter a song, and cease to be.
(T.B.Hagigah 14a)

And why is that God more loves the Seraphim
Than he does love a Gnat?
(Angelus Silesius)

Seraphim[1] in the Hebrew Bible are throughout associated with
hybridity, transformation, and the conjunction of opposites. In this
essay, I propose to examine the major texts in which seraphim occur
(Isaiah 6; 14:28–32; 30:6; Num 21:4–9), exploring the inter-
connections and transformations between them. It is both a delineation
of a metaphorical field, and an investigation of the poetic process
which the seraphim make manifest. This is evidently the case with

---

[1] There has been much debate on the nature and provenance of seraphim. Most
scholars identify the seraph with the *uraeus*, the winged cobra that was part of the
iconography of Pharaohs and Egyptian deities. Othmar Keel, in particular, has
argued for the prevalence of four-winged *uraei* in seals and amulets of eighth-
century Judah; he suggests that Isaiah both magnifies the numinosity of the
seraphim by bestowing six wings on them, and subordinates them to YHWH, to
communicate YHWH's transcendent majesty. Manfred Görg (29, 33, 34), on the
other hand, identifies the seraph with a flying and demonic serpent of the
wilderness, known as *sfr* or *srf* in Egyptian, which is quite distinct from the *uraeus*;
only in Palestine were the two combined (32). John Day (149) argues that they are
personifications of the lightning, as indicated by their name, and derive from Baal's
seven thunders and lightnings; their form is that of the *uraeus*, but their function is
Canaanite.

Isaiah 6, in which the seraphim, as visionary speakers, are alter egos for the prophet and the divinity who speaks through him. They become metaphors of metaphor, of the interfusion of words and creatures, the point of articulation between the ineffability of the divine and the differentiated world. They preside also over Isaiah's commission, with its retraction of meaningful communication. The metaphor is both overdetermined and signifies a collapse of meaning. In a second passage, the oracle against the Philistines in Isa 14:28–32, the seraph is associated with the Judean monarchy and the ideal kingdom in Isa 11:1–9. In the third passage I will be discussing, Isa 30:6, the seraph connotes the desert between Judah and Egypt, the empty interim that infuses all political and linguistic structure. In the fourth intertext, Num 21:4–9, the transformation of the seraph, from an animate instrument of death to a metallic agent of healing, partakes in the narrative poetics of Numbers, and of the Moses legend in general, in which rods and serpents interchange. This narrative cannot be discussed in isolation from its return in 2 Kgs 18:21, in which the bronze serpent is broken, a fractured circularity contemporaneous with the putative era of Isaiah, to which we now return.

Isaiah 6:1–4, 6–7

> Seraphim were standing about him; six wings, six wings for each one; with two it would cover his face, and with two it would cover his feet, and with two it would fly. And one would call to the other and say, "Holy, holy, holy YHWH of Hosts, the whole earth is full of his glory." . . . And one of the seraphim flew to me, and in his hand a coal; with tongs he took from the altar. And he touched my mouth and said, "Behold, this has touched your lips; your iniquity has turned away, your sin is purged."

In Isa 6:1–4, the gaze passes from the vision of God sitting on his throne, to the hems of his robe,[2] the seraphim, their wings, before

---

[2] The meaning of שׁוּלָיו in v. 1 has been much debated. Eslinger (146–55) has argued recently that it refers to the divine pudenda, rather than to skirts, as conventionally rendered, and seeks to interpret all the instances in which it occurs accordingly. The case in which it most clearly denotes an article of clothing, in the description of the priestly vestments (Exod 28:33, 34; 39:25, 26), he either discounts (148) or treats as a metonymy (170–72). His interpretations are not self-evidently superior to those they displace, and rely on a dubious emendation of Isa 47:2 (149–51), as well as an unwarranted exclusion or figurative explanation of the evidence from Exodus. The

finally coming to rest on the threshold of the Temple and the house obscured with smoke. There is a progressive displacement and filtering of the vision, which compounds the transgressiveness Isaiah laments in v. 5. In this process the seraphim are liminal, since they mark the periphery of the divine vision, the first things Isaiah sees when he turns his eyes away. In the seraphim, the various domains of creatures are represented: serpents, humans, birds, angels and fire. As angels, they mediate between God and humanity, and symbolize the deity as well as the creaturely realm. They are consequently figures for the prophet, as emissaries of God who embody the divine word. In an inaugural scene,[3] they are prefigurations of the prophet's career, from which its complex significations diverge, and in which they are mirrored. As initiator, the seraph transmits his own essence to Isaiah; his lips touched with the coal, he acquires some of the seraph's power and personality.

Seraphim are fire creatures;[4] fire is a familiar metaphor for God, as well as one of his most frequent attributes.[5] Fire consumes,

---

conception of YHWH sitting on a high and uplifted throne and his testicles filling the Temple does, however, put a strain on the visual imagination. Keel (62–70), in an extensive discussion, holds that שׁוּלִים means not only the hem but the lower parts of the divine garments, and that they constitute a zone of dangerous liminality between the divine and the human. Müller (168) notes that שׁוּלִים, the hem of the cloak, belongs to the iconography of divine kingship from the third millenium onwards. The analogy with the priestly vestments would suggest that YHWH is here presented as the divine priest. Hurowitz (42 n. 3), following an oral communication from Aaron Schaffer, thinks that it may refer to YHWH's priestly retinue. Hakham (65 n. 4b) suggests that the possessive suffix could apply to the throne as well as YHWH, in which case שׁוּלִים would be flaps interconnecting heaven and earth.

[3] Most critics identify Isaiah 6 as a call-vision (cf. Sweeney: 136; Wildberger 1980:239, ET:256–57; Vermeylen 1977: 191–92). Some have, however, argued that it does not fit the standard pattern of a prophetic call (e.g. Steck: 189–91); others hold that chronologically it succeeds chaps. 1–5 (e.g. Milgrom, 1964). Neither argument is compelling. The first applies a Procrustean standard to which call-visions should conform; the second confuses literary with historical sequence.

[4] Weiss (94–95) suggests that the choice of seraph over all the other possible terms for angels is dictated by a wish to emphasize the fiery aspects of the divinity. Miscall (34) sees the play on "fiery ones" as participating in the intertextuality of the book, and associates it with the close homophone צָרַף, "refine," in Isa 1:25 and its permutation into רִצְפָּה "coal" in 6:6.

[5] For examples of fire as a metaphor for God, see Deut 4:24 and the symbol of the burning bush. For an interesting discussion of the latter account, see Robinson, 1997. In Ps 104:4 God's angels are fire; elsewhere God is surrounded or preceded

eradicates the distinction between things. The seraphim thus represent the world in its diversity and its absorption into the divine. Fire also imparts light and warmth, and so becomes a symbol for creative energy. Fire may be a metaphor for the poetic and divine word,[6] which burns and gives life to the world, for the metaphoric process of dissolution and recreation.

As serpents, seraphim are associated with the wilderness, death, as well as metamorphosis, wisdom and immortality. Serpents are antonymic to God throughout the Hebrew Bible, for instance, as personifying the irredentism of the sea. For God to be attended by serpents suggests a conjunction and transformation of the wilderness into the divine, death into life, animosity into liturgical celebration.

The seraphim have six wings, which radiate from their bodies, distracting the eye yet again from the centre of vision. With their wings they cover their faces and feet,[7] concealing themselves from our view, but also from the perception of God. The detail augments the distance between the seraphim and God, as well as between the seraphim and ourselves.

Verse 2 is alliterative, distinguished especially by the doubled fricatives of שׁשׁ, "six," and מְעוֹפֵף, "fly."[8] It is also repetitive, the doubling of שׁשׁ כְּנָפַיִם, "six wings," followed by the ternary repetition of

---

by fire (e.g. Ps 97:3, Ezekiel 1). The sacrificial flame is the most common medium of communication between God and humanity. Likewise theophany is generally accompanied by appearances of fire e.g. Exodus 19, 1 Kgs 19:12; 2 Kgs 2:11.

[6] The metaphor, while not so pervasive as in other poetic traditions such as the Vedas, is explicit in Jer 23:29 and implicit, for instance throughout Deuteronomy. In my work on the Song of Songs, I have argued that fire in the Song functions as a metaphor both for God and for poetic process. See also Ps 39:4.

[7] Many critics hold that the feet are a euphemism for the genitals (Eslinger: 161; Clements: 74). However, there is no necessity for this assumption, which obscures the merismus of "face" and "feet" (Keel: 76). For the shame arising from exposure of the legs in a sacerdotal context, see Exod 20:23. Eslinger (160–65) argues at length that the referent of the "face" and "feet" is YHWH; the immediate antecedent, however, as well as the subject of the final clause in the verse ("with two it would fly") suggest that the face and feet are the seraphim's. Weiss (96) suggests that their concealment expresses their shame and a feeling of guilt before the throne of YHWH, corresponding to that of Isaiah. Keel (112–14) remarks that from being protective agencies like the *uraei*, they become self-protective, their wings shielding their faces and feet rather than those of the deity.

[8] Alonso-Schökel (226) discusses how alliteration and ternary repetition contribute to the solemnity of the chapter.

בשתים יכסה פניו ובשתים יכסה רגליו ובשתים יעופף, "with two it would cover its face, with two it would cover its feet, and with two it would fly." Repetition augments the process of bifurcation in the scene, from the vision of YHWH sitting on his throne to the indeterminate number of seraphim, multiplied by their wings, and subdivided among the parts of the body. Repetition suggests symmetry and multiplicity, as we turn from one set of wings to the other. But it also slows time down, and contributes to the static (Müller: 164) and numinous quality of the scene. Refrain, with its high level of redundancy, is the medium of liturgical and magical poetry, and directs attention from the significance of the words to their sound, supported by the onomatopaeic alliterations of שש and עופף. It anticipates the threefold repetition of קדוש, "holy," in the seraphim's doxology.[9]

What the seraphim say gives us further insight into their subjectivity. On the one side there is the ineffable holiness of God, radiating from its source, on the other side there is the world full of his glory.[10] The seraphim stand in between, "above" God, who is at the centre of this vision, and mediating between him and the seer, blinding his eyes, burning his lips so that he can speak, and instituting the paradoxes of percipience and incomprehension wherewith he is commissioned.

Isaiah 14:28–32

> In the year of the death of King Ahaz there was this burden. Do not rejoice, Philistia, all of you, for the rod of your smiter is broken, for from the root of the serpent will come forth a viper, and its fruit a flying seraph. And the firstborn of the poor will graze, and the needy will pasture in safety, and I will kill your root with hunger, and your

---

[9] Marks (67–68) notes how the multiplicity of wings and the repetition of the word are techniques for "filling the [mental] house with smoke," and thus suggesting infinity.

[10] There are numerous discussions of the trisagion. Most critics find in the first part an allusion to God's otherness and transcendence (Magonet, 1985:92; Kaiser, 1972:77, 1983:127; Clements: 74). Wildberger (1980:249, ET:266) cautions against applying contemporary notions of holiness, e.g. derived from Rudolf Otto's *The Idea of the Holy*, to Isaiah's use of the word קדוש. However, its pervasiveness in Isaiah, for instance in chap. 2, would seem to me to justify such an interpretation. Williamson (43) comments, "Unlike anything that we find in the Psalms, Isaiah seems to have regarded the holiness of God as something that was threatening to his people."

remnant he will slay. Wail, O gate, cry, O city, Philistia, all of you, is melted, for smoke comes from the north, and there is no deserter in its ranks. And what will he answer the envoys of a people, for YHWH has founded Zion, and in it will the destitute of his people find refuge.

Isa 14:28–32 is linked to Isaiah 6 through the mention of the seraphim and the introductory notice dating it to the year of the death of a king.[11] The death of king Ahaz might lead us to expect a new era, like that of king Uzziah; instead the Philistines are promised more of the same. Most commentators connect the broken rod with the demise of one or other Assyrian monarch;[12] the context, however, would suggest that the referent is the Judean king. 2 Kgs 18:8 records Hezekiah's wars against the Philistines;[13] Sweeney (234) argues that

---

[11] Williamson (162–63) suggests that the dating formula marks the beginning of originally major sections of the book, separating what the compiler regarded as the phases of Isaiah's career. Conrad (119) argues that chaps. 6–39 are structured round the death of kings: Uzziah at the beginning of his career, Ahaz in the middle, and Hezekiah at the end. Likewise Jenkins (59–60) sees a chronological progression as a structuring device in the book. Gosse too supposes an intentional affiliation between 6:1–2 and 14:28–32.

[12] Wildberger (1989:577, ET:92), Sweeney (233–34), Vermeylen (1977:298–99), Childs (60), Clements (149), Jenkins (48), Gosse (98), who thinks it must have originally referred to the death of Sargon in 705. The reason is that the smoke that comes from the north in v. 31 would identify the enemy as the Assyrians. Vermeylen (1977:300) proposes that the date was added to the oracle at a late stage, so as to permit a rereading, whereby the "rod" became the Judean king; at this point the Philistines are a code term for a Jewish faction opposed to that of the author. Kaiser (53) identifies the conqueror with Alexander the Great; this is based, however, on very little evidence (for older proponents of this hypothesis, see Donner: 112). Vermeylen's argument is overly complex; it would be simpler to regard Ahaz as the original subject, certainly on a synchronic plane. The transition from Judeans to Assyrians is not atypical of Isaiah. Cf., for example, chaps. 17 and 22. Jenkins (59–63) proposes similarly that the death of Ahaz and v. 30 were introduced at a late stage so as to enable a rereading of the oracle idealizing the Davidic dynasty. The year of the death of Ahaz is uncertain, owing to inconsistencies in the regnal data. Critics consequently relate the oracle to the deaths of different Assyrian kings. For a history of Philistia in the period see Tadmor and Ahlström (665–716). Ahlström (690) warns sensibly against seeking precise historical contexts for this oracle.

[13] Tadmor (88 n. 12) notes that according to the Chronicler (2 Chr 28:12) the reign of Ahaz was a period of Philistine expansion, and associates this with the crisis of 734–33 BCE. Jenkins (61) likewise argues that the mention of the death of Ahaz emphasizes his failure as a king, and refers to the evidence from Chronicles.

the new reign might have encouraged hope for a breach in Ahaz's Assyrian alliance.[14] If so, the seraph is Hezekiah.[15] The burden itself, though brief, is complex, with extreme contrasts of imagery, a symmetrical structure underlined by wordplay,[16] and thematic associations both with the neighbouring משׂאות—between which it forms a bridge—and passages further afield in the book.[17]

I would like to focus, however, on the metaphorical chain itself.[18] A rod becomes a root which turns into a common snake (נחשׁ) which undergoes metamorphosis into two more exotic, and presumably more deadly, נחשׁ species before achieving fruition and flight. Tree and serpent are the common elements in this chain, interfused with the

---

However, 14:29 implies continuity between Ahaz and Hezekiah as aggressors against the Philistines. The biblical evidence is of course sketchy and unreliable. For a discussion of the schematized contrast between Ahaz and Hezekiah in Kings and even more in Chronicles, see Ackroyd and Ahlström (689).

[14] See similarly Wildberger (1989:584, ET:99), and Donner (112–13).

[15] Jenkins (52) thinks it doubtful that serpent imagery would have originally been used of the Davidic king, given the negative connotations of serpents. This ignores their pervasive ambiguity in the ancient Near East.

[16] Wildberger (1989:580, ET:99) observes the parallels between vv. 29 and 31, both of which combine initial imperatives to Philistia to lament or not to rejoice with predictions of destruction. The framing verses (28 and 32) are similarly linked through their reference to Zion or the Judean monarchy. That leaves the central verse (30), which consists of two contrasting segments. The first, which promises security for the poor and the needy, corresponds to the concluding prophecy that Zion will be a refuge for the destitute; the second, in which YHWH declares that he will kill Philistia's root, reverses the mention of the serpent's root in v. 29. Many critics spoil the structure by holding that v. 30a is an intrusion or misplaced (Wildberger 1989:579, ET:94; Clements: 149; Vermeylen: 302–3). Jenkins (51) removes the whole of v. 30 from the original oracle, though he admits that none of the arguments are in themselves conclusive. Wordplays include the sequence שׁרשׁ, "your root," שׁאריתך, "your remnant," and שׁער, "gate," in vv. 30 and 31; the near homonymy of מלך, "king," and מלאך, "envoy," in the outer frame (vv. 28, 32); and the alliteration of צפע, "adder," and צפון, "north," in the inner ring (vv. 29, 31).

[17] In the immediate context, it is transitional between oracles against Assyria or Babylon, and those against neighbouring peoples. A similar assertion of the invulnerability of Zion is central to the succeeding oracle against Moab (16:8). Echoes further afield are the founding of the cornerstone in Zion (28:16); the messengers from the land "beyond the rivers of Kush" in 18:2; the motif of the seraphim, which I have already noted; and solicitude for the poor (3:15). For other intertextual connections, see Miscall (51).

[18] Several critics find the metaphor "strained" (Clements: 149) or "verunglückles" (Wildberger, 1989:581); possibly this is a symptom of intolerance for complex metaphor.

frequent combination, in iconography and myth, of trees, especially trees of life, and serpents throughout the ancient Near East—and indeed world. Serpents are, as it were, the animal equivalents of trees; both are long and thin. Serpents differ from trees in their quickness, their flexibility, and their capacity to change. The sap of trees is life; that of serpents is death. Trees of life, fixed and solid, grant immortality, at the centre of the garden or world; serpents wrapped around them signify change and death. In our context, the tree, as Kirsten Nielsen shows in her wonderful study of the metaphor of the tree in Isaiah, is the Davidic dynasty at the centre of the world in Zion, whose foundation concludes the oracle (130, 133–35, 153). "The root of the serpent" may be a cliché for insemination; more indefinitely, it suggests an analogy between roots and serpents, that they inhabit the same spaces, are nourished from the same sources, are twisty, insert themselves in crevices and holes. Similarly, literally the fruit denotes the child, or the child's actions, but implicitly it makes fruit, the culmination of the growth of the tree, into a metaphor for seraph, the angelic serpent manifested in flight and fire. The death of the old king, the sequence asserts, is a change of skin; death is birth or, better still, sex. Royalty, immortality, snakes, trees, fruit, birds, angels and fire are interconnected in a continuous process of metamorphosis. However, its direction reverses that of Isaiah 6. In Isaiah 6, the passing of the old king is the prelude to the revelation of divine sovereignty; the prophet is situated at the centre of an impure and uncomprehending people. The vacant throne portends the coming desolation and an emptiness at the centre of the sacred and poetic world. The seraphim, creatures of chaos and wilderness, are transformed into agents of the divine will. Here the movement is outwards: the king/tree becomes a seraph to harrass the Philistines. The king is also associated with fire and therefore perhaps with seraphim in chap. 33, where, salamander-like, he survives the eternal flames.

The closest parallel, however, as Miscall (51) says, is with chap. 11.[19] There the fruit of the shoot from the root of Jesse rules over a paradisal world, and simultaneously smites the earth with his breath. Similarly, in 14:30, the flying seraph presides over, and permits the existence of, a zone of immunity, where the poor and needy peacefully

---

[19] Jenkins (54) also notes the close verbal associations with chap. 11, and posits a similar background in royal imagery.

graze. As in 14:29, rod and tree are complementary images; that which brings death to the nations is the Tree of Life. Under its aegis, the serpent, as the archetype of natural animosity, is placated; the suckling plays on its hole, the weanling pats its den. The images are powerful, not only because the words in Isa 11:8 for suckling (יוֹנֵק) and playing (שִׁעֲשַׁע) are elsewhere used for shoots and tendrils (most notably in Isa 53:2),[20] but because the serpent substitutes for maternal dependence. The infant plays with the world, separate from the mother, but secure, because it does not feel abandoned. The mountain on which none hurt or destroy (11:9) is endowed with that security, which, as the verse develops, encompasses the entire earth. One may see in this a regression to, or projection of, the womb; at any rate, as in 6:3, we are incorporated in a plenitude of glory and knowledge. In this idyll, the figure of the serpent is dissonant; in the place of the mother's nipple there is an absence, in which the serpent resides or from which it has vanished. The venom has not, or at least not at this juncture, been transformed into milk or the sap of the tree, but neither is it potent. Death is present in this garden, but only as deferred or displaced outside it.

Isaiah 30:6

> The burden of the beasts of the south, in a land of distress and ordeal, lion and growling leonine, viper and flying seraph; they bear their wealth on the shoulders of asses, their treasures on the humps of camels, to a people who profit not.

In Isa 30:6, the "flying seraph" occurs at the end of a series of desert phenomena that comprise, or at least comprise the first part of, a burden of the beasts of the south.[21] The burden is strange, because it is isolated from the corpus of burdens in Isaiah 13–23. It is accordingly

---

[20] For שַׁעֲשֻׁע as "tendrils," see 5:7.

[21] Wildberger (1982:1157–59) argues against מַשָּׂא being a superscription here, comparable to the Oracles against the Nations, since its real subject is Egypt; he would see it as having its primary meaning of "burden," anticipating the loads carried by domestic beasts later in the verse. Sweeney (399–400) sees a pun here, as does Irwin (76), according to whom the passage is characterised by pervasive ambiguity. It seems somewhat improbable that, as an initial word in a poetic discourse, מַשָּׂא should refer to a genre in every instance except this. The objection that it does not specify its target is not compelling, since several מַשָּׂאוֹת have indirect and enigmatic titles.

what Mieke Bal calls a "wandering rock," an evocation of one kind of discourse in another, that acts as a sounding board against which it plays. The burdens, like the one on the Philistines in 14:28–32, are ostensibly delivered against the nations; the weight of the prophecy is transferred from the prophet and his people to the ever-antagonistic other. So, at least, it is in theory whose spectre is raised only to disconcert the reader. Especially is this true of burdens with allegorical designations, such as "the burden of the wilderness of the sea" (Isa 21:1) and "the burden of the valley of vision" (Isa 22:1). There the real subject of the oracle is either different from the ostensible subject, or turns out to be Judah. In chap. 30, the insertion of a burden in the midst of denunciation of the inanity of Judean foreign policy may promise welcome relief; the addressees, "the beasts of the south," would, however, prove puzzling objects of divine judgment, as well as an unreceptive audience. One would suppose metonymy with desert tribes, such as those mentioned in chap. 21;[22] however, as the oracle develops, it reverts to the subject of Judean diplomacy. The beasts of the south evoke the landscape the emissaries pass through on their way to Egypt.[23] The burden is displaced from the indigenous wildlife of the desert to the pack animals which transport their useless inducements. The figure of the serpent is transposed from the seraph of the wilderness to Egypt, whose illusory pretensions and immobility are satirized as those of Rahab, the sea monster.[24] But we must focus on the sequence itself: "The burden of the beasts of the south: in a land of straits and ordeal, lion and growling leonine, viper and flying seraph." Six terms, paired through synonymity and alliteration,[25] of which the

---

[22] Wildberger (1982:1161) and Clements (245) cite this view, for which there is little evidence.

[23] Various critics (e.g. Wildberger, 1982:1160–61; Kaiser, 1980: 289) hold that the emissaries had pass through Sinai since the coastal route had already been occupied by Assyrian forces. But the coastal road also passed through desert, and could be imagined, in a poetic description, as being haunted by fabulous terrors.

[24] We do not know how Rahab was depicted. It appears as a designation for Egypt also in Ps 87:4, without apparent animus. The association of Egypt with the Nile facilitated identification with a water-creature, such as the תנין in Ezek 29:3–6. It may be noted that Rahab parallels תנין in Isa 51:9.

[25] See the analysis of Alonso-Schökel (513), who comments on the extraordinary poetic quality of the passage. He imitates the alliteration in his translation, which may be quoted: "Leones y leones 'rugen', dragones y endriagos revuelan, a lomo de burros sus bienes" (509–10).

last two—the two pairs of beasts—are embodiments of the first pair of abstractions, צרה וצוקה, the horror, thirst and desolation of the wilderness. What the emissaries pass through, then, is a liminal terrain, which also represents an absence, the ever-presence of death, that renders their efforts useless and is the backdrop to the whole book of Isaiah. As in 14:29 and 6:2, the seraph is a hybrid creature, combining flight and serpentine motion; the coupling with אפעה, "viper," suggests both the diversity of species of snakes, and hence the multiplication of terror, and their coalescence. אפעה, "viper," for instance, alliterates with מעופף, "flying." The parallel couplet, לביא וליש, "lion and leonine," subdivides the species of lion, suggesting its immense poetic and mythological valence,[26] and matches it with the snakes; the desert is represented by a composite of lion and serpent.[27] The motif of the desert recalls the Mosaic period, and takes us to our fourth intertext, Num 21:4–9.

Numbers 21:4–9

> They marched from Hill's Hill by the Reed Sea Road, to go-around the land of Edom, and the people became short-tempered on the way. The people spoke against God and against Moshe: Why did you bring us up from Egypt to die in the wilderness? For there is no food and no water, and our throats loathe the despicable food! So YHWH sent upon the people vipers, burning-snakes (*seraphim*); they bit the people, and there died many people of Israel. The people came to Moshe and said: We have sinned! For we have spoken against YHWH and against you. Intercede to God, so that he may remove from us the vipers. So Moshe interceded on behalf of the people. And YHWH said to Moshe: Make yourself a burning-snake (*saraph*) and put it on a banner-pole; it shall be: whoever has been bitten and then sees it, will live. So Moshe made a viper of copper, and he put it on a banner-pole, and it was: if a viper bit a man and he looked upon the viper of copper, he would live (trans., Fox).

As in Isa 30:6, here the seraphim are creatures of the wilderness, animated and half-fabulous figures of its virulence. They signify the dead land, the liminal space between Egypt and Israel, and Israel's dependence on God, as their transformation from purveyors of death to bringers of life shows. Their intervention at this point is especially significant, since it follows the death of Aaron at Mt. Hor ("Hill's Hill"

---

[26] See, for example, the parade of five synonyms for lion in Job 4:10–11.
[27] The parallelism is underscored if מהם, "growling," matches מעופף, "flying."

in Fox's translation), on the edge of the Promised Land (Num 34:7–8).
As Olson (137) suggests, they mark the transition between death and
life, the passing of the old generation and the transference of power to
the new, the narrative of the wilderness and that of the conquest. But
they are also a throwback: the episode begins with a return towards the
Red Sea, a recapitulation of regret for the departure from Egypt, and it
is followed by a song, introduced, like the Song of the Sea, by אָז יָשִׁיר,
"thus it sang" (Num 21:17). As many critics have noted, including
Robert Culley, it is closely interlinked with the other narratives of
rebellion in the wilderness. The old generation is perpetuated in the
new, despite the breaking of the forty years' spell marked by the
reversal of the debacle at Hormah in 21:1–3.

הַנְּחָשִׁים הַשְּׂרָפִים, "the burning serpents," recall especially the fire of
YHWH that burns around the edge of the camp in the first of the
accounts of rebellion in Numbers, in 11:1–3. The seraphim are
embodiments of divine fire; if 11:1–3 is paradigmatic of the stories of
rebellion, simplifying them to their essentials,[28] that of the seraphim
closes the sequence where it began, with Moses' intercession and the
removal of the peril. But it also augments and overwhelms it with
detail. As we have seen, the seraphim are composite creatures, angelic,
demonic, fiery, serpentine, winged, and human.[29] They represent all
domains of existence, and in particular the intersection of the natural
and supernatural, the miraculous and the everyday, in the wilderness.
The celestial food that the Israelites despise (21:5) is transformed into
the poison injected by the seraphim; the fire of YHWH becomes venom
in their bloodstream. Like the seraphim in Isaiah 6, the burning

---

[28] For the terseness, see Culley, 1990:28–29. Culley also compares the two texts in
Culley, 1976:101–4, as does Van Seters (223). Another example of a narrative
stripped to its essentials so as to establish a paradigm against which to measure
ensuing variations is the first of the deliverance stories in Judges (Judg 3:7–11).
Van Seters (221), citing H. H. Schmid, notes the correspondence of the narrative
schemata in Numbers and Judges.

[29] Many commentators, especially conservative ones, naturalize and try to identify
the serpent, ignoring the possibility that it may be angelic, or winged, as in the
references in Isaiah (e.g. Davies: 215; Wiseman). Milgrom (1990:174), however,
considers the seraph that Moses erected to be a "winged snake," similar to *uraei*.
Keel (83) thinks that Nehushtan was probably not winged, on the basis of
Phoenician parallels. Its identification as a "seraph" tells against this, however. See
also the note on "Seraphim and Fiery Serpents" by David Goodman in Douglas
(213–15).

serpents become metonymies for the divine wrath, fire, and the capacity for metamorphosis; they are both hostile entities and emissaries. The demonic realm is co-opted into, and absorbed by, the divine. The seraphim in Isaiah 6 heal the prophet, enabling him to speak through cauterizing his lips; his word, however, will destroy the people. In Numbers 21 there is a further transformation. Moses makes a bronze seraph, corresponding to the metallic representations of the cherubim. Statuary freezes and perpetuates the image; the flexible violence of the incendiary serpents, on the boundary between form and energy, is reproduced and controlled at the centre of the human community, as human creations. The proliferation of images at the periphery of the divine contrasts with the aniconism mandated by the text. A transgression is instituted in the midst of the community, outside, moreover, the concealed paraphernalia of the Tabernacle. The serpent is an alibi for God's transformative power. Gazing at it is an antidote for snakebite because it displaces, and stands for, the unmediated and fatal vision.

The cure is homeopathic, and is amply attested in Egypt and elsewhere. Joines provides evidence for the healing and regenerative properties of serpents, and for the apotropaic and therapeutic powers of amulets.[30] Veneration of the icon turns the demonic power into an ally, puts one into its orbit; it may have cultic associations antipathetic to the exclusive worship of YHWH. Only the instruction of YHWH and the Mosaic fabrication grant it at least temporary sanction.[31] As with the seraphim in Isaiah 6, as hypothesized by Keel, the cult of winged seraphim is accommodated through subordination to YHWH. The instability of the approbation of the image is evident from its uncertain location, its setting outside the sanctuary,[32] as if its status with relation

---

[30] See also Milgrom (1990:459), Wenham (157). Seebass (227–28) argues that the widespread apotropaic use of serpents in Egypt is evidence for the antiquity of the tradition, as well as its association with the motif of the return to Egypt.

[31] Coats (118, 123), for instance, holds that the narrative served to legitimate the serpent cult. Seebass (226) argues that certain elements in the story presuppose Hezekiah's abolition of it. For a contrary view, see that Asurmendi, who considers that the story originates in the close connection between Moses and the Midianites.

[32] Seebass (228–29) rejects the general assumption that it was situated in the Jerusalem Temple, arguing that the temples in Beersheba and Arad are equally possible. See also Coats (117–18). Milgrom (1990:460) suggests that it was the visibility of the serpent, as opposed to other memorabilia of the wilderness, that rendered it vulnerable to iconoclasm.

to the sacred and symbolic centre of Numbers is indeterminate. It is analogous to the Nazirite, a sacred person outside the order of the priesthood,[33] and like the Nazirite, has Dionysian connotations,[34] and is the source of tension and ambiguity.[35] The metaphorical transmutations and infusions—angel/demon, serpent, victim and image— intervene between the destructive fire of God, which threatens all distinctions, and his invisible but no less fearful presence. They may be representative of the poetics of Numbers, whose narratives, laws, and spatial and social organization work out the problems and dangers of proximity to YHWH.

What is the somatic process and the scopic economy? The sufferer looks at the icon, beseechingly, and the icon heals him, filling her with a vision of itself. Perhaps the bronze serpent looks at him, certainly God does, behind the transgressive alibi, the scrawl on the field of vision. The master of the gaze is abject, in need of recognition, and sight. If the fire in his veins is that of the serpents, and hence of the wrath of God, that which fills her eyes is light. As in the priestly blessing in Num 6:25, the illumination by God's face is that which is seen and imagined.[36] Light neutralizes fire; the two, however, are metaphorically equivalent, transformatively linked to each other.

---

[33] As Milgrom (1990:355) points out, not only is the Nazirite comparable to a priest, but approximates the greater sanctity of the High Priest. Wenham (85–89) likewise examines the similarities and differences between priests and Nazirites, e.g. that both men and women could take Nazirite vows.

[34] The serpent is Dionysian, not only in that Dionysus is associated with serpents, but because it mediates between life and death, wildness and the sacred. The Dionysian connotations of the only figure in the Hebrew Bible who is explicitly Nazirite, Samson, have often been remarked. The Nazirite is prohibited from drinking wine or eating grapes, the fruit of Dionysus, just as priests are forbidden to drink wine in the sanctuary; the abstention corresponds to his avoidance of impurity. On the other hand, Nazirites have unshorn hair, which is antonymic to the priestly code (e.g. Lev 21:10), and associated with licentiousness (Num 5:18), social and sacred disorder (e.g. Exod 32:25), and leprous exclusion (Lev 13:44). Unshorn hair and abstention from wine are structural opposites, expressing the marginality and ambivalence of Nazirites, as sacred persons outside the sacred system. Samson is the boundary-crosser *par excellence.*

[35] The tension surrounding the Nazirite is emphasized by his or her extreme vulnerability to sudden death (Num 6:9).

[36] Likewise in Pss 36:10 and 42:3 seeing and being illuminated by the face of God is the source of life and the object of the Psalmist's desire.

Against the background of divine fire and light, the figures are sketched, and maintain their fragile existence.

In Isa 14:29, serpent and tree are identical; the tree of life that nurtures the poor is the serpent that harries the Philistines. In Isa 11:1–9, the tree at the centre of the paradisal world flourishes harmoniously with the child-friendly serpent. Here the tree corresponds to the caduceus, the pole on which the serpent is mounted; it is focal point of the narrative, the vertical axis round which the serpent twists. In Isa 11:10, the tree becomes a "banner" (נס) to which the peoples come. Here the same word (נס) means both "pole" and "miracle." The homonym furnishes a further linguistic and metaphoric regress. The pole is the base for the sign that counteracts and preserves the agents of God's retribution; at the same time, it is the sign for the signs of unconditioned divine power. The pole is reassuringly fixed and solid, and worshipped as such for centuries; it represents, however, the contingency of life in the wilderness, the dependence on the divine capacity to transform reality. The pole is the miracle, what is seen is the unseen reversal of death into life, natural into supernatural. There is another pun, often remarked, linking the words for "serpent" and "bronze" (נחש, נחשת).[37] "Serpent" and "bronze" are antonyms, opposed as animate and inanimate, flexible and motionless. They may share an affinity of colour,[38] and perhaps hybridity, if נחשת is an alloy of copper and tin.[39] Both are the products of fire. The pun suggests a fluidity of language, mimicking the creative process that makes a serpent out of bronze, and hence also the fluidity of phenomena, the metaphorical overdetermination, that we have found especially associated with the seraphim. Everything solid may dissolve, into language and miracle; everything mobile may be arrested. That which poisons may also heal.

The narrative has numerous correlations with others in the Mosaic traditions. Mary Douglas (210–12), in the concentric structure

---

[37] Milgrom (1990:175) suggests that the wordplay adds to the homeopathic powers of the icon. Cf. also the discussion in Douglas (213–14).

[38] Wenham (158). Wenham also suggests that red is the colour of purification.

[39] Milgrom (1990:175) and Wenham (157) prefer to translate נחשת as "copper" rather than "bronze," in view of the discovery of an image of a copper serpent at Timna dating to the early Iron Age. On the other hand, as Joines (253) points out, bronze images of serpents were extremely common in Palestine and elsewhere in the ancient Near East. Milgrom's and Wenham's interpretation, like that of Asurmendi (284), is clearly motivated by a wish to provide a Mosaic context for the narrative.

that she attributes to Numbers, matches it with the story of the quails, winged creatures whose consumption brings death; she also sees a parallel with the golden calf. Wenham (157–58) suggests that an inversion of pollution into purification is typical of the entire ritual system. In the story of Korah, divine fire devours the offerers of incense who challenged the sacred hierarchy (Num 16:35); Eleazer is enjoined to hammer their bronze censers into a covering for the altar (Num 17:3).[40] Punitive fire, as in the story of the seraphim, is transformed into bronze, and incorporated within the sacred order. In the next major narrative block, Balaam claims that there is no נחש in Jacob (Num 23:23), evoking yet another meaning of the word— "magic" or "divination." Balaam the seer evidently has blind spots.

The clearest echo, however, is the story of Moses' call. Moses is instructed to cast his rod to the ground, where it changes into a serpent; he picks it up by the tail, and it reverts to being a rod (Exod 4:2–4). Aaron's rod likewise becomes a serpent, to swallow those of the Egyptian magicians (Exod 6:8–12). The metamorphosis of rod into serpent is a sign of the perils and ambiguities of Moses' mission. Moses' rod is his most abiding metonym, signifying potency, but also pastoral care, determination, and the difficulty of the journey. It is an axis round which the narrative revolves, and an index of divine agency. In the previous chapter, however, it has been Moses' undoing (Num 20:6–10), and has paradoxically brought sanctity and vitality to the community. Here the emblems of rod and serpent are combined in one image, closing the sequence of rebellions, culminating in Moses' (inadvertent?) rebellion, and in a vision of healing.[41]

In 2 Kgs 18:4, however, Hezekiah breaks the bronze serpent,[42] since the people, like Korah's followers, have been offering incense to it, and calling it Nehushtan, a name suggesting affection, and personification. The magical connotation of the word נחש predominates. The writer of Kings approves of Hezekiah's acts: "he

---

[40] Another parallel is suggested by Robinson (1985:17–18), who compares the narrative with that of the defeat of the Amalekites in Exod 7:8–16, largely on the basis of the shared terms נס and שם.

[41] For these parallels, see also Douglas (211).

[42] Long (194–95) suggests that a parallel is drawn with Moses' smashing the golden calf, since the same verb כתת is used as describes his destruction of the calf in Deut 9:21. Long, like Jones (562) and Joines (255), thinks the serpent was in fact a fertility symbol. See also Ahlström (702).

did what was right in the eyes of YHWH" (18:3). Nevertheless, the detail that this was the serpent that Moses erected conveys regret and intimates Hezekiah's iconoclastic daring. There is no permanent symbol that may not be appropriated, no icon, or metaphorical chain, that is not there to be broken. The seraph touches Isaiah's lips, permitting him to prophesy. The prophecy will bring healing to those who understand, but also presages incomprehension and death to the listeners. The remedial serpent will become the object of devotion, the source of estrangement from YHWH, as perhaps do all our words and images. Yet the story remains, to transfix us with its gaze.

To Robert Culley, a great storyteller.

Bibliography

Ackroyd, Peter
1984   "The Biblical Interpretation of the Reigns of Ahaz and Hezekiah." Pp. 247–59 in *In the Shelter of Elyon: Essays on Ancient Palestinian Life and Literature in Honor of G. W. Ahlström*. Ed. W. Boyd Barrick and John R. Spencer. JSOTSup 31. Sheffield: JSOT.

Ahlström, Gosta W.
1993   *The History of Ancient Palestine from the Palaeolithic Period to Alexander's Conquest*. Ed. Diana Edelman. JSOTSup 146. Sheffield: JSOT.

Alonso-Schökel, Luis
1963   *Estudios de Poética Hébrea* Barcelona: Juan Flor.

Ashley, Timothy R.
1992   *The Book of Numbers*. NICOT. Grand Rapids: Eerdmans.

Asurmendi, Jesus
1988   "En Torno a la Serpiente de Bronce." *EstBib* 46:283–94.

Childs, Brevard S.
1967   *Isaiah and the Assyrian Crisis*. Studies in Biblical Theology, 2nd Series 3. London: SCM.

Clements, Ronald E.
1980   *Isaiah 1–39*. New Century Bible Commentary. Grand Rapids: Eerdmans/London: Marshall, Morgan and Scott.

Coats, George W.
1968   *Rebellion in the Wilderness*. Nashville: Abingdon.

Conrad, Edgar
1991   *Reading Isaiah*. OBT. Minneapolis: Fortress Press.

Culley, Robert C.
1976   *Studies in the Structure of Hebrew Narrative.* Philadelphia:
            Fortress Press; Missoula: Scholars Press.
1990   "Five Tales of Punishment in the Book of Numbers." Pp. 25–
            34 in *Text and Tradition: The Hebrew Bible and Folklore.* Ed.
            Susan Niditch. Atlanta: Scholars Press.

Davies, Eryl W.
1995   *Numbers.* NCBC. London: Marshall Pickering.

Donner, Herbert
1964   *Israel unter den Völkern.* Leiden: Brill.

Douglas, Mary
1993   *In the Wilderness: The Doctrine of Defilement in the Book of
            Numbers.* JSOTSup 158. Sheffield: JSOT.

Eslinger, Lyle
1995   "The Infinite in a Finite Organical Perception (Isaiah VI 1–5)."
            VT 45:145–73.

Fox, Everett
1999   *The Five Books of Moses: Genesis, Exodus, Leviticus,
            Numbers, Deuteronomy: A New Translation with Introduc-
            tions.* New York: Schoken.

Görg, Manfred
1978   "Die Funktion der Serafen bei Jesaja." *BN* 5:28–39.

Gosse, Bernard
1991   "Isaïe 14, 28–32 et les traditions sur Isaïe d'Isaïe 36–39 et Isaïe
            20,1–6." *BZ* 35:97–98.

Hakham, Amos
1984   *Sefer Yeshayahu.* Vol.1. Jerusalem: Mossad Harav Kook.

Hurowitz, Victor
1989   "Isaiah's Impure Lips and Their Purification in Light of
            Akkadian Sources." *HUCA* 60: 39–89.

Irwin, William Henry
1977   *Isaiah 28–33: Translation with Philological Notes.* Biblica et
            Orientalia 30. Rome: Biblical Institute.

Jenkins, Allan K.
1980   "Isaiah 14: 28–32—An Issue of Life and Death." *Folia
            Orientalia* 21:47–63.

Joines, Karen Randolph
1968   "The Bronze Serpent in the Israelite Cult." *JBL* 87:245–56.

Jones, Gwilym H.
1984   *I and II Kings.* Vol. 2. NCBC. Grand Rapids: Eerdmans.
            London: Marshall, Morgan and Scott.

Kaiser, Otto
1972   *Isaiah 1–12.* 1st ed. Trans. R. A. Wilson. OTL. London: SCM.

1980   *Isaiah 13–39*. 2nd ed. Trans. R. A. Wilson. OTL. London: SCM.

1983   *Isaiah 1–12*. 2nd ed. Trans. John Bowden. OTL. London: SCM.

Keel, Othmar
1977   *Jahwe-Visionen und Siegelkunst*. SBS 84/85. Stuttgart: Katholisches Bibelwerk.

Long, Burke O.
1991   *2 Kings*. FOTL 10. Grand Rapids: Eerdmans.

Magonet, Jonathan
1985   "The Structure of Isaiah 6." Pp. 91–97 in *Proceedings of the Ninth World Congress of Jewish Studies: Division A (The Period of the Bible)*. Jerusalem: World Union of Jewish Studies.

1991   *A Rabbi's Bible*. London: SCM.

Marks, Herbert
1990   "On Prophetic Stammering." Pp. 60–80 in *The Book and the Text: The Bible and Literary Theory*. Ed. Regina M. Schwartz. Oxford: Blackwell.

Milgrom, Jacob
1964   "Did Isaiah Prophecy During the Reign of Uzziah?" *VT* 14:164–82.

1990   *Numbers*. JPSA Torah Commentary. Philadelphia: JPSA.

Miscall, Peter
1993   *Isaiah*. Readings. Sheffield: JSOT.

Müller, Hans-Peter
1992   "Sprachliche und religionsgeschichtliche Beobachtungen zu Jesaja 6." *ZAH* 5:163–85.

Nielsen, Kirsten
1989   *There is Hope for a Tree: The Tree as Metaphor in Isaiah*. JSOTSup 65. Sheffield: JSOT.

Olson, Dennis T.
1996   *Numbers*. Interpretation. Louisville: John Knox.

Robinson, Bernard P.
1985   "Israel and Amalek: The Context of Exodus 17.8–16." *JSOT* 32:15–22.

1997   "Moses and the Burning Bush." *JSOT* 75:107–22.

Seebass, Horst
1993   *Numeri*. BKAT 4. Neukirchen-Vluyn: Neukirchener Verlag.

Sonnet, Jean-Pierre
1992   "Le motif de l'endurcissement (Is 6,9–10) et la lecture d'Isaïe.'" *Bib.* 73:208–39.

Steck, Odil H.
1972   "Bemerkungen zu Jesaja 6." *BZ* 16:188–206.

Sturdy, John
1976   *Numbers*. Cambridge Bible Commentary. Cambridge: Cambridge University Press.

Sweeney, Marvin
1996   *Isaiah 1–39, with an Introduction to Prophetic Literature*. FOTL 16. Grand Rapids: Eerdmans.

Tadmor, Hayim
1966   "Philistia under Assyrian Rule." *BA* 29:86–102.

Vermeylen, Jacques
1977   *Du prophète Isaïe à l'apocalyptique: Isaïe I-XXXV, miroir d'un demi-millenaire d'expérience religieuse en Israël*. Tome 1. Paris: Gabalda.
1989   "L'unité du livre d'Isaïe." Pp. 11–53 in *The Book of Isaiah. Le Livre d'Isaïe: Les oracles et leurs relectures, unité et complexité de l'ouvrage*. Leuven: Leuven University Press.

Wenham, Gordon J.
1981   *Numbers: An Introduction and Commentary*. Tyndale OT Commentaries. Leicester: Inter-Varsity.

Weiss, Meir
1973   "Temunah Weqol Bepirqê Mare'ot Hannebuah." Pp. 91–99 in *Proceedings of the Sixth World Congress of Jewish Studies Division A (Period of the Bible)*. Jerusalem: World Union of Jewish Studies.

Wildberger, Hans
1989   *Jesaja 13–27*. 2nd ed. BKAT 10/2. Neukirchen: Neukirchener Verlag; English translation Thomas H. Trapp. Minneapolis: Fortress Press, 1991.
1982   *Jesaja 28–39*. BKAT 10/3. Neukirchen: Neukirchener Verlag.
1980   *Jesaja 1–12*. 2nd ed. BKAT 10/1. Neukirchen: Neukirchener Verlag; English translation Thomas H. Trapp. Minneapolis: Fortress Press, 1991.

Williamson, Hugh G.M.
1994   *The Book Called Isaiah: Deutero-Isaiah's Role in Composition and Redaction*. Oxford: Clarendon.

Wiseman, D.J.
1972   "Flying Serpents?" *TynBul* 23:108–10.

WHAT IS MY BELOVED? ON EROTIC
READING AND THE SONG OF SONGS[1]

Fiona C. Black

You have heard it said that in the beginning was the word. I make this somewhat audacious robbery of John's eminent opener in order to locate a place for a beginning. Do all beginnings start this way? I am not asking about the capital-w word. I mean the word that teases, that allures, the word that entices exploration—intimate discovery of its curves and hollows, its warm, forbidden places; the word that must be covered up—for modesty's sake, or is it for fear of vulnerability?; the word that is made bare again, for explorers are ever curious, attracted, urgent. Lover-like, this word beckons, it seduces, it possesses, is possessed, then is cast away, only to be sought again, forever.

Like a great matriarch (why not?), I shall name this word the Song of Songs. Not because the Song is the only way of speaking, but because it is such a word. Through the twists and turns of lyrical language, through deception of image and the temptation of narrative, it entices its readers, confounds them, seeks union, begs knowledge, spurns, pouts, requires protection, demands possession, refuses ownership. One could say that the Song engages its readers *as a lover*, that the reading relationship is amatory, even erotic. The Song, if any Hebrew Bible text does, demands a little extra of the personal from its readers. They respond in feeling and in writing, perhaps imposing

[1] An earlier version of this paper was presented to the Reading Biblical and Extra-Biblical Texts Section of the Canadian Society for Biblical Studies, Annual Meeting, June, 1998.

upon the Song (and not simply the characters in it) the profile of an "ideal" relationship. Moreover, the text-amante seems to bring out in its lovers a reluctance to tarnish—and, better still, encourages them to protect and makes them blind to its faults. Discovering an idyllic world, readers seem loathe to suggest that it may be flawed or spoiled in any way. It is a skilful lover indeed that can do all that.

> *I am interested in language because it wounds or seduces me.*
> (Barthes, 1990b:38)

Roland Barthes's investigation into an "erotics of reading" (Barthes, 1994: viii) in *Pleasure of the Text* and his later reproduction of a "structural portrait" (Calvet: 220) of the lover in *A Lover's Discourse: Fragments* provide a provocative background against which one might investigate readerly relationships to the Song of Songs. Influenced by the whimsical and musing spirit that characterizes these works, I am not tempted to "apply" Barthesian "theory" or "method" to the Song. Rather, in a less precise fashion,[2] I wish to play a little: to inquire how Barthes's pondering and instancing of amatory discourse might elucidate reading the Song of Songs. Could Barthes help to explain readers' loyalty, their profuse, written acclamations of the text's charms, and their matching of the Song's language in critical writing, as if the courted must respond to the one courting, in kind? Could his work elucidate the difficulty that many readers have in reading this text, and their compulsion to continue trying?[3] What I purpose here is to borrow some of the Barthesian themes and discourse used in the two above-mentioned texts (and also in his "autobiography," *Roland Barthes*) and to employ Barthes's well known metaphor of the erotic, textual body, with a view to investigating the reading relationship between readers and the Song. Naturally, I could not hope to give a full account of love's many

---

[2] The admission of an intentionally imprecise reading is potentially embarrassing in a volume dedicated to Robert Culley. As an M.A. student of Culley's, I cut my teeth on his careful, focused attention to detail and I have learned much from his precise scholarship. In fact, it is in attending to the Song's detailed convolutions that I have become aware of its resistance to definitive readings and to the pleasure it affords the reader; thus, I take the liberty of being imprecise with Barthes in order to elucidate my text.

[3] These characteristics of reading are ubiquitous in Song of Songs scholarship; it is not necessary to instance them here.

textures here, if anywhere. Instead, I consider the Song's amatory technique, the display of its erotic subject matter which is intermingled and veiled with its imagery and its flirtation with a plot. The responses of a few readers will also be considered throughout, as an attempt to gauge the Song's effectiveness as a lover.

Pleasure of the Text and *A Lover's Discourse* do not provide a theoretical definition of eroticism. Rather, together with *Roland Barthes*, which comes between them, they represent an investigation of writing as pleasure. The two books are intimately concerned with the marginalization of amatory discourse, *A Lover's Discourse* the more so, because its goal is to recover this lost speech not by studying it, but by recreating it (Barthes, 1990a:1). And in trying to recover it, Barthes is very much playing—with the subject, with his writing, with us, perhaps even with himself. The books are designed to tease and show evidence of textual teasing. Further, they irresistibly brush up against each other. The fragments of *A Lover's Discourse* inevitably find their way to the mouths of all lovers, including the text which Barthes has embodied and personified. The books' style is intentionally fragmented and incomplete, therefore appropriately imprecise for my purposes and Barthes's (because both the Song and the erotic are imprecise arts). They reveal and subsequently invite, thus, not an analytical systematization of their subject and themselves, but treatment in kind. This means that any use of them needs to be carried out in the same spirit, with an emphasis not on the *theory* of reading, but its affect. In the same way that amatory discourse has been marginalized (so Barthes), so too has discussion of the affect of the Song. Perhaps Barthes's work might be able to assist in righting the balance.

To speak of the affect of the text turns out to be useful for addressing the theme of the volume for which this essay is written. The labour of reading Barthes, which can be quite marked, owing to the density and sometimes obscurity of this phase of his writing (an expected outcome from work that is self-consciously introspective and self-pleasing—auto-erotic?), is also a pleasant, even pleasurable exercise. As Naomi Schor observes, Barthes's major strategy is seduction, and many have succumbed (99). And as I noted above, reading the Song is also hard going sometimes, but tantalizingly pleasurable. In reading Barthes and the Song, and indeed in reading them together, labour and pleasure become inseparable, indistinguishable, so that one must then say in this case that work is pleasure, or maybe more provocatively, pleasure is work.

So let us proceed to the pleasure of the text. When Barthes speaks of the eroticism of a text, he is not saying that its subject matter has to be erotic love, though it can be. A text, like the human form, has several bodies, one of which is erotic. Barthes explains:

> Apparently, Arab scholars, when speaking of the text, use this admirable expression: *the certain body*. What body? We have several of them; the body of anatomists and physiologists, the one science sees or discusses: this is the text of grammarians, critics, commentators, philologists (the pheno-text). But we also have a body of bliss [*jouissance*] consisting solely of erotic relations, utterly distinct from the first body: it is another contour, another nomination; thus with the text: it is no more than the open list of the fires of language…. Does the text have human form, is it a figure, an anagram of the body? Yes, but of our erotic body. The pleasure of the text is irreducible to physiological need [*Le plaisir du texte serait irréductible à son foncionnement gramarien [phéno-textuel], comme le plaisir du corps est irréductible au besoin physiologique*; 1973:30]. (1990b:17)

This erotic body, moreover, is erotic not because of certain "erogenous zones," but because it is intermittent, showing itself like skin through gapes in a garment ("Is not the most erotic portion of the body *where the garment gapes?*"; Barthes, 1990b:9); the flash of skin, or the "staging of appearance-as-disappearance" (Barthes, 1990b:10) is what seduces the reader. It is a fetish object, but in a typically Barthesian paradox, the fetish also desires the reader, through "a whole disposition of invisible screens, selective baffles: vocabulary, references, readability, etc.…" (Barthes, 1990b:27). Sexy sentences stand out/stand alone, and, like sexy bodies which invite the viewer to envision or imagine their erotic practice (Barthes, 1995:164)—not because of their beauty but because of the viewer's fantasy—they invite the reader to glimpse their eroticism through linguistic practice.[4]

---

[4] Something could be made here of Barthes's homosexual orientation, and the proposition in scholarship that this phase of his work (especially *A Lover's Discourse*) represents a gay relationship. Critics do not agree, however, that Barthes's so-called erotics of reading, or *A Lover's Discourse*, are explicitly gay (compare Schor, Heath, Saint-Amand). Barthes's work seems diffuse enough that it is suitable for a text like the Song of Songs, but it could also prod interesting homoerotic readings.

Here is what I did with my body one day ....
(Barthes, 1995:61)

So, following Barthes, "lover" would not be a throwaway metaphor for the Song and its exercising of its desires and charms; the text is active in interacting with its readers.[5] In Barthes' terms, we might say that it is embodied, it desires its readers, it has an erotic body that is an anagram of ours. The Song's display of itself is intermittent, carried on through language that teases, baffles, attracts. It is, moreover, a jealous lover; it closely guards the enjoyment and liberties readers take in it. With its orchestration of erotic content, imagery and plot, it prevents the easy assumption of various readerly pleasures, such as skipping through a text, reading selectively.[6] It commands constant attention, demands that readers always ask, "What does this mean? What is happening here?"

If the Song is erotic, it is doubly so, for it is also in part about erotic love. Thus, we encounter a duality of which Barthes would doubtless have been pleased: the Song is eroticized (in Barthesian terms, as above) by way of its erotic content. But what does it mean to say that the Song is about erotic love? That it depicts two people in love with each other who express their desire in lyrical, sometimes cryptic, language, need not be disputed. It is more difficult to assess whose desire is actually being revealed and how (what are the gender politics of the Song), and whether the Song hints at sexual love more than actually portrays it. In comparison to the Hebrew Bible's more regulated and efficient, "and · he · knew · her · and · she · conceived"— sex undertaken (or inflicted) for procreative purposes—the Song's lyrics seem highly irregular, in Barthes's terms they are perverse, for they showcase sexual activity which is pursued or enacted for its own end.[7] More often than not, however, the "good stuff" in the Song is

---

[5] To speak of the Song as a lover is, naturally, a decision about reading, a move to position the text as a (fictional) speaking, feeling subject, in order to identify and give voice to an "other" party in the reading process. This seems an appropriate enterprise given the Song's subject matter.

[6] Some might say that the nature of the Song's composition allows for selective reading. Indeed, one of the issues in Song scholarship is whether the book should be read as a series of unrelated poems, or as a unified poem (see below).

[7] Perversity is not a morally loaded term for Barthes in the way that it might ordinarily be used.

obfuscated by cryptic imagery or is disappointingly *coitus interruptus*, so that what actually takes place remains clouded.

To speak of the Song's erotic content is also to ask about readers, to posit, erotic for whom? Readers vary on whether the Song teases us with showing-of-the-ankles suggestion or clobbers us with full frontal. To some, references to sexual intercourse are obvious; so obvious, in fact, that they are added in where one might be hard pressed to find them—which sometimes says more about interpreters' sexual interests than anything else. A small example from Michael Goulder illustrates my point. Of Song 8:5, "under the apple tree I awakened you," he writes:

> ... it could be that the place where she aroused him is an anatomical place as well as a place in a glade; and that it is thought of as an apple-tree by virtue of the two fruits hanging down above the 'trunk'; that there is a special force to 'under', because it is at the under end of this tree that the nerves are concentrated that make for such arousal; ....(7–8)

Such a reading, still euphemistic in its own way, tells us an awful lot about the reader as well as the fluidity of the text. Goulder himself makes the point, too, that the Song "can sail nearer the wind than this," meaning that it can be more overt in terms of its erotic content (8).

> *I tell myself: the signs of this passion run the risk of smothering the other. Then should I not*, precisely because of my love, *hide from the other how much love* ...?

I do not want to eclipse the politics of the Bible's portrayal of sexuality, and, though this would be relevant here, there is not space to address the issue in any detail. Feminist critics are quick to point out that sexual politics and sexual conduct in the Song seem to be "equal," in the sense that the woman's sexual needs and desires are pursued as much as the man's, some would say more so. But this is a limited way of looking at the Song's gender politics, for various factors, such as the descriptions of the body and the attack (rape?) of the woman in 5:7, among others, challenge these usual feminist assertions. It is true that sex in the Song seems to be pursued without consideration for procreation, however, and in this way I would grant that the Song is unique—in Barthes's terms, perverse. In other cases where non-procreative sex happens in the Hebrew Bible, if the woman is shown to be a willing participant, or even the instigator, it is so that the reader may be shown the waywardness and risks of female sexuality. It would be difficult to read this message into the Song, but I do not want to exclude the possibility that female sexuality is yet a dangerous entity there.

(Barthes, 1990a:42)

In my view, the text is purposely fluid in presenting its erotic material, that is to say, purposely suggestive. Moreover, its suggestiveness is what makes it realistically and most effectively erotogenic. The speculations by commentators that seek to "fix" and map out sexual events confirm this proposition. The key is in the speculation, not the definitive mapping, for, as Barthes observes, should the "event" actually occur, there would be "disappointment, deflation" (1990b:58). That is, the all-too-available pattern in modern erotic literature of excitement/foreplay/consummation becomes dull and disappointing for those who read it (Barthes, 1990b:58). Goulder's propensity to hammer the point home, and on texts that might not even warrant it, is a case in point. In asking, thus, "have they done *it* yet?" or, "did they do *it* here?" (a crude but accurate rendering of some commentators' interest in the lovers' consummation of their desire), readers of the Song participate in its strategy; they become willing objects of its amatory designs. They become enticed by the text. The Song's apparent ability to hold off from climaxing—we might call it its stamina—is a key to the success of its strategy. By teasing the reader (who, the Song might assume, reads it because he or she is interested in its contents), the Song keeps its lovers interested. *Is not the most erotic portion of the body where the garment gapes?*

The Song's erotic artistry can be more fully illustrated by looking at 5:1, the widely posited "consummation" scene of the book: "I come to my garden my sister my bride; I gather my myrrh with my spice, I eat my honeycomb with my honey, I drink my wine with my milk." This text has been the (or one of the) frequently acknowledged "moment(s) of truth" for the lovers chiefly because it appears to be the man's response to an apparently direct invitation for sex from his partner (4:16):[8] "Let my beloved come to his garden, and eat its choicest fruits" (Bloch and Bloch: 178, Fox: 138–39; Goulder: 39; Lavoie: 145; Murphy: 162; Pope: 504–6; etc.). "Come into" (בוא) here is understood in its sexual sense, and "his garden," refers to the woman, so named by the man in 4:12 and 4:15. Verbs of eating and

---

[8] Other factors have also influenced the decision, such as the expectation in earlier commentaries that the couple, once married (chap. 3), would have to have a wedding night (e.g. Delitzsch and Budde, as cited in Pope [504]).

drinking, moreover, conjure up various consummatory proclivities (see Prov 5:15, 19; Fox: 139).

But is this scene as straightforward as commentators seem to think it is? In the first instance, the verbs of consumption in 5:1 are a series of four perfects, a tense which is usually translated to give a present, past or past perfect meaning, but which may also refer to that "which is *represented* as accomplished, even though it [is] continued into the present time, or even [is] actually in the future" (Kautzsch: 125 n.1, original italics). Depending on their views of what is happening in the Song at this point, then, commentators may play with the tenses and take advantage of their relative fluidity, making the consummation either a past or a future event. Pope lists some of the translations that have been employed to date: past, present (implying either imminent— but not yet completed—action, or future action), future perfect, the *perfect confidentiae* (future action, but so certain that it may be spoken of as having occurred), and so on (504).

The greater context of texts such as this one may also influence interpretation, as we saw with 4:16. Quite a different state of affairs occurs in 5:2–8, however. There, an apparently failed encounter results in the woman searching for her lover who has abandoned her, and being beaten for her efforts. One easily becomes embroiled in the logistics of the situation: have they just consummated their love/ marriage? If so, why is the meeting being attempted all over again? Why is he knocking at her "door" when he has just entered her "garden" (compare Fox: 144–46, Keel: 192, Murphy: 165, 170–71, Pope: 517–19)? Does the scene imply that the lovers have not yet come together, or that they must make another attempt, or even that they are doomed never to be united?

In the case of 5:1, concern with the continuity of the Song's texts and grammatical choices such as decisions about verb tenses, indicate, among other things, commentators' desires to make of the Song a story.[9] I see readers' motivations to understand what is happening and indeed their quest for coitus in the text as part of a novelistic drive that arises when they are confronted with the Song of Songs. In this we see the second aspect of its amatory technique.

---

[9] The separation of the Song into scenes also reflects this interpretive move. One finds, for example, that in most commentaries 5:2–8 has been separated from 5:1 (Bloch and Bloch, Fox, Goulder, Keel, Murphy. Pope is an exception), thereby removing the potential contradiction.

Whereas we may say that readers of any texts typically try to "make sense" of what they read, reading the Song is a unique enterprise because of its structure and its content. I am not suggesting that readers approach the book with the intention to render it into a narrative. Rather, owing to the Song's meandering, lyrical style and its apparent mixture of genres, they face questions about how they should go about reading this text, almost as soon as they start: is the Song comprised of a series of poems? How, if at all, are they related? Who are the characters in the Song? Is the book telling their story? Once readers identify the Song's apparent intentions toward, or its baffling ignorance of, a tangible structure, they are better situated to make sense of its lyrical maze. Or so they figure. Added to the Song's display of brief, veiled, sexual encounters which has also been stimulating the readers' drive, the quest for plot in effect becomes a kind of coital quest itself. As with the Song's erotic subject matter, it is not the outcome that is the attraction (the completed and unified plot), rather its titillation, its promise. What better way to pursue the encounters of the lovers than to construct them into a narrative, where the excitement builds to a satisfying climax? Hard on the heels of such drives is the question, What happens?

> *I am nailed to the scene and yet very wide awake:*
> *my attention constitutes a part of what is being acted out,*
> *nothing is external to the scene, and yet I read it.*
> (Barthes, 1990a:123)

The Song entices us with the question, What happens? as soon as the credits go by (1:1), with its opening shot of a man and a woman in love (1:2). But it is more than a static glimpse of the couple at work or at play. This first text, "let him kiss me," is hardly an idle moment of wishful thinking. The statement has narrative currency, an urgency that jump starts the plot into motion. It infers that the presence of the one she seeks is imminent, so much so that we are not surprised when she addresses him in the next verse, or when she meets up with him in his chambers. Then, *what happens*, when, two verses later, we learn that the woman's siblings are angry with her: will they prevent the lovers from seeing each other again? The woman's first meeting with her lover in 1:4 was merely a tease. Sometimes, she calls and he is absent. Or she will send him away. Or maybe he will be the one looking for her. Sometimes they might meet each other. Sometimes obstacles prevent their uniting, be they watchmen, siblings, mothers, foxes, or the lovers' own whimsies. Then, even the last word in the book is ambiguous: does בְּרַח mean that the woman is telling her lover to hurry to her (the mountains of spices), or to flee? If it is the latter, the ending is most unsatisfactory for us old romantics. After all that chasing, seeking, finding and missed encounters, why wouldn't the book end with the protagonist finally getting the kiss she looked for in 1:2, and more besides?

Part of reading the Song, then, involves keeping track of the "narrative" movement, and, additionally, of who is speaking, who is searching, whose desire stimulates whatever action is occurring. Readerly desire persists, not merely to know what happens, or when *it* happens, but because what happens is accessible at constantly shifting intervals. In keeping track of its constant shifting, readers become personally involved in the Song, they feel the impetus to search and are devastated by missed encounters. The lover's quest for his or her beloved in effect becomes the reader's own.

> *The image is presented, pure and distinct as a letter:*
> *It is a letter of what pains me ....*
> *The image is peremptory, it always has the last word;*
> *no knowledge can contradict it, "arrange" it, refine it.*
> (Barthes, 1990a:132)

If the reader decides that the Song tells a story, and that, as in the case of 5:1, the story includes an identifiable consummation of the couple's relationship, there is yet more that influences the picture, that acts to effect readerly confusion—that keeps the Song's lovers interested. In terms of the book's amatory technique, we come here to the third aspect, its use of imagery. A key role in the ambiguity or suggestiveness of 5:1 has to be the enticing and confounding nature of the images. In the first place, here, as elsewhere throughout the Song, readers are always confronted with the question, How do we know how the images are to be understood? Do we know that coming into a garden, plucking myrrh, eating honey and drinking wine with milk are to be taken as euphemisms for sex? In an obvious, literalizing alternative, if the identification of the garden and various foodstuffs with the woman's body is denied, a man simply walks into a garden and has a nice (?) meal. If we allow that these elements do represent the woman's body (as we might, since he uses them to describe it in

4:10–15 [garden is also used by the woman to describe herself in 4:16b]), who is to say that eating, drinking or plucking (ארה)—verbs of taking and consumption, agreed—need indicate that coitus occurs here? Might these actions, whatever they intimate, not still be relegated to foreplay, or some other private peculiarity between the lovers of which we are not aware? The images used in the lover's description, and indeed elsewhere in the Song, offer little help in deciding the matter. In 4:10, wine describes her דדים, as it does his in 1:2. In 4:11, we see that honey and milk are under the woman's tongue. A long list of spices (including myrrh; מר) describes her "groove" in 4:14.[10] Do drinking, eating and plucking these various items correlate to particular parts of her anatomy or specific sexual activities? Moreover, what do their combinations in 5:1 signify? Is it important for the Song's erotic message that milk and wine are consumed together, for instance?

The opacity of the Song's imagery is no stranger to lovers of the Song. The so-called "dream scene" that follows 5:1 in vv. 2–8 is another, immediate example. There, hands, bolts, doors, and myrrh— all arguably parts of the lovers' bodies—give a suggestive but in-complete picture of what is happening. Elsewhere in the Song, yet more concentrated body imagery is exemplary. It is frequently a source of confusion for readers, one could even say a source of anxiety. Over the years, a lot of energy has been expended in commentaries and poetic translations on the descriptions of the lovers' bodies (4:1–5 [6:4 7]; 5:10–16; 7:1–8), in order to give an account of what various images mean for the body parts they describe. Most writers acknowledge the difficulty in interpreting the images, which reveal odd, sometimes ridiculous bodies that are amalgamations of natural and military imagery; as Murphy notes, there is at the least a "certain poetic playfulness" evident in them, and in some cases, they are

---

[10] The word שלחיך (שלח; shoot, weapon, missile, sprout) in 4:13 is problematic. Pope translates it as the singular "groove" (491); Keel as "canals" (174-78); Görg debates between "canals" (*känale*) and "branches" (*zweige*); the NRSV renders it "channel." (See also Vg: *emissiones tuae*; LXX: *apostolai sou*; Pope: 490). It is usually taken as a euphemism for vagina (even though plural), especially when coupled with פרדס which gives a meaning something like "your groove is a park/enclosure (of pomegranates)." An enclosed "grove" is in keeping with commentators' expectations of the chastity of this "virgin" (a locked garden). The spices in question come as a list in 4:14 which continue the metaphor of 4:13: Her "groove" is an enclosure of pomegranates, with the choicest fruits, with nard . . . and then the list begins.

comical, or even grotesque (71). One assumption generally governs the interpretive enterprise: the descriptions must be explained as contributing to a loving and complimentary portrait of the intended (this is their story).[11] For example, the woman's teeth being compared to sheep depicts perfectly arranged, neatly matched, white teeth (Murphy: 155, 159), and the comparison of her neck to the tower of David shows that it is "bespangled" and manifests her "erect and bold carriage" (Pope: 465). This trend witnesses to the ideals of readers and their expectations of what should be involved in "love poetry."

> *Language is a skin: I rub my language against the other.*
> *It is as if I had ... fingers at the tip of my words.*
> (Barthes, 1990a:73)

A measure of the Song-as-Lover's ploy to attract its readers, then, is the variance in clarity—or opacity—of the imagery. At times, the text is bold: "Let him kiss me with the kisses of his mouth" (1:2); at others, it veils its meaning a little: "with great delight I sat in his shadow and his fruit was sweet to my taste" (2:3). At its most enigmatic, the Song's imagery makes one ponder whether it is really expressive of desire at all, as in the four descriptions of the lovers' bodies. The variation of imagery in the Song flirts with innuendo and clarity and thus with readerly understanding. The Song's imagery is compelling, because it is sometimes clear, sometimes confuses, thereby displaying its erotic content openly and concurrently secreting it away.

> *Every contact, for the lover, raises the question of an answer:*
> *the skin is asked to reply.*
> (Barthes, 1990a:67)

The Song may be a jealous lover, ensuring that it constantly has the attentions of its readers, but it is not unjust. It does seem to allow the right of reply. The intermingling of erotic content, images and narrative play allows for the participation of readers, as we have seen. There is yet more, however, in that the Song maybe offers more than readers will take on, or, allows some of its overtures to be resisted. I want to turn here in a slightly different direction and return to the Song's erotic content. If the Song is by no means clear about sex as we

---

[11] Brenner is one exception. See also Black.

have seen, even when commentators think it is at its most blatant, another aspect of its eroticism must also be acknowledged, that the reverse can be true as well. Sometimes, the Song may actually suggest what commentators do not wish to acknowledge. This feature of Song scholarship was the impetus behind Goulder's focus in his commentary (8), but even he has limits as to what he will and will not write about.

I consider here what is a more extreme example than Goulder's work. Stephen Moore has recently called for a "carnal allegory" of the Song (Boer, 2000), which Roland Boer postulates "would be concerned with a range of questions: the function of sexual language and poetry, narrative and sexual description, explicitness and realism, repetition, fetishism, and the range of sexual practices suggested in the Song...."[12] Though he does not undertake this project here, in another work (1999), he takes us a step closer to it in a provocative *ménage* (*à quatre, cinq ou six*, depending on who you count) of author, book, and a host of fictional porn stars who inevitably act out the play.

Boer's porn-essay raises the question, however, How much is too much? One is uncomfortably forced to play the voyeur in his reading, and it is not so much that one must question how comfortable one is with reading about explicit sex (pornographic sex being still another issue), but whether the Song hasn't been taken advantage of quite unfairly. That is, in Boer's reading, the pleasure of the text becomes, as Barthes has referred to it, like the spectator who leaps on stage to hasten the stripper's unveiling (1990b:11), only I am not so sure, as Barthes stipulates, that the order of the ritual has been respected here. Boer's reading, I think, in effect denies the text its erotic freedom by rushing through foreplay, stripping and *taking* it before it has had the chance to show a little skin.

As a reader, it is therefore obvious that I have "sensibilities" of my own about the Song's erotic material which make me critical or uncomfortable with how other readers have read it; all readers do. I also have my own ideas about what the Song is and is not trying to say in terms of its erotic content. Thus, the manner in which or the degree to which readers *want* to read the erotic content of the Song is also a significant feature of the amatory relationship between Song and

---

[12] Boer continues, "... such as sex between variously gendered partners, bestiality, inter-generational sex, group sex, water sports, menstrual sex, fisting, discipline and so on. However, this is not my task here." (2000, page unavailable).

reader. The fact that the Song can support readings as varied as Bernard's[13] and Boer's indicates not only that its imagery is opaque and can be read in a variety of ways—that, as a lover, it is quite versatile—but also that there are restrictions (a kind of censorship?) in terms of what can be discussed around the eroticism of the Song. This is extremely significant for its success as a lover.[14]

A less "obvious" (in terms of sexual content) or controversial text, 2:3 and its counterpart in 8:5, might further illustrate my point. In 2:3, the woman compares her lover to an apple tree: "As an apple tree among the trees of the wood, so is my love among young men. With great delight I sat in his shadow, and his fruit was sweet to my taste." We already saw how Goulder[15] (in the introduction to his commentary) provocatively identified the tree in 8:5 with the (male) lover's genitalia. After that reading, I expected to find a rather explicit explanation of 2:3. Perhaps he might have commented on the lover's priapic prowess (a tree among trees?), and maybe explicated—or at least alluded to—the "oral arts" of the woman who sits in his shadow and enjoys his fruits. Boer certainly doesn't shy away from the opportunity.[16] Instead, however, Goulder's reading of the apple tree's significance in 2:3 is quite moderate and is almost missed, it is so veiled: "... the apple forms a suggestive pair to the lily ["singled out for its deep calyx"; 18], with its fruit often borne in pairs along a rising spur" (19). The connection is made not between the tree and the mouth, as the text intimates, but the tree and the lily of the previous verse (2:2). Moreover, a comment in the following paragraph seems to contradict Goulder's earlier, quietly uttered suggestion as to the phallic significance of the tree here in 2:3: "The sweetness of the fruit to her

---

[13] Allegorical readings of the Song would provide a fruitful field of inquiry for this topic. In one of his sermons, Bernard of Clairvaux makes a reference to the garden in 5:1 as representative of one of the stages of scriptural history: "The man who thirsts for God eagerly studies and meditates on the inspired word, knowing that there he is certain to find the one for whom he thirsts. Let the garden, then, represent the plain, unadorned, historical sense of Scripture..." (28 [Serm. 23:2]).

[14] See Boer's comments on the relationship between censorship and pornography (1999).

[15] I do not wish to appear to be picking on Goulder, who, as I said above, is undertaking a much needed step in Song criticism. It is, in fact, for this very reason that I make use of his work so often in this paper, for he is one of the few who actually has sustained discussions on the Song's erotic material.

[16] Though he doesn't explicitly mention oral sex (1999).

palate suggests that they now kiss ..." (19). This, he decides, is what occurs because of the context of the verse (2:4–6 and 1:2).[17]

Goulder's reading is not unique. Something prevents him and other commentators from being tempted by the apples in 2:3 and 8:5 (compare Murphy: 132, 136; Fox: 107; Keel: 82; among others). It is not, moreover, the case that only a few ambiguous references are being ignored in Song scholarship, such as these ones in 2:3 and 8:5 and, for example, in 7:10. The Song abounds with references to eating and drinking and is a catalogue of comestibles (see Lavoie).[18] Though Goulder and others have been quite willing to venture into discussing sexuality in the Song, at times somewhat explicitly (even when it involves female genitalia),[19] there remains a definite barrier at the point of what might be considered "polite" discourse about (conventional) sex. Boer's work is a good example here: it promotes the question of whether it is necessary to break through the barriers (in Boer's case, to cross over into "pornography") before one can actually discuss what might be seen as the full erotic range of the Song. And in doing so, will it be necessary to take the kind of risks of marginalizing oneself from

---

[17] Pope also writes of kissing and intercourse (the reference in 8:5 is cited to support his reading) (371–72); Murphy, the "delights of love" (136); Fox, of kisses, and also the egalitarian nature of the relationship: here she is in his protection (shade), in 1:3, he was in hers (108); Keel, the "tenderness and erotic attention of the lover" (82); Lavoie that he is "l'aphrodisiaque," the lover who, "loin d'assouvir la faim de sa bien-aimée, lui creuse l'appétit" (133).

[18] A detailed inquiry into the Song's sexual content will eventually have to take these on board and consider them seriously as part of an erotic vocabulary. Boer's work (1999) is the only exception of which I am aware (though see Landy: *passim*). Even Lavoie, who promises a discussion of "tendresse canibalique," doesn't take the step.

[19] Interestingly, commentators, primarily male to date, seem to be significantly more comfortable with discussing female genitalia in (explicit) detail than male. If the penis is referred to, it will usually be called the phallus (e.g. Pope: 517, 517), or treated euphemistically, as in Goulder's discussion of the apple tree and the "tusk" of ivory (5:14). This does not mean that female genitalia is not also referred to euphemistically—Pope will sometimes use euphemisms ("evermoist receptacle" is one of the most creative; 617) in addition to the regular, anatomical terms (vagina, vulva). Compare, however, Goulder's and Eslinger's detailed anatomical descriptions of the woman's sexual organs (Goulder: 38, Eslinger: 276–77). One could pursue this matter further with respect to investigating the fantasies of readers. Boer's work would be another interesting field for this topic.

"polite" and conventional academic discourse that Boer does?[20] Further, are these the only risks of such a reading?

Indeed, reading the Song in any way seems risky: to read it is effectively to replay the book. Readers interpolate themselves into the text's contours as they become personally involved in them, as they arc compelled to ask What happens? Or, What does this mean? But their interpolation is hardly objective, rather, it is deeply personal and affective (*What does this mean for me?*). They might identify with the lovers in the Song, but they also become lovers of it themselves and are subject to the desires and whimsy of the text, which teases them by playing at display and hiding. Moreover, they respond with their own demands and restrictions, so that there is constant dialogue and negotiation between the two. So it is that both lovers may say,

> I am caught in this contradiction: on the one hand, I believe I know the other better than anyone and triumphantly assert my knowledge to the other ("I know you—I'm the only one who really knows you"); and on the other hand, I am often struck by the obvious fact that the other is impenetrable, intractable, not to be found; …. Who is the other? I wear myself out, I shall never know. (Barthes, 1990a:134)

To replay the book is thus to encounter the contours of intimate relationship. In Francis Landy's words, "we find ourselves spoken there" (7).

Bibliography

Barthes, Roland
    1973   *Le Plaisir du texte.* Paris: du Seuil.
    1990a   *A Lover's Discourse: Fragments.* Trans. Richard Howard. London: Penguin.
    1990b   *The Pleasure of the Text.* Trans. Richard Miller. Oxford: Basil Blackwell.
    1995   *Roland Barthes.* Trans. Richard Howard. London: Papermac (Macmillan General Books).

---

[20] Boer is not uncomfortable with this position (2000). Of course, one must also ask if the risk of marginalization from mainstream academic discourse is not such a bad thing.

Bernard of Clairvaux
　　1983　　　*On the Song of Songs, II: Sermons 21–46.* Trans. Kilian Walsh.
　　　　　　　Cistercian Fathers Series 7. Kalamazoo: Cistercian Publica-
　　　　　　　tions.

Black, Fiona C.
　　2000　　　"Beauty or the Beast? The Grotesque Body in the Song of
　　　　　　　Songs." *BibInt* 8/3 (forthcoming).

Bloch, Ariel and Chana Bloch
　　1995　　　*The Song of Songs: A New Translation with an Introduction
　　　　　　　and Commentary.* Berkeley: University of California Press.

Boer, Roland
　　1999　　　"Night Sprinkle(s): Pornography and the Song of Songs."
　　　　　　　Chap. 3 in *Knockin' on Heaven's Door.* London: Routledge.
　　2000　　　"The Second Coming: Repetition and Insatiable Desire in the
　　　　　　　Song of Songs." *BibInt* 8/3 (forthcoming).

Brenner, Athalya
　　1993　　　"Come Back, Come Back the Shulammite' (Song of Songs
　　　　　　　7:1–10): A Parody of the *wasf* Genre." Pp. 234–57 in *A
　　　　　　　Feminist Companion to the Song of Songs.* Ed. Athalya
　　　　　　　Brenner. Sheffield: JSOT.

Calvet, Louis-Jean
　　1994　　　*Roland Barthes: A Biography.* Trans. Sarah Wykes. Cam-
　　　　　　　bridge: Polity Press.

Eslinger, Lyle
　　1981　　　"The Case of an Immodest Lady Wrestler in Deuteronomy
　　　　　　　XXV 11–12." *VT* 31:269–81.

Fox, Michael V.
　　1985　　　*The Song of Songs and the Ancient Egyptian Love Songs.*
　　　　　　　Madison: University of Wisconsin Press.

Gallop, Jane
　　1986　　　"Feminist Criticism and the Pleasure of the Text." *North
　　　　　　　Dakota Quarterly* 54:119–34.

Görg, Manfred
　　1994　　　"'Kanäle' oder 'Zweige' in Hld 4,13?" *BN* 72:20–23.

Goulder, Michael D.
　　1986　　　*The Song of Fourteen Songs.* JSOTSup 36. Sheffield: JSOT.

Heath, Stephen
　　1983　　　"Barthes on Love." *SubStance* 37/38:100–106.

Kautzsch, E., ed.
　　1910　　　*Gesenius' Hebrew Grammar.* Trans. E. Cowley. Oxford:
　　　　　　　Clarendon Press.

Keel, Othmar
　　1994　　　*The Song of Songs.* Trans. Frederick J. Gaiser. Minneapolis:
　　　　　　　Fortress Press.

Landy, Francis
    1983   *Paradoxes of Paradise: Identity and Difference in the Song of Songs*. Sheffield. Almond.

Lavoie, Jean-Jacques
    1995   "Festin érotique et tendresse cannibalique dans la Cantique des Cantiques." *SR* 24:131–46.

Murphy, Roland
    1990   *The Song of Songs*. Hermeneia. Minneapolis: Fortress Press.

O'Neill, John
    1984   "Breaking the Signs: Roland Barthes and the Literary Body." Pp. 182–200 in *The Structural Allegory: Reconstructing Encounters with the New French Thought*. Ed. John Fekete. Manchester: Manchester University Press.

Pope, Marvin
    1977   *Song of Songs*. AB 7C. New York: Doubleday.

Saint-Amand, Pierre
    1996   "The Secretive Body: Roland Barthes's Gay Erotics." *Yale French Studies* 90:153–71.

Schor, Naomi
    1987   "Dreaming Dissymmetry: Barthes, Foucault, and Sexual Difference." Pp. 98–110, 272–76 in *Men in Feminism*. Ed. Alice Jardine and Paul Smith. New York: Methuen.

TO LOVE THE LORD
AN INTERTEXTUAL READING OF JOHN 20

Adele Reinhartz

Introduction

In his introduction to the first *Semeia* volume on *Textual Determinacy*, Robert Culley reflects on the necessary interplay between reader and text in determining meaning (vii). Since the publication of that volume, the field of biblical studies, at least that part of biblical studies that is represented by *Semeia*, has increasingly called into question the very notion that textual meaning can be determined in any fixed way. This shift in language and assumptions, however, only serves to underscore the sense that meanings float in the space between reader and text, held aloft by the interplay between them.

One aspect of this interplay is intertextuality—the reading of one text against the background of another, at the discretion and choice of the reader. In this essay I attempt an intertextual approach to John 20, in which I argue that John 20 allows for two divergent readings of Mary Magdalene *vis-à-vis* the authority structure set out in the Gospel. One of these readings employs the tropes and imagery of discipleship that emerge through a study of specific elements of the chapter and its links to other sections of the Gospel. A second reading focuses on the tropes of physicality and sensuality that emerge when John 20 is read in conjunction with biblical love stories. I dedicate this effort to Bob, in appreciation of his long-standing participation in the Canadian

Society of Biblical Studies through which so many of us have learned so much from him.

Mary Magdalene and Discipleship

Is Mary a Disciple?

It is amply clear that Mary is an apostle, commissioned by Jesus to deliver "the good news of Easter" to his his ἀδελφοί (brethren; 20:17, Schneiders: 160–61). Like the biblical prophets, she is commissioned directly by "the Lord," given the text of the message, and sent off to deliver it to the designated recipients. More difficult to discern, however, is whether, in addition to being an apostle, emissary, or prophet, Mary is also to be included among that group formally designated "the disciples" (μαθηταί).

The argument rests on the interchange between Jesus and Mary in 20:15–16. Jesus initially addresses her as "woman" (γύναι) and asks two questions: "Why are you crying? Whom are you seeking?" (20:15a). Mary takes him to be the gardener, hence her response: "Sir, if you have carried him away, tell me where you have laid him, and I will take him away" (20:15b). Jesus then calls her by name, "Mariam" (20:16); she recognizes him and calls him "Rabbouni" (Ραββουνι, which is not Hebrew, as the narrator maintains, but Aramaic).

A number of arguments support the view that Mary is a disciple of Jesus. First, by addressing Mary as "woman," Jesus links her with his mother Mary, who is addressed in similar fashion in 2:4 and 19:25–27. Both women, it is argued, are disciples; this common mode of address emphasizes this similarity between them (Schüssler Fiorenza: 330; O'Day: 301). Second, in asking her, "Whom are you seeking?" Jesus evokes the call of the first disciples in 1:38 and thus establishes continuity between Mary and the first disciples (O'Day: 301). Third, in identifying her by name, Jesus is acting out the role of the good shepherd who calls his own sheep (10:26). Mary's recognition of Jesus as "Rabbouni" indicates that she is a member of his flock (10:27) and demonstrates that she is a true disciple who recognizes the resurrected Jesus as teacher (Schüssler Fiorenza: 333).

The contrary view, however, may also be supported. Alison Jasper, for example, argues that although Mary is commissioned as a messenger, she is not more than this. The message she takes to Jesus' brethren is addressed not to her but to them (113). In Jasper's reading, Mary is a mere vehicle for the message; what is important from Jesus' perspective is not that she understand, but that the disciples hear and comprehend. Claudia Setzer points to a more straightforward exegetical basis for questioning whether Mary is a disciple. John 21:14 enumerates Jesus' appearance in Galilee as the third of the risen Jesus' encounters with his disciples. This enumeration implies, of course, that there were two previous visits. John 20 clearly recounts two such appearances, 20:19–23 and 20:26–29, in which Jesus appears to a group of disciples in Jerusalem. One may therefore infer that the Gospel narrator does not consider 20:1–18 to recount an appearance to a disciple and hence that Mary is not among the group formally designated as "disciples" (Setzer: 268).[1]

Certainly part of the dispute centers on the definition of discipleship. If discipleship is understood broadly as referring to followers of and believers in Jesus as the Messiah, Son of God, then it is obvious that both men and women are included in this group. All of the women characters in the Gospel are, or become, followers of Jesus and can therefore be called "disciples" under this general definition. In favor of the broad definition are passages such as John 6:60 and 6:66, which describe, respectively, the puzzled reaction of "many of his disciples" to Jesus' teaching concerning the bread of life and the departure of many of the disciples from the fold. A similar use is evident in John 15:8, in which Jesus urges his listeners to bear much fruit and become his disciples. These passages support an inclusive reading of the term μαθηταί (disciples), as well as of the related term ἀδελφοί (literally, brethren; 20:17).[2]

---

[1] It must be noted, however, that the Johannine narrative as it now stands is not always consistent in its enumeration. John 4:54 refers to the healing of the nobleman's son as the "second sign that Jesus did after coming from Judea to Galilee," though it would seem that in fact this healing was Jesus' third sign as narrated in the Gospel. For this reason the enumeration of Jesus' appearances may also be construed as inconsistent, in that it omits the appearance to Mary Magdalene. On the other hand, the enumeration as it stands implies that the appearance to Mary did not count in the enumeration of appearances to disciples because she was not considered such.

[2] Schneiders (161) translates ἀδελφοί in 20:17 as "brothers and sisters." She deplores the masculine form in 20:17 which reflects the androcentric character of the Greek language and the culture of the times, but argues that "in reading and translating it we should honor its obviously inclusive meaning" (166).

In other passages, however, the Gospel exhibits a more limited use of the term "disciples" to designate that group of followers who accompanied Jesus on his travels and were his most regular audience. The question then becomes, were women in general, and Mary Magdalene in particular, part of this group according to the Gospel narrative? In my view the answer is no.

Most telling is the fact that no individual woman is explicitly designated as a disciple, nor are women included among the group identified as such. The listing of Jesus' mother, brothers and disciples as those who returned to Capernaum after the wedding at Cana (2:12) suggests that these are not overlapping categories. The fact that Jesus' disciples marvel that he was talking to a woman in 4:27 suggests that no women were among them. No women are mentioned in John 6, in which the disciples follow Jesus from one side of the Sea of Galilee to the other, nor in the foot washing scene in John 13. Of course, it may be that we should read women *into* this silence rather than read them out of it, but I would argue that doing so lets John off the hook too easily.

What, then, of the above arguments in favor of identifying Mary as a disciple? In my view the exchanges between Jesus and Mary do no more, and no less, than confirm the observation that Mary is a believer in and follower of Jesus. They do not label her as a disciple in the formal sense of belonging to the group with which Jesus travelled and associated with most closely.

Far from linking Mary with others who are formally designated as disciples, Jesus' use of the word "woman" to address Mary connects her closely both with Jesus' mother (2:14; 19:25–27) and the Samaritan woman (4:21). Though not formally designated as disciples, all three women are significant within their respective pericopes. The mother of Mary prompts the first sign that Jesus performs. The Samaritan woman receives Jesus' direct proclamation of his messianic identity using the powerful "I am" formulation (4:26), and becomes an apostle to the Samaritans. Mary Magdalene is the first to witness the risen Lord and she receives her own apostolic commission.

Another element linking these three women is the sexual subtext of their narrative portrayals. Jesus' mother is encountered in the context of a wedding at which she inexplicably takes over the role of hostess by worrying about the availability of wine. Jesus reveals knowledge of the Samaritan's chequered sexual history. He seems quite prepared to drink from the cup of a woman with whom Jews would not normally associate, and who might have expected a lusty rather than sermonic reception from a thirsty man she meets at a well (cf. Eslinger). There are also sexual connotations to Jesus' directive to Mary, that she refrain, or perhaps, desist, from touching him (20:17). In having Jesus address Mary as "woman," the narrator may indeed be linking her to Jesus' mother and to the Samaritan woman, and drawing attention to the complexities of these relationships as well as to their public roles, but the form of address does not identify them as disciples.

Second, Jesus addresses the question "Whom are you seeking?" to three other individuals: the two disciples of John the Baptist who trail Jesus at the outset of his ministry (1:38) and the delegation that accompanies Judas at the moment of betrayal (18:4, 7).[3] Elsewhere the verb "to search for" (ζητέω) is used in a variety of ways, to refer to the seeking of Jesus or of God (e.g. 4:23; 5:44), to speak of the Jews' search for Jesus in order that they might kill him (e.g. 7:1, 19), and to warn that the Jews, or the disciples, will soon be seeking Jesus, unsuccessfully (7:34–36; 13:33). Though the verb may also have a technical meaning, such as to study (Schüssler Fiorenza: 333, Culpepper: 291–99), it does not appear to be a specific or exclusive marker of discipleship.

Third, the exchange during which Jesus calls Mary by name and she calls him her teacher (20:18) does indeed evoke John 10 and thereby identifies Mary as one of Jesus' own. Jesus' "own" include the disciples such as Peter, but are not limited to those who travelled with Jesus. Indeed, according to Jesus' prayer in John 17, his "own" include not only those who received Jesus' word directly but also those who will believe the testimony of his followers (17:20). Furthermore, the hallmark of those who are his own is that they too will experience resurrection. The Good Shepherd parable as well as the story of Lazarus's resurrection echo the language of 5:25–29, in which Jesus proclaims that the hour is coming, and is now here, when the dead will hear the voice of the Son of God, and those who hear will live. "Do not be astonished at this," he continues, "for the hour is coming when all

---

[3] In 4:27 the narrator notes that the disciples refrained from asking Jesus this question, puzzled though they were to find him speaking with the Samaritan woman.

who are in their graves will hear his voice and will come out—those who have done good, to the resurrection of life, and those who have done evil, to the resurrection of condemnation." The exchange between Mary and Jesus therefore not only marks her as one of his own, but also as one who will experience the resurrection of life.

To summarize. If a disciple is defined solely by faith in Jesus as the Messiah, Son of God, then it is abundantly clear that Mary Magdalene is a disciple. But the weight of the evidence does not support the view that the Gospel identifies Mary as a disciple in the narrower and more specific role of a person who lives and travels with Jesus. This conclusion does not preclude the possibility that the historical Jesus had female followers or that the historical Johannine community may have included women in leadership positions; the Gospel is not a clear window into the life of Jesus or the Johannine community.[4]

Mary and the Disciples

Far from identifying Mary as a disciple, John 20 sets up a relationship of some tension between Mary and those to whom the "disciple" designation is applied. Mary runs to Simon Peter and the beloved disciple immediately after discovering that the stone had been removed from the tomb. Although she has apparently not yet looked within the tomb, she reports that "they" have taken the Lord out of the tomb (20:2). That she turns to them so quickly demonstrates her recognition of their authority, to which she is subordinate. Her report implies not only their "need to know" but also the hope that they will be able to remedy the situation, that is, find the body or explain its absence.

The disciples disappoint. Although they respond to her report with some urgency, they fail to understand, and they fail to remain. Without investigating further, they simply return home and leave Mary at the empty tomb without any answers or help.

---

[4] According to Witherington (182), the positive portrayal of Mary Magdalene and other women is at least in part a reaction against negative views of women among Jews, a point that Witherington makes abundantly elsewhere. For a critique of Witherington's views on the role of women in Judaism, see Reinhartz, 1992:164–66.

Mary's final scene both recalls and reverses this set of events. A second time she runs to the disciples. Her second report solves the mystery concerning the whereabouts of Jesus' body; whereas the disciples could not explain the puzzle to her, she now explains it to them. Her prefatory comment, "I have seen the Lord" (20:18), is not simply a description of a wondrous experience but her badge of authority as messenger.

Mary's words, "I have seen the Lord," echo the words uttered by Hagar after her first encounter with the angel (Gen 16:13). This parallel is particularly interesting because it is part of a similar progression, or conflation, of sensation. It is not stated that Hagar had seen the angel; the text refers only to a conversation. Yet her conclusion after the angel's words is that she has seen the Lord, and she names a well after the experience. This suggests that her auditory experience is interpreted by her as sight. Similarly, Mary recognizes Jesus not by seeing him but only after she hears him call her name. Yet she relates this event to the disciples as a visual experience. The point in both cases is not to indicate that these women were imprecise and unable to distinguish between hearing and seeing, but rather, that the notion of seeing can be interpreted more broadly in the sense of experience or perception.

Mary's exclusive knowledge of the risen Lord could have signalled a shift in the formal structures of authority as the Gospel moves towards its conclusion. The narrative could have continued with a series of events that would have consolidated Mary's own authority based on the pivotal fact that Jesus had provided her alone with the solution to the puzzle and acted through her to convey the solution to the disciples. We could imagine a scenario in which the disciples rejoice at hearing the word, just as the noble father of the ill child in 4:53 rejoiced when his servants reported that his child was now well. Such a scenario would have fit in very well with the Gospel's emphasis on belief through hearing the word, as expressed in Jesus' words to Thomas, "Blessed are those who have not seen and yet have come to believe" (20:29). Finally, how delightful it would have been had Jesus conferred the holy spirit and its attendant authority over sin upon Mary, as the one who had "abided," remained at the tomb, sought him out, and believed.

But the narrative does not unfold in this way. Instead, the Gospel is completely silent on the disciples' reception of Mary's proclamation.

This silence dismantles Mary's authority that had been built up so carefully in 20:17–18, and instead restores the reader's attention, as well as the locus of authority, to the disciples through the three resurrection appearances they are granted and, even more so, through the elevation of Simon Peter to the role of shepherd of the flock. Mary appears no more.

Therefore as a communication to the disciples, Mary's report is superfluous and abortive. Although some scholars, such as Karen King, suggest that there is no evidence that disciples doubted or rejected her witness (1997a:3) I would counter that there is no evidence that they accepted her report. In this respect, Mary Magdalene's portrayal differs from that of the other two women whom Jesus calls "woman." Whereas the words of Jesus' mother contribute to the turning of water into wine, and the testimony of the Samaritan woman causes her compatriots to believe in Jesus (4:40), the words of Mary Magdalene have no discernible effect on their audience within the narrative. The disciples' rejoicing at Jesus' return comes only after he has shown them his hands and his side (20:21); a change in their own role occurs only after he breathes the holy spirit upon them (20:22–23).[5]

If her report to the disciples is without effect, the same should not be said with respect to the reader, however. As a communication to the reader, Mary's portrayal in John 20 is powerful. This power stems from the details of the passage itself, but emerges even more forcefully from an intertextual reading of the passage which draws Mary into connection with a range of biblical women and link her concerns in this passage with the central themes of other texts. Scholars have long discussed the possibility that John 20 contains biblical allusions and echoes. My aim is not to debate whether the author(s) of John intended these allusions, but rather to explore the impact of an intertextual reading on our perceptions of Mary, with particular attention to the questions of gender and authority.

---

[5] Note, however, that Jesus does not explain again the content of the message that he had commissioned Mary to convey to the disciples.

Mary Magdalene and Jesus' Body

Throughout her narrative, Mary is preoccupied with the body of Jesus. Her concern is made explicit in her own response to the empty tomb, and in Jesus' directive in 20:17, "Do not touch me." This explicit concern receives substance and texture when it is read against the background of other biblical passages which encode expressions of physicality and sensuality. The intertextual subtext attributes a role to Mary dramatically different from that conveyed through the explicit story.

Mary's Response to the Empty Tomb

As we have already noted, Mary interprets the missing or displaced stone as an indication that Jesus' body is absent from the tomb. Mary's hypothesis, as reported to the disciples, is that the body has been taken away by parties unknown and laid in some other place. After the disciples depart, leaving her no wiser, she weeps. Mary's weeping may simply express grief at the death of a loved one, similar to the grief displayed by Jesus at Lazarus' tomb (11:35, 38). But that it entails also worry, frustration, or despair at the absence of Jesus' physical body is confirmed by her comments to the angels and "the gardener," which reiterate her fear that the body has been stolen.

Mary expects the body to be present; in its absence, she is anxious to arrange for its retrieval and proper care. Marianne Sawicki suggests that Mary Magdalene's real fear is that the body, left outside the tomb, would not undergo normal decomposition and hence the bones would not be prepared for resurrection and the messianic age by the family and/or disciples (257). Gail O'Day suggests that Mary's confusion reflects the world-shattering dimension of the empty tomb; Mary does not yet have any categories other than grave-robbery through which to understand the empty tomb (300–301). Certainly, from a commonsense perspective, Mary's hypothesis is the only available one given that even the disciples closest to Jesus "did not know the scripture, that he must rise from the dead" (20:9).

Mary's Identification of Jesus as "the Gardener"

Mary's thrice-repeated alarm concerning the whereabouts of Jesus' body focuses our attention on the notion of Jesus' physicality. In the third iteration of her concern, she politely accuses "the gardener" of having carried the body away (20:15). Ben Witherington considers Mary Magdalene simply to have been mistaken in her identification of Jesus as the gardener (179). Others, however, recognize 20:15 as a moment of typical Johannine irony. As in all examples of irony, the scene depends upon communication between the reader and the narrator to which the character is not privy. Indeed, as O'Day notes, the power of the scene comes from the reader's anticipation of Mary's moment of recognition (301). In Schneiders's view, Mary Magdalene identifies Jesus as precisely who he is while completely missing the symbolic point (162; cf. O'Day: 301).

It is not Mary, however, who must comprehend the symbolic point, but rather the reader. According to Schneiders, Mary's behavior in the first part of the passage symbolizes the inner turmoil of early followers who felt they had to choose between the synagogue and faith in Jesus as the Messiah. Schneiders suggests that in turning away from the angels (20:14), Mary turns momentarily towards the things that lie behind her, that is, to what she has left behind, namely, Judaism. By insisting that the absence of Jesus' body means his absence from the world, Mary turns back to the previous dispensation which ended with the cross. But in turning towards Jesus and identifying him as "Rabbouni," Mary seals her choice of Jesus over Moses as her teacher (Schneiders: 161–62). Schneiders's interpretation seems far removed from the text itself, for there is no indication that Mary is in conflict over whether to be loyal to the synagogue or to Jesus. Rather, the garden setting, in which Jesus and Mary are alone together, calls to mind other biblical gardens, in particular the primordial garden of Eden of Gen 2–3, and the garden which symbolizes the female lover in Canticles. The theory that John 20 alludes to the Garden of Eden is considered tenuous by R. E. Brown (990). Nevertheless, John 20 readily calls Genesis to mind. Schneiders points out that God walks around the Garden of Eden (Gen 2:15–17; 3:8) just as the risen Jesus walks about the garden which holds his tomb (161). In more detail, Wyatt argues from biblical and postbiblical literature that the Garden of Eden was profoundly associated with royal motifs. From a Christian perspective, the cross is the tree of life from which the first man had been driven away. After his death, Jesus becomes the new gardener of Eden, reversing the decree of banishment that had been passed on the first Adam (38).[6] To Wyatt's points may be added that the allusion to Eden in John 20 also recalls the creation symbolism and imagery of the Johannine prologue (1:1–18).

Does reading Jesus as the new Adam transform Mary into the new Eve? The passage does not portray her using the familiar Genesis images. She does not evoke the woman who is made from Adam's body, converses with the serpent, eats the forbidden fruit, offers it to Adam, and is banished with him from the garden. Nevertheless, some echoes of Genesis may be heard. Jesus calls her "woman," just as the first man called his mate in Gen 2:23, and then calls her by name, as Adam did the first woman (Gen 3:20). Jesus' directive that Mary not cleave to him challenges the physical basis of the male-female relationship as described in Gen 2:24, according to which a man leaves his father and his mother and clings to his wife and they become one flesh. This echo suggests a contrast between the sexual relationship which developed between the first man and woman and the relationship of devotion between Jesus and Mary. In doing so, it also draws attention to the sexual potential of an encounter between man and woman in a garden.

The sexual undertones of the passage emerge even more clearly against the backdrop of another biblical garden. The garden of Canticles is identified with the body and person of the female lover. Mary's search for the body of Jesus echoes the search of the lover for the beloved in Cant 3:1–4.[7] This passage depicts the woman as seeking him whom her soul loves, but not finding him, calling him but receiving no answer. She asks the sentinels of the city, "Have you seen him whom my soul loves?" She then finds him, holds him and declares that she will not let him go until she brings him into her mother's house. The verb "to seek" ($\zeta\eta\tau\acute{\epsilon}\omega$) appears four times in these verses.

---

[6] The allusion to the Garden of Eden is reminiscent of the Pauline description of Jesus as a second Adam (Rom 5:12–20).

[7] That the Fourth Gospel as a whole contains numerous allusions to the Song of Songs is argued in detail by Ann Robert Winsor. See also Schneiders, who argues that the encounter between Jesus and Mary Magdalene is intended to evoke both the garden of Gen 2:15–17; 3:8 and the garden of Canticles understood as "the hymn of the covenant between Israel and Yahweh" (161).

Other parallels between Canticles and our chapter include the use of the verb παρακύπτω to mean "peering in" (John 20:5; Cant 2:9; Schneiders, 161), and the emphasis on spices associated with both gardens (John 19:39; Cant 1:12; 3:6; 4:6, 10; 5:1, 13). These parallels suggest that Mary Magdalene is symbolically presented as the beloved of the Lover in the Canticle, the spouse of the New Covenant mediated by Jesus in his glorification, the representative figure of the New Israel which emerges from the new creation (Schneiders: 168).

Touching/Not Touching

John 20:17 does not explicitly state that Mary attempted to touch or succeeded in touching Jesus. Jesus' command that she not touch him, or desist from touching him, presumes some such act or intention on her part. The question is: why the prohibition? Most readings place Jesus' command in the context of the words which follow: "For I have not yet ascended to the Father." These words are most frequently taken as an explanation of why Mary may not touch Jesus: he is too insubstantial, perhaps, to be touched physically. Or perhaps it is not fitting that a human embrace delay his ascension to the Father through which his glorification will be complete (Brown: 1012). Other aspects of the discussion focus on the precise translation of the phrase μή μου ἅπτου. The traditional "touch me not," though defended by some scholars such as Mary Rose D'Angelo (536), is modified by some, such as Schneiders, who suggests that we read the clause as "do not continue to touch me." Schneiders argues that the directive teaches Mary that she should not encounter Jesus as if he were the earthly Jesus resuscitated (164). O'Day suggests that Jesus teaches Mary that he cannot and will not be held and controlled (301). On the basis of Matt 28:9, Pheme Perkins, along with Rudolf Schnackenburg, suggest that the original point of Mary's action may have been an act of worship as it is in Matthew. This reading is supported by the fact that "my brothers" is found in both passages (Matt 28:10; John 20:17). An act of worship is prohibited because Jesus' return to the Father is not yet completed (Perkins: 175–76; Schnackenburg: 317).

Related to this question is the issue of the relationship between the two commands of 20:17. Michael McGehee challenges the usual punctuation of 20:17 and suggests that the verse should be read: "Do not cling to me. Since I have not yet ascended to the Father, go to my brothers and tell them." In other words, she should not cling to him because there is a job to be done. Schneiders suggests that 20:17b should be seen not as a statement, "I am not yet ascended," but as a rhetorical question, "Am I not yet ascended?" the answer to which is, "No, you are indeed ascended, that is, glorified" (164). D'Angelo points to an interesting parallel in Apocalypse of Moses 31:3–4 in which Adam tells Eve: "When I die, leave me alone and let no one touch me until the angel of Lord shall say something about me . . . do not rise to pray to God until I shall give back my spirit into the hands of the one who has given it" (532). This parallel suggests that touching is postponed until after the angel of the Lord speaks. Perhaps, then, we are to understand that Mary's touch is not rejected but only postponed until after she has delivered his message as the Lord's messenger (or angel). Far from showing the inadequacy of Mary's faith, argues D'Angelo, the story intends to confer on her a unique privilege in this encounter (535).

The notion that the touching of Jesus is to be postponed until after the delivery of the message draws attention to the encounter between Jesus and Doubting Thomas. Whereas Mary is told not to touch, Thomas is invited to "put your finger here and see my hands. Reach out your hand and put it in my side" (20:27). In contrast to Brown, who argues that these two episodes should not be brought into comparison with each other (1011), Dorothy Lee suggests that Mary Magdalene and Thomas are in a narrative partnership that encircles the giving of the spirit. Hence Jesus' prohibition of Mary's touch and invitation of Thomas's touch draws attention to the giving of the spirit as the essential act of the risen Lord (37–38).

These are all plausible interpretations. But allow me to add another. Reading through the lens of Canticles casts Mary and Jesus in the role of lovers. Mary's search for the body of her beloved is fuelled by love as expressed through her desire to hold him and touch him. Had she found the body in the tomb as she had expected, she would have touched it and cared for it, perhaps anointing it with spices as in Mark 16:1. But imagine the joy of the lover in finding that her beloved is not dead after all. How else could the joy be expressed other than to touch and to hold, and to vow never to let go (Cant 3:1–14)?

This reading suggests two directions that our interpretation of 20:17 might take. One is a negative direction, in which Jesus' words are a rebuke, a rejection of the woman longing to be united with her lover. Jasper (112–13) argues that Jesus' rejection of Mary carries undertones of a decided brutality which cannot be smoothed away. For Jasper, this act parallels the Eden story which also recounts a brutal expulsion from innocent intimacy subsequent upon the demonstration of inappropriate knowledge. Others have read this act less harshly. Jesus' words may imply not so much outright rebuke as a mild, impersonal chastisement, not so much a rejection of Mary herself as a statement that physical contact is not possible or appropriate, given Jesus' liminal location between the grave and his father's house. The Johannine Jesus may be attempting to teach Mary, and the reader, that the ascension is Jesus' glorification and an essential part of process that began on the cross (Brown, 1012). Mary must grow and pass from the known dimension of her relation to Jesus to a new one (Ricci: 144). In this line of interpretation, 20:17 indicates that the Canticles paradigm is aborted at this time, with the woman and man never again being together or achieving the consummation of their relationship (Derrett: 178). The message to Mary may be that she must endure their physical separation, as she goes off to the disciples with Jesus' message while Jesus ascends to the Father. On this reading we imagine Mary as tearful and angry at her lover's rebuke, or perhaps stoically accepting of a necessary separation.

Of course, in the absence of narrative clues as to her mood or the tone of voice, we may only guess at Mary's state of mind as she does Jesus' bidding. But the joyful and awestruck tenor of the resurrection narratives in all the Gospels argues against the negative reading we have explored above. It seems more natural to imagine that Mary's tears are now dry, and that she hastens eagerly to do her teacher/ lover's bidding. Her report of what she has seen—the Lord—and heard —the things he had said to her (20:18)—may support an alternate reading of Jesus' response to the lover who has searched for him.

This alternate reading requires us to redefine our notion of what might constitute consummation in the Johannine context. The Gospel is silent on the prior relationship between Jesus and Mary Magdalene. Even if we posit a prior sexual relationship, as is suggested in Scorcere's film *The Last Temptation of Christ*, for example, John 20 clearly rules out the possibility of such after the empty tomb. Instead, the words of Mary suggest that her relationship to her beloved is expressed not through touch but through speech and vision. Its consummation is not an embrace but Mary's testimony to the disciples of what she has seen and what she has heard. Although the beloved is not accessible in the flesh, she has his image in her mind's eye, and his words upon her lips.[8]

The subtext of the Gospel that emerges through the intertextual reading attempted here creates an authority structure that is at odds with that which plays upon the text's surface. Whereas the Gospel's surface upholds the authority of the disciples as an exclusive group within the community of Jesus' followers, the subtext defines Mary as the one who exemplifies the intimacy and love of the believer and the risen Lord. If the subtext is not acknowledged by the disciples, it is accessible to the reader, to whom the experience of Mary is available through the Gospel, particularly when it is read together with other biblical texts. The Gospel not only allows readers to learn of and appreciate Mary's experience but also to experience the intimacy of relationship with the risen Lord by seeing, hearing, and almost touching him through the "signs that are written in this book" (John 20:30–31). If some readers choose not to enter into this intimate relationship, they may nevertheless appreciate the experience of Mary as she moves from sorrow and anger to joy and profound understanding, from uncertainty and deference to confidence and authority.

Bibliography

Brown, Raymond E.
1970   *The Gospel According to John XIII-XXI.* AB 29A. New York: Doubleday.

Culley, Robert C.
1993   "Introduction." *Semeia* 62: vii-xiii.

Culpepper, R. Alan
1975   *The Johannine School: An Evaluation of the Johannine-School Hypothesis based on an Investigation of the Nature of Ancient Schools.* Missoula: Scholars Press.

D'Angelo, Mary Rose
1990   "A Critical Note: John 20:17 and Apocalypse of Moses 31." *JTS* 4:529–36.

---

[8] According to Craig Koester (345), Mary's story confirms that seeing alone does not guarantee faith. Only when she heard Jesus speak her name did she recognize him. What she heard enabled her to make sense of what she saw, although the command to stop touching Jesus (20:17) indicates that she did not fully comprehend the significance of the resurrection.

Derrett, J. Duncan M.
1993   "Miriam and the Resurrection (John 20,16)." *The Downside Review* 111:174–86.

Eslinger, Lyle
1987   "The Wooing of the Woman at the Well." *Journal of Literature and Theology* 1:167–83.

Jasper, Alison
1993   "Interpretative Approaches to John 20:1–18: Mary at the Tomb of Jesus." *ST* 47:107–18.

King, Karen
1997a   "Mary Magdalene in the New Testament and Other Early Christian Literature." Working Paper, American Bible Society.
1997b   "Who are the Disciples?" Working paper, American Bible Society.

Koester, Craig
1989   "Hearing, Seeing, and Believing in the Gospel of John." *Bib* 70:327–48.

Lee, Dorothy A.
1995   "Partnership in Easter Faith: The Role of Mary Magdalene and Thomas in John 20." *JSNT* 58:37–49.

McGehee, Michael
1986   "A Less Theological Reading of John 20:17." *JBL* 105:299–302.

O'Day, Gail
1992   "John." Pp. 293–304 in *The Women's Bible Commentary.* Ed. Carol Newsom and Sharon Ringe. Louisville, KY: Westminster/John Knox.

Perkins, Pheme
1984   *Resurrection: New Testament Witness and Contemporary Reflection.* New York: Doubleday.

Reinhartz, Adele
1992a   "From Narrative to History: The Resurrection of Mary and Martha." Pp. 161–84 in *"Women Like This": New Perspectives on Jewish Women in the Greco-Roman World.* Ed. Amy-Jill Levine. SBLEJL 1. Atlanta: Scholars Press.
1992b   *The Word in the World: The Cosmological Tale in the Fourth Gospel.* Atlanta: Scholars Press.

Ricci, Carla
1994   *Mary Magdalene and Many Others: Women Who Followed Jesus.* Minneapolis: Fortress Press.

Sawicki, Marianne
1994   *Seeing the Lord: Resurrection and Early Christian Practices.* Minneapolis: Fortress Press.

Schnackenburg, Rudolf
    1982   *The Gospel According to St. John.* Vol. 3. New York: Crossroad.

Schneiders, Sandra M.
    1996   "John 20:11–18: The Encounter of the Easter Jesus with Mary Magdalene—A Transformative Feminist Reading." Pp. 155–68 in *What is John? Readers and Readings of the Fourth Gospel.* Ed. Fernando F. Segovia. Atlanta: Scholars Press.

Schüssler Fiorenza, Elisabeth
    1986   *In Memory of Her: A Feminist Theological Reconstruction of Christian Origins.* New York: Crossroad.

Setzer, Claudia
    1997   "Excellent Women: Female Witnesses to the Resurrection." *JBL* 116:259–72.

Winsor, Ann Robert
    1999   *A King is Bound in the Tresses: Allusions to the Song of Songs in the Fourth Gospel.* Studies in Biblical Literature 5. New York: Peter Lang.

Witherington, Ben
    1988   *Women in the Earliest Churches.* Cambridge: Cambridge University Press.

Wyatt, Nicolas
    1991   "Supposing Him to be the Gardener" (John 20,15): A Study of the Paradise Motif in John." *ZNW* 81:21–38.

IN THE EYE OF THE BEHOLDER
WISHING, DREAMING, AND *DOUBLE ENTENDRE* IN THE SONG OF SONGS

J. Cheryl Exum

How much of the Song of Songs is wishing for the beloved, as opposed to description of intimate encounters taking place? Kissing, for example, is wished for, but not actual kissing ("Let him kiss me," 1:2; "If only you were my brother . . . I would kiss you," 8:1).[1] How much of the Song is a dream? Describing it as a dream is, at least, the way some commentators deal with the woman's nighttime search for her elusive lover (3:1–5; 5:2 7). There is a good deal of dreaming, or fantasizing, in the Song, but does anything explicitly sexual ever happen between the female and male protagonists of this beguiling love poem?[2] She invites him to come out to the countryside, where she will give him her love (8:11–13), but this is something yet to take place. He takes her to the house of wine (2:4); she takes him to her mother's chamber (3:4). But do they consummate their love there?[3] Or anywhere else in the poem, for that matter?

---

[1] Though the root נשק does not appear, kissing seems to be intended in Song 4:11 ("your lips distill nectar, bride; honey and milk are under your tongue") and 7:10 [ET 7:9] ("and your palate like the best wine...gliding over lips and teeth/the lips of sleepers"); but the first case is a description of her lips/kisses and the second is a wish.

[2] The Song's unity, or lack of it, has little bearing on my discussion; I am reading the text as we now have it as a poem.

[3] She would like to, she says, not only kiss him in public but also, in the privacy of her mother's house, give him spiced wine, the juice of her pomegranates, to drink—if only she could (8:1-2).

The place where sexual union takes place in the Song of Songs is not in the vineyards or the country bower or the king's harem or even the mother's house, but on the level of *double entendre*. Coition is represented by means of figurative language, through the indirection of language described perceptively by Albert Cook. "[C]oition, the center of desire in the poem, is veiled by circumlocution, by metaphor, or by roundabout description of the delights of love play" (110). The male lover is an apple tree whose fruit is sweet to the woman's taste (2:3). She is a lotus (2:1) and a garden (4:12, 15), and he goes down to his garden to feed among the lotuses (6:2–3), "carelessly cropping flowers" (Landy: 69). She invites him to come to his garden and eat its choicest fruits (4:16). Since just before this he has tasted honey and milk under her tongue and sampled her orchard of pomegranates, with all choicest fruits and spices (4:11–14),[4] it is a rare reader who would mistake the sexual innuendo in his reply for a light snack *al fresco*:

> I come to my garden, my sister, bride;
> I gather my myrrh with my spice,
> I eat my honeycomb with my honey,
> I drink my wine with my milk. (5:1)

But what form intimacy takes, here and elsewhere, though it may be strongly suggested is never literally described. Moreover, an imaginative reader can find *double entendre* everywhere. Attempts to match obscure images to specific body parts or specific sexual activities often lead to ludicrous results. So how is the interpreter to proceed, how to steer a wary course between the Scylla of reticence, leaving intimate encounters to the privacy of the page, and the Charybdis of explicitness, turning startling metaphor into anatomical tedium? Is it any wonder that a tradition arose about Jews not permitting a man to read the Song until he had reached maturity (and, one presumes, a woman not to read it at all)?[5] Reading the Song of Songs is a risk; the labour is complicated by the pervasiveness of figurative language and numerous *hapax legomena*, obscure refer-ences, and strange metaphors. Indulging in the labour of reading that

---

[4] If he hadn't sampled them, how would he know about the honey and milk and choice fruits? One could say that he simply assumes this will be the case—and this is my point: sexual knowledge both is and is not represented (see below).
[5] Mentioned by Origen in his commentary on the Song of Songs; for a discussion of its possible meaning, see Scholem: 38-40.

becomes the pleasure of the text (and I don't expect to be the only contributor to this volume to make this connection), this essay explores the interplay among modes of wishing, dreaming, and so-called veiled descriptions of coition as a function of the Song's poetic artistry.

I am using "wishing" and "dreaming" loosely, to refer to all the ways desire is expressed in the Song, and not as a literary category, such as the Egyptian "wish song" (Fox: 281–82), or as a state of consciousness (wakefulness or sleep) to be decided upon. Wishing includes what I have elsewhere (1999) described as the erotic imperative, the call to love by means of imperatives, jussives, and cohortatives that lend urgency to longing: "let him kiss me," "draw me after you," "come away," "let me see/hear," "turn," "let us run," etc. Dreaming is a kind of wishing. Desire is such stuff as dreams are made of, and lovers typically indulge their fantasies in daydreams. Roland Murphy observes that whether or not 3:1–5 and 5:2–7 are reports of dreams is not at all certain (146, 168), and of the latter says, "The woman is relating an episode, whatever the degree of the reality" (168). Where in the text, one wonders, would the dream end and reality begin? Murphy here exemplifies a prevailing tendency among commentators to treat literary creations as if they were real people.[6] This is neither reality nor a dream; it is a poem, and the man and woman are literary personae created by the poet. They have no relationship, no existence, apart from what is on the page before us, or in the reader's consciousness. Francis Landy duly appreciates this fact throughout his study of the Song's aesthetic dimension, but otherwise Michael Fox is virtually alone in taking seriously its significance for interpretation: "[I]f the speakers are personae we must ask not only

---

[6] Murphy is certainly aware that a dream can be a daydream (170); it is the consideration of reality that bothers me. I keenly recognize the difficulty here; one does not want to say each time "the female persona" or "the male persona" when one wants to refer to the woman and man/women and men who inhabit the poem, but it would help to keep this distinction in the foreground as much as possible; cf. Keel: "Wie bei 3,1-5 kann es sich auch hier, wenn man das literarische Genus der Liebeslyrik beachtet, nicht um die realistische Schilderung eines wirklichen Vorgangs oder eines Traumes handeln . . . Allein schon die Tatsache, daß ein Mädchen oder eine Frau allein in einem Zimmer mit Tür zur Straße schläft, ist unwahrscheinlich" (176). The Song's status as a written poem, with all that poetic license includes, similarly gets pushed into the background; cf. Clines's criticism of Murphy and Fox for ignoring the textuality of the Song (96-98, 97 nn. 3, 4).

what the lovers are like, but also how the poets view them and present them to us" (253; cf. Landy: 62).

The notion of reality when applied to a lyric poem like the Song is problematic. Reality is not the same thing as realism in literature, fidelity to nature or real life;[7] one could argue that the Song is too idealized to be realistic. The Song may be realistic in some ways— people live in houses, there are streets and squares, and even watchmen who patrol them—but even here one could question the degree of realism, as Murphy, in fact, does when he criticizes what he calls historicizing the situation by asking practical questions like: would the man not have aroused the woman's family? How would they have responded to her opening the door? (170 n. 11, with reference to Nolli). The distinction that is blurred in the Song is not between fantasy and reality (Murphy; Pardes: 136) but between desire, or anticipation of sexual enjoyment, and sexual experience or knowledge of love, between the young lovers, amazed by budding romance, and the mature poet, who knows the power of eros to transform the world. The speakers are the voices for the poet's knowledge and allow the poet a space in which to investigate, with all the senses, the nature of love (Fox). The poet presents the lovers to us as knowing all there is to know about love but also as explorers discovering the delights of intimacy.

This is where *double entendre* comes so significantly into play. Like beauty, *double entendre* is in the eye of the beholder. While recognizing it as a reader's conundrum (do we find what we are looking for?), I also want to treat it as a feature of the text: a poetic quality of the Song that allows it to be read as both very explicitly and very delicately erotic. The Song is, first and foremost, a love poem; it encourages reading for sexual meanings. As Fox, who worries about his conclusions while appreciating the fun of speculating, says, "Love poets tease us with sexual *double entendre*. Sexual innuendoes, not to mention explicit sexual references, start us looking for more of the same until we begin seeing them everywhere" (298). Sexuality is pervasive in the Song, even though we may disagree where and how,

---

[7] Mariaselvam creates a false dichotomy between dreams and fantasies and "down-to-earth realities" (32-33); Fisch sees the whole Song as like a dream vision or dream, with its free flow of images (88-90), though he also finds in it an "anti-dream" or "aborted dream poem . . . invaded by the sense of historical time" (98-100).

exactly, it gets expressed or what correspondence there may be between a suggested image and its possible sexual referents. *Double entendre* is an important feature of the Song's erotic lyricism; encoded in the text, it is activated by the reader (cf. Eagleton: 119–20). Like the beholder who cannot look away from the Shulammite but contemplates what her features are like from foot to head (7:1–10), the reader's eye is captivated by the text's semantic and metaphoric contours and looks beneath the surface for what its images "stand for."

It is surely an artistically sophisticated poem that can be read as both delicately erotic and sexually overt at the same time, an achievement deserving the distinction, "the Best of Songs." The Song is roundabout, insinuative, but not coy; it does not tease. *Double entendre* gives the impression of gratification taking place even as it is longed for. Desire in the Song is always on the brink of fulfillment, has an urgency about it (come! tell me! make haste!); and fulfillment is simultaneously assured, deferred, and, on a figurative level, enjoyed. The slippage from one mode to another, the blurring of distinctions between the more literal level of wishing, dreaming, desiring and the figurative level of consummation is central to the Song's poetic artistry and erotic persuasiveness. So the question is not, is sexual union represented as taking place in the Song? It both is and is not (just as the Song both is and is not about Solomon, who is not the lover but who keeps cropping up and whose Song it is [1:1]). But even the distinction between literal and figurative, like that between reality and fantasy, is not very helpful when it comes to the Song. Jill Munro remarks on the poet's omission of markers to set the lyrics in time and space and the blurring of the distinction between absence and presence, dream and reality, that results (126).[8] We find, for example, the boundaries between anticipation and experience already blurred in the temporal slippage of the opening lines, "let him kiss me . . . the king has brought me . . . we will rejoice," where wishing, experiencing, and anticipating coalesce.

Before examining *double entendre* more closely, in the much disputed case in Song 5:2–6, I would like to consider briefly a few places where distinguishing wishing or anticipating from references to

---

[8] In addition to "reality," I have a problem with the terms "presence" and "absence," because poetic representation is an attempt to make present what is absent, but Munro's discussion shows how important the handling of time and space is as part of the Song's artistry.

love already enjoyed proves difficult. The exegetical issues are more complex than I am able to go into here (e.g. context is important, though it does not seem to have helped much), and I am not arguing that they are unresolvable but only that the solutions are not self-evident.

Let us start with kisses. "Let him kiss me" is so sudden and unexpected a beginning, and thus so powerful –a voice conjures up an Edenic world, as in those first moments of creation. Desire bursts onto the scene with an appeal for something specific and tangible: kisses. The verb could be translated as an imperfect (thus some confusion already exists): "He will kiss me." But in any event, he isn't kissing her now nor has he just kissed her. Why does she want kisses? The next words seem to answer the question: because his love play is better than wine. Does this not assume some prior knowledge of his lovemaking (דדיך is sexual activity) on her part? We could translate כי as asseverative, with W. F. Albright (followed by Pope and Murphy), "Surely your love play is better than wine!," so that sexual intimacy remains a future possibility. There is, however, no reason to seek an explanation of כי by recourse to Ugaritic when its most basic meaning of "for" or "because" works so well: she wants his kisses because lovemaking, which includes (within the semantic range of דדים) and often begins with kissing, is better than wine, sweet and intoxicating. And so we have in Song 1:2 a situation where either the man's lovemaking is imagined as something that will be (must be) deliciously stimulating or it is known to be. Here at the beginning, as throughout the poem, we cannot disentangle the lovers' experience of each other from their wishes or desires.

Particularly noteworthy is the so-called refrain of adjuration:

> I adjure you, daughters of Jerusalem,
> by the gazelles and hinds of the field,
> that you do not arouse or awaken love
> until it pleases/is ready. (2:7; 3:5; cf. 8:4)

Is the woman telling her companions that love is not the sort of thing to be rushed, that sexual desire should not be aroused prematurely? In other words, is sexual intercourse yet to take place? Or, has it taken place already? Is this an adjuration not to disturb the couple in their lovemaking before they are satisfied? It is much debated in the literature whether "love"—used here with the definite article—is to be understood as an abstract, an emotion (Murphy: 133; Ayo: 108), or the act of lovemaking (Fox: 108–10; Rudolph: 131; Loretz: 83; G. Krinetzki: 97; Snaith: 33);[9] whether עור, "arouse, stir up," has the sense of exciting to action (Pope: 386–87; Murphy: 133) or disturbing or interfering with (Gordis: 82; Fox: 110); and whether חפץ refers to eagerness in the sense of readiness, "until the time is right" (Pope, Murphy; Pardes: 131; Block and Bloch: 152; NRSV) or is elliptical for "until it wishes to be disturbed, woken up" (Gordis, Fox, Snaith, Rudolph, Loretz, G. Krinetzki). The extent of disagreement over the meaning of this injunction is symptomatic of the difficulty of distinguishing between anticipating and enjoying.

Preceding this refrain on two occasions (2:6 and 8:3) the woman speaks of her lover's embrace. If we translate the imperfect verb in her declaration as future, we get: "His left hand under my head, and his right hand will embrace me," as the Septuagint understood it. But the action can also be understood as taking place in the present, and this is how a number of commentators take it (Pope; Murphy; Fox: 107, 165; Rudolph: 130; L. Krinetzki: 117, 235; Ringgren: 265, 267, 289; G. Krinetzki: 94, 213–14; Keel: 89, 242; Snaith: 32): "His left hand is under my head, and his right hand embraces me." In its first appearance (2:6), the declaration is preceded by imperatives ("sustain me with raisin cakes, revive me with apples") and a participle ("for I am lovesick"), so it would make sense to take what follows as describing a present state of affairs. But in 8:3, the declaration is preceded by what is probably an optative (if it continues the wish begun in 8:1, "Would that you were my brother . . . I would kiss you . . ."), so should the optative mood continue here?: "O that his left hand were under my head, and that his right hand embraced me!" (NRSV; Falk; Rudolph: 178–79). If so, should we also translate it as an optative when it appears earlier in 2:6? Pope says there is no reason to take the nominal sentence as optative rather than indicative (384); Murphy, who translates it as a nominal sentence, says it can be understood as a wish (133; Rudolph: 131). What, if not the slippage between anticipation and experience in the Song, makes it so difficult to decide which interpretation to adopt?

---

[9] Yet another, less likely interpretation is that אהבה refers to the woman (Vg., *dilectam*) or the man (KJV), who is not to be wakened from sleep.

In the above examples sexual intimacy may be anticipated or may already have occurred; in the case of *double entendre* it is both not happening and happening at the same time through the suggestiveness or indirection of the language. Song 5:2–6:3 offers a good opportunity to explore the power of allusion and the forms it can take. It has the advantage of being a unity (even Falk, for example, who divides the Song into 31 poems, sees 5:2 6:3 as a "composite poem" [121]) and so provides us with a context, and even more of a "plot" than any other part of the Song. It begins with a narrative that also blurs distinctions, the nebulous boundary between sleep and wakefulness ("I was sleeping but my heart was awake"). The woman recounts a nighttime visit by her lover, who seeks entry to her chamber. On a literal reading, it seems that he is outside the door in the damp night air, calling to her. She makes some rather weak excuses for not letting him in, at which point he tries to open the door by putting his hand through the keyhole or latch. She then gets up to let him in, dripping the myrrh with which she has anointed herself (in preparation for his visit?) on the handles of the bolt, but when she opens the door he is gone (5:2–6c).

The discovery of the lover's departure is the fulcrum of the poem, the point at which the mood changes. The rest of the poem revolves around the motif of seeking and finding, concluding with what can be described as finding-by-praise (Cook: 134). The woman goes out looking for her lover, but is unsuccessful; instead the seeker is found by the watchmen and beaten (5:6de–7). With v. 8 she stops narrating and addresses the daughters of Jerusalem. A dialogue ensues in which (1) they ask her what is so special about her lover, and she responds with a metaphoric description more meaningful to her than to anyone trying to pick him out in a crowd, and (2) they ask her where he is, and she responds that he has gone down to his garden to feed and to gather lotuses, and that she and he, "the one feeding among the lotuses," belong to each other (5:8–6:3). Thus, at the end of the poem she reveals that she knows where he is—in his garden; that is, with her, indulging in sexual divertissements. So she did not need to look for him at all, and this has some bearing on the interpretation of 5:2–6. As I intimated above, it is difficult to miss the *double entendre* in 6:1–3, which brings the poem to closure.

In view of the sexual innuendo at the end of the poem, is it reasonable to find a veiled account of coition in 5:2–6 as well? A

notoriously graphic reading of these verses is that of Pope, though
Eslinger outdoes him in anatomical detail (275–76). Pope sees "feet"
(v. 3) as a possible euphemism for the genitals ("I have washed my
feet, how could I soil them?"). But the key is v. 4: "my beloved
stretched forth his hand through [?][10] the hole and my insides were
stirred for him." Pope concludes:

> Given the attested use of "hand" as a surrogate for phallus, there can
> be no question that, whatever the context, the statement "my love
> thrust his 'hand' into the hole" would be suggestive of coital
> intromission, even without the succeeding line descriptive of the
> emotional reaction of the female. (519)

One assumes Pope takes the woman's reaction as orgasm, though he
digresses at this point to expound on the movement of bowels. Ilana
Pardes follows a similar path as Pope in dealing with this "daring,
though curiously indirect, description of sexual arousal" (131), and,
further, likens the dripping of myrrh to the woman's "genital juices
[that] 'flow forth' in quest of an opening." She also allows that "[t]he
nocturnal encounter . . . comes close to a masturbatory fantasy (the
dripping fingers)" (132).

Michael Fox is not convinced. This *double entendre* for coition
in v. 4, he points out, interferes with the course of the narrative, for it is
not until v. 5 that the woman arises to open to her beloved (144;
Gordis: 90; Sasson: 196). It is hard to argue with that. Furthermore,
Fox thinks that v. 6 makes it clear that the young man has not entered
the woman's house, and, if this were a veiled description of coition, it
would produce an "ugly picture" of a man who has sex with a woman
and then leaves. But that rather depends on whether one takes his
withdrawal literally or figuratively. I can see a way to make *double
entendre* work here that would answer Fox's objections, but it would
say more about me than about the poem. More important, I think, is to
ask how the poem works, how it manages not simply to be suggestive

---

[10] מִן normally means "from," but שׁלח is motion toward something, and how does
one stretch forth one's hand from something? Pope, citing Ugaritic evidence, takes
מִן as interchangeable with בּ. Fox and others, following Delitzsch, take the
preposition to represent the perspective of one who is inside (thus, "in from
outside") and point to the similar usage in Song 2:9. For its *double entendre*
possibility, I quite like one of Munro's suggestions: that he puts his hand to the
door and withdraws it in the same movement (130).

(as Fox admits) but to reflect sexual union at the same time that, for all appearances, it tells about a missed encounter. The specifically erotic and delicately suggestive are superimposed in such a way that what the poet has so brilliantly and beautifully constructed cannot be taken apart and retold in terms of the kind of one-to-one correspondence some interpreters seek.[11]

Neither dream nor fantasy, but playing on their potential, Song 5.2–6:3 is a carefully wrought poem. At the beginning (5:2–6c), it works on different levels at once, one of which may be to suggest to its audience that the couple would have had intercourse if the woman had opened the door sooner and the man hadn't left so suddenly, as Fox proposes (145). Another is to represent sexual passion poetically, not only through allusion but also by the configuration of the poem, something neither Fox nor Pope takes into account. While the woman's narrative ostensibly moves in one direction (a missed encounter), the poetic composition moves in another (coition)—through its choice of vocabulary and imagery and, particularly, in its artistic design.

This dual capacity of the poetry can be illustrated with a musical analogy. In Hector Berlioz's dramatic legend in four parts, "La Damnation de Faust," Marguerite sings of the desire that overwhelms her. She is waiting for her lover, like the woman in the Song, but Faust, unlike the man in the Song, does not come. Her song begins softly and plaintively, as she sings of the burning flame of love that consumes her and of his unbearable absence (the tempo is given as *poco riten.*, slightly slowing).[12]

D'amour l'ardente flamme	The burning flame of love
Consume mes beaux jours.	Consumes my youth away,
Ah! la paix de mon âme	Ah, peace has fled
A donc fui pour toujours!	From my soul for ever.

---

[11] I agree with Fox: "I would like to emphasize at the outset the place of eroticism in these songs: everywhere. Sexual desire pervades the songs, and sexual pleasure is happily widespread in them. But their eroticism is not concentrated where commentators most often seek it: in specific allusions to genitalia and coitus" (298).

[12] Part 4, Scene 15; the text is by Berlioz and Almire Gandonnière after Gérard de Nerval's translation of Goethe's *Faust*, and the English translation of the libretto by David Cairns from Deutsche Grammophon.

The tempo picks up as she sings of the emptiness of life without him and the loss of her senses, but it slows again in a musical interlude, first soft and wistful but gradually gaining momentum. The pace becomes faster and pulsing, as she sings of Faust's charms in a *wasf*-like fashion reminiscent of Song 5:10–16. She is effectively conjuring up her lover through the power of language (like her counterpart in the Song [Exum, 1999]) and the sensuous beauty of the music.

Sa marche que j'admire,	His walk that I marvel at,
Son port si gracieux,	His graceful bearing,
Sa bouche au doux sourire,	His mouth with its gentle smile,
Le charme de ses yeux,	The charm of his eyes,
Sa voix enchanteresse	His bewitching voice
Dont il sait m'embrasser,	With which he can set me on fire,
De sa main la caresse,	The caress of his hand,
Hélas! et son baiser . . .	And, alas, his kiss . . .

The slowing and quickening of the tempo mimics the rhythm of sexual intercourse. Next comes a repetition of the plaintive beginning melody, followed by a dramatic change of pace—more animated and agitated (*più animato ed agitato*), faster and faster—as she sings of watching at her window, or outside, hoping for his return. The tempo at this point is almost breathless, having almost doubled (from a quarter note = 50 beats to a minute to a quarter note = 96), and reaching an orgasmic height as she describes, and we hear in the music, the pounding of her heart:

Mon cœur bat et se presse	My heart beats faster
Dès qu'il le sent venir.	When it feels him near.
Au gré de ma tendresse	Would that I could keep him here
Puis-je le retenir!	Just by the power of my love!

Having reached the height of passion, the tempo begins to slacken (*ritenuto*) but remains extremely passionate (*tempo 1mo [primo] appassionato assi*) as she wishes her soul could sigh out in the flame of his kisses. A connection with *la petite mort* (and to the exclamation, "my *nephesh* went forth"—often translated, "I swooned"—"when he spoke/because of him," Song 5:6) is easily drawn, especially in view of an earlier instance of *double entendre* in the beautiful duet between Faust and Marguerite (Scene 13). Nothing takes place on stage except rapturous expressions of love, but here also the tempo grows ever more erotically frantic until Faust cries, "Viens!," and Marguerite exclaims, "Ah! je meurs!"

The scene is equally suggestive in Franz Schubert's setting of "Gretchen am Spinnrade," from *Faust*, Part I, Scene XV. The music conveys the movement of Gretchen's spinning wheel, while at the same time its rise and fall is a sexual rhythm. She begins by singing of her heavy heart and the anguish that Faust's absence causes her, and of watching for his return, but, as in Berlioz's "Faust," when she comes to describe him (conjuring him up, finding-by-praise), the music becomes feverish, reaching a breathtaking crescendo with "sein Händedruck/ Und, ach! sein Kuß!"

Sein hoher Gang,	His lofty gait,
Sein' edle Gestalt,	his noble appearance,
Seines Mundes Lächeln,	his mouth's smile,
Seiner Augen Gewalt	his eyes' power
Und seiner Rede	And his speech
Zauberfluß,	magically flowing,
Sein Händedruck	the touch of his hand
Und, ach! sein Kuß!	and, O! his kiss!

As in the Song's emphatic "let him kiss me with the kisses of his mouth!," the lover is absent, yet he is musically (as poetically) available. After the powerful musical climax reached on a high G with the word "Kuß," there is a brief pause for her to recover, to catch her breath, then the tempo modulates and she begins again, repeating the first stanza about her disquiet. With the last two stanzas, the tempo again builds, rising to a second climax, only slightly less dramatic than the first but gaining force through repetition. Twice she repeats the last stanza; and three times, the last two lines—each time more emphatically, more insistently, and reaching a high A on the last two repetitions of *verGEHen sollt'*.

Mein Busen drängt	My soul yearns
Sich nach ihm hin.	for him. Ah,
Ach, dürft' ich fassen	if only I could seize
Und halten ihn!	and hold on to him!
Und küssen ihn,	And kiss him
So wie ich wollt',	As much as I like,
An seinen Küssen	On his kisses

Vergehen sollt'!   I might expire!

Like the woman in the Song, she wants to seize her lover and not let him go; she desires his kisses, to the very point of extinction—or *la petite mort* or the "swooning" of the woman in Song 5:6. After this, passion having exhausted itself, the music becomes doleful and her voice fades as she repeats the first two lines (Meine Ruh' ist hin, /Mein Herz ist schwer [my peace is gone, my heart is heavy]).

In these musical examples, Marguerite/Gretchen sings of Faust's enchanting attributes, his touch, and his kiss, but Faust is not there, and, in fact, he will not come. The music, however, through its erotic intensity, conveys sexual arousal to the point of orgasm. I propose that the poetry of the Song in 5:2–6c functions the same way that the music does in these cases. Just as Berlioz and Schubert represent orgasm musically,[13] the Song represents it poetically. Sexual intercourse is not to be found in Song 5:2–6c by matching verbal clues to body parts or sexual functions; it is found in the poem's progression and emphases.

In Song 5:2–6c, three actions by the woman, underscored by the appearance of the personal pronoun אני, mark the division of her narrative into three parts: "I was sleeping" (v. 2), "I arose" (v. 5), "I opened" (v. 6). Each of these parts contains a reference to opening (פתח), and, significantly, פתח never has a direct object, which makes its erotic suggestiveness stronger: first, the request by the man to "open to me," v. 2; second the woman's intention "to open to my beloved," v. 5; and third, the act itself, "I opened to my beloved," v 6 (Exum, 1973:50–53). Like the music of Berlioz and of Schubert that gets faster and faster as the climax approaches, the parts of the poem grow shorter as the woman's narrative (and coition, on the level of *double entendre*) reaches its climax in v. 6. But even in the "absence" of the lover, both

---

[13] Performances, of course, will vary. I have three recordings of Berlioz's "Faust"; for me the definitive performance is that of Seiji Ozawa and the Boston Symphony Orchestra, Tanglewood Festival Chorus, and Boston Boy Choir, with Frederica von Stade as Marguerite: the pounding of the heart and the breathlessness are more emphasized. But in the performance by Myung-Whun Chung and the Philharmonia Orchestra, Philharmonia Chorus, and Eton College Boys' Choir, with Anne Sofie von Otter as Marguerite, the second climax is even more pronounced. In that of Pierre Monteux and the London Symphony Orchestra and Chorus (Regine Crespin as Marguerite), in contrast, the second climax is rather muted. Similarly, one of my recordings of "Gretchen am Spinnrade," sung by Arleen Auger, is more sensual and dramatic that the other, sung by Kathleen Ferrier.

music and poetry suggest sexual climax, and Song 5:6 is like "Gretchen am Spinnrade" in that, after the climax, the mood of the poem modulates in her report of seeking and not finding him. Thus, while allusive terms and imagery in Song 5:2–6c present an impressionistic picture of sexual intimacy, the poetic arrangement strengthens the impression by reflecting sexual union. Whether the reader recognizes it or senses it in the way we intuitively perceive the structural intricacies of a musical composition even if we cannot read the score, the artistic manipulation of sexual innuendo, imagery, and patterning that we find here contributes significantly to the effectiveness of the Song of Songs as erotic poetry. The result is a work of art, a thing of beauty. Of course, beauty, like *double entendre*, is in the eye of the beholder.

Bibliography

Albright, William F.
    1963   "Archaic Survivals in the Text of Canticles." Pp. 1–7 in
                *Hebrew and Semitic Studies Presented to Godfrey Rolles
                Driver*. Ed. D. Winton Thomas and W. D. McHardy. Oxford:
                Clarendon.

Ayo, Nicholas
    1997   *Sacred Marriage: The Wisdom of the Song of Songs*. Words by
                Nicholas Ayo and Paintings by Meinrad Craighead. New
                York: Continuum.

Bloch, Ariel and Chana Bloch
    1995   *The Song of Songs: A New Translation with an Introduction
                and Commentary*. New York: Random House.

Clines, David J. A.
    1995   *Interested Parties: The Ideology of Writers and Readers of the
                Hebrew Bible*. JSOTSup 205; Gender, Culture, Theory 1.
                Sheffield: Sheffield Academic Press.

Cook, Albert
    1968   *The Root of the Thing: A Study of Job and the Song of Songs*.
                Bloomington: Indiana University Press.

Delitzsch, Franz
    1885   *Commentary on the Song of Songs and Ecclesiastes*. Trans. M.
                G. Easton. Grand Rapids: Eerdmans.

Eagleton, Terry
    1983   *Literary Theory: An Introduction*. Minneapolis: University of
                Minnesota Press.

Eslinger, Lyle
1981   "The Case of an Immodest Lady Wrestler in Deuteronomy XXV 11–12." *VT* 31:269–81.

Exum, J. Cheryl
1973   "A Literary and Structural Analysis of the Song of Songs." *ZAW* 85:47–79.
1999   "How Does the Song of Songs Mean? On Reading the Poetry of Desire." *SEÅ* 64:33–49.

Falk, Marcia
1990   *The Song of Songs: A New Translation and Interpretation*. San Francisco: HarperSanFrancisco.

Fisch, Harold
1988   *Poetry with a Purpose: Biblical Poetics and Interpretation*. Bloomington: Indiana University Press.

Fox, Michael V.
1985   *The Song of Songs and the Ancient Egyptian Love Songs*. Madison: University of Wisconsin Press.

Gordis, Robert
1974   *The Song of Songs and Lamentations: A Study, Modern Translation and Commentary*. Rev. and augmented ed. New York: Ktav.

Keel, Othmar
1986   *Das Hohelied*. ZBAT 18. Zürich: Theologischer Verlag.

Krinetzki, Günter
1981   *Kommentar zum Hohenlied: Bildsprache und theologischer Botschaft*. BET 16. Frankfurt am Main: Peter Lang.

Krinetzki, Leo
1964   *Das Hohe Lied: Kommentar zu Gestalt und Kerygma eines alttestamentarischen Liebesliedes*. Düsseldorf: Patmos.

Landy, Francis
1983   *Paradoxes of Paradise: Identity and Difference in the Song of Songs*. Sheffield: Almond.

Loretz, Oswald
1963   *Gotteswort und menschliche Erfahrung: Eine Auslegung der Bücher Jona, Rut, Hoheslied und Qohelet*. Freiburg im Breisgau: Herder.

Mariaselvam, Abraham
1988   *The Song of Songs and Ancient Tamil Love Poems*. AnBib 118. Rome: Pontifical Biblical Institute.

Munro, Jill M.
1995   *Spikenard and Saffron: A Study in the Poetic Language of the Song of Songs*. Sheffield: Sheffield Academic Press.

Murphy, Roland E
1990   *The Song of Songs: A Commentary on the Book of Canticles or the Song of Songs*. Hermeneia. Minneapolis: Fortress Press.

Nolli, Gianfranco
1968   *Cantico dei Cantici*. La Sacra Biblia. Torino: Marietta.

Pardes, Ilana
1992   *Countertraditions in the Bible: A Feminist Approach.* Cambridge: Harvard University Press.

Pope, Marvin H.
1977   *Song of Songs: A New Translation with Introduction and Commentary*. AB 7C. Garden City, NY: Doubleday.

Ringgren, Helmer
1967   *Das Hohe Lied*. Göttingen: Vandenhoeck & Ruprecht.

Rudolph, Wilhelm
1962   *Das Buch Ruth, Das Hohe Lied, Die Klagelieder*. Gütersloh: Gerd Mohn.

Sasson, Jack M.
1978–79   "On M. H. Pope's Song of Songs [AB 7c]." *MAARAV* 1/2:177–96.

Scholem, Gershom G.
1965   *Jewish Gnosticism, Merkabah Mysticism, and Talmudic Tradition*. New York: Jewish Theological Seminary.

Snaith, John G.
1993   *The Song of Songs*. New Century Bible Commentary. Grand Rapids: Eerdmans.

SING US ONE OF THE SONGS OF ZION
POETRY AND THEOLOGY IN THE
HEBREW BIBLE[1]

Robert B. Robinson

Introduction

The labour of reading suggests our operations upon a literary text. My interests in this paper lie in the contrary direction, in the ways that a literary text works upon us. That interest is explicitly theological, is the interest of a confessedly biblical theologian who recognizes that scriptural texts have work to do, indeed central and irreplaceable work to do within the life of communities of faith. Throughout the history of the Christian church, my own tradition, scriptures have worked to reveal the reality and nature of God, to call to faith and to nurture faith, to shape the distinctive form of the faithful life. Important work.

Emphasis on the work that the text does within a community does not deny that the community acts upon the biblical texts. The community continually interprets its sacred writings as it lives with those scriptures, continually turning and returning to scripture in

---

[1] This paper represents my inaugural lecture as Anna Burkhalter Professor of Old Testament and Hebrew given at The Lutheran Theological Seminary at Philadelphia, delivered April 20, 1999. My original plan was to hark back to my earliest collaboration with Robert Culley by presenting a paper on the sophisticated historiography introduced into 1 and 2 Kings by the Josiah prophecy in 1 Kings 13. Unfortunately, much of what I initially thought true wasn't. The substitution of this address preserves the coveted opportunity to honor a remarkably fine man.

situations that change yet are bound to the continuities of the faithful life. That interpretation of necessity and quite naturally responds to different situations in the community of faith and ongoing developments within the community of faith because scripture never moves outside the community, never becomes an object somehow outside the vital moment of the community's life. Reading is a continual labour, but a labour deeply rooted in the desire of the community for the scriptures to do their own work of shaping and expressing the faithful life.

As Hans Frei and a number of other scholars have stressed, narrative has a privileged position in shaping the Christian life because of the uniquely fit way in which narrative renders the life, death, and resurrection of Jesus. Much of the Old Testament, however, is not narrative. The present paper is a meditation on the way that certain poetic texts do their work of orienting us in the world and with God, or cultivating Christian emotions or dispositions, or drawing us into silences within which reflection takes place, or providing powerful analogies for our relationship with God. The studies offered here are exemplary or suggestive of ways in which the poetry of the Bible can affect us. They are not meant to be either prescriptive or exhaustive. Stipulating the function of biblical poems in disregard of actual situations in which they are interpreted is at best perilous and dubiously restrictive of the creativity of the interpretive community. Nor can any suggested interpretation of a poetic text exhaust the generative potential of the text, as even a glance at the history of interpretation confirms.

It is a great pleasure to dedicate this address, with which I began a new phase in my own work, to Robert Culley, as he completes a stage in his own. Beyond being a scholar whose work has contributed greatly to the present direction of biblical studies, Bob is that rarest of beings, a truly modest and good man whose friendship enriches our lives.

* * * * *

Consider for a moment two related and very familiar passages from the book of Exodus.

Exod 14:21–25 (RSV): Then Moses stretched out his hand over the sea, and the LORD drove the sea back by a strong east wind all night, and made the sea dry land, and the waters were divided. And the people of Israel went into the midst of the sea on dry ground, the waters being a wall to them on their right hand and on their left. The Egyptians pursued, and went in after them into the midst of the sea, all Pharaoh's horses, his chariots, and his horsemen. And in the morning watch the LORD in the pillar of fire and of cloud looked down upon the host of the Egyptians, and discomfited the host of the Egyptians, clogging their chariot wheels so that they drove heavily, and the Egyptians said, "Let us flee from before Israel, for the LORD fights for them against the Egyptians."

Exod 15:1–10: I will sing to the LORD, for he has triumphed gloriously, the horse and his rider he has thrown into the sea. The LORD is my strength and my song, and he has become my salvation; this is my God, and I will exalt him. The LORD is a man of war, the LORD is his name. Pharaoh's chariots and his host he cast into the sea; and his picked officers are sunk in the Red Sea. The floods cover them; they went down into the depth like a stone. Thy right hand, O LORD, glorious in power, thy right hand, O LORD, shatters the enemy. In the greatness of thy majesty thou overthrowest thy adversaries; thou sendest forth thy fury, it consumes them like stubble. At the blast of thy nostrils the waters piled up, the floods stood in a heap; the deeps congealed in the heart of the sea. The enemy said, "I will pursue, I will overtake, I will divide the spoil, my desire shall have its fill of them. I will draw my sword, my hand shall destroy them." Thou didst blow with thy wind, the sea covered them; they sank as lead in the mighty waters.

Somewhere behind these two passages lies the same event, yet how different they are from one another. The first is marked by its linearity, the strict adherence to the familiar sequence of events: Moses stretches his arms, a strong wind swirls, the waters split, the people of Israel enter the now-dry seabed, the Egyptians heedlessly pursue, their chariots founder, the waters return and drown the hapless Egyptians in a maelstrom of crashing waves. Depiction does not vary from expected sequence, nor does the language rise above the factually descriptive. That word "discomfited" may stand for the nature of all the language, a fine business-like descriptive term.

The second passage disdains the normal sequence of events. Contrary to what must be the first rule of good storytelling, the decisive event appears at the very beginning, "The horse and its rider he has thrown into the sea;" no care expended to build to a climax. A rough description of the event may be constructed, but the passage does not aid us greatly in the task. Apostrophes addressed to the victorious God and even to God's right hand cut across the retelling of events. The heat of battle is broken by shouts of praise to God. Quotations embodying the enemy's arrogant confidence sound, stopping the action. Even the imagery retards progress through the event. We are challenged to imagine waters standing as walls or congealed in the deep.

Were we asked to explain the difference between the two passages, given their similarity of reference, we would be inclined to say, "It's simple. The first is prose and the second is a poem." We would, of course, be right and may have said something profound, perhaps without recognizing it. Only one event, but two types of literature respond to it. Those two types of literature, the prose narrative and the poem, require different means of interpretation and, here is the one tentative thesis of this paper, they serve different theological purposes. My reflection will begin with narratives, but you will quickly see that my interest lies in the theological function of poetic texts.

I

But first narrative. Recent years have witnessed a remarkable convergence among theologians of different schools on the importance of the narrative texts of the Bible. Scholars from as diverse intellectual backgrounds as Stephen Crites and Paul Ricoeur have stressed what Crites called the narrative quality of experience, that as a matter of phenomenological description, narratives mimic the way we experience the world. Both Ricoeur, in the hermeneutical tradition of Schleiermacher, Dilthey, and Heidegger, and Crites, whose intellectual star is the work of Ludwig Wittgenstein, return to St. Augustine's well-known paradox of time in Books 10 and 11 of the *Confessions;* the future, which does not yet exist passes into the past, which no longer exists through the present, which constitutes no more than a fleeting "quasi-mathematical point." The human experience of time described by Augustine and the narrative rendering of temporal sequence are identical, bestowing on all narratives, including the biblical narratives, a privileged status as mode of representation of human reality. More specifically my own mentor, Hans Frei, argued that narrative was the uniquely fit form of expression to render the incarnation of Jesus

Christ. Indeed, for Frei narrative was a privileged form not because of some phenomenological correspondence with human experience of time or anything else, but because of the simple fact that the Gospels rendered the identity of Jesus Christ, preeminently revealed in his death and resurrection, through narrated stories. The aptness of narrative was shown by that one story. That one central story then drew into itself the stories of the life of Israel that led up to the life of Jesus, giving the narratives of the Old Testament a special prominence. But that central story also established a narrated line on which could be found all subsequent stories, including our own and all the history intervening. Students of Frei, such as Charles Wood and the ethicist Stanley Hauerwas, explored the manner in which aligning our own stories with the biblical stories gave the Christian life, both of the individual and the Christian community, a determinate shape. Living within the biblical narrative schooled us in patterns of trust, hope, and gratitude to God characteristic of the Christian life and, through story, rather than abstract ethical principle, taught us the pattern of the caring, serving Christian life.

The emphasis on narrative is important. But the central place in theology ascribed to the narrative raises a serious question for the Old Testament. Much of it is not narrative. The phenomenon with which I began, a single event refracted in both narrative and poetic texts, is by no means isolated. More pressingly many poetic passages in the Old Testament are far less directly related to the biblical narratives and some, particularly in the wisdom literature, may not be related at all. If narrative is privileged, what are we to make of the poetic texts in the Bible which are not themselves narrative in form? Still further, although the biblical narratives can be construed as constituting a single unified narrative, biblical poetry embraces many different genres and types. It would be a mistake of the first order to oppose a "poetic theology" to "narrative theology," as if all poetry were alike. My method will therefore be to work with a number of poetic passages exegetically and then to generalize somewhat modestly from the interpretations.

II

Before turning to the exegesis it seems necessary to provide some definition of biblical poetry which will allow us to identify poetic texts in the Bible. The task of definition is not easy. Earlier efforts have suggested parallelism or meter, yet neither parallelism alone nor meter nor the two together appears adequate to define biblical poetry. What then? Are we consigned to intuitions? Our minimal requirement is a conception of poetry that defends the multitudinous ways that poetry exploits, explores, and indeed continually expands the resources of language. Robert Alter's snap definition, "The best words in the best order," is immensely attractive (Alter: x). Or listen to Barbara Herrnstein Smith's simple reflection, "As soon as we perceive that a verbal sequence has a sustained rhythm: that it is formally structured according to a continuously operating principle of organization, we know that we are in the presence of poetry and we response accordingly" (Smith: 23–24). Or, more technically, here is Benjamin Hrushovsky in *The Jewish Encyclopedia*: Hebrew poetry is marked by a "free rhythm," "[a] rhythm based on a cluster of changing principles," principles involving meaning, syntax, semantics, or phonetics, all interacting, open to change (Hrushovsky, col 1201). Rhythm implies order, yet the principles of order shift and intermingle without thereby flowing together into some vast estuary of indistinctiveness. The poem seeks revelation, disposing the orderly rules of language and poetic convention yet willfully breaking their strictures; artificial limits are the poem's nemesis.

Reflection on the relationship between poetry and prose by the literary theorist Michael Riffaterre is also pertinent. For Riffaterre poetry is, well, not-prose. Poetry of course presupposes familiarity with prose but primarily so that we may recognize poetry's daring departures and negations of the mimetic function of prose, the ways that prose too extensively describes the world (Riffaterre: 1–3). Poetry takes flight from the mimetic function of prose in order to *simplify* and reorganize the complexity of the mimetic world. Given the daunting complexity of poetic interpretation there is something paradoxical about Riffaterre's notion that poetry simplifies. Many avoid poetry because it is so demanding. It is possible to curl up with a good novel but I, at least, have never found it comfortable to curl up with a book of poetry. Poetry requires a straight back. Yet Riffaterre touches a truth, which might be carried further than he himself would take it. Poetry has the power to structure and organize the multiplicity of experience, a truth more easily recognized if we do not persuade ourselves that any organization implies over-simplification. Poetry grants perception of order within the multiplicity of experience, order which is rich, profound, and, I believe, liminal, the very boundaries of understanding. Here I touch again on the central thesis of this paper. The order revealed through biblical poetry is ultimately the order constituted by God, in all God's own richness and profundity, God moving through and across boundaries of experience, not as one unknown or unknowable, resident outside of those boundaries, but as one founding the boundaries which poetry sounds and explores.

III

Let me begin with an exegetical exploration of the theological function of biblical poetry "in the beginning...," that is, with the first verses of Genesis. This may require some preliminary justification, since the opening of Genesis is not self-evidently poetic. Yet the opening verses are full of poetic devices. The first two words of the first verse begin with the same three letters, ב, ר, and א: ברא בראשית. The third word, the word for God, breaks the alliteration of the first two, but directly links to the act of creation by beginning with an *aleph*, the same letter with which the second word concludes. The fourth word and the last in the verse begin with that same *aleph*. There is an internal rhyme in the same line, all this certainly sufficient to signal that we must pay attention to much more than the simple narrative sequence, that is, in Riffaterre's terms, more than the mimetic capacity of language is drawn upon. We may treat this as poetry.

The specific poetic effect of the first lines can then begin to emerge. In the first verse the compactness of the line plus the mounting up of literary devices creates the effect of an epigram, although whether just to this chapter or the whole of the Bible is intentionally open. Even in the English the effect is not lost, although most of the original Hebrew devices do not translate. "In the beginning God created the heaven and the earth." The break in the alliterative pattern at the name of God places God at the center of this simply ordered creation, all creation divisible into a balanced pair, heaven and earth. With the second verse all the orderliness of the first is abandoned. There is no alliteration, even the grammar is unsettled and slightly unusual. But the line is dominated by a series of striking and strikingly threatening images. The earth itself is formless and void. The English here is far too descriptive. The Hebrew has "the earth was *tōhû wābōhû* (תהו ובהו)," a pairing that mocks translation. Were it to be translated, we might suggest helter-skelter, or higgledy-piggledy or, as a colleague suggested, hurly-burly, although none is sufficiently threatening to capture the original. In other biblical passages, equally poetic, the land that is (תהו ובהו) is tractless and deserted, hawks and porcupines its only denizens (Isa 34:11). Jeremiah applies (תהו ובהו) to a land desolated by invading armies, fruitful earth now desert, cities wasted, the very mountains quaking in dismay. תהו ובהו sends a chill up the spine. The figure of darkness that follows perpetuates the foreboding and threat. Darkness here is not mere night, but before night, primordial negation, Milton's "visible darkness," restless, threatening, ominous and full of dread. And in this short line a final image, the deep (תהום), roiling, fathomless, again Milton's "dark, illimitable sea," later haunt of Leviathan in Job, and for Jonah the power of death itself, rising to engulf him. The imagery does not describe but evokes a mouldering chaos, without foundation or sanctuary, gaping in its vastness, swallowing comfort and hope, yet, decisively not alien to God. The spirit or wind of God hovers over this brooding chaos. The text employs a rare and somewhat uncertain word, "hovering" (רחף), found only one other time in the Bible, to defer the manner of God's specific relationship to the chaos—we are given an image, not a cosmogonic speculation. The composite image of threatening chaos and hovering God recognizes within experience the sobering reality of chaotic disorder and threat and its dank foreboding; there is no whistling past the graveyard. Yet God is present, and God's presence carries a lightness and anticipation to match the foreboding darkness. The juxtaposition of images is poetry at its highest powers, defining the limits of the world soon called into existence.

Then God sweeps into action, or better, into voice. If the language of the description of chaos is itself alarmingly chaotic, the language of the first words of creation could not be more clear and compressed: "Let there be light and the was light." The Hebrew is, if anything, still more compressed: יהי אור ויהי אור. Within language itself order emerges, all the more evident in contrast to the chaos. There is a pleasant rhythm to the naming of day and night, based of parallelism, "God called the light day and the darkness he called night." Most striking is the rhythm of the closing of the day, which comes through in every language, "There was evening, there was morning, one day." The rhythm is of a wave rising, then falling along the long run-out of a gentle shore, only to rise again. Or it is the rhythm of breathing itself, filling the chest, then gently released with a moment of peace before the next breath.

The rhythm of this poem of creation runs from the cold fingers of chaos upon our very nerves to the soothing assurance of the orderliness of succeeding days. Within this movement light dispels darkness or, more fully, comprehending the movement, God dispels dread. The decisiveness of God's command and the immediacy of its glorious enactment as light breaks everywhere upon the earth pay no attention to the threatening turbulence of the chaos. Chaos commands no power to impede and at the end of the first day no hint of threat darkens the serene confidence of, "There was evening, there was morning, one day." The force of the poem is to allow us to experience God's triumph of order over chaos, to breath with the confident rhythm of the days, to find ourselves within a world marked by God's purposeful creativity.

IV

The opening chapter of the book of Lamentations offers a far less confident and much more painful orientation to a world aflame not with the light of creation but with the smouldering fires of walls and houses burning, a world under the judgment of God. The poetic quality of the text is beyond question, thanks to the acrostic arrangement of verses which provides an obvious instance of Barbara Herrnstein Smith's "continuously operating principle of organization." The poem opens with an immensely sympathetic image, "how lonely sits the city, how like a widow." We mark the widow's bitter tears in the night and feel her precipitous fall from fortune, from princess to vassal. Even more affectingly her friends have betrayed her, dealing treacherously and becoming her enemy. Betrayed. Abandoned. Our heart goes out to her.

With our sympathies aroused by the images, we are shown their import. The husband who died is Jerusalem, the widow is those who survived Jerusalem's fall only to be carried into exile. Even though the emotive imagery gives way to Judah named by its own name and exiles called exiles, the tone is still immensely sympathetic as we imagine the plight of refugees. Our own troubled times provide the emotions.

The concrete depiction of Judah's fall and exile intersect with other biblical passages in 2 Kings that portray the same event in narrative form. But Lamentations functions very differently from the narrative. Lamentations does not show us Jerusalem in flames. It shows us the faces and hearts of those driven from Jerusalem by the flames as they look back and weep. And it shows still more complex emotions. Once our sympathies are thoroughly engaged on the side of the exiles, it acknowledges, "For the LORD has made her suffer for the multitude of her transgressions." This widow beside whom we have wept and mourned brought her downfall upon herself. That is a complex emotion, sympathy mixed with blame. And it is the LORD who made her suffer, the LORD who is the instrument of her downfall. Images that move us to pity continue to weave amongst the harshest words of judgment. Listen to the way the poem has two adjoining verses confront one another:

> Jerusalem remembers in the days of her afflictions and bitterness
> all the precious things that were hers from days of old. When her
> people fell into the hand of the foe and there was none to help her,
> the foe gloated over her, mocking in her downfall.

Are we not moved? But then:

> Jerusalem sinned grievously, therefore she became filthy.

Sympathy. Blame, the reality of the fall of the city, brought upon themselves yet heartrending in the suffering endured. One step deeper than both sympathy and pain lies the realization that it is God who inflicted this suffering, although justly. To this swirling emotional mix the poem adds one more level to complete its simplification. Even though the people know that it is God who sold them into the hands of their enemies, it is to God they turn to deliver them from their mourning. "O LORD, behold my affliction, for the enemy has triumphed." And, again, as the people groan and search for scraps of bread amidst the ruins of their homes, they cry out, "Look, O LORD, and behold, for I am despised." In *extremis*, in guilt and in mourning, the people turn to the one who has destroyed them as their only hope. Poetry simplifies!

Yes, it simplifies, by drawing the experience of the fall of Jerusalem into the tortured emotions of those who survived that horror. But it does not oversimplify. Pitiable mourning confronts merited guilt, confronts by a certain ruthless juxtaposition. No attempt is made to rationalize the connection between the two responses, no linkages appear in the text except the personal link. The same refugees experience both the profound pain of loss and the desolating certitude of guilt, pain and guilt sweep the exiles in waves, one on the back of the other. Emotions roll in turmoil, yet out of the turmoil emerges a cry to God who alone can deliver.

In this way Lamentations schools us, teaching the full range of emotions known to those who feel their lives under judgment. And it teaches the proper turmoil of their interrelation. Were Lamentations to offer only the mourning of the widow, the destruction of the city would seem simply tragic and the response of the people would be self-pitying. The dimension of judgment would be lost. But were only the guilt of the people reflected in the poem, judgment would appear juridical and bloodless. It is in the turmoil of these conflicting emotions that we learn the proper response to the reality of judgment. And it is out of that turmoil that the cry to God for deliverance becomes our own cry.

V

Hosea is a gloomy book, evoking in often horrifying language—all the power of poetry to shock and disgust—Israel's abandonment of its own faithful and patient God for the false promises of the gods of Canaan and God's incendiary anger at Israel's betrayal. God's accusations and anger are passionate and personal, broken only occasionally by introspections of immense tenderness, which I will come to later. Near the end of the book is a passage of a different spirit, nearly overwhelming in its beauty. Chapter 14 begins with a call to Israel to repent. The voice speaking apparently belongs to the prophet and not directly to God, since God is mentioned in the third person. Israel is bidden to return to the Lord and there is a summarizing reference, we must suppose, to the unhappy relations of God earlier in the book, "For you have stumbled because of your iniquity." The prophet instructs Israel to take with it words when it returns to God. This is a striking contrast to the earlier parts of the book in which it is Israel's actions that have characterized its dismal relations with God, actions stigmatized as harlotry and betrayal. If normally actions speak louder than words, here it is words that are required to commit Israel to repentance. Israel will render to God the fruits of its lips and it will stop saying the false words "Our god" to the insensible constructions of its own hands. Repentance here means the right words addressed to the right God.

Then God says, "I will heal their unfaithfulness, I will love them freely, for my anger has turned from them." But wait. I have overlooked the most important thing. Between the prophet's call to repentance and God's assurance of God's love—nothing but silence. It is as if between the call to confession and the assurance of pardon in the liturgy there were nothing at all! The prophet's call and God's assurance are "one part against another across a silence," to recall John Ciardi's definition of a poem (Ciardi: 995). Here is the key insight, in the words of a line from a student paper on this passage, "When you stand next to someone, whether or not there are words exchanged, something is said" (Hitt: 8).

But what exactly is said here? That is precisely the wrong question. If the poem had sought to make certain the movement from call to repentance to God's assurance it surely could have done so, a simplification indeed. It could have described in suitably poetic terms Israel's actual cry of repentance, the words that Israel took to God. It could have constructed a univocal narrative of the course of forgiveness. The narrative sequence would have clarified the logic of forgiveness: first, call to repentance, then response to that call, then God forgives. But that movement, so natural to assume, is not certainly present here. The movement must pass through the silence and the silence allows other possibilities than the most logical and linear. The interpreter must actively enter the silence as well. The silence allows the two halves of the poem to be read, for instance, as simultaneous movements. While Israel is called to repent, God is forgiving and expressing love toward the people. The poem then becomes a meditation of God's merciful nature, always prepared to forgive without condition. Or perhaps the silence is to allow us to think that God's forgiveness and mercy is in advance of Israel's repentance, beckoning to Israel in hope, forgiveness already granted even as the call is given by the prophet. The silence does not allow the reflection on repentance and God's grace to rest on any single interpretation; reflection is continually forced deeper. The silence insists on our involvement in the interplay.

The poem also guides that reflection beyond the silence. Just after the assurance of God's love and pardon comes one of the loveliest, most tender passages in the Bible. God will be as the dew to Israel, a lovely, peaceful image, the dew more gentle than rain. The image is so striking because it involves a reversal. On two earlier occasions in Hosea the dew is a figure of the inconstancy of Israel: "Your love is like a morning cloud, like the dew that goes early away" (Hos 6:4). And, "Therefore they shall be like the morning mist or the dew that goes early away, like the chaff that swirls from the threshing floor or like smoke from a window" (Hos 14:3). With God all inconstancy is gone. God will be the dew that leads to image after image not just of growth and solidity, but of beauty, the beauty of the lily in blossom or of the olive tree, valued not for its rich fruit but for its pleasing form and sweet fragrance. The vine, too, blossoms, its fragrance like the wine of Lebanon, but is not yet laden with fruit. God's forgiveness brings not just sustenance to life, but beauty, even an extravagance of beauty. Again these images must pass into the silence. Does the beauty God promises encourage us to repentance? Or is that beauty a metaphor for the tenderness of God's mercy? It is within the poetic resources of that silence to suggest both and much more, but not to resolve the matter nor narrow our thought. The very beauty of the poetry and that beckoning silence lures us to continual reflection, and that continual reflection is the life of faith.

VI

Song of Songs must seem the most unlikely book of the Bible to yield theological insight from its poetry. Nearly all modern commentators regard it as a secular book, a book that does not so much as mention God, an anthology of love poems. The frankly erotic nature of much of the poetry has gained acceptance and even appreciation in a cultural setting much less inhibited than formerly about sexuality. But a judgment accompanies acceptance of the Song as love poetry. The erotic tells us nothing about God. So contemporary readers are puzzled why this celebration of human love is found in the Bible.

The Song is indeed in our Bible. It is scripture and its status as scripture insists that we draw deeper into this book. The deeper we go into the Song of Songs the more we will find the categorization of it as erotic poetry not wrong exactly but inadequate to the richness of the book. It is important to be clear. The point here is not to deny the obvious nature of the book or to be a bluenose. The poetry celebrates the attraction between a couple, their yearning for one another. A strongly erotic atmosphere charges the book. But the erotic movement is linear, from attraction and desire or yearning to consummation. The natural medium of that linearity is the narrative. The Song is not a narrative of erotic yearning leading to consummation. At points there are narrative vignettes, but they are juxtaposed to one another and do not either form or imply a connected narrative. Nor is there explicit consummation of love in the Song, although interpreters content with a simple erotic reading of the poetry can suggest passages in which consummation is an inference. The movement from yearning and desire to consummation, the movement characteristic of the erotic, is too linear for the poetry of the Song of Songs.

Recently the philosopher Paul Ricoeur, in a most sensitive reading, has drawn attention to a different movement in the Song, a movement of intense attraction between the lovers and celebration of their love which is followed by a withdrawal and searching for one another. On several occasions the one lover searches through the streets for the absent one, on another the lover is expectantly at her gate, but when she turns to him, he has vanished. This rhythm of drawing together and moving apart, only to return to one another with undiminished ardor, suggests to Ricoeur an image of mutual commitment, continually renewed, which draws its energy from erotic attraction, but deepens it by incorporating desire in a fuller relationship. Again to be clear: the commitment between the lovers is not institutionalized or conventionalized through marriage or any other external commitment. Ricoeur is not moralizing the Song. The commitment is intensely between the lovers, it is the form their desire takes, the desire to know the other fully through delight in their presence and physical attributes and through devotion expressed in each renewed approach to one another. Ricoeur finds the climax of this relationship near the end of the book, "Stamp me in your heart, upon your limbs. Sear my emblem deep into your skin. For love is strong as death, harsh as the grave, its tongues are flames, a fierce and holy blaze." Ricoeur calls this rich blending of erotic attraction and deep commitment the nuptial bond, a coinage that helps move away from the linearity of the erotic movement and also frees us from our cultural identification of the erotic exclusively with sexuality.

Intertwining with the nuptial bond is another movement in the Song of Songs, a movement to identify the lovers with the world of nature. Listen to this lovely poem: "In sandy earth or deep in valley soil, I grow, a wildflower thriving on your love. Narcissus in the brambles, brightest flower—I choose you from all the others for my love. Sweet fruit tree growing wild within the thickets—I blossom in your shade and taste your love." That is just the way of metaphor, we might say. But in the Song of Songs the metaphors of nature become so exuberant, as the critic Robert Alter points out, that they interconnect and form a world of their own, into which the lovers are drawn. Or consider the little narrative vignette in Song of Songs that figures the lover as a deer or gazelle. The lover hears her beloved coming to her over the hills, bounding like an anxious deer. As he approaches her window he slows, hesitant and shy, all alertness, ready to bound away at any disturbance. The identification of lover and deer is so complete that, at the window, we do not know which is meant. Then the lover begins to speak, wooing his beloved to come out to him, calling her out to become part of nature's celebration, "The rains have fed the earth and left it bright with blossoms." Birds gambol through the air, songbird and dove sweeten the air with their songs. Come out. Let us join the celebration.

It is in the conjunction of the nuptial bond with the identification with nature that we begin to see the first theological import of the Song of Songs. That import becomes most clear in contrast with another biblical book, the book of Ecclesiastes. Ecclesiastes is known by its refrain, "Vanity, vanity, all is vanity and a seeking after wind." The pessimism of the speaker in Ecclesiastes has a precise source, his inability to become a part of his world, the world that God has created. He looks around him and notices that everything passes through cycles. Creation is constantly renewed. Waters flow through rivers to

the seas, then return. The winds blow from the four quarters, then
return to their sources. The whole world returns to its starting point and
is renewed. Except he himself. His life flows in a line, from birth to
death. He is fundamentally alienated from the world of creation. Songs
of Songs presents a far more optimistic understanding of our
relationship to the world God created. Through their desire for one
another, deepened in the nuptial bond, the lovers are one with all the
created world, they take their natural place in that world. This is what
the lover says as he approaches his lover's window: Come out to me in
love and join all the world. His call is recognized as true. There is, to
be sure, no common pattern to which all of nature conforms. Humans
remain uniquely and delightedly human in their desire for one another.
The man must woo and wait, not hurrying or compelling. The woman
must be coy, honoring the shy reticence of love. The rhythm of desire
and withdrawal that deepens desire into commitment must be
observed. But if it is, if love is genuinely and fully human, then the
lovers take their full and rightful place within the order God created in
the beginning. Once more the theological import of the poetry is to
orient us into the world which God created, even if God is not
explicitly mentioned in the book.

A still deeper theological import for the nuptial imagery of the
Song is suggested by the judgment of Rabbi Aqiba on the Song at the
time of the Council of Jamnia, "Had the Torah not been given, the
Song would have sufficed to guide the world." To place the Song of
Songs beside Torah! What could have been his thought? The honor
was justified because Aqiba read the Song of Songs as an allegory of
the love of God for Israel, and in the strength of the attraction of the
lovers in the Song he saw a fit analogy with the strength of God's love
for Israel and Israel's reciprocal nuptial love for God. Indeed, with
such mutual commitment Torah was not essential.

What is striking is that Aqiba did not shy from the nuptial image
with its strongly erotic component as an appropriate representation of
God's love for Israel. But not only Rabbi Aqiba adopted the imagery of
love in the Song as a fit metaphor for God's love. Allegorization of the
Song as God's love for the Church, of Christ's love for baptized
individuals, marked early Christian interpretation of the book. The
Song, for instance, was early incorporated into a baptismal liturgy in
the time of Ambrose. As those seeking baptism approached the altar it
was said, "You have come to the altar; the Lord Jesus calls you—both

your soul and the Church—and He says, 'Let him kiss me with the kiss of his mouth'" (Ambrose: 311). Origen, best known of early church allegorizers, made repeated use of the Song for a reason nicely indicated by Paul Ricoeur: "The spiritual world lacks a means of expression," it must draw on images from the everyday world (Ricoeur and LaCoque: 284). What is significant in the early Christian drawing on Song of Songs is that the nuptial imagery was accepted as completely appropriate both to render the church's love of God and, still more strikingly, God's love for the Church.

In time the use of nuptial or erotic imagery to speak of God's love for God's people receded, except in some mystical circles. Catherine LaCugna suggests that for some theologians concerned with God's essence the erotic imagery of yearning suggested that God was not impassive but had emotions and, still more seriously, that God might be in need of something, namely human affection (352). Paul Ricoeur suggests that by destroying the distinction between the monastic state and lay-people the Reformation demolished the ascetic discipline in which the eroticism of the Song could safely be applied to God (Ricoeur and LaCoque: 293). And of course the Reformation principle that scriptures interpreted themselves finally undercut all allegorical interpretation. None of these explanations is adequate alone, but what may not be denied is the abandonment of the erotic, or, still better, Ricoeur's nuptial bond, to speak of God's relationship to God's people. That abandonment strikes me as an exegete as a great impoverishment of our possibilities of reading biblical texts aright. It is not only in the Song of Songs that we encounter the language of yearning and the passion of God for God's people. Listen to this passage from Jeremiah: "For the wound of the daughter of my people is my heart wounded. I mourn and dismay has taken hold on me." This is the soul of yearning, here under the figure of a different relationship, the parent for the child. Or again, feel the yearning in Hosea 11, "How can I give you up, O Ephraim? How can I hand you over, O Israel." God is not impassive, loving from a distance in these passages. God has entered a nuptial relationship and yearns for the beloved, aching at the pain of separation. Song of Songs offers us in the full play of nuptial or erotic imagery the language by which we experience the power and depth of God's desire for us, the depth of yearning of a God who will not give us up. Rabbi Aqiba was right: "The entire world is not worth the day on which the Song of Songs was given to Israel."

VII

Four studies, four different ways in which poetry shapes our life with God. Is it possible to generalize in even a cautious, preliminary way about how biblical poetry functions to shape Christian faith? Only with great hesitancy rooted first in the exegete's preference for interpretation over theorizing and then by a deep conviction that poetry's implication is inexhaustible, or is only exhausted by prescription in advance of the act of reading.

Still, poetry simplifies, Riffaterre tells us, and it is in that simplifying of the complexity of experience that we must look to poetry in scripture to shape life. Poetry does not simplify by analysis, imposing a more highly abstract set of categories above the narrated course of experience. It offers images and figures, conjunctions and hesitancies, productive silences and the turmoil of contradictions, that in unanticipated ways bring experience itself into arrangement, arrangement that is experienced concretely. From that arranged experience come new capacities for seeing the world and moving through it, new language as new sight and hearing, new modes of experience. When the poetry that schools us in new capacities is the language of scripture, those capacities and the dispositions associated with them such as hopefulness, gratitude, a trust in God, assume a determinate Christian (or Jewish, within that tradition) character. Poetry does not provide categories to understand events, as if we were able to stand outside events looking in. It provides the language and complex yet simplifying emotions by which we live experience faithfully. Poetry can also influence the pace with which we move along the line of our lives with God, as was the case in the silence in Hosea 14, silence according time and space for reflection. And poetry can lead us deeper into the heart of God, to know something not just of our own experience but of that of God as well, as in the Song of Songs or that haunting cry in Hosea, "O Ephraim, how can I give you up?" Again, the poetry of the Song or the prophets does not provide us categories of analysis of our relationship to God or of God's inner life. It provides the language of yearning and makes us feel the depth and power of that yearning, both God's yearning for us and our yearning for God.

Poetry simplifies, simplifies by bringing order to experience. Biblical poetry provides order in our lives, an order offered us by God in God's poetic word, the order finally of the faithful life tuned to God.

Bibliography

Alter, Robert
    1985   *The Art of Biblical Poetry*. New York: Basic Books.

Ambrose
    1963   "On the Sacraments." Trans. Roy J. Deferrari. In *Theological and Dogmatic Works*. Vol. 44. *The Fathers of the Church*. ed. Roy J. Deferrari. Washington: Catholic University of America Press.

Ciardi, John
    1959   *How Does a Poem Mean?* Boston: Houghton, Mifflin.

Crites, Stephen
    1989   "The Narrative Quality of Existence." Pp. 65–82 in *Why Narrative? Readings in Narrative Theology*. Ed. Stanley Hauerwas and L. Gregory Jones. Grand Rapids: Eerdmans.

Falk, Marcia
    1982   *Love Lyrics from the Bible: A Translation and Literary Study of the Song of Songs*. Sheffield: Almond.

Frei, Hans
    1974   *The Eclipse of Biblical Narrative*. New Haven: Yale University Press.

Hitt, Jennifer Schoonmaker
    1997   "Exogesis of Hosea 14·1–7." Unpublished.

Hrushovsky, A.M.
    1971   "Prosody." *Encyclopedia Judaica*. New York: McMillan.

LaCugna, Catherine
    1991   *God For Us: The Trinity and Christian Life*. San Francisco: Harper.

Petersen, Davil L. and Kent Harold Richards
    1992   *Interpreting Hebrew Poetry*. Minneapolis: Fortress Press.

Ricoeur, Paul and Andre LaCoque
    1998   *Thinking Biblically: Exegetical and Hermeneutical Studies*. Trans. David Pellauer. Chicago: University of Chicago Press.

Riffaterre, Michael
    1982   *Semiotics of Poetry*. Bloomington: Indiana University Press.

Smith, Barbara Herrnstein
    1968   *Poetic Closure*. Chicago: University of Chicago Press.

Wood, Raymond
    1981   *The Formation of Christian Understanding: An Essay in Theological Hermeneutics*. Philadelphia: Westminster.

IMAGINING ARRIVAL
RHETORIC, READER, AND WORD
OF GOD IN DEUTERONOMY 1–3

Susan Slater

Cynthia Ozick reflects as follows on the combination of discipline and focused imagination that she finds in rabbinic writings: "The rabbis' call to imagination was a call to imagine arrival: homecoming, deliverance, fruition, resolution, an idealism of character, right conduct, just determinations, communal well-being" (227). Her words come close to expressing the heart of Deuteronomy's rhetorical purpose as I would understand it.[1] I would draw out one further element—perhaps implicit in Ozick's view of the rabbinic literature as well—that in Deuteronomy, the call to imagine arrival in all its aspects is yoked with a powerful imperative for active love of God in covenant obedience, and this is understood as the way from imagination to actualization. Of course, as Moses came late to realize, there is no assurance that all will experience this homecoming and the fullness of its rest. In fact, it is probably no accident that the people of Israel, to whom Deuteronomy addresses itself, are asked to situate themselves

---

[1] For a discussion of the purpose of Deuteronomy that develops more of a historical orientation see Mayes (1993). Mayes is concerned to elaborate ground for determining the purpose of Deuteronomy and for adjudicating amongst differing views on this topic. He believes that something approaching objective historical analysis ("quasi-objectivity"; 24) can be achieved through critical reflection informed substantially by Habermas's reconstruction of historical materialism, in which the hermeneutic of suspicion plays a significant part.

outside the land looking towards it, in order to hear the words that will be addressed to them governing life within the land that God gives.

This brings me to Deuteronomy 1–3, chapters in which readers are is invited to assume a stance that will likewise allow the deeper hearing of what follows in the book as a whole. What I would like to do here is, first, to outline some key elements of the rhetoric of these first chapters. Second, I will turn to questions of the reader's interpretive contribution, moving through critical dialogue with aspects of the rhetoric of Deuteronomy 1–3. In my reading, this dialogue will focus on questions raised for me as a reader who is Christian, a woman, and living in a world where practices such as "ethnic cleansing" and its more readily accepted cognates are in evidence all around us, not infrequently in connection with issues of national destiny. My perspective as reader is theologically interested, in ways that reflect both my professional context in theological education and the commitments that help situate me within its many-voiced project. This leads, third, to reflection on hermeneutical implications of such a reading. Fourth, I will situate this present exploration within a broader and theologically animated conversation in biblical studies in which active roles for readers are envisaged, in "acts of dialogical imagination" (Kwok: 30), readings that move "from context to context" (Ringe: 283), and critical engagement with biblical values on the basis of those values that animate readers and their communities (eg. Mosala; Segovia and Tolbert; Sugirtharajah).

Key Elements of the Rhetoric of Deuteronomy 1–3

Deuteronomy 1–3 is mainly speech addressed by Moses to the people of Israel just before they cross over into the promised land. In this speech Moses recalls events experienced by the people over the past forty years since the exodus, events which have brought them to the present moment, the brink of entry into the promise. Primarily, Moses speaks of two sequences of events which stand in sharp contrast to one another. The first of these centers around the scouting expedition to Canaan which led to the people's fearful refusal to go up into the land, and which ended with the death of the generation involved in the wilderness outside the land. The second sequence of events centers around the trans-jordanian victories over Sihon and Og, with the division of their territories afterwards. Between these two major episodes there is a lapse of some thirty-eight years and one full generation of Israelites, although the text does not emphasize these distances.

Moses is speaking to a people who stand once again before the call to go up into the land given by the LORD. They are called to leave the familiar and to come home. How will they respond this time? It is in this area—the cultivation of response—that the rhetoric of Deuteronomy 1–3 can be seen to operate. The response Moses seeks to elicit from his audience is, in particular ways, also sought from the reader. The reader's identification with Moses' audience is promoted by the use of second person address throughout, and compounded by features in the text that blur distinctions among different times and audiences, thus loosening the text from any particular audience or historical setting.

One of the most persuasive examples of this loosening of reference is in the glossing over of the generational shift that occurs during the wilderness years. The first generation to leave Egypt dies in the wilderness, we are told, for their lack of faith. This means, of course, that from the beginning of Deuteronomy, Moses is addressing the *children* of this first generation. He addresses them, however, as if they were the parents, as if the two generations shared a common identity and experience. And when the time comes to record the death of the first generation, in Deut 2:14–16, Moses' audience—and readers with it—is gently excised from that group by a grammatical sleight of hand. All at once the first generation has become "them" and the "you" whom Moses continues to address is clearly the second generation. And no attention is given to the fact that Moses could only have been speaking to that second generation from the beginning of his speech. This helps crystallize an understanding of the use of second person address as a rhetorical technique used to draw readers into identification with those Moses is addressing in his speech. The reader, after all, is the only actual "you" addressed from the beginning of Moses' recollection to its end.

Besides this blurring of the particular identity of those addressed by Moses' words, there is a further, temporal, blurring between Moses' words spoken forty years ago and those addressed now, just before entry into the land. Deut 1:29–33 is a case in point.

> I said to you, "Have no dread or fear of them. The LORD your God,
> who goes before you, is the one who will fight for you, just as he did
> for you in Egypt before your very eyes, and in the wilderness, where
> you saw how the LORD your God carried you, just as a man bears his
> son, all the way that you traveled until you reached this place. Yet in
> spite of this word, you did not trust in the LORD your God, who goes
> before you on the way to seek you out a place to pitch your tents, in
> fire by night, to show you the way in which you should go, and in
> the cloud by day."[2]

In this speech Moses is repeating the words of encouragement
he had addressed to the people some forty years ago. But, in the last
verse, his exhortation slips from those past circumstances to continue
in the present of his speech. Moses slips almost unnoticeably from past
to present, from exhortation of the parents to that of the children.

At times, Moses' words even seem to address later generations,
as when he speaks of Sihon and Og's land as being "across the Jordan"
(3:8), or when he uses expressions rooted in settled agricultural
practice (2:7a; cf. 14:29; 16:15; 24:19; 28:12; 30:9). Blurring of
temporal references works with other features to loosen Moses' words
from particular times and references and to position readers as those
most immediately addressed by Moses' words.

Readers, then, are to identify with those who, sinning, perished
in the wilderness and, faithful, now stand before the promise. But as
much as readers are drawn back towards the circumstances of Moses'
contemporaries, there are recurring indications, more frequent and
insistent as the text moves towards a close, that the fidelity towards
which they are being called has their own much later historical setting
as its actual context. These indications come from features in the text
that work to re-establish contact with a perspective that is external to
Moses' recollection.

For example, the antiquarian notices in chaps. 2 and 3
recurrently break into Moses' recollection and initiate a process of
reflection and application from a later time and another place (2:10–12,
20–23; 3:9, 11, 13b–14). They do this in a few ways. First, there is the
simple fact that these notices, with their preference for circumstantial
clauses, their subject changes and intrusions of strange characters,
stand out from the material around them. Second, the antiquarian

---

[2] The RSV, used here, preserves rhetorically significant gendered language.

notices reflect a perspective later than Moses' speech. This is visible in the reference to the conquest of the promised land as already accomplished in 2:12, the phrase "to this day" in 2:22 and 3:14, and the reference to the display "to this day" of Og's bedstead in Rabbah in 3:11.

Third, as interruptions made from the perspective of a time after the conquest, the antiquarian notices seem to come from a different voice. Whose? Apart from Moses, the reader has been introduced to only one voice: that of the narrator who introduced Moses' speech in 1:1–5. The narrator was speaking from a time after the conquest, since he spoke of Moses as making his speech "across the Jordan," revealing his own position within the land. It would seem to be his voice that speaks in these notices, editorializing in parentheses.

What is the intended effect on readers of these interruptions of Moses' speech in which readers, without warning, find themselves addressed by another voice, from another time, and concerning other people than those Moses is discussing? Robert Polzin discusses the rhetorical effect of these notices as "breaking frame," a term he takes from Erving Goffman.

> By breaking frame five times, the Deuteronomist may very well be forcing the reader to shift back and forth a number of times between narrated past and narrator's present . . . These frame-breaks force the Deuteronomic audience to shift from a subsidiary awareness that they are descendants of these earlier Israelites, and therefore distant hearers of Moses' teaching, to a momentary focal awareness of this situation, and then back again to the continuing focal awareness of the earlier context of the story. (32)

In other words, Polzin is arguing that most of the time the audience of Deuteronomy 1–3 has a strong sense of being close to the situation Moses is recalling, with only a peripheral awareness that they are in fact historically distant from it. Through the frame breaks, though, these two awarenesses shift, with the sense of historical distance becoming the stronger awareness for the duration of the notice. In terms of their frame-breaking strategy, these notices provide readers with a momentary awareness of the real distance between them and the events of Moses' recollection, an awareness that is quickly lost as Moses' recollection becomes once more the focal reality.

While the antiquarian notices serve to establish only a momentary sense of distance, other features appear in the text that maintain this sense more consistently. The principle vehicle used to achieve this is the repeated phrase, "at that time," which occurs in 2:34 and 3:4, 8, 12, 18, 21, 23. This phrase indicates an end to the forward movement that characterized Deuteronomy 2. Bumpily, it slows Moses' recollection down to a standstill. The real movement forward ended with the conquest of Sihon's kingdom. It was in reflection on that conquest that the first "at that time" was introduced (2:34). The conquest of Og, which follows, is already conceived of in terms of a repetition of that which happened with Sihon. From there on, Moses' recollection begins a winding down. There is no longer any significant passage of time.

Beyond indicating the end of the action, this phrase seems also to advert to a lapse of time greater than that which the chronology of Moses' speech would indicate. (The material of chap. 3 completes the move up to the present moment of the speech, but it is presented as if distantly recalled: "at that time.") A sense of distance from these last recollected events is promoted.

At the same time as the action slows, the all-inclusive second person address begins to break up, with Moses' speech focusing more on particular groups and individuals, rather than on a corporate "you": for example, Reuben, Gad and half-Manasseh in 3:18–20, Joshua in 3:21–22 and the LORD in 3:23–25. Second person address shifts to third. Since second person address is one of the features that draws the reader most strongly into identification with Moses' recollection, its interruption has the effect of weakening that identification. We are being moved towards the periphery of the text.

In addition, the text itself becomes increasingly difficult as it approaches its close, requiring readers to work more actively and self-consciously in construing it: filling in blanks, making connections, perhaps glossing over inconsistencies. One example of this can be seen in the curious relationship between the last antiquarian notice (3:13b–14) and the material from Moses' recollection which follows it. Typically, these notices have been highly interruptive and work to evoke in readers a consciousness of the real distance between themselves and the events being recalled. For most of the text, this consciousness is peripheral, and the central consciousness is of the events being recollected, into which the reader is drawn as a participant. Now, as we move towards the outside of this recollection of the wilderness time, it is striking to see that the discontinuity between text and antiquarian notice is no longer so great. The two frames are closer together. This final antiquarian notice manages to be both interruptive and so close to the main line of Moses' presentation that it contributes directly to it. Both the notice and the following sentence of Moses' speech are taken from the same passage in Numbers 32.[3] Together, the notice and the following verse fill out Moses' presentation of the Manassite territories in Gilead and Bashan. And not only does the antiquarian notice seem more integrated into the main line of Moses' recollection, but Moses' recollection by the same token seems affected by the logic of the notice. The introduction of strange characters has, to this point, been the territory of the notices. Here, for the first time in our text, Moses introduces a certain Machir, without any preparation. While this would be out of place elsewhere in the text, here it contributes to the mounting sense that things are breaking up, and readers are being brought back to their present time—that later time in which they are addressed by the narrator.

Another example of the text's growing complexity occurs in reading 3:18–20. Moses, having assigned trans-jordanian lands to Reuben, Gad and half-Manasseh, goes on to charge the community that they should continue on to the conquest of the land across the Jordan, until their "brethren" have rest. The reader is here delivered the task of wrestling between the text's rhetorically driven reference to the whole community ("you") and the fact that it makes narrative sense only as applied to the two and one half tribes. In the process, the labour of the reading self provokes that very self—wrestling, sifting, judging—towards consciousness of its own operations.

As readers move through Deuteronomy 3, then, they are repeatedly called to consciousness of the artificiality of the narrative situation. Moses is not really giving a speech to a group of people that includes readers. Rather, this is a literary situation in which Moses' words are part of a bigger picture that includes interruptions from the narrator, as well as other rhetorical manipulations. As readers are put in a position to become more conscious of the literary character of this situation, they are maneuvered again to a position external to it.

---

[3] The question of the literary relationship between the two passages is taken up in some detail in my dissertation (204–7).

Readers are encouraged to step outside the chalk drawing before it becomes completely blurred by the rain.

The rhetoric of these chapters is not so much propositional as experiential. Deut 30:19–20 *says* "I set before you this day life and death, blessing and curse, therefore choose life that you may prosper in the land." Deuteronomy 1–3 does not *say* this. Rather, it brings readers through the experience of disobedience and death, fidelity and prosperous life, and sets them before the moment of decision to enter the land in obedience to the LORD's command. It offers the identity required to hear the law and understand the urgency of its imperative, while at the same time reminding readers that this imperative is addressed to them in their own present circumstances, and not in some far off long ago. Identification with the people positions readers to hear the law addressed to Israel in Deuteronomy, while awareness of their own context positions readers to respond faithfully in their own time and place.

Engaging the Rhetoric of Deuteronomy 1–3

The text tenders its invitation, naive of the audience that will pick it up. Now, it may happen that a real disjuncture is experienced by particular readers or reading communities between the call for identification with the people of Israel and their common memories, and the call to faithful response within the context of their own identity, time and place. This, at least, has been the case for me. Aspects of the call to faithful response in the context of community, a call which I hear loudly from these chapters and the book of Deuteronomy as a whole, prevent an easy assumption of the identity with the people of Israel and the theologically freighted memories that go with it in Deuteronomy. The invitation to imagine arrival is powerful; the way home, though, is not at all clear.

For instance, there are problems raised for Christians and Jews when Christians too easily take on the identity of the people of Israel. Here I speak as a Christian. The problem, of course, is not that the feat cannot be accomplished. It is rather that there is a long history of its being accomplished at horrible expense to Jews. Such assumption of the identity of the people of Israel by Christians has most commonly proceeded in the theological garb of supercessionism. This view, for example, shines through the kindly meant words which, many years ago now, I heard attributed to a Christian participant in Jewish-Christian dialogue: "Après tout, monsieur le rabbin, nous ne sommes que des juifs perfectionnés!" It is troubling to realize that such views are still not at all uncommon, are still expressed quite unreflectively and kindheartedly in our classrooms and our churches, by persons who are not engaged in any such potentially mind-opening dialogue with Jewish partners. And, as Mary Boys notes with some anguish, supercessionist interpretations are also common in preaching:

> Among the assertions I hear with disturbing frequency: (1) The Jews could not accept Jesus as the messiah because they were looking for a royal figure; (2) Jesus has freed us from the law, but Jews are still bound by it; (3) Christians *are* the people of God, though the Jews *were* God's people before Christ came; (4) the prophets preached the word of judgment to sinful Israel, but the Jews refused to listen to their prophets, just as they later refused to heed the prophetic preaching of Jesus; and (5) the God of the Old Testament is a God of justice, but the God of Jesus Christ is a God of love. (174)

Claims such as these have helped to shape a spiritual landscape in which it has been possible to dismiss and despise Jews. Still, the extent of the evils practiced against Jews and Judaism, either in the name of Christianity or with active Christian complicity over two millennia, goes wildly beyond what one might imagine could flow from even such claims. At least, it would if we did not have a history of institutionally sponsored and condoned atrocity to provide us with an interpretation of what these claims have meant as lived in Christian communities. As Emil Fackenheim and others continue to remind us, Christians cannot get past Auschwitz alone (89, 99).

Another constellation of questions is raised for me as a woman reading this text. What place do I have in a community that mentions women only once, in company with livestock (and children), in 3:19: "Only your wives, your children, and your livestock—I know that you have much livestock [!]—shall stay behind in the towns that I have given to you." Here the women and children of the two and one half tribes are exempted from the solidary participation in the conquest that is required of their men. Not only do we discover here that that which is essential for the men of Reuben, Gad, and Manasseh is not required of the women; we see what we might already have suspected—that they are not actively addressed by the inclusive second person discourse. They are attached to the moral actors, faithless and faithful, but they were not among those addressed by Moses as actors in the rebellion.

In Deuteronomy 1–3, women are not included among those enjoined to faithful and solidary action. Neither are their actions mentioned in the description of the people's first and faithless response. And yet, while they are classed with the children and the livestock as exempt from the requirements of solidarity in chap. 3, they are not granted the parallel exemption from death outside the land for faithlessness, in chap. 1. The women of the first generation, we assume, perish in the wilderness along with the men. Only the children are exempt, since they "do not yet know right from wrong" (1:39). In point of fact the women do not seem to be a concern for the writer. They are simply not on the horizon except as a logistical issue.

The Deuteronomist's understanding of the community here can be seen to work against the inclusive and familial vision of social life in the promised land. We are but slowly waking up to the severely destructive consequences for the whole society of the violence and distortions that are part and parcel of maintaining women's invisibility.

The women of Israel are not the only invisible ones in Deuteronomy 1–3. Equally overlooked are the "men, women and children" in all the towns of Sihon and Og who were righteously struck down by the men of Israel in demonstration of their faithfulness to the LORD: "We left not a single survivor." These are killed because of their relation to Sihon or Og: "Do not fear him, for I have handed him over to you, along with his people and his land" (3:2). "We struck him down until not a single survivor was left . . . utterly destroying men, women and children" (3:3b, 6b). The women of Israel stand, or fall, with the populations of the trans-jordanian territories as accidents of the narrative, mentioned only along the path of defining the moral stance taken by the men *vis-à-vis* God's call to faithful action.

This kind of diminishment of human persons on the basis of gender or ethnicity, or simply because they stand in the path of one group's sense of destiny, has sinister and familiar resonances in the world through which we journey today. Is it possible to read *past* this kind of language, possible not to hear the rhetoric of the conflicts in Bosnia and Kosovo, of Jewish settlers in the West Bank, of the

European settlement of North America, of Nazi Germany and so very
many other conflicts that can readily be named?

This is another point from which dialogue with the text leads to
an appreciation that the practice, the mode, is not consistent with the
vision, but works tragically against it. Nobody gets home from here:
neither settled nor settlers, women nor men, Christians nor Jews. What
is at fault? Is it the very notion of homecoming promoted within the
text? Is it the freighted imaginations of the comers-home? (Is there any
other kind of imagination?) Is it the way the two, in the end, are
inseparable? We begin to see that it may be for good reason that people
approaching Deuteronomy are asked to understand themselves as
situated outside the land, straining towards it, but not established
within it.

Some Hermeneutical Implications

I have named three areas in which I encounter obstacles to
cooperation with the rhetoric of inclusion that is at work in
Deuteronomy 1–3. Others might focus on different areas. At this stage
I would like to reflect briefly on some hermeneutical implications of
readings from context to context such as that begun above.

Michael Fishbane views as one of Judaism's greatest contributions to the history of religions the assertion that "the divine Reality is
communicated to mankind [*sic*] through words" (128). This brings
with it both positive and negative consequences. He writes,

> Our hermeneutical hope is in the indissoluble link between the
> divine and the human *textus*—the divine *textus* being the texture of
> truth as it converges upon itself, and the human *textus* being our
> rationalized versions of this divine *textus* in culture. On the other
> side our existential poverty is an unawareness of this link, and our
> exegetical proclivity to cross over too fast from one *textus* to
> another. Too soon do we close the terrifying gap between the divine
> infinity and a human world of words. (129)

The Bible lives in the human world of words, and within the
constraints of that world it witnesses to the divine *textus*, the
communication of the divine reality. Its witness calls those who read to
discern the divine *textus* in their reality, acknowledging the imperative
of divine communication in their lives even while acknowledging that

discerning its content is an ongoing search and does not lead to secure possession. As Fishbane further writes, "The Bible . . . dramatizes the linkage between the human and divine *textus* and expresses the hopes and terrors of this necessity. It is, in truth, the Book of the *Ivrim*: the Book of the Over-Crossers" (130). It is the book of the Over-Crossers: the nomads, not the arrivers. Crossing over is the lived actuality, but homecoming is the goal nourished by the divine *textus* in the heart and the imagination. This goal allows the reader, especially the later reader, to see at times where the human *textus* is working against the divine.

There may seem to be more of Exodus than of arrival in the dissonances I have named above, but Exodus begins in the recognition that the people are not yet home, and in the discovery that there is a home towards which they are called to journey, through Sinai and towards the land. This is the call to the imagination that Cynthia Ozick likewise has discerned in the rabbis' writings: "A call to imagine arrival: homecoming, deliverance, fruition, resolution, an idealism of character, right conduct, just determinations, communal well-being" (227).

The Broader Conversation

Talk of crossings over brings me towards the broader discussion of the role of context in biblical interpretation. Dialogue with contemporary cultural-political realities is, in a variety of circles globally, being pressed to the heart of the interpretive process. The phrase "reading from context to context" is used by Sharon Ringe to characterize feminist hermeneutics and its contribution to liberation theologies (283). Asian scholars such as Kwok Pui-lan have called similarly for the re-interpretation of biblical texts through "creative acts of dialogical imagination" (30). The South African black liberation theologian and biblical scholar Itumeleng Mosala speaks of the necessity to engage the text critically "on the basis of the questions and agenda emanating out of the history and culture of struggles today" (11).

In part these calls recognize that the interpreter's context impinges upon reading whether or not this is acknowledged. Further, though, they set a positive value on a dialogical and critical relation between text and reader, viewing this as in fact essential for a theologically and socially-politically fruitful relationship with the biblical material. Theologically as well as practically, this tends to be accompanied by a shift in the location of scriptural authority—from text to interpreting community. At the same time, there are those who situate the revelatory character of the text in the full and dialogical engagement of reader with text, within the reading process itself. Sandra Schneiders's work, *The Revelatory Text*, develops this approach. And Katherine Doob Sakenfeld's notion of "authority in community" is similar.

Such dialogical approaches often make use of the space opened up by the tension between awarenesses of the Bible as revelatory (or at least liberative) text and as oppressive (or at least seriously muddled) text, and in a range of significantly different ways. Fishbane's proposal, for example, would likely be greeted with hermeneutical suspicion by some practitioners of contextually committed readings. One reason for this may have to do with its way of drawing qualities of ineffability and transcendent mystery into hermeneutically key positions: "Too soon do we close the terrifying gap between the divine infinity and a human world of words" (129). "Not nearly soon enough," might be the rejoinder of many biblical interpreters whose work is strongly motivated by a desire to find resources in Scripture for practices of liberative struggle by the communities within which they stand committed. This has to do with an ideological critique of notions related to mystery and the mystical. The critique is exemplified, for instance, in Michael Welker's work with David Tracy's term "prophetic-mystical," which Tracy applies to what he discerns as a globally emerging movement towards polycentric and experientially based theology. Welker recognizes the prophetic element as an apt descriptor, but finds the mystical to be an "externally imported" addition. He views it as "burdened . . . with various associations of subjectivism, cognitivism, and elitism," and as "invit[ing] indeterminacy" (49). But does indeterminacy wait for an invitation, or does it not just inevitably crash the epistemic party? How we deal with this is a large question.

For those who read from somewhere in this conversation, the labour of reading is ancillary to another, longer labour. I would look for ways to hold in dialogue the revelatory and oppressive dynamics not only of the biblical text but also of the interpretive process. Fishbane's perspective allows this to go forward in a way that preserves the notion of a sacred text without trivializing the understanding of divine communication. Both the Bible and our experience are inscribed with the divine *textus*, and both are expressed in the human world of words. This has an effect on how we see life—and biblical interpretation.

> This new Bible-sponsored sacrality would allow the awesome transcendence of the divine reality to chasten our constructions of order and sacrality. . . . The Bible itself, with its own pretension to present a humanly conditioned divine voice, would also be radically transcended. Here, I suggest is the final prophetic voice of the text. Or is it the divine voice which speaks to Job, and asks: Do you love God more than tradition, more than all your versions of the sacred? (131, 133)

Deuteronomy 1–3 may call me to embrace the vision of life towards covenanted society in the land given by God. It provides hints of what such life might look like. Some of these hints, these particular elements of Deuteronomic vision, shatter against particular elements of contemporary vision and practice. Our own visions have no more eternal quality, but form the basis for our engagement with the biblical text and the world of our experience, an engagement out of which we may discern something of the vital, dynamic and unimaginable divine *textus*. The visions draw us forward, but we are separated from the reality by more than a river. Moses has a lot of company on that mountain top, looking towards the land, living towards the land, but not able to embrace the rest promised within it.

Bibliography

Boys, Mary
1991   "An Educational Perspective on Interreligious Dialogue: A Catholic's View." *Religious Education* 86:171–83.

Fackenheim, Emil
1990   *The Jewish Bible after the Holocaust: A Re-reading.* Bloomington: Indiana University Press.

Fishbane, Michael
1989   *The Garments of Torah: Essays in Biblical Hermeneutics.* Bloomington: Indiana University Press.

Haynes, Stephen
1991   *Prospects for Post-Holocaust Theology: "Israel" in the Theologies of Karl Barth, Jurgen Moltmann, and Paul Van Buren.* Atlanta: Scholars Press.

Kwok, Pui-lan
1989 "Discovering the Bible in the Non-Biblical World." *Semeia* 47:25–42.

Mayes, A. D. H.
1993 "On Describing the Purpose of Deuteronomy." *JSOT* 58:13–33.

Mosala, Itumeleng J.
1989 *Biblical Hermeneutics and Black Theology in South Africa.* Grand Rapids: Eerdmans.

Polzin, Robert
1980 *Moses and the Deuteronomist: A Literary Study of the Deuteronomistic History.* New York: Seabury.

Ozick, Cynthia
1991 "Bialik's Hint." Pp. 22–39 in *Metaphor and Memory: Essays.* New York: Vintage International.

Ringe, Sharon
1990 "Reading from Context to Context: Contributions of a Feminist Hermeneutic to Theologies of Liberation." Pp. 283–92 in *Lift Every Voice: Constructing Christian Theologies from the Underside.* Ed. Susan B. Thistlethwaite and M. P. Engels. San Francisco: HarperSanFrancisco.

Sakenfeld, Katherine Doob
1989 "In the Wilderness, Awaiting the Land: The Daughters of Zelophehad and Feminist Interpretation." *Theology Today* 46:154–68.

Schneiders, Sandra
1991 *The Revelatory Text: Interpreting the New Testament as Sacred Scripture.* San Francisco: Harper.

Segovia, Fernando F. and Mary Ann Tolbert, eds.
1995a *Reading from this Place.* Vol. 1. *Social Location and Biblical Interpretation in the United States.* Minneapolis: Fortress Press.
1995b *Reading from this Place.* Vol. 2. *Social Location and Biblical Interpretation in Global Perspective.* Minneapolis: Fortress Press.

Slater, Susan
1991 "I Have Set the Land before You: A Study of the Rhetoric of Deuteronomy 1–3." Ph.D. diss., McGill University.

Sugirtharajah, R.S., ed.
1995 *Voices from the Margin. Interpreting the Bible in the Third World.* Rev. ed. Maryknoll: Orbis; London: SPCK.

Van Buren, Paul
1980 *A Theology of the Jewish Christian Reality.* Vol. 1. *Discerning the Way.* San Francisco: Harper and Row.

1983   A Theology of the Jewish Christian Reality. Vol. 2. A Christian Theology of the People Israel. San Francisco: Harper and Row.

1988   *A Theology of the Jewish Christian Reality*. Vol. 3. *Christ in Context*. San Francisco: Harper and Row.

Welker, Michael
1997   "God's Power and Powerlessness: Biblical Theology and the Search for a World Ethos in a Time of Short-lived Moral Markets." Pp. 39–56 in *Power, Powerlessness and the Divine: New Inquiries in Bible and Theology*. Ed. Cynthia L. Rigby. Studies in Theological Education Series. Atlanta: Scholars Press.

YEARNING FOR JERUSALEM
READING MYTH ON THE WEB[1]

David M. Gunn

I

WELCOME to the Israel Foreign Ministry Home Page (www.Israel.org). I'm looking for something official on Jerusalem. I need an authoritative account. Given the five main options, I choose *Facts about Israel*, and then, under the general heading *State*, I select *Jerusalem* and contemplate the page that opens:

> Ten measures of beauty were bestowed upon the world;
> nine were taken by Jerusalem
> and one by the rest of the world.
> (Babylonian Talmud, Tractate Kiddushin 49:2)

---

[1] My thanks to Edward McMahon who assiduously marshaled resources and pointed me to the website in the first place, and to Claudia Camp who encouraged and criticized in about equal measure. Neither, of course, are to blame for the result.

I met Robert Culley first, several decades ago, in the library of the University of Melbourne, Australia, where I came across his article on oral tradition in biblical studies. His interest in the work of Parry and Lord on Serbo-Croatian heroic songs intersected with my interests as a student of Homer. Later as a fledgling biblical critic I was delighted to come across him in person at a meeting of the IOSOT in Uppsala. It was a turning point for me. Bob invited me to write for a new journal, *Semeia*, in an issue (it was to be number three) that he was editing on "classical Hebrew narrative." He urged me to be "experimental," to write a "literary" piece. I tried, he published the essay, and set me on a course I am traveling still. Robert Culley, fellow journeyer and friend, I salute you.

After this modest beginning, I read further of "the capital of Israel, . . . located in the heart of the country," with its

> incandescent glow, golden in sunshine, silvery by moonlight, . . . rivaled in impact only by the kaleidoscope of its people—some the descendants of generations of Jerusalemites, others who have come from the four corners of the earth. Mingling with people wearing the spectrum of modern fashion are dark-suited ultra-Orthodox Jews, Arab women in brightly embroidered shifts and Christian clergy in somber robes.

Small wonder this technicolor marvel has been "praised by the Prophets, enshrined in literature and liturgy, and sung by poets, near and far, down through the generations." I hesitate to be reminded of Chateaubriand's description of "extraordinary desolation," Edward Lear's phrase, "that vile place, the foulest and odiousest on earth," or Mark Twain's "pauper village . . . knobby with countless little domes as a prison door is with bolt-heads" (cf. Elon: 134, 142–43), Instead I click on *Capital* to find a brief survey of *Jerusalem the Capital of Israel*.

> And the days that David reigned over Israel were forty years; seven years reigned he in Hebron, and thirty-three years reigned he in Jerusalem. (1 Kings 2:11)

The biblical epigraph provides the proof text for Jerusalem's political role as "capital of the Jewish people." This function, it would appear, is of the very essence of the city.

> Throughout the millennia of its existence, Jerusalem has never been the capital of any other sovereign nation. Jerusalem has stood at the center of the Jewish people's national and spiritual life since King David made it the capital of his kingdom in 1003 BCE. The city remained the capital of the Davidic dynasty for 400 years, until the kingdom was conquered by the Babylonians. Following the return from the Babylonian exile in 538 BCE, Jerusalem again served as the capital of the Jewish people in its land for the next five and a half centuries.

The Christian link with Jerusalem is essentially a religious one, we are assured, with no political or secular "connotations" (apart from the "short-lived" Crusader kingdom). As for Muslim rule, whether

Arab or otherwise, Jerusalem was never the capital of any political entity "or even a province." Though British administration made Jerusalem its seat during the Mandate, it was not until 1948 that the city was restored once more to its place as a Capital, "the capital of a sovereign Jewish state." Divided between 1948 and 1967, it was "reunited" in June 1967 as the gates of the Old City were opened and "the eastern sector was reintegrated into the nation's capital."

So while Christians and Muslims may have religious investments in Jerusalem it is "the Jewish people" who alone have a millennia old stake in the city. I click on *History* to open *Jerusalem through the Centuries*.

> If I forget thee, O Jerusalem,
> may my right hand forget it[s] cunning.
> May my tongue cleave to the roof of my mouth,
> if I do not set Jerusalem above my highest joy.
> (Psalms 137:5–6)

Below the biblical warrant appears an untitled photograph of an imposing ancient city, currently, if I am not mistaken, to be found in the grounds of the Holyland Hotel at Bayit Vegan. (An uncharitable reader might take it as an apt emblem of the website's "facts.") At any rate, the "history" proceeds with brief biblical paraphrase, starting once more with David in "1003" but quickly moving to Solomon in order to configure the temple as "the religious and national center of the people of Israel" (are these the same as "the Jewish people"?) and the city as "the prosperous capital of an empire extending from the Euphrates to Egypt." The account comes to rest with the "reuniting" of the city in June 1967, the restoration of the Jewish Quarter of the Old City, and the opening of their holy places to Israeli citizens.

So Jerusalem's is a story of sovereign glory, displacement (exile), and restoration (redemption), in other words, the story of "Israel" in microcosm. That story, Jerusalem writ large, is repeated constantly throughout the website (see, for example, *Israel in Brief* [.../facts/brief.html], *History* [.../facts/hist/fhist1.html], *Zionism* [.../facts/ state/zionism.html], *Society: Jewish Society* [.../facts/soc/fsoc2.html], or *Aliya and Absorbtion* [.../mfa/zionism/aliya.html]). In one form or another the narrative runs as follows. The Jewish people/nation along with their religion and culture are born in the Land (Eretz-Israel). However, they are forcibly removed, exiled from the Land. They endure vicissitudes in far lands (prosperity, oppression), looking always with yearning to their lost Land. Then, after long centuries, the Zionist movement begins to forge for them a Return, an "ingathering of exiles," to their ancestral homeland. On return they (are to) redeem Israel/the Land, establish law, and exercise justice and equity. One does not need the constant reminder of biblical quotations as web page epigraphs to recognize how thoroughly "biblical" is this story As the biblical story of return from Egypt (and possession of the land) is recapitulated in the return from Babylon (and possession of the land), so now a new post-biblical story of exile and return (and possession of the land) recapitulates both biblical stories (cf. Neusner, 1987, 1997). What we have here might well be described as a "foundation myth" (cf. Lemche: 86–97) or a "master commemorative narrative" (Zerubavel: 3–12). Indeed, one notable rendition of the narrative, to which others on the website make rhetorical allusion constantly, is the "Declaration of the Establishment of the State of Israel" (May 14, 1948; …/peace/independ.-html).

While the myth can be recounted in brief without mention of Jerusalem, the city frequently appears. Clearly, by way of synechdoche, Jerusalem/Zion is the land or the state. The city is often freighted also with the role of "capital," a characteristic which marks the myth of Exile and Return as a story of *sovereignty* lost (at Exile) and rightfully regained (at Return).

As Yael Zerubavel, among others, has observed, however, the Zionist myth, like all such master commemorative narratives, conceals as well as reveals, harboring within it deepseated ideological tensions and contradictions relating to the society that makes and maintains it (cf. Neusner, 1997:223–28). Moreover, the myth, as the web exemplar makes plain, derives authority in part from an appeal to "history." Yet subject it to serious historical critique and some of that assurance ebbs. In the case of Jerusalem as capital, for example, as Keith Whitelam (1998) points out, "the notion of 'the city of David' as 'capital' is not something which emerges naturally from the biblical text or the archaeological remains." The Bible nowhere uses any term equivalent to "capital" and the archaeological remains of the tenth century support neither a centralized "state" of Israel or Judah nor an "empire" of David for which the small, out of the way town might have been the political and administrative center (cf. Finkelstein, 1996; Knauf, 1997: 81–82; Thompson, 1999:161–67).

In the present paper I indicate some lines of inquiry arising from my encounter with the myth in its website manifestations, seeking in particular to "unpack" the topos of Jerusalem. I enumerate here six main points which appear (and reappear) in the essay in no neat order. First, Jerusalem, in the myth, is characterized as an object of desire ("yearning"). Second, yearning drives the plot of the main narrative and validates the outcome by warrant of emotion. Third, yearning constitutes the subject of the narrative, namely "the people," in the myth's middle episode, Living in Exile. Fourth, yearning is a pivotal term which allows (pre-Zionist) expressions of religious imagination to be co-opted as (Zionist) expressions of ("romantic") nationalism or geopolitics. Fifth, yearning constitutes the historical "memory" of an unbroken bond, through several millennia, between "the people" and "the land." (How do we know there was this unbroken bond? Because the people yearned.) Sixth, the Bible is used, in the manner of a proof text, to lend authority to yearning: because their yearning originates in the Bible, the people's claim to possess the object of their yearning, namely Jerusalem, Zion, the Land, is justified. In all of this I neither bring nor argue a normative understanding of "yearning" beyond assuming its primary use as a term of affect. Rather my point is to track some of the varying ways the term appears in "Jerusalem" rhetoric, to track, in short, some intriguing migrations between diverse contexts.

II

Jerusalem is a key element in the Living in Exile episode of the plot, inasmuch as it is cast as the object of desire whose attainment exile thwarts. If we move on, click on *Holy City*, and bring up *Jerusalem the Holy City*, this function of the city becomes clearer. As usual, first comes the religious proof text, then the historical "facts."

> Rejoice thee with Jerusalem, and be glad with her,
> all ye that love her:
> rejoice for joy with her,
> all that mourn for her.
> For thus saith the Lord,
> Behold, I will extend peace to her like a river
> and the glory of the nations like a flowing stream.
> (Isaiah 66:10–12)

Sanctified by religion and tradition, by history and theology, by holy places and houses of worship, Jerusalem is a city revered by Jews, Christians, and Muslims. It reflects the fervor and piety of the three major monotheistic faiths, each of which is bound to Jerusalem by veneration and love.

> The Jewish bond to Jerusalem was never broken. For three millennia, Jerusalem has been the center of the Jewish faith, retaining its symbolic value throughout the generations. The many Jews who had been exiled after the Roman conquest and scattered throughout the world never forgot Jerusalem. Year after year they repeated "Next year in Jerusalem." Jerusalem became the symbol off [sic] the desire of Jews everywhere to return to their land. It was invoked by the prophets, enshrined in daily prayer, and sung by Hebrew poets in far-flung lands.

So here we have it, full-blown: yearning for Jerusalem. The topos is, in fact, ubiquitous in accounts of the founding of modern Israel. In a brief article, a few clicks away on the Ministry website (.../mfa/ariel/102efron.html), Zusia Efron begins an article ("'If I Forget Thee...'") on longings for Jerusalem in Jewish folk art of Eastern Europe:

> Longings for Zion and Jerusalem have accompanied the Jewish people in their exile, for more than 2,500 years, from the time of the Babylonian Exile (by Nebuchadnezzar in 598–537 BCE), and since the conquest of Jerusalem and its destruction by the Roman army of Titus in 70 CE, after which began the great dispersion of the Jewish people. Longings for Jerusalem are mentioned more than 1,000 times in the Bible as well as in the Talmud, and in daily and holiday prayers—and are summed up in vision and hope at the end of the Passover Haggadah; in the supplicatory words, "Next Year in Jerusalem."

> Some of the most poignant expressions of these feelings were composed by the author of the Psalms:

> By the waters of Babylon, there we sat down and wept when we remembered Zion. On the willows there we hung up our lyres (137, 1–2).

> If I forget thee, O Jerusalem, let my right hand wither, let my tongue cleave to my palate if I do not remember you, if I do not set Jerusalem above my highest joy (137, 5–7).

> Praise the Lord, O Jerusalem! Praise your God, O Zion! (147, 12)

In Meron Benvenisti's *City of Stone* (145), the topos even causes the author to desert his customary, more sanguine style:

> The Jewish people, powerless to rehabilitate their Holy City [after the Roman destruction], expressed their longings in dreams of a "celestial Jerusalem." However, the restoration of the earthly Jerusalem was perceived not as a task for God alone, but as an undertaking within human capabilities. Year after year, for nearly 2,000 years, Jews vowed, "Next year in Jerusalem," mourning over its destruction and longing to work for its rebuilding. Time did not diminish their yearning, and it burst forth with irresistible force when the political conditions necessary for its fulfillment were attained.

Amos Elon's offering in *Jerusalem: Battlegrounds of Memory* (33–34) rounds out my sampling with its inclusion of Judah Halevi's long treasured language of love:

> Among the many vanquished capital cities of the ancient world, only Jerusalem survived in the imagination of her exiles and in that of their descendants from generation to generation. . . . As they wandered from land to land, they remained stubbornly a people of Jerusalem: "If I forget thee, O Jerusalem. . . . If I do not remember thee. . . ."

> Jerusalem became their great Capital of Memory. Memory gave them their culture and their identity. . . . Under the iron skies of northern Europe, the Jewish festivals remained tied to the seasons of the city. Passover and Yom Kippur services ended with the exhortation "Next year in Jerusalem." For centuries, Jews turned in prayer toward Jerusalem three times a day: "Return in mercy to your city Jerusalem and dwell in it as you have promised; rebuild it soon, in our own days. Praised are you, O Lord, builder of Jerusalem." The words of the Spanish-Hebrew poet Yehuda Halevi (c. 1075–1141) reaffirmed this devotion.

> Could I but kiss thy dust
> so would I fain expire.
> As sweet as honey then,
> My longing and desire.

How long, indeed, could such longing be constrained? And what North American reader of this topos is not going to be swayed by the expression of such deep desire coming to fulfillment? Yearning not only drives the plot of return and rebuilding. At the same time, to an audience schooled in popular romance, it validates the outcome, namely possession of the yearned for, the beloved. Jerusalem is a woman, waiting for her lover's embrace (the metaphor has a long rhetorical history). As Mr. Falwell put it, commenting on the invitation of his friend, Mr. Netanyahu, to send Liberty University students to visit Israel, "What we are talking about is 3,000 young people who will return forever lovers of Israel." (Indeed, among the settlers of the First Aliyah at the end of the nineteenth century were members of the Russian associations called Lovers of Zion [Laqueur: 75–83].)

III

That we are dealing with the language of romance is an observation of no small matter. Desire for Jerusalem is desire for Zion is desire for the Land. An American audience's enthusiasm for consummation in the plot of popular romance is certainly one dimension of the myth's contemporary consumption. The language of romance also takes us to some historical roots of the myth's formation in the wake of the romantic revival and the rise of "romantic" nationalism in the nineteenth century. Zerubavel (cf. Evron: 61, 102) has argued that:

> For the Zionists the major yardstick to evaluate the past was the bond between the Jewish people and their ancient land. Influenced by European romantic nationalism on the one hand and drawing upon a long, distinctively Jewish tradition of longing to return to the ancient homeland on the other, Zionism assumed that an inherent bond between the Jewish people and their ancient land was a necessary condition for the development of Jewish nationhood (15; cf. 22).

Let us look a little further at this connection between the language of longing and the construction of Jewish nationhood (and, in due course, the Jewish State). Nationalism assumed the need for a land in which "nationhood" could be fully realized. To some early (secular) Zionists, particularly those motivated by the desire to alleviate the predicament of Jews arising from the pogroms of the 1880s, the precise territory to be occupied was a debatable matter. Within a few years, however, the issue was settled: Palestine was to be the land of settlement. Jewish traditions of longing to return to Jerusalem were invoked to show that there had always been a desire to return to this particular geographical region. Hence the traditional language of longing was, and is, construed in terms of the innate desire of an exiled people to become a fully fledged nation state. Longing becomes the motive power for a geopolitical (ad)venture in Eretz-Israel by those who, irrespective of their prosperity or oppression, construed themselves as "exiles."

Michael Seidel points us to a rich body of "exilic" writing, with which, I would suggest, the Zionist narrative has obvious affinities. Among the stories:

> . . . the Tartarian and Luciferian expulsions, the trek east from Eden, the sagas of Io and Europa, the flight of Daedalus, the exposure of Oedipus, the voyage of the Argonauts, the Exodus, Captivity, and Diaspora of the Jews, the wanderings of Odysseus, the displacement of Aeneas, the trials of the prodigal son, the medieval and gothic myths of the Wandering Jew, the journey of Dante the pilgrim, the outlawry of El Cid, the "fugitive" fable of the castaway Robinson Crusoe, the river odyssey of Huck Finn, even the intercontinental trauma of Tarzan and the intergalactic adventure of Superman. In the exilic plot the extraneous becomes foundational, the blighted and ill-fated from one sphere become instigators and originators in another. The powers of exilic imagining represent desired territory, lost or found, as narrative fate (8).

The Zionist myth taps into this tradition. "Longing" then provides a bridge from this world of "exilic imaginings" to a narrative of national aspiration in which the desired is reified as actual land, configured politically.

IV

Yehuda Halevi is invoked by Elon, as he is by many others, to buttress his exposition of the (geopolitical) Zionist master narrative. The assumption is that Halevi's yearning is one rendition of an ancient desire for possession of the land/Jerusalem which has been passed on from generation to generation of Jews until it has found its culmination in the romance of Zionist settlement and state-building. But Halevi is writing in a quite other vein of romance, typical of twelfth-century Spain (and elsewhere in western Europe) and not without its cognates in modern literature. He is as adept at penning love poetry for his imagined lovers as for any far off holy city, perhaps rather more so. He is writing of yearning itself, and not simply of its object. The language of yearning has a peculiar power which it draws from being situated in the space-time between desire and attainment, between passion (suffering) and consummation. As Seidel notes, speaking of exile and desire in Vladimir Nabokov's *Lolita* and *Pale Fire*, "As is the case with the homeland, the desire for the object of love grows in proportion to the distance placed between it and the disorienting, displaced mind" (Seidel: 176). The power of yearning is represented in the space between Tristan and Isolde, a space occupied by a drawn sword.

That space "between," where desire can flourish as longing, is also the condition of religious yearning. Indeed the language of romantic love is often the language of adoration and worship even when its topic is not ostensibly religion: the yearning lover "adores" and "worships" the beloved. By the same token, the language of religion draws on the language of love. Such metaphoric crossover makes it easy to understand how in the Middle Ages the yearning lover of the Song of Songs was the soul seeking the divine, the bride of Christ her husband, or Israel yearning for God (cf. Astell). Such a literary context is the location of Halevi's poetry and in such terms it would seem reasonable to interpret it.

As it happens, he did in fact set off on pilgrimage to Palestine, suggesting that he may indeed have attempted to collapse the space where yearning thrived by attaining the place of his desire. Yet were he to have reached the physical place, we could not be sure that he would have found his yearning space collapsed and a new space attained where yearning was absent. He might equally have found his yearning space simply displaced. We do not know because he does not write of it. Halevi may have taken his poem sufficiently literally to have actually attempted to kiss the dust of Jerusalem (though it seems he tarried in Egypt and never reached his destination). He may also have taken a lover or two (perhaps that's why he tarried). But whether or not any of this happened, his poetry lived because its admirers found in its conjuring of yearning a conceit that they could easily transpose into many and various dimensions of their emotional and spiritual lives. Many Jews (and indeed many Christians) have regularly, over the centuries, understood "Jerusalem" metaphorically as a transcendent object of spiritual longing. Halevi was a master at constructing religious sensibility out of such conceits, as witness his beautiful poem on the Sabbath as beloved. The Zionist co-option of his language into a geopolitical program envisioning the conquest and physical rebuilding of Jerusalem by Jews is then a remarkable one—quite a "stretch," one might say. Indeed it is hardly surprising that by the end of the nineteenth century the apparent abandonment of traditional spiritual, metaphysical, or messianic meanings of exilic longing in favor of geopolitical/historical constructions prompted strong opposition to Zionism from Orthodox Jews (cf. Zerubavel: 14–16; Evron: 54–55). Yet plucked thus from its former context, the language of yearning admits of this, as of any other, transposition and now in these (Crusader?) clothes, lives on.

Once questions of metaphor and the functions of language are raised, the liturgical phrase so frequently cited in the myth's construction of yearning, namely "next year in Jerusalem," becomes as problematic a witness as Halevi's poetry. Without entering into a full discussion here, it will suffice to say that the possibilities for understanding the phrase range from the purely performative, whereby the end of the service is enacted, to the literal, with boat passage in mind, and any number of metaphorical conjugations in between. Plainly the cryptic phrase has the potential to have meant a variety of things to a variety of people over a good many centuries and in many different places. Given, however, the relative dearth of literal action (travel to Jerusalem) consequent on the phrase's countless recitations over the times (the subject of another discussion!) when it was actually in liturgical use, it is not difficult to conclude that a literal meaning was the least prevalent of the possibilities.

V

As the Ministry website's epigraphs and texts make clear, it is of the essence of the foundation myth that it is biblically warranted (no small irony in a largely secular society), and Efron, too, is eager to claim this stamp of approval. No less than one thousand times are longings for Jerusalem expressed in the Bible as well as in the Talmud, the writer tells us. An impressive figure. I can only suppose (for I have not ventured to track the details) that either there are a very large number of occurrences in the Talmud, close on one thousand to be precise, or Efron's definition of "longings for Jerusalem" is rather broad, since the Bible's expressions of such sentiments is sparse, to say the least. My paper has already listed most of them, since most appear on the website. Psalm 137 tops the list and Lamentations is frequently invoked. The latter part of Isaiah is full of calls to return, of course, but curiously little "longing."

Both Psalm 137 and Lamentations are themselves witness to the complexity of "longing" as a literary construct. In neither case is it obvious that they are the direct product of "exile." Psalm 137 invokes the traditional (one might say "generic") emblem of Jewish "exile," namely Babylon, and speaks of an experience in the past. As with most of the psalms, there is nothing in the poem to convey any particularity that might disclose a personally lived experience, though generically lived experience is exquisitely apparent. Through the traditional forms, the poet is cultivating a nostalgia by which the readers or reciters may constitute themselves as "exiles" too, whether or not they are in actuality dispersed from their homes. Likewise Lamentations is a literary product at some distance from any actual siege of Jerusalem. Women (not men) eat their children in literary sieges (Lam 2:20; 2 Kgs 6:24–31; see Fewell and Gunn: 171–73) because this patriarchal reversal of maternal norms ratchets up the horror quotient in a spectacular way, as no end of commentators bear witness, while leaving the men to do the manly stuff. Again Lamentations may be seen as a product of a "returnee" community that is intent on maintaining its identity as a *golah* community (cf. Thompson: 217–25; Lemche: 88; Linville: 25–37; Neusner, 1997).

If this analysis is cogent, it suggests that, broadly speaking, the deployment of these texts in the making of a modern legitimating myth recapitulates their early life at the end of the first millennium BCE. Yet there is also a striking difference between the modern and ancient literary contexts of the passages. These "longing" passages do not specify political independence or sovereign "nationality" as objects of desire, whether past or future. But neither do the biblical (con)texts to which they belong. Indeed, it is notable that the literature that touches most the theme of political sovereignty, the accounts of the Maccabean revolt in the second century BCE, is not accorded canonical status within early Judaism. Hence, at least in this specific regard, there is

something decidedly "un-biblical" about the Zionist rallying song, now
the Israeli national anthem, "Hatikva":

> As long as deep in the heart,
> the soul of a Jew yearns,
> and towards the East
> an eye looks to Zion,
> our hope is not yet lost,
> the hope of two thousand years,
> to be a free people in our land,
> the land of Zion and Jerusalem.

Here is a concept never expressed in the oft-cited biblical passages of
yearning: to be a "free people" in the land is the *summation* of desire.
The orthodox community of Jerusalem at the end of the nineteenth
century would not have looked kindly on such a conceit. Nor do the
Haredim today.

Myths mask structural, social and ideological tensions. I have
indicated already at several points where the Zionist myth conceals the
divide in Jewish and Zionist thinking (and behavior) between the
religious and the political—terms that themselves risk hiding the
complexity of a "divide" which is in reality multiple "divisions." The
myth of exile, yearning, and return masks an ongoing and bitter
struggle over Jewish identity. Today I read in my local newspaper (in a
report culled from a longer New York Times version) of an incident at
the Western Wall:

> In an ugly confrontation 100 strictly Orthodox yeshiva students
> surrounded a group of American Reform rabbis who went to pray at
> the Western Wall this morning, booing loudly and hurling insults
> past officers from the border police. What was most chilling to the
> Americans was that the youths, their faces contorted in anger under
> their black hats, screamed that the rabbis should "go back to
> Germany," to be exterminated, one explained later. . . . "They are
> nothing but biological Jews," said an Orthodox member of
> Parliament, Avraham Leizerson, who entered the pen [in which the
> rabbis were confined for their service] to yell at the Americans.
> (Deborah Sontage; Jerusalem, Feb. 1, 1999; Fort Worth Star-
> Telegram, Feb. 2)

There are mere biological Jews and there are true Jews according to
this fault line. Another of Mr. Leizerson's associates might have put it

in terms of secular Jews versus religious Jews, or for yet another the term "biological" might conjure the ghosts of the "political" and "practical" Zionisms that, a century ago, shaped the future that is now the present. Actually, of course, there are any number of combinations and permutations bridging and confounding the divide (witness the Reform rabbis) but structurally speaking the divide is widely recognized. Historians speak routinely of the invention of Zionism in the latter part of the nineteenth century as a predominantly secular movement. Since then, the construction of Jewish identity has been contested in terms of shifting polarities: secular politics and (apolitical?) religion, Zionism and Orthodoxy, and political Zionism and religious Zionism, to name but a few of these constructions and leave ethnicity out of the mix. In Israel in recent years, the permutations of the "religious" side of the spectrum have produced some striking ironies, such as the Gush Emunim as a Zionist looking "settler" movement bitterly opposed by many who stand in the secular labor Zionist tradition. But broadly speaking, as Boas Evron persuasively argues, there remains a secularist versus religionist divide at the heart of the society. Though his is but one effort to sketch the contours of the chasm, his sense of the deep fractures of Jewish identity and Israeli society is widely shared. What interests me here is, on the one hand, the widespread recognition of the identity (and societal) divide(s) and, on the other, the strenuous efforts of the myth makers to mask the chasm(s).

The question of the "divide(s)" prompts me to return to the website and ask of the myth: who is the subject of yearning in this particular narrative of exile and return? The answer, of course, is "the Jewish people." So yearning not only motivates the plot's transition from exile to return, it also constitutes the narrative's subject. (It is important to note that in both regards—motivation and subject construction—yearning, the affect of exile, works in tandem with suffering, the affect of persecution, specified, most often, as the Russian pogroms of the late nineteenth century and, ultimately, the great German destruction of the mid-twentieth century.) This function of the topos, namely subject construction, is of crucial importance for the myth, because without "yearning" the singularity and continuity of the subject would be less apparent.

While the Zionist myth from its beginnings in the nineteenth century has tended to make strenuous efforts to collapse all experience of Exile into the negative of persecution and suffering (Zerubavel: 16–20), this erasure of manifold positive dimensions of Jewish life over many centuries has proved a difficult eclipse to sustain. As seen in more recent, post-State, versions (like the website), the pressure of alternative memories of flourishing communities, distinctive ethnic customs, and rich cultural contributions, has begun to make inroads into the myth, straining the Zionist characterization (caricature?) of Exile as only Disaster. (From "Facts" click on *Culture* or *Society*; and see, on Jerusalem, Benvenisti: 169–84.) Under the strain, the singularity of the subject, the Jewish People who Suffer in Exile, begins to break down. Yearning, unlike suffering, is an affect that unites the subject across all periods and places, and through the rough and the smooth. No matter what was happening, the myth could confidently assert, "the Jewish people" continually "yearned." Not that yearning has been wholly immune to contradiction. The Zionist movement has had to struggle, from its beginnings, to persuade people to come to Israel; most, even in the face of persecution, would rather have gone somewhere else, the United States most notably. Fifty years after the foundation of the State, however, this unitary, yearning (and/or suffering) subject is under even greater stress: as the web is forced to acknowledge (the State that wants their money can hardly render them invisible), most of "the Jewish People" continue to live "in Exile" or in "Diaspora" (a term that nicely fudges the problem) or, as Zionist (Orwellian?) vocabulary would have it, in "voluntary Exile" (Eisen: ix). If this people is yearning, it does not appear to be too mightily. A puzzled reader of the myth might well wonder: was it ever thus?

Yearning constitutes the unitary mythic subject. But, from my vantage point as a North American web viewer, the (Ultra-Orthodox) men in black hats and dark suits "mingling with people wearing the spectrum of modern fashion" (.../facts/state/jerusalem.html) disturb this singularity. Here is a reconstitution of southwest Asian space as eighteenth-century eastern Europe. At the same time, here and elsewhere on the website, the space is being reconstituted as late twentieth-century western Europe or North America, not to speak of mid-twentieth-century Iraq or, from some times that I cannot exactly pick, Russia or Ethiopia. The Jewish People is a collective of myriad disparities, religious, ethnic, political, and cultural. According to the myth, however, the members of this people share both a name and a yearning (whether unfulfilled or assuaged). While "Israel" is a collective that attempts to supplant the disparities of the "People" with its own synthetic, "indigenous" culture (Zerubavel: 27–28), the men in black hats prove a stubborn reminder that the synthesis is a recent invention of immigrants sharing little (or nothing) in common—unless it be a name, a suffering, and, of course, a yearning. Yearning restores the people as it restores the romance.

The rhetoric of yearning is powerful and slippery. A narrative of yearning which issues in fulfillment may engage its consumers for a time. But arrival risks dissipating the power that the "longing" generates. So the Odyssey ends with its hero preparing to set out once more. The master commemorative narrative of Zion, the more it becomes the narrative of the "eternal and undivided capital of Israel," risks becoming "passionless," its yearning empty, a hollow mask. By the same token, yearning's passionate imaginings may indeed empower, yet blind the yearning subject to an Other subject's "country."

Bibliography

Astell, Ann W.
1990   *The Song of Songs in the Middle Ages*. Ithaca: Cornell University Press.

Benvenisti, Meron
1996   *City of Stone: The Hidden History of Jerusalem*. Trans. Maxine Kaufman Nunn. Berkeley: University of California Press.

Boyarin, Jonathan
1992   *Storm from Paradise: The Politics of Jewish Memory*. Minneapolis: University of Minnesota Press.

Diamond, James S.
1986   *Homeland or Holy Land? The "Canaanite" Critique of Israel*. Bloomington: Indiana University Press.

Elon, Amos
1995   *Jerusalem: Battlegrounds of Memory*. New York: Kodansha International [First edn. 1989 as *Jerusalem: City of Mirrors*].

Efron, Zusia
1992   "'If I Forget Thee . . .': Longings for Jerusalem in the Jewish Folk Art of Eastern Europe." *Ariel* 102 [www.Israel.org/mfa/ariel/102efron.html].

Evron, Boas
1995   *Jewish State or Israeli Nation?* Bloomington: Indiana University Press.

Finkelstein, Israel
1996   "The Archaeology of the United Monarchy: An Alternative View." *Levant* 28:177–87.

Flapan, Simha
1987   *The Birth of Israel: Myths and Realities*. New York: Pantheon.

Grabbe, Lester L., ed.
1998   *Leading Captivity Captive: 'The Exile' as History and Ideology*. JSOTSup 128. European Seminar in Historical Methodology 2. Sheffield: Sheffield Academic Press.

Hassassian, Manuel S.
1994   "The Emigration of Soviet Jews to Palestine and Israel." *Palestine-Israel Journal of Politics, Economics and Culture* 2: 86–93.

Israel Information Center
1996   *Facts about Israel*. Jerusalem: Israel Information Center/ Hamakor Press.

Khalidi, Walid, ed.
1971   *From Haven to Conquest: Readings in Zionism and the Palestine Problem Until 1948*. Washington, DC: Institute for Palestine Studies.

Knauf, Ernst Axel
1997   "'Le Roi est mort, vive le roi!' A Biblical Argument for the Historicity of Solomon." Pp. 81–95 in *The Age of Solomon: Scholarship at the Turn of the Millennium*. Ed. L. K. Handy. Leiden: Brill.

Kolsky, Thomas A.
1990   *Jews Against Zionism: The American Council for Judaism, 1942–1948*. Philadelphia: Temple University Press.

Laqueur, Walter
1989   *A History of Zionism*. New York: Schocken Books.

Lemche, Niels Peter
1998   *The Israelites in History and Tradition*. Library of Ancient Israel. Louisville: Westminster/John Knox.

Linville, James Richard
1998   *Israel in the Book of Kings: The Past as a Project of Social Identity*. JSOTSup 272. Sheffield: Sheffield Academic Press.

Myers, David N.
1995   *Re-Inventing the Jewish Past: European Jewish Intellectuals and the Zionist Return to History*. New York: Oxford University Press.

Neusner, Jacob
1987   *Self-Fulfilling Prophecy: Exile and Return in the History of Judaism*. Boston: Beacon. Reprint, with a new introduction, Atlanta: Scholars Press, 1990.

1997   "Exile and Return as the History of Judaism." Pp. 221–37 in *Exile: Old Testament, Jewish, and Christian Conceptions*. Ed. James M. Scott. SJSJ. Leiden: Brill.

Pappé, Ilan
1998   "Israeli Television's Fiftieth Anniversary 'Tekumma' Series: A Post-Zionist View?" *Journal of Palestine Studies* 27/4:99–105.

Ravitzky, Aviezer
1996   *Messianism, Zionism, and Jewish Religious Radicalism*. Trans. Michael Swirsky and Jonathan Chipman. Chicago: University of Chicago Press.

Reinharz, Jehuda and Anita Shapira
1996   *Essential Papers on Zionism*. New York: New York University Press.

Schweid, Eliezer
1985   *The Land of Israel: National Home or Land of Destiny*. Trans. Deborah Greniman. London: Associated University Presses.

Scott, James M., ed.
1997   *Exile: Old Testament, Jewish, and Christian Conceptions*. SJSJ. Leiden: Brill.

Seidel, Michael
1986   *Exile and the Narrative Imagination*. New Haven: Yale University Press.

Silberstein, Laurence J.
1997   "Towards a Postzionist Discourse." Pp. 95–101 in *Judaism Since Gender*. Ed. Miriam Peskowitz and Laura Levitt. New York: Routledge.

Thompson, Thomas L.
1999   *The Bible in History: How Writers Create a Past*. London: Jonathan Cape.

Wheatcroft, Geoffrey
1996   *The Controversy of Zion: Jewish Nationalism, the Jewish State, and the Unresolved Jewish Dilemma*. Reading, MA: Addison-Wesley.

Whitelam, Keith W.
1996   *The Invention of Ancient Israel and the Silencing of Palestinian History*. London: Routledge.
1998   "Constructing Jerusalem." Unpublished paper delivered at the Society of Biblical Literature, Annual Meeting.

Zerubavel, Yael
1995   *Recovered Roots: Collective Memory and the Making of Israeli National Tradition*. Chicago: University of Chicago Press.

READING THE LAND
HOLY LAND AS TEXT OF WITNESS

Burke O. Long

This essay is drawn from a larger study of how American biblical scholars experienced Palestine in the late nineteenth and early twentieth centuries, and how they imagined Palestine as objects of fantasy and desire.[1] These scholars' contacts with, and notions about, holy land not only complicated their commitments to ideologies of scientific discovery; they were entangled with identity-forming values, and political and cultural debates in the United States as well. Moreover, scholarly talk of "holy land" was part of a long tradition of vernacular literary and visual representations of "holy land" as pilgrims, tourists, missionaries, preachers, settlers, explorers, archaeologists, and diplomats acted on their deep affection for this piece of earth and sought physical contact with Ottoman, later British Mandate, Palestine (Vogel; Ben-Arieh, 1979; M. Davis, 1977, 1983, 1991, 1995, 1997; J. Davis, 1996; Greenberg, 1994). These social realities partially shaped the direction and substance of professional research on the Bible, which in part gave definition to a field called biblical studies.

An important ideological pillar supporting much of this holy land consciousness was the belief that the land itself was a direct witness to divine revelation. As geoscripture, Palestine's landscapes, peoples, even ruins, attested to the truths of biblical prophecy and

[1] With sincere gratitude, I acknowledge that this project is supported in part by the American Council of Learned Societies and the William R. Kenan Charitable Trust, both of which awarded research fellowships to me during 1997–98.

Christianity. Perhaps more than any other writer, William A. Thomson, a missionary in Ottoman Syria and Palestine, gave this ancient Christian idea popular currency. His lavishly illustrated study-travelogue *The Land and the Book*, which sold more than 200,000 copies, considered the holy land as a "vast tablet whereupon God's messages to men have been drawn, and graven deep in living characters by the Great Publisher of glad tidings, to be seen and read by all to the end of time. The Land and the Book—with reverence be it said—constitutes the ENTIRE and ALL-PERFECT TEXT, and should be studied together." (Thomson: 2. xv).

An especially interesting example of a university biblical scholar negotiating the borders between technical scholarship and the materials and convictions of popular culture is Charles Foster Kent (1867–1925). A student of William Rainey Harper at Yale University in 1889–91, Kent taught briefly in Chicago during 1892–94 when Harper became president of the newly organized University of Chicago. He subsequently was Professor at Brown University, and in 1901 returned to Yale as the Woolsey Professor of Biblical Literature, a post he held until his death in 1925. An active churchman, religious educator, biblical historian and geographer, Kent wrote and lectured widely for professional and popular audiences, and in 1914 and 1924 offered two series of courses at the Chautauqua Institution, an upstate New York center for vacation, study, and evangelistic training (Kent, 1924, 1935; Dahl). He was remembered as the young scholar whom Jesse Lyman Hurlbut (1843–1930), a leading force in Sunday school education and one of Chautauqua's dynamic leaders, consulted to assure that the lakeside assembly's large topographical map of biblical Palestine was accurate in all its features (Booth: 8).

Kent traveled to Palestine in 1892, as a graduate student, and again in 1910, to collect material for a revised edition of his *Biblical Geography and History* (Kent, 1900a) and accompanying photographic illustrations (Kent, 1900b). In 1914, Kent collaborated with Chautauqua's Jesse Lyman Hurlbut in publishing *Palestine through the Stereoscope*, a tour of the holy land using two hundred dual image photographs printed on cards, a hand-held viewer that enhanced the illusion of three dimensional sight, and commentary on each photograph (Hurlbut and Kent).

The parlor tour offered rewards assumed to derive from intimate experience of Scripture. Its words (landscapes, peoples and ruins) witnessed to divine manifestation (the Word), which would be made plain if one but got the geography right.

> (Biblical) geography is a description of the divine character and purpose expressing itself through natural forces, in the physical contour of the earth, in the animate world, and, above all, in the life and activities of man. Biblical geography, therefore, is the first and in many ways the most important chapter in that divine revelation which was perfected through the Hebrew race and recorded in the Bible. . . . Through the plains and mountains, the rivers and seas, the climate and flora of the biblical world, the Almighty spoke to men as plainly and unmistakably as he did through the voices of his inspired seers and sages. (Kent, 1900a:v)

In *Palestine through the Stereoscope*, Hurlbut and Kent repeatedly urge their charges, like scientists, to plot their journeys on detailed topographical maps of Ottoman Palestine. Each stereoptic card was numbered and correlated with dots on these maps, from which bold lines extended outward, "V" shaped, in an expanding two dimensional cone of vision.

Fig. 1: "Jerusalem," from Kent, *Biblical Geography and History*.

A viewer pilgrim thus participated in an infinitely expanding portion of sacred land, subjugating it to a commanding Christianizing vision (J. Davis: 75–76). In their commentary, Hurlbut and Kent provide the rhetorical counterpart. They move pilgrim-viewers from where they stand, beyond foregrounded objects, encompassing more and more space, until all is swept into the limitless realm of remembered biblical event. Typically, the holy land that emerges is set within a meta-narrative of Christian redemption.

Experiencing "holy land" as a witnessing text provided affective support for believing the Bible's historical accounts and religious claims, enhanced commitment to Christianity felt to be challenged by modernist skeptics and historians, renewed fervor for Christian missions, a heightened sense of possessing the Bible and, by right, penetrating and dominating the land of its origin.

Such a feminized holy land seems fraught with ideological consequence. In the spaces between photographic image and commentarial text, I try to discern bundles of ideological commitments: romantic expectations, assumed cultural values, scientific rationality, theology, and exclusionary Christian vision. Out of these visio-literary texts of geopiety, Hurlbut and Kent enacted Thomson's "entire and all-perfect text" as they created and re-created didactic and inspirational "holy lands" quite at odds with the actual conditions they encountered in Ottoman Palestine.

Hurlbut and Kent read the land, and I read them, and try to set them within a specific social and cultural context. Whereas they sought truths more tangible and assured than those to be gained from the Bible alone, I seek contingent and ideologically burdened truths, the constructs of holy land and revelatory witness rooted in the material culture and values of Hurlbut's and Kent's Protestant America. Their tour offers me an extraordinary glimpse into the interactive spaces between image and commentary along the permeable borders between university and church, professional and popular. Here, reader-viewers—the authors presume them to be pilgrims—were led into pleasurable fantasies of holy land and helped to negotiate those realities of Ottoman Palestine that they found to be disconcerting.

I am pleased to offer a few examples of such entanglements as promise of what a more complete study might offer, and as tribute to Robert Culley. Friend and colleague, Culley stirs in me a sense for the ironic and the playful, while encouraging innovative ways to construe what biblical scholars study (no longer exclusively a Bible of late antiquity) and what they see (complicated, contingent constructions of knowledge and truth-telling).

The True Woman of Amwas

Viewing Position 5a: "The Village of Amwas [Emmaus]" (Hurlbut and Kent: 21–23) [Fig. 2]). Three Arab women, water jars lifted up, constitute the main visual subject, and they impede Hurlbut's and Kent's desire to visualize biblical Emmaus amidst contemporary Palestine.

Fig. 2: "Village of Amwas," from Hurlbut and Kent, *Palestine through the Stereoscope.*

The authors meet the challenge by drawing boundaries between themselves (and their pilgrim charges) and these voiceless women of nonbiblical otherness, while suggesting what is to them self-evident cultural superiority. They assume notions of true womanhood—motherly virtues of passivity, domesticity, piety, moral purity, cleanliness—that were widely shared by Protestant writers of post-civil war

America, and often invoked to distinguish middle class Protestant "America" from working-class (often immigrant), even morally deficient, "America" (Smith-Rosenberg). In the end, the women of the photograph are absorbed into Hurlbut's and Kent's ambivalent compassion, and swept away by their conjury of remembered associations with Jesus.

The opening in the ground just to the right of the nearest woman, the authors write, is a spring "from which the village people get supplies for drinking, cooking, and such little cleaning as they are disposed to do." Viewer-pilgrims, Hurlbut and Kent imply, are to forgive the "unbearably dirty" village houses (hardly visible on the distant hillside), and pardon the inadequacy of the women (very visible in the commentary), because it is such a "toilsome undertaking" to carry water into that distant village for "thorough-going house-cleaning." Besides, they add, "fuel is pitifully scanty, and can ill be spared for heating water" (Hurlbut and Kent: 22).

Hurlbut and Kent instruct their pilgrims to "notice how erect and graceful is the poise of the women, even though they evidently belong to the poorer class." Perhaps surprised that such graces of true woman could be associated with these Arab women and particularly with "the poorer class," the commentators explain: "The habit of carrying such burdens on the head gives to the working women of oriental lands a much finer figure and carriage than belong to the women of the wealthy class" (Hurlbut and Kent: 22). Do heavy work and graceful posture, after all, become the female poor and expose the corpulent and ill postured body language of idle wealth?

Eventually, Hurlbut and Kent avert their eyes from the water-bearers who have become entangled in this orientalizing thicket of attitude, desire, assumption, and proffered expertise. They ask their pilgrim charges to look away, too. "Do you know," they write, "that this very path around the little hill, where those women are walking with their water-jars freshly filled from the spring, may have been trodden by the torn feet of our Saviour, on that glorious day when He rose from the dead?" (Here the authors footnote Luke 24:13–32.)

Thus diverted, pilgrim-viewers are encouraged to embrace familiar accounts of the risen Jesus' appearance on the road to Emmaus. Hurlbut and Kent paraphrase Luke's narrative, urging their charges to "sweep away from the landscape yonder the Amwas of to-day, with its squalid clay huts and its poverty-stricken inhabitants."

Imagine a time of innocent receptivity to Christ, they suggest, plainly in contrast to the "squalid village" and the "poverty-stricken," not quite acceptable, yet appealing women in the photograph. Invoking a myth of Edenic prosperity, from which modern Palestine has fallen, the authors imagine Jesus and two disciples breaking bread (are the photographed women now transformed, missionized, into followers of Jesus?). "They see their Master for a moment," Hurlbut and Kent write, and then, "He vanishes from their sight. That is the one event which gives to yonder village a thrilling universal interest—for it is typical of the deeper spiritual revelation which comes to every disciple who yearns to behold the face of his Master" (Hurlbut and Kent: 22–23). They had no need to add that the barren and uninviting Ottoman landscape itself, surely not those troublesome water carriers, evoked those deep rhythms of exegetical passion and Christian devotion.

The Tired and the Wretched

Viewing Position 54: "Women Grinding at the Mill" (Hurlbut and Kent:176–77 [Fig. 3]). Viewing Amwas, the main strategic problem was how to evoke biblical presence from a photographic image that might pull a viewer in a contrary direction. When guiding their charges to look upon "Women Grinding at the Mill," Hurlbut and Kent imagine the Bible more directly, a biblical land that had providentially remained unchanged by time. A Palestine "held back to the life and customs of an antiquated [biblical] past," Kent had earlier written his teacher William Rainey Harper, teaches the world that the Bible is true (Kent, 1892). Now, commenting on this stereograph some years later, Hurlbut and Kent exclaim, "How completely the life of to-day in these Oriental lands copies that of two thousand years ago!" (Hurlbut and Kent: 176). As they describe the scene, the authors construct a holy land of value-laden conceptual juxtapositions—prosperity, technology, and cultural superiority implicitly laid opposite poverty, primitiveness, and cultural inferiority.

Fig. 3: "Women Grinding at the Mill" from Hurlbut and Kent, *Palestine through the Stereoscope.*

It is "women's work" glimpsed here, they write, a scene of natural, approved of domesticity. And yet, the process is quaint, primitive, and emblematic of how far technology and rising wealth have carried American society. "But what a slow and laborious process of making flour!" Although almost every town has a grist mill turned by water power, they add, the photograph shows "poorer people [who] save expense by having their own little mills" (Hurlbut and Kent: 176).

The scene seems exotic, despite its evident backwardness. Perhaps the women are a little seductive in their slight immodesty, even if defined by laborious poverty and the authors' desire to visualize the Bible. Notice the bracelets, Hurlbut and Kent instruct— the "bangles, like coins" fastened around the child's forehead; the "veils left open more than is usual" when men, presumably the photographer and entourage, are near; the large hole for "an oriental key . . . always a clumsy affair"; the rough pavement, a "fair sample" of what must be endured in any town "advanced enough to have its streets paved at all"; the mat, not chairs, on which the women are seated. "How forlorn and hopeless they look!," the authors declare, with apparent sympathy, perhaps dismay, and evident conflict. Maybe the women do not conform to the authors' expectations of virtue and beauty, even as they represent the revered Bible. Perhaps their land is *not* the Bible land, which was, as Hurlbut and Kent repeatedly assert, formerly prosperous. "The lot of woman," they declare, "in a land where almost every family is desperately poor, and where women are regarded as little better than beasts of burden, is such as to give to all women of the working class a tired, wretched, almost despairing look" (Hurlbut and Kent: 177).

Yet Hurlbut and Kent cannot entirely sweep the photographic contemporary out of sight. Their orientalizing gaze imparts to the scene an unredeemed, "wretched, almost despairing" quality. Perhaps this moment is an encounter with direct, textual witness after all. What would one have imagined, if not abject need, when the choice of Christianity was first offered? Perhaps the women suggest a needy twentieth-century Palestine, too, when Muslim rule, widely regarded as hostile and fanatic, restrains Christian missions. It may be, as Kathy Gutierrez argued, that for most Protestant travelers to Palestine, indigenous women had their insufficient piety inscribed on their bodies in lack of beauty and in immodesty (186).

Christianity the Truly Picturesque

Viewing Position 11a, "Jerusalem, Beautiful for situation, from the Southeast, Showing the Temple Site" (Hurlbut and Kent: 45–47 [Fig. 4]). Looking toward walled Jerusalem from a hillside to the southeast, the pilgrim's eye travels downslope, across the Kidron Valley, and fixes on the city's most prominent landmark, the Dome of the Rock. A favorite vantage point for depicting Palestine, especially Jerusalem, as a picturesque and aesthetic object of Christian affection, the scene also foregrounds one of the most prominent landmarks in Muslim configurations of Palestine. Like many other Christians of the day, Hurlbut and Kent summon up specifically Christian memories, while marginalizing contemporary Muslim presence in their construal of "holy land."

Fig. 4: "Jerusalem, Beautiful for Situation" from Hurlbut and Kent, *Palestine through the Stereoscope.*

"That open square . . . is the Haram-es-Sherif (sic), or 'Noble Sanctuary,'" Hurlbut and Kent inform their pilgrim-viewers, "covering in part the area occupied in ancient times by the Temple and its courts" (Hurlbut and Kent: 45–46). The building, nevertheless, "is of surpassing interest, for directly under that dome is the great slanting rock on which stood the altar in the Temple of old" (here the authors refer to 2 Chr 3:1). In the manner of commonly published panoramic engravings, the authors take their pilgrims' eyes from point to point on that distant background hill, mentioning a few Muslim sites, but in general creating a landscape of Christian piety, even ownership. The Turkish governor's castle stands on the site where Jesus was condemned to death, and where St. Paul was taken for refuge; the modern tower barely visible beyond a clump of trees marks the headquarters of crusaders organized to "defend the city from the Saracens"; nearby is the Church of the Holy Sepulchre, the site of Jesus' burial; next to that is a hospice for "pilgrims of the Latin [Roman Catholic] church." Moving their learned eye toward the foreground of the photograph, Hurlbut and Kent focus attention on the walled-in road at which the viewer pilgrims stand. It "would lead, if we could follow it, past the Garden of Gethsemene and then up the Mount of Olives" (Hurlbut and Kent: 46–47). The Arab woman looking back at the camera is invisible, or at least merits no comment, along that pathway of Christian topography.

Viewing Position 89: "Traditional Capernaum, Christ's Home by the Sea of Galilees" (Hurlbut and Kent: 256–58 [Fig. 5]). Jews held a similarly ambiguous place in Hurlbut's and Kent's "holy land." Gazing down on the tumbled ruins at "Traditional Capernaum," the authors fold moral lesson and prophecy fulfilled into an ideology of paradise lost. Palestine's former prosperity, repeatedly asserted, has become ruin and degradation, just as the prophets, and in the case of Capernaum, Jesus had foretold.

Fig. 5: "Traditional Capernaum" from Hurlbut and Kent, *Palestine through the Stereoscope.* Courtesy Pitts Theological Library, Emory University, Atlanta, Georgia.

"Can this be Capernaum [biblical Chorazin], once exalted to heaven?" they ask, footnoting Matt 11:21–24 where Jesus prophesied that the unrepentant Jewish town would be cast down into Hades. "How it has been brought down to the depths! All that is left of it is a dozen or more miserable huts, outside the range of our vision." At least the sea remains, they add, as though asking themselves how a fallen and degraded Palestine can yet witness to Christian truth. The sea is a powerful witness to Jesus' remembered presence. It looks "just as it looked of old, except that we see it deserted, and he saw it alive with ships and fishermen" (Hurlbut and Kent: 257).

Viewing Position 89a: "Shattered Remains of Old Chorazin" (Hurlbut and Kent: 258 [Fig. 6]). Moving closer to Capernaum at the "Shattered Remains of Old Chorazin," the pilgrims view fragments of broken columns and building stones sprawled akimbo and partially hidden in tall grasses.

Fig. 6: "Old Chorazin," from Hurlbut and Kent, *Palestine through the Stereoscope.* Courtesy Pitts Theological Library, Emory University, Atlanta, Georgia.

An Arab youth—he seems a sculpted part of the pillar on which he sits—carries the viewer-pilgrim's eye through a gentle "S" curve, traversing the ruins, moving through the distant valley pass, and out of frame at the top left. There, Hurlbut and Kent report, "We catch a glimpse of the Sea of Galilee" (Hurlbut and Kent: 258).

The photograph converts ruins into aesthetic object. The commentary shapes it into a metaphor of Christian supersessionism. In its ruined and picturesque Jewishness, Chorazin (Capernaum) requires the Sea of Galilee and memories of Jesus for its fullest significance. "This mass of broken columns and ruined walls is all that remains of the once prosperous city of Chorazin," the authors write, alluding again to the New Testament prophecy. The ruins evidently belong to a synagogue, and therefore, "they interest us deeply," confess Hurlbut and Kent. Memorials to Jesus' activity, the ruins mark the spot where Jesus rebuked Chorazin and other cities "because they did not repent." It was a place "where mighty works were wrought" (Hurlbut and Kent: 258).

For Hurlbut and Kent, images of ruination often elicit supplanting symbols of Christian redemption. In this case, the Sea of Galilee and recollections of Jesus' "mighty works" trump the foregrounded remnants of prosperity—that mythic world before its fall into backwardness and poverty. Even the Arab, pure ornamentation in many of the stereographs, is anchored to this vanquishing ideology. "The native at the right," they add, "is sitting upon the pedestal of a pillar which once stood before the synagogue" (Hurlbut and Kent: 258). It is his gaze, stripped of any Islamic or indigenous Christian elements, that encourages pilgrim-viewers to move through the scene to the distant and remembered biblical Sea of Galilee. Hurlbut and Kent guide them to hear, once again, a geoscripture that speaks the voice of God.

Holy Land, American Style

Viewing Position 37: "A Barley Harvest near Bethlehem" (Hurlbut and Kent: 119–21; Fig. 7). "If we go there," Hurlbut and Kent tell their travelers, "we may look upon a scene which takes us back to the times of the Old Testament" (Hurlbut and Kent: 119). The camera eye gathers together ten figures, evidently Arab, pleasingly posed during a moment at harvest time. Some walk toward the camera, carrying sheaths of grain; others bend into the cutting work; two figures, apparently women at rest, pass a jug between them; a bearded man and a distant figure in the rear stand facing the camera, and with the woman in the foreground lower right, engage the pilgrims' gaze. Assuming a culturally static "East," Hurlbut and Kent see a harvest scene directly illustrative of the Book of Ruth. But they also load the image with affirmations of values they evidently cherish: individualism, frugality, industry, piety, and self-directed political independence.

Fig. 7: "Barley Harvest," from Hurlbut and Kent, *Palestine through the Stereoscope.* Courtesy Pitts Theological Library, Emory University, Atlanta, Georgia.

Kent and Hurlbut urge upon their charges an egalitarian's suspicion, perhaps disdain, for the boss and the wealth they supposedly see in the photograph. "That gray-bearded, turbaned farmer stands there at ease, while everybody else is hard at work!" they declare. They suppose him to be the "master of the reapers," or perhaps the "owner of the field." In any case, the scene, with its implicit heirarchy of owner (boss) and worker, is biblical. "His name might be Boaz, for aught we know" (they footnote reference to Ruth 2:1–4 [Hurlbut and Kent: 119]). Describing "primitive" harvesting methods, and noting a baby in the sheltered cradle ("perhaps the woman with an armful of sheaves is his mother"), Hurlbut and Kent presume a contemporary Palestine stratified between wealthy and poor, land owner and peasant. They also evaluate it simplistically as degraded and oppressed. It is not at all like the United States, where freedom (and Christianity) have fashioned a superior social order, they intimate.

Women and men work "from sunrise to sunset, for a few cents," and take little time for lunch right in the fields, presumably in contrast to the at-ease man standing beside the harvest laden donkey. "Ruth may have looked like one of these women," the authors aver, with heads wrapped in a "coarse veil," and dressed in "common" garments. Yet pilgrim-viewers are urged to imagine harvesters in the days of Ruth and Boaz as "somewhat less ragged and common." For these days in Palestine (typically understood to be a time of suffering under Turkish rule) are "days . . . of oppression and robbery, when the poor are kept wretchedly poor." The era of Ruth and Boaz, by contrast, were "days of quiet, and in the main, of prosperity," not at all anarchic. Weaving a fantasy of pre-industrial, pre-state, agrarian and Edenic self-sufficiency (is this the biblical paradise lost to Turkish or Muslim rule?), Hurlbut and Kent continue:

> Except at rare intervals of invasion and subjection the Israelites lived on their mountain summits in peace, tilling their fields, obtaining at home all the necessities of food and clothing, having absolutely no foreign relations, and with little use for a government. They were contented, frugal, and industrious; and when at times foreign foes held sway over them, there was always a Gideon or an Ehud, or an Othniel to appear as the champion of Israel and break the chain of oppression. The whole period of the Judges from Joshua to Samuel sweeps before us as we look upon this harvest field....Each man did what was right in his own eyes, and, while there was a neglect of the rites and ceremonies of the law, there were, upon the whole, prosperity and progress. (Hurlbut and Kent : 120–21)

The land witnesses to a former biblical prosperity; but perhaps as importantly, it evokes a biblical archetype for a political and economic Eden, the true heir to holy land, now in America.

A Retrospective

Hurlbut's and Kent's parlor tour of Palestine is a complexly layered rendering of "holy lands" for their Christian charges. The authors read the place as witness to specifically Christian, evangelical convictions and affirmation—against sceptics—of the Bible's historical trustworthiness. Like modern day crusaders, Hurlbut and Kent try to subdue an unruly Ottoman Palestine, making its geography conform to images of biblical realities generated from a mix of textual recollections, theological intepretation, and values rooted in Protestant America. Palestine, and especially its women, are somewhat repugnant to them, but tolerable as evidence of biblical (Jesus') prophecy fulfilled and America's cultural superiority; the contemporary land they encounter is explainable within an etiological myth that plots an Edenic (and biblical) past ending in contemporary (Turkish inspired) degradation; Muslim and Jewish presence is eclipsed by supersessionist Christianity, which also happens to be entangled with assumptions of United States exceptionalism—notions of political independence, economic progressivism, agrarian virtues, cultural advancement, and economic prosperity. *Palestine Through the Stereoscope*, and the biblical scholarship on which it in part relies, tells its truth, and like the poet, tells it slant.

Bibliography

Ben-Arieh, Yehosua
  1979 *The Rediscovery of the Holy Land in the Nineteenth Century.* Jerusalem: Magnes Press; Detroit: Wayne State University Press.

Booth, Edwin
  1965 "A Biography of Dr. Jesse Lyman Hurlbut." Typescript. Archives, Smith Library, Chautuaqua Institution, Chautauqua, New York.

Cutter, C.
  1996 "Jerusalem: A Select Bibliography of Books in English." *Jewish Book Annual* 53:29–40.

Dahl, George
  1933   "Charles Foster Kent." P. 343 in *Dictionary of American Biography*. Vol. 10. Ed. Dumas Malone. New York: Charles Scribner's Sons.

Davis, John
  1992   "Holy Land, Holy People? Photography, Semitic Wannabes and Chautauqua's Palestine Park." *Prospects* 17:241–71.
  1996   *The Landscape of Belief: Encountering the Holy Land in Nineteenth-Century American Art and Culture*. Princeton: Princeton University Press.

Davis, Moshe
  1977   *America and the Holy Land*. With Eyes Toward Zion 1. New York: Arno.
  1983   Themes and Sources in the Archives of the United States, Great Britain, Turkey, and Israel. With Eyes Toward Zion 2. Westport, CT: Praeger.
  1991   *Western Societies and the Holy Land*. With Eyes Toward Zion 3. Westport, CT: Praeger.
  1995   *America and the Holy Land*. With Eyes Toward Zion 4. Westport, CT: Praeger.
  1997   *Jerusalem in the Mind of the Western World*. With Eyes Toward Zion 5. Westport, CT: Praeger.

Field, James A.
  1969   *America and the Mediterranean World, 1776–1882*. Princeton: Princeton University Press.

Finnie, David H.
  1967   *Pioneers East: The Early American Experience in the Middle East*. Cambridge, MA: Harvard University Press.

Gal, Allon, ed.
  1997   *Envisioning Israel: The Changing Ideals and Images of North American Jews*. Detroit: Wayne State University Press.

Goell, Y.
  1983   "America and the Holy Land. A Select Bibliography of Publications in English." *The Jerusalem Cathedra* 3:327–33.

Greenberg, Gershon
  1994   *The Holy Land in American Religious Thought 1620–1948: The Symbiosis of American Religious Approaches to Scripture's Sacred Territory*. Lanham, MD: University Press of America.

Gutierrez, Cathy
  1996   "Representation and Ideals: The Construction of Women in Travel Literature to the Holy Land." Pp. 181–94 in *Pilgrims & Travelers to the Holy Land*. Ed. Bryan Le Beau and Menahem Mor. Omaha, NB: Creighton University Press.

Handy, Robert T.
1981   *The Holy Land in American Protestant Life, 1800–1948. A Documentary History*. New York: Arno.

Hurlbut, Jesse L.
1900   *Traveling in the Holy Land through the Stereoscope*. New York: Underwood & Underwood.
1921   *The Story of Chautauqua*. New York: G. P. Putnam and Sons.

Hurlbut, Jesse L. and Charles F. Kent
1914   *Palestine through the Stereoscope*. New York: Underwood & Underwood.

Kent, Charles F.
1892   Letter to William Rainey Harper. In *Presidents' Papers, 1889–1925*. Archives, University of Chicago. Box 51, Folder 6.
1900a   *Biblical Geography and History*. New York: Charles Scribner's Sons.
1900b   *Descriptions of One Hundred and Forty Places in Bible Lands to be Seen through the Stereoscope or by Means of Stereopticon Slides*. New York: Underwood & Underwood.
1914   "Rhythm in Hebrew Life and Literature." *Chautauquan Daily* 39/6 (July 9):2.
1924   "Charles Foster Kent, B.A., 1889." *Obituary Record of Graduates of Yale University* 84:1380–83.
1935   "Charles Foster Kent." Pp. 28–29 in *National Cyclopaedia of American Biography*. Vol. 24. New York: James T. White.

Morrison, Theodore
1974   *Chautauqua: A Center for Education, Religion, and the Arts in America*. Chicago: University of Chicago Press.

Nir, Yeshayahu
1985   *The Bible and the Image: The History of Photography in the Holy Land 1839–1899*. Philadelphia: University of Pennsylvania Press.

Peters, Francis E.
1985   *Jerusalem. The Holy City in the Eyes of Chroniclers, Visitors, Pilgrims, and Prophets from the Days of Abraham to the Beginnings of Modern Times*. Princeton: Princeton University Press.

Purvis, James C.
1988   *Jerusalem, the Holy City: A Bibliography*. 2 vols. Metuchen, NJ: American Theological Library Association and Scarecrow Press.

Queen, Edward L.
1996   "Ambiguous Pilgrims: American Protestant Travelers to Ottoman Palestine, 1867–1914." Pp. 209–28 in *Pilgrims & Travelers to the Holy Land*. Ed. Bryan M. Le Beau and Menahem Mor. Omaha, NB: Creighton University Press.

Said, Edward
    1978   *Orientalism*. New York: Pantheon.
Shepherd, Naomi
    1987   *The Zealous Intruders. The Western Rediscovery of Palestine.*
                San Francisco: Harper & Row.
Smith-Rosenberg, Carroll
    1985   *Disorderly Conduct: Visions of Gender in Victorian America.*
                New York: Alfred A. Knopf.
Thomson, William A.
    1859   *The Land and the Book: Or, Biblical Illustrations Drawn from
                the Manners and Customs, the Scenes and Scenery of the Holy
                Land.* 2 vols. New York: Harper & Bros.
Van De Bilt, Eduardus F.
    1985   "Proximity and Distance: American Travellers to the Middle
                East, 1819–1918." Ph.D. diss., Cornell University.
Vincent, John H.
    1886   *The Chautauqua Movement*. Boston: The Chautauqua Press.
Vogel, Lester
    1993   *To See a Promised Land: Americans and the Holy Land in the
                Nineteenth Century.* University Park, PA: Pennsylvania State
                University Press.
Wilken, Robert L.
    1992   *The Land Called Holy: Palestine in Christian History and
                Thought.* New Haven: Yale University Press.

PART 2

WRITERS, POWER AND
THE ALIENATION OF LABOUR

DAVID IS A THING

Roland Boer

Introduction

I propose to do a rather simple thing. I want to read various sections from the work of Slavoj Žižek alongside some biblical texts. This is somewhat anachronistic, but, given that all interpretation of ancient literature is anachronistic, it is worthwhile to be willful about this task. What I am going to do, then, is place Žižek's reflections on "The King is a Thing" (1991a:253–73), the "transferential relationship" (1993:125–26), and the "theft of enjoyment" (1993:201–5) beside the narratives of David and Solomon in Samuel and Kings. In particular, I am interested in 1 Samuel 8, in which Samuel explains to the people all that they might expect from a king. In doing so, I undertake that which is always so important to the work of Robert Culley, namely, an unquenchable interest in that which is new, that which offers fresh angles on the biblical text. At the same time, there is no excuse for not giving careful and diligent attention to both the theoretical text and the biblical text, for the labour of writing can never provide satisfaction without the labour of reading.

On Dialectical Lacanianism

But let me introduce Slavoj Žižek, who is still trying to come to terms, as he says, with the epithet "the giant of Ljubljana," coined by *The Village Voice*. The publication of nine books (although that will no doubt soon change) in as many years (from 1989 to 1997), as well as his role as editor of four other volumes (1992, 1994, 1998; Žižek and Salecl, 1996) and a series each with Verso and Duke, has established Žižek as one of the most arresting thinkers in philosophy, psycho-analysis, and critical and cultural theory today. His work might best be described as a dialectical psychoanalysis, or dialectical Lacanianism, that draws its subject matter from popular culture, although at times of an older and more conventional type—Hitchcock, Chandler, Highsmith, Kafka, and, of all things, opera. Only his interest in film breaks out and ranges high and low.

Along with a number of other writers such as Joan Copjec, Alenka Zupancic and Renata Salecl, Žižek has been concerned to extend the viability of Lacan's work into the realms of popular culture and politics, to recover, as it were, Freud's own project of psycho-analysis as a highly illuminating tool for the consideration of a wide range of social as well as individual phenomena. I need to make it clear, however, that this paper is concerned specifically with Žižek's work, for the simple reason that the focus on one thinker is more manageable (and that his frenetic writing incorporates hoards of others). One other attraction to Žižek lies in the critical socialism or post-Marxism he brings to his work, nourished in the long Eastern European tradition, but also in the thick of the profound challenges and changes that have arisen there more recently.

The King is a Thing

What interests me in this paper is Žižek's development and use of certain ideas of Kant—in particular *das Ding*, the Thing—via Lacan. In the Žižek text under scrutiny, the section on "The King is a Thing" (1991a:253–73), the argument moves by way of the Jacobin dilemma as to whether they should kill the king, Louis XVI, to the theory of the king's two bodies—the sacred, immaterial body and the destructible earthly one; the divine and the human, as it were (and Žižek's religious language is not by accident). However, in contrast to some other well known theories of human-divine interaction, it is not so much that the earthly one is the incarnation of the sacred one, but that the one becomes the other: "As soon as a certain person functions as 'king,' his everyday, ordinary properties undergo a kind of 'transub-stantiation' and become an object of fascination" (Žižek, 1991:255).

But the phrase "ordinary properties" refers not only to the everyday properties of human existence, to its processes of birth and decay and human interaction, but also to those aspects of life that are more sordid and scandalous, to those things that people not in power wish they had or could do for themselves. And it is all of these things—intrigues, affairs, corruption, humiliations and scandals—that actually enhance the charisma of the king. So much so that royals (and indeed others in positions of ruling power) unintentionally incite rumors about precisely these things. The royal family of England is perhaps the best contemporary example. The dialectic here works at full tilt: "At the very moment of his greatest abasement, he arouses absolute compassion and fascination" (Žižek, 1991:255).

I want to make a few connections with this stage of the argument and the story of David in a few moments, but there is one other point in Žižek's argument that I need to follow first. It is important to note that Žižek is not talking about an empirical person and that person's symbolic function: the original formulation is between the earthly body and a sublime, sacred body. The reason for postulating two bodies is that the dialectical process of the symbolic function "redoubles his very body, introducing a split between the visible, material, transient body and another, sublime body, a body made of a special, immaterial stufflings" (1991a:255).[1] The problem with all of this is that it begins to move into explicitly theological terminology as an explanation of the function of kingship (and then the ruling classes in general). In order to save himself from this move, Žižek appropriates a common motif from the work of Lacan—*objet petit a*. In contrast to the king's earthly body, the sublime, immaterial body is designated *objet petit a*, or, borrowing from both Shakespeare[2] and Kant, the "Thing."

---

[1] "It is no less crucial to avoid confusing *objet a* with an ordinary material object. Even in the late 1950s, Lacan distinguished between ordinary and sublime body—a distinction that is perhaps best exemplified by the subjective position of a nun. A nun radically refuses the status of the sexual object for another human being—this refusal, however, concerns only her ordinary, material body, while enabling her to offer all the more passionately her sublime body, that which is 'in her more than herself', to God qua absolute Other" (1994:179).

[2] Rosencrantz: My lord, you must tell us where the body is, and go with us to the king.
  Hamlet: The body is with the king, but the king is not with the body. The king is a thing—

For Žižek *objet petit a* "is what philosophical reflection lacks in order to be able to locate itself, i.e., to ascertain its nullity" (1991b:6). Not unexpectedly, the dialectic is in full operation here: *objet petit a* is that which constitutes something by its very absence, that void, that unnecessary item which is absolutely necessary for the existence of the whole, whether that be desire, the subject, or the nation itself. "We could thus define *objet petit a*, the object-cause of desire embodying surplus enjoyment, precisely as the surplus that escapes the network of universal exchange" (1991b:167). Žižek draws in a series of items under the auspices of *objet petit a*: Freud's kernel, Kant's *das Ding*, Lacan's *l'extimité*, Plato's *agalma* and Hershey chocolate bars.[3] They are all part of "this point of the Real in the very heart of the subject which cannot be symbolized, which is produced as a residue, a remnant, a leftover of every signifying operation, a hard core embodying horrifying jouissance, enjoyment, and as such an object which simultaneously attracts and repels us—which divides our desire and thus provokes shame" (1989:180). So, the Thing, *das Ding*, is "the pure substance of enjoyment resisting symbolization" (1992:8).

Rather than more theoretical pronouncements, I will draw on two examples. First, there is the MacGuffin, Hitchcock's famous cause that is not a cause, the item that gets the story going in the first place but is in itself nothing. The example here is the package on the train's luggage rack: upon being asked, the owner indicates that it is a MacGuffin. "'What's a MacGuffin?' 'Well, it's an apparatus for

---

Guildenstern: A thing, my Lord!
Hamlet: Of nothing: bring me to him. Hide fox, and all after.
(Shakespeare 1943:895)

[3] "Rather than a pure 'this', the object without properties, *a* is a bundle of properties that lacks existence. In a brilliant essay, Stephen Jay Gould . . . extrapolates *ad absurdum* the long-term tendency in the relationship between price and quantity of Hershey chocolate bars. For some time the price stays the same, while the quantity gradually diminishes; then, all of a sudden, the price goes up and, with it, the quantity, yet the new quantity is still less than what we had gained with the previous rise. . . . The quantity of chocolate bar over a temporal span thus follows a zigzag: it gradually declines, then it suddenly jumps up, then it gradually declines again, and so on, with the long-term tendency towards decline. By extrapolating this tendency to the senseless extreme, we can calculate not only the exact moment when the quantity will reach zero—that is, when we will get a nicely wrapped void—but also how much this void will cost. This void—which, none the less, is nicely wrapped and has a definite price—is an almost perfect metaphor for the Lacanian *objet petit a*." (Žižek, 1994:179)

trapping lions in the Scottish Highlands.' 'But there are no lions in the Scottish Highlands.' 'Well, you see how efficient it is.'" For Žižek, "the MacGuffin is the purest case of what Lacan calls *objet petit a*: a pure void which functions as the object-cause of desire" (1989:163). The second example is that of the vampire. In his discussion of the mirror stage, or the mirror relationship, Žižek notes: "It is therefore clear why vampires are invisible in the mirror: because they have read Lacan and, consequently, know how to behave—they materialize *objet a* which, by definition, cannot be mirrored" (1992:126).

The king, then, may be understood as *objet petit a*, as that extraneous item that is crucial to the social body. The king, as a Thing, is "a foreign body within the social texture" (Žižek, 1992:122), yet it is what "'holds together' the social edifice by means of guaranteeing its fantasmatic consistency" (Žižek, 1992:123). I would like to take one further step in the argument and pick up a very Hegelian, and therefore dialectical, reflection on royalty as the "place-holder of the void." For Hegel (as for the terrorist among the Jacobins), the monarch functions to protect the "empty locus of Power" (Žižek, 1991a:269). That is, by being in what appears to be the location of Power, the king, as an empty, extraneous entity, prevents those who exercise Power (the executive) from being able to identify with the locus of Power itself. "The 'monarch' is nothing but a positivization, a materialization of the distance separating the locus of Power from those who exert it. It is for this reason—because his function is purely negative—that the question of 'who should reign' could be, even must be, left to the contingency of biological lineage—only thus is the utter insignificance of the positivity of the monarch effectively asserted" (Žižek, 1991a:269). There are two outcomes that are important for my discussion: the most effective monarchs are therefore those who are not "fit" for the job, since in their very negativity (understood not only as inability, but also as blunders, lapses and crimes) they fulfil their role. Second, if a monarch is then removed from the locus of Power, someone else takes the monarch's place, most notably the President of a republic, or perhaps a totalitarian dictator. I don't think I need to dwell for too long on the immense popularity of a Kennedy or a Reagan to back up my point.[4]

---

[4] Indeed, it is as though Žižek's characterization was written on the basis of presidents of the USA, none of which has seemed "fit" for the job in an ordinary

How then does this work itself out in the story of the rise of the monarchy in 1 Samuel? In what way is it possible to speak of the king as a Thing, as the *objet petit a*, in this text? Let me begin with 1 Samuel 8, the text in which the issue of a king for Israel is broached explicitly, albeit negatively, only to be counterbalanced by the direct involvement of Samuel in the selection and appointment of a king in 1 Samuel 9–10. In these three chapters of Samuel, the one (8) where Samuel attempts to warn the people away from a king, and the others (9–10) where he actively takes part in his appointment, the two sides, pro and con, come textually face to face. But it is 1 Samuel 8 that interests me more directly.

A reverse reading of the chapter—Samuel's warning about a king (1 Sam 8:10–20), Yahweh's words to Samuel (1 Sam 8:4–9) and then Samuel's sons (1 Sam 8:1–3)—is required here in order to see the logic of Žižek's argument more clearly. In the main section of 1 Samuel 8, Samuel follows the advice of Yahweh to listen to the people's request for a king, yet warn them "of the ways of the king who shall reign over them" (1 Sam 8:9). And so, in response to the request of the elders to "appoint for us a king to govern us like all the nations" (1 Sam 8:4), Samuel iterates all that having a king will mean: the king will take the people's sons for chariots, horsemen, runners, army officers and ordinary soldiers; he will take labourers for agriculture, to plough and reap; he will take others for the war industry, to make weapons, chariots and other implements; he will take daughters for domestic labour, "perfumers and cooks and bakers" (1 Sam 8:13); he will take agricultural produce for his army and court; he will take slaves, livestock, and the people themselves as slaves for labour. The list closes out with: "And in that day you will cry out because of your king, whom you have chosen for yourselves; but the Lord will not answer you in that day" (1 Sam 8:18). Resounding through this oppressive list is the verb "he will take" (six times from 8:11 to 8:17 except 8:12 where "he will appoint" appears) with no sense of reciprocity, of what the king might give in return, such as protection, patronage or state welfare.

---

sense: one has only to recall Kennedy's uncontrolled libido, Nixon's crime, Carter's ineffectual smile, Reagan the airhead, Bush the wimp, Clinton's uncontrolled libido. . . .

A gloomy picture? A powerful piece of propaganda? A clever effort at dissuasion? It appears not. In response to all of this the people insist on a king: "No! but we are determined to have a king over us, so that we may be like other nations, and that our king may govern us and go out before us and fight our battles" (1 Sam 8:19–20). It is not so much that the people refused to listen (1 Sam 8:19), nor that they opposed to Samuel's diatribe what they felt to be positives—keeping up with the neighbours, strong government, leadership and military protection—but that the people listened too well: it is only through these demands and expectations on their offspring, produce, land and their own bodies that the king may govern and fight. Without the taxes, armies, corvée labor, appropriation of livestock and land, there would be no army and there would be no king. In other words it is precisely the negatives that make the king desirable: or rather, the more Samuel lists the negatives, the more he misses the point of kingship: the king is there to fill the void, to do all of these terrible things, so that he can be king and so that the people will love him all the more. This is, after all, what a king is like, and this is why we want a king. A king who does not take our children, our labour, our cattle and flocks, our grains and our land is not worthy of our respect.

The contradiction I have been tracing bears all the marks of the king as a Thing, as the uncontainable excess that is crucial for the operation of the social body, the figure who is required to do all of the things that no one else in the social body may do in order to secure that body. In 1 Samuel 9–10 is found the distinction between the corporeal and sublime body that is crucial for the notion of the king as a Thing: the focus on Saul's body indicates the establishment of his sublime body as *objet petit a*. He was, the text notes with a drooling admiration, "a handsome young man. There was not a man among the people of Israel more handsome than he; from his shoulders upward he was taller than any of the people" (1 Sam 9:2). Indeed, in the curious doubling of the selection process in 1 Sam 10:20–24—why choose by lot one who has already been anointed (1 Sam 10:1)?—it is precisely his body, his height to be precise (1 Sam 10:23 in a phrase that repeats 9:2), that is the marker by which Samuel acclaims him king: "Do you see him whom Yahweh has chosen? There is none like him among all the people" (1 Sam 10:24). The dialectical switch here is that he already is the sublime body, for God has given him another heart (10:9) and the spirit of God is upon him (10:10). Anything he does merely enhances this sublime body, even hiding in the baggage at the big moment (10:22). In the end, however, Saul is only an imperfect embodiment of *objet petit a*, for it is David who comes to realize this logic more profoundly.

However, before considering David further, I need to step back in 1 Samuel 8 to the second item in the sequence, which is the speech of Yahweh to Samuel. Here, the character of Yahweh speaks to Samuel after he has told Yahweh of the words of the elders in 1 Sam 8:4: "Listen to the voice of the people in all that they say to you; for they have not rejected you, but they have rejected me from being king over them" (1 Sam 8:7). Is this not the pure form of Žižek's notion of the empty locus of Power? For Žižek, the king is ultimately one who occupies an empty position so that the real locus of Power—advisors, faceless bureaucrats, nameless officials—is never named. This is precisely why the king may be, indeed must be, a tyrant, inept, corrupt, one who shamelessly exploits his subjects and makes an ostentatious show of it, for he occupies a void and does not have Power *per se*. But here, in 1 Sam 8:4, we find that while the king may be the place-holder of the void, the void itself, the empty place of Power, is in fact occupied by God. Is Yahweh, then, the ultimate nameless official, or the void itself? Is the king a front for this real Power, or is Yahweh in turn a front for another source of never-to-be-named Power?

All the same, the contradiction of 1 Samuel 8–10, as well as that of the depiction of Saul, is fully realized in the figure of David. It seems to me that Žižek's argument regarding the king may well have been written for David himself, for it promises an answer to a deep contradiction between the representation of David in the books of Samuel and that in the books of Kings. In the latter, he is elevated to the status of ideal figure, a Judahite counterpoise to the evil Israelite Jeroboam. In contrast to the "sins of Jeroboam" that marked Israel's kings (for example, 1 Kgs 15:26, 34; 16:19, 31), David is the benchmark by which all the kings of Judah are measured. He is the one who "followed Yahweh" (1 Kgs 11:6), whose heart was "wholly true to the Lord his God" (1 Kgs 15:3), for "David did what was right in the eyes of Yahweh, and did not turn aside from anything that he commanded him all the days of his life, except in the matter of Uriah the Hittite" (1 Kgs 15:5; see also 15:11 and so on). Indeed, it is this marker, the notation of Uriah (not Bathsheba!), that points up the contradiction. For the depiction of David in the books of Samuel hardly bears up to the ideal king that he rapidly becomes in Kings.

David's story is a continual saga of sordid deals, deception, bloodshed, and an unruly court. He is "loved" by all of Saul's family and Israel, exploiting this affection for his own gain and the path to kingship that is abdicated by Jonathan (1 Samuel 18–20); works for the Philistines when he is on the run from Saul, particularly Achish of Gath, to whom he feigns madness (1 Samuel 21, 27, 29); runs a protection racket with a gang of four hundred runaway criminals and outlaws (1 Sam 22:1–2; 25); leaves his parents in the protection of the king of Moab (1 Sam 22:3–4); engages in guerilla warfare (1 Samuel 23–24, 26–27); slaughters indigenous inhabitants (1 Sam 27:8–11); acquires and abducts women, such as Abigail (1 Samuel 25) and Bathsheba (2 Samuel 11–12) by killing off their husbands, or Michal (2 Sam 3:12–16), by taking her from her husband Paltiel (see also 2 Sam 3:2–5; 5:13–16); has a dubious connection to the deaths of Saul and Ishbosheth (1 Samuel 31; 2 Samuel 1, 4); engages in civil war on his way to the throne (2 Samuel 2–3); turns on the Philistines and Moabites who formerly sheltered him (2 Samuel 8) oversees a brood of offspring who engage in incestuous rape (2 Samuel 13) and plots for the throne, which then requires familial war between Absalom and David (2 Samuel 13–19); hands over seven of Saul's grandchildren to be killed by the Gibeonites (2 Sam 21:1–14); and, finally, is responsible for a divine plague over Israel (2 Samuel 24).

The contradiction between these two Davids is between story and narrative memory, between the devious character of the books of Samuel and the one who is represented in Kings as the ideal king who walked with God, whose heart was right with God. It seems to me that Žižek's reworking of the "Thing" is helpful here. I want to suggest that, in dialectical fashion, the contradiction between Samuel and Kings provides the very reason for their connection, that the sordid life of David in Samuel is the very reason for his elevation in the formulae of Kings. Rather than the more usual argument that the account of David in 1–2 Samuel is an effort at propaganda to clear his name of suspicion (if this is so, it is a rather sorry effort), it seems that the story itself provides the basis for his status in 1–2 Kings.

This dual, contradictory, story of David intersects with each stage of my discussion of Žižek above. Most obviously, there is the suggestion that it is precisely the king's excesses that lead to his elevation: David's corrupt, devious, abased and bloody life becomes an object of fascination for the narrative, because he is destined to be king. The very production of the narrative of David may be read as an unconscious production of rumour—however late it may be—so that his figure might be enhanced all the more. Secondly, like Saul, there is a focus on his real, earthly, body, an attention that is placed in the sight of Yahweh himself. In the story of his anointing by Samuel, the narrator, oozing desire, writes, "Now he was ruddy, and had beautiful eyes, and was handsome" (1 Sam 16:12). Even Yahweh is smitten, the one who supposedly "looks on the heart" (1 Sam 16:7), for he says immediately after David's luscious entrance, "'Arise, anoint him; for this is he'" (1 Sam 16:12). Like Saul, he too received the Spirit of Yahweh (1 Sam 16:13) that now passes on from Saul (1 Sam 16:14). He is the "lamp of Israel" (1 Sam 21:17), the sublime body upon which the social body depends. At the other end of his reign it is once again David's body that is the focus of attention: now unable to generate its own warmth, the king's body is warmed by the "very beautiful" Abishag the Shunammite, "the king's nurse" who "ministered to him" (2 Sam 1:4).

Thirdly, David comes through as *objet petit a*, as the excess that provides the structures of the social body, as the item that is beyond the experience of the people that is at the same time their focus of attention and admiration, as the void that is necessary for the social body to exist. He occupies the extraneous place that is outside the social body and yet is crucial for it: he is that enjoyment that will not be symbolized, the leftover or the remnant that is outside the system of exchange. *Objet petit a* is the point where all the elements of his earthly life and body are transformed into dimensions of the sublime body, which is, finally, what we find in the annals of 1–2 Kings.

The ideal king of 1–2 Kings is, then, not the mistaken ideological memory of David, a misshapen messianic promise: rather, this ideal king is precisely what one would expect from the narrative of his life provided in 1–2 Samuel. 1–2 Kings embodies, as it were, the sublime body of King David that relies on the Real body of 1–2 Samuel. David, to adapt a quotation from Žižek, "'holds together' the social edifice [of Israel] by means of guaranteeing its fantasmatic consistency [in 1–2 Kings]" (1992:123). And then he becomes the basis of messianic expectation. Is not Jesus, for Christians, the ultimate *objet petit a*?

To conclude this section I will return to Žižek more directly for a few moments. The contradiction between the narrative representation of David and the formulaic memory of him in Kings, as also the contradiction between the objections to a king and the people's demand for one in 1 Samuel 8, may be described in terms of the "transferential relationship," something we encounter in love stories, or melodramas: someone (a plotter or friend) tries to persuade the hero or heroine to leave his or her lover by listing all of the latter's weak points—he has a bad temper, he is untrustworthy, he is lazy, he is a criminal, etc.—yet all these points merely serve to reinforce the affection of the hero or heroine ("for those reasons I love him all the more"). So also with Ronald Reagan: the more the liberal media played up his slips of tongue, his *faux pas* and general inability to govern, the more popular he became. Or Bill Clinton: the more the Republicans and the media focused on the lurid details of his sexual affair with Monica Lewinsky, including the cigar dildo, the blow jobs in the oval office, the semen-stained dress—all of which (at least the information) was available on the Internet after the Senate judicial enquiry had perused it—the greater was his popularity (73% after the vote to impeach him in late 1998). So also with David: the more the text enhances his amorphous sexuality, his double-dealing, his bloody plots, his ambiguous alliances and his tumultuous personal life, the more he becomes the ideal king, forerunner of the messiah.

Conclusion: The Theft of Enjoyment

However, the pattern I have traced—the king as a Thing, as *objet petit a*, as an excess that is crucial for the social body itself—does not always apply. The contrast is already found in the first section of 1 Samuel 8, where Samuel's sons, Joel and Abijah, do not make it as judges over Israel. They take bribes and pervert justice (1 Sam 8:3), something that David, and Saul to a lesser degree, seem to be able to carry out with impunity. They are, of course, not strictly kings, but they do function as the immediate narrative trigger to the request for a king by the elders of Israel in 1 Sam 8:4.

Joel and Abijah foreshadow a much greater failure of the logic of *objet petit a* that I have been tracing, namely that of Solomon himself. Even a cursory reading of the Solomon material (1 Kings 1–

11) is able to pick up a significant contrast with the texts on David: Solomon is, to begin with, too good. There is little if any reference to intrigue (at least after the succession), but rather a depiction of an ideal Solomonic Jerusalem. In this case I am not so much interested in what social contradictions are marked in the text and to which the text is a response: the image of Solomon is so good it sets my dialectical sensors itching, particularly in the light of the negative turn (preempted to be sure in the positive material) in either I Kings 9 or 11. The Solomon of the great temple, of wealth, wisdom, judicial and diplomatic skills, becomes a Solomon who uses his wisdom for personal gain, whose libido is out of control, and who consequently ends up in apostasy. He is the precursor to the breakup of the kingdom under his son Rehoboam (1 Kings 12).

Somewhere Solomon has lost it (I am speaking of the narrative), and I would like to attempt some explanation through the idea of the "theft of enjoyment." For Žižek, enjoyment itself is implicitly tied up with *objet petit a*, particularly the idea of "surplus enjoyment," which is the residue of pure enjoyment that remains outside the signifying system. It is an enjoyment that is not the same as pleasure, but rather goes beyond pleasure, it is the "impossible/traumatic/painful enjoyment beyond the pleasure principle" (1992:182). The king, as the Thing, is thereby this enjoyment incarnated, this surplus or residue, that which cannot finally be articulated or identified. For Žižek what is crucial about the Thing is that "it means something" to people, that others believe in it as well as myself (his examples are the nation and the Holy Spirit). It is then possible for such a Thing to be under threat, for people to feel that the "national Thing" may well be stolen by the Other, by immigrants or refugees. "The basic paradox is that our Thing is conceived as something inaccessible to the others and at the same time threatened by them" (1993:203). Thus the foreigner either steals our jobs or is a sponge on our welfare system (with both charges being levelled simultaneously); the immigrant wants to steal our enjoyment yet has access to a greater enjoyment than us, of which we catch glimpses through his language, his celebrations, the smell of his food, their social practices and so on; the worker who enjoys weekends, has the occasional sick day, looks forward to the end of the working day, slacks off when possible, somehow enjoys herself at the expense of the boss or the work place, and therefore she cannot be truly committed to her job.

I would like to extend this notion of the theft of enjoyment to the biblical narrative under question. The king is also the location, through the Thing, of surplus enjoyment, of the enjoyment that cannot be attained and yet is there. Thus, the people seem to accept it when glimpses of that enjoyment are provided—sumptuous feasts, great wealth, interesting sexual practices, even crime and corruption. Yet there is a moment when all this somehow falls away, when all of these trappings of power are no longer regarded as the expectation of the king, but rather as drain on public resources, as unfair taxation of the populace, as self-indulgence rather than the right of the monarch. It is at this moment that the king is guilty of the "theft of enjoyment," of stealing the enjoyment of the people. The king becomes the "thief" of enjoyment and loses the status of *objet petit a* or the Thing. The narrative signal of the beginnings of such a process is in the overwhelmingly "positive" image of Solomon in the first chapters of Kings: he is too good, and there is none of the ambivalence, the sordid life and devious politics, that makes David a Thing. The king is never worthy of the excesses that are taken (the lack of worth is the secret to adoration of the king), and as soon as the king is represented as worthy, as deserving of all the wealth and power, then the breakdown has begun. This means of course that the signs of Solomon's decline are found not in the final sections that deal with his libido and apostasy, nor even in the hints of problems in the rosy picture that is depicted initially, but rather in the descriptions of the glorious temple, in his influence, wealth, economic expansion, judicial skill, wisdom and obedience to the Torah. The theft of enjoyment has already begun.

Bibliography

Shakespeare, William
    1943   *The Complete Works of William Shakespeare*. Ed. W. J. Craig. London: Oxford University Press.

Žižek, Slavoj
    1989   *The Sublime Object of Ideology*. London: Verso.
    1991a   *For They Know Not What They Do*. London: Verso.
    1991b   *Looking Awry: An Introduction to Jacques Lacan through Popular Culture*. Cambridge, MA: MIT Press.
    1992   *Enjoy Your Symptom: Jacques Lacan in Hollywood and Out*. New York and London: Routledge.
    1993   *Tarrying With the Negative*. Durham, NC: Duke University Press.

1994   *The Metastases of Enjoyment: Six Essays on Women and Causality*. London: Verso.

1996   *The Indivisible Remainder: An Essay on Schelling and Related Matters*. London: Verso.

1997   *The Plague of Fantasies*. London: Verso.

Žižek, Slavoj, ed.

1992   *Everything You Always Wanted to Know about Lacan (But Were Afraid to Ask Hitchcock)*. London: Verso.

1994   *Mapping Ideology*. London: Verso.

1998   *Cogito and the Unconscious. Sic 2*. Durham, NC: Duke University Press.

Žižek, Slavoj and Renata Salecl, eds.

1996   *Gaze and Voice as Love Objects. Sic 1*. Durham, NC: Duke University Press.

A BETTERED WOMAN
ELISHA AND THE SHUNAMMITE IN
THE DEUTERONOMIC WORK

David Jobling

The labour of reading a biblical text is a dialectic work, constantly passing between the particular text and the larger biblical context, and between theory and praxis. Robert Culley is one who never lets the opposite sides of these dialectics get out of sight of each other. In this essay I read and theorize about the story of Elisha and the woman of Shunem (2 Kgs 4:8–37; 8:1–6) as it informs and is informed by its context: the Elijah-Elisha cycle, and eventually the whole Deuteronomic History.

In my recent book on 1 Samuel (Jobling, 1998), I found the Deuteronomic History (DH)—in the context of postexilic reimagining of Jewish identity, and consequent canon-building—to be caught up in a systematic "forgetting" of the political ideal of old Israel. Ironically so, since the Deuteronomists were the lineal heirs to that ideal.

DH provides the only literary record of how Israel moved to monarchy from its earlier constitution. But the process of creating the record is a process also of reconceiving that which is being recorded. DH preserves traces of an old egalitarian and antimonarchical ideal. But it is also involved in a process of turning the premonarchical time into an *anti-ideal* (a process which will culminate, at a post-Deuteronomic stage, in the creation of the book of Judges), and of positing monarchy as a substitute ideal (by means of the compromise that kingship is ideal if and only if it is Davidic). DH remembers egalitarian Israel as *that which must be forgotten*.

The only available analogue is provided by psychoanalysis. The DH's "forgetting" is a national process of repression. The reading of the text must therefore be an attempt to talk to the text's "unconscious." If there was an historical "fall" from an ideal, it is available to us only as a fall that is repeated in the process (perhaps centuries long) of DH's creation. Our only access, uncertain at best, is through the manifold contradictions in the Deuteronomic text which the paradoxical process of its production—turning an ideal into an anti-ideal, creating a substitute ideal—has left behind as symptoms.

Through a reading especially of Hannah, but also of other women in 1 Samuel, I further argued that the dynamics of gender are an necessary element in DH's labour of reading Israel's past and our labour of reading DH. The text's transmuting of ideal into anti-ideal, and its positing of a substitute ideal, involve a systematic diminution of the active role of the women characters. Gender is not, of course, the only factor in play, but it is certainly among the most important.

I shall show in this essay how these same dynamics are repeated in a different way in the Elijah-Elisha sequence (1 Kings 17 to 2 Kings 13), and how the story of Elisha and the Shunammite is pivotal for the creation of the textual effect.

Literary-Feminist Reading of the Story

A woman of Shunem, seeing that the prophet Elisha regularly visits her town, builds for his use a small furnished room. After he has been using it for some time, Elisha decides that the woman should be rewarded for her trouble. He first offers to put in a word on her behalf with the king or the general. The woman rejects this offer in the mysterious words which first drew me to the story: "I live among my own people" (2 Kgs 4:13). At a loss, Elisha consults his servant Gehazi, who reminds him that the woman has no son and that her husband is old. Without consulting the woman, Elisha informs her that she will have a son. Her response seems less than enthusiastic.

The son is born, grows, and suddenly dies. Leaving his body in Elisha's room, the woman travels to fetch the prophet, who agrees to come. After unsuccessfully trying to achieve resuscitation by the agency of Gehazi, Elisha succeeds in raising the son himself. The woman does obeisance to Elisha. This completes the part of the story that appears in 2 Kings 4.[1]

Several chapters later, Elisha warns this same woman that there is a famine coming, and that she should temporarily emigrate. She does so. The famine over, the woman comes with her son to petition the king of Israel for the restoration of the property she abandoned. They arrive as Gehazi is recounting to the king the miracles of Elisha, and he identifies the woman and son as the recipients of the greatest of these miracles. The king enthusiastically grants the woman's petition.

Mary Shields provides an excellent feminist-literary reading of this story, which is basic to mine, at least so far as 2 Kgs 4:8–37 is concerned. She notes how the story develops as a competition for prestige between Elisha and the Shunammite woman (59; cf. Bergen, 1999:90–93). Elisha eventually wins this competition, when the woman is brought to worship at his feet (4:37; Shields: 66). But there are many indications in the story of admiration for the woman and a diminution of the prophet's standing.

The Shunammite is described as a "big woman" (אשה גדולה, 4:8), the only biblical use of this adjective for a woman (Bergen, 1990:90). It is usually translated "wealthy," but her bigness extends beyond wealth (Shields: 60; cf. Long, 1991b:54, "esteemed"). She belongs to a line of biblical women whose narrative importance, and especially initiative-taking, put their husbands in the shade (Shields: 60). Her husband plays a passive role in the building of the spare room, and later he responds ineptly to the death of their son (4:23; Shields: 64). The Shunammite projects a sense of independence and lack of need (Long, 1991a:17); this may be the meaning of "I live among my own people" (Shields: 62). She is not afraid to rebuke Elisha, probably in 4:13, 16, certainly in 4:28 (Long, 1991b:57). She steals the initiative in the story from Elisha when she insists that he go with her to Shunem (4:30; Shields: 65; Bergen, 1999:100–101; Long, 1991b:58). Elisha constantly tries to keep his distance from the woman, but she vigorously breaks the distance down (Shields: 64–65; Bergen, 1999:100).

The strongest part of Shields's essay is her impatient rejection of the clichés about women and children who have been almost universal

---

[1] Robert Culley made one of the early contributions to the literary clarification of this part of the text. See 1976:46–49, 90–91.

in previous interpretations of the story. Biblical women do not automatically want children (67). The Shunammite "is described neither as barren nor as desiring a child" (63), and her words in 4:16 may be a rejection of Elisha's "offer" (62). Regarding these words Shields chillingly notes that the repeated negative אל . . . אל ("no . . . don't") is characteristic of the scene of rape (2 Sam 13:12; Judg 19:23). Elisha does not seek the woman's consent, overpowers her with his wonder-working ability, and makes her pregnant—what else is this than rape? For me, "No, my lord" also resonates across the chapters of DH with the almost identical words of Hannah (1 Sam 1:15)—the very first words ascribed to Hannah, and spoken to no less a one than the high priest of Israel. Just as firmly, the Shunammite negates the prophet of Israel.[2]

Anxious for Elisha's reputation, the narrator of 2 Kings 4 conjures the memory of the divine gift of a child to many barren women in the Bible. This evocation of other annunciations makes the Shunammite seem faithless and/or ungrateful; as Long notes, the story so manipulates things that "the woman puts herself on the side of Sarah" (1991b:56). But this is merely "a parody of the annunciation type-scene" (Shields: 63). There is no divine gift, only the inept effort of a prophet whose descent into futility begins (as we shall see) with this episode.

Even Shields and others whose work on 2 Kgs 4:8–37 I admire fail to see the absolute necessity of the resumption and conclusion of the Shunammite's story in 2 Kgs 8:1–6.

A story—even a brief one—in which a "lay" person, a woman, simply gives, and a famous prophet simply receives, seems to be an intolerable irritant. The text's resources must be marshalled to counteract and, so far as possible, erase the prophet's "obligation" to the woman. The woman must be put under an even bigger obligation to

---

[2] In the development of my work, the Shunammite has become a lineal heir to Hannah. The two have much in common: their domination over their husbands, their childlessness. Long has noted a striking number of detailed parallels of style and substance between their two stories (1991b:53, 54, 57). Reading the secondary literature on Hannah was for me the same stultifying experience of wading through clichés that Shields must have had with the literature on the Shunammite. Hannah, I decided, cannot be read as desiring a son for any "normal" maternal reason, since she intends from the outset to give him away. So I was ground well prepared for Shields's suggestion that the Shunammite doesn't want a son at all! See Jobling, 1998:131–42.

the prophet. This is partly accomplished in 2 Kings 4. The narrator, uncomfortably aware that the gift of the son failed to elicit her gratitude, so arranges things that the son is given to her again, but this time as a grown child whom she has brought up, with whom she has bonded, to whose existence she can no longer be indifferent.

The strategy appears successful. The woman's prostrating herself in humble gratitude (4:37) is no doubt most satisfying both to Elisha and to the narrator. But a discerning reader may wonder whether the narrative task has been *fully* accomplished. The woman has been put down, but only for her refusal of the child. Does not her offense go deeper? What about her refusal of Elisha's first offer, to speak on her behalf to the high and mighty? What about her energy and initiative that created the story in the first place? That was perhaps her archcrime! True, her energy and initiative have been commended in 4:8–37. But women are supposed to act energetically *on behalf of their families*; the patriarchy can tolerate a great deal of female power when it is thus safely channeled. Building add-ons for prophets, refusing the gifts of prophets, such power falls into a different category.

The reader may, then, not be too surprised at the long-delayed dénouement. 2 Kgs 8:1–6 is an ending totally contrived for the purpose of completing Elisha's victory and the woman's defeat. The sheer atrocious precision with which these verses finish the job compels our reluctant admiration. Is this a woman proud that she lives among her own people (4:13)? Then let her be removed from her people and made to live elsewhere (8:1–2). Is this a woman who scorns Elisha's offer to curry favour for her with the king (4:13)? Then let her be obliged to petition the king, and so contrive things that Elisha's servant assists her petition (8:3–6). But the trick is achieved by making the woman unrecognizable as the person we knew in chap. 4, even though we are solemnly told she is one and the same. Would the Shunammite of chap. 4 have left home even at Elisha's suggestion? Would she have petitioned the king under any circumstances?

As to narrative technique, the final scene deserves to be laughed off the stage. When the woman arrives, with whom should the king *happen* to be talking but Elisha's servant? What should they *happen* to be talking about but Elisha's miracles? And which particular miracle should Gehazi's recitation *happen* to have reached but the resurrection of her son—who just *happens* (we were not previously told this) to be beside her. What can the king do? PR like this can't be bought with money! Of course he gives her what she asks, and beyond what she asks.

There is one last connection between the beginning and the end of the story. It began with a "big woman" (אשה גדולה, 4:8) but ends with Elisha's "big deeds" (כל הגדלות, 8:4—even the chapter and verse numbers are reversed!). The story has made the big woman into merely the occasion for the biggest of the prophet's big deeds. What he has done for her has finally swamped what she did for him. In the game of favours, Elisha has "bettered" this woman into submission.

No less critical than the content of 2 Kgs 8:1–6 is its narrative separation from the earlier part of the story. The numerous stories between 2 Kgs 4:37 and 8:1 have been made part of the large narrative space defined by the Shunammite's story. To explore the "exchange of meaning" between the containing and the contained text is a non-optional step in such a case (Jobling, 1986:70–83). What do the Shunammite's story and the stories it contains (4:38–7:20) have to say to each other, and how does this exchange of meaning contribute to the textual work of "forgetting" Israel's egalitarian ideal?

To begin with a minor point, the two brief stories which immediately follow 4:37—vv. 38–41 and vv. 42–44—both stress Elijah's role as *provider* rather than as *provided for*. This tends to cast a shadow on the Shunammite's provision for Elisha's needs. We may extend the point to the next story: Elisha's refusal of a present from Naaman (5:15–16) suggests that the prophet intends to put himself under no more obligations!

There are two major points to be made. First, Elisha's relationship to the king improves and intensifies between 2 Kgs 4:8 and 8:6. 2 Kgs 4:13 is the first time Elisha (or Elijah) refers to a king of Israel in any positive way. In 2 Kgs 5:6–8 and 6:9–10, 21–23 a tendency still to ridicule or insult the king (5:7; 6:22) fails to disguise a new ethos of cooperation. The progression is even more interesting in 2 Kgs 6:24–7:20. First the king vows death to Elisha (6:31), but this aggression quickly dissipates into a muted appeal (6:33). Even when the king demonstrates a culpable lack of faith in Yahweh, this is not in the long run held against him, for his doubt and its punishment are neatly displaced onto his captain (7:2, 17–20). The rapprochement between prophet and king perhaps proceeds rather jerkily, but it is real, and it prepares us for the coziness that we find in 8:1–6.[3]

The second point is even more compelling. The narrative space defined by the Shunammite's story is precisely the space within which Elisha has a *personal servant* (not always specified as Gehazi: see 4:38; 6:15). Especially when combined with the rapprochement with the king, this suggests an important *class* dimension in the narrative. Gehazi figures not only in the Shunammite's story but also in the story of Naaman (chap. 5). The reader is startled to find the leprous, disfigured Gehazi of 5:27 chatting merrily with the monarch about miracles in 8:4–5. This highlights how contrived 8:1–6 is. It also highlights an overloading of the role "servant of Elisha." The servant appears as everything from incompetent, doubter, liar and thief, to the prophet's plenipotentiary and ambassador to the king.[4]

Within six verses (4:8–13) a "big" woman, a servant of Elisha, and favourable mention of the king of Israel all make their first appearance. In six final verses (8:1–6) this servant and this king join in adulation of Elisha and in the diminution of this woman. Must we not suppose that these observations summarize, at some level, the basic agenda of 2 Kgs 4:8–8:6?

The "Historical Scenario"

I believe that DH "forgets" what it is about, loses touch with Israel's egalitarian ideal, in the Elijah-Elisha cycle just as much as in the transition to kingship in 1 Samuel (see the discussion with which I began). Specifically, my thesis is that the Shunammite's story constitutes the key moment in this "forgetting."

The school of Norman Gottwald, refining a much older scholarly tradition, has created an image of the circumstances of Elijah and Elisha.[5] The dynasty of Omri greatly hastened state centralization in

---

[3] The geography of the chapters confirms the point. Elisha's itinerancy continues and the different stories find him in a considerable number of places. But there is a steady focussing in on Samaria, the royal capital.

[4] All these roles appear in the two Gehazi stories and/or in the mentions of an unnamed servant (4:38–44; 6:15–17).

[5] Gottwald has himself contributed to our understanding of the Elijah and Elisha tales, in an old essay very different from most of his work, but remarkably reminiscent of the work of Robert Culley! See Gottwald and compare Culley, 1992.

the northern kingdom of Israel, deepening class division and pauperiz-
ing the peasantry. Concomitant with this sociopolitical process was a
takeover of the national religion, sponsored particularly by Ahab's
Phoenician wife Jezebel: Baal-worship was replacing Yahweh-wor-
ship. In this situation, Elijah and then Elisha arose as partisans of
Yahweh, leaders of a resistance movement. They were itinerant
prophets, travelling from place to place in Israel, stirring up, organizing and nurturing groups of resisters, for whom one name was "sons of
the prophets." These communities suffered hardship, and the prophets
are remembered as performing miracles which often were of a directly
economic kind.[6]

I shall refer to all this as the "historical scenario." I use the quote
marks first because many biblical scholars are deeply sceptical of our
ability to recapture the ninth century BCE. But there is an even more
important reason, intrinsic to my method. I like the "historical
scenario," and hope that it is near the truth. Access to such historical
truth, however, here as in 1 Samuel, is caught up in the Deuteronomic
process of repression or "forgetting." According to the scenario, Elijah
and Elisha resist the royal system by drawing on the ideological
resources of egalitarian, premonarchical Israel (perhaps they even seek
a restoration of that Israel). But the text of DH is much more
ambiguous. At one level DH *does* depict the northern prophets as
representatives of the old ideal—but simultaneously at another level it
is losing touch with the ideality of that ideal and casting doubt on its
very existence.

In 1 Samuel, as I noted earlier, DH makes a fundamental and
fatal compromise over monarchy: monarchy is good if it is Davidic,
bad if it is non-Davidic. This is an avoidance of the real question,
whether monarchy is a good or bad mode of government for Israel, and
in the crunch the compromise leaves no stable ideology to defend. It
comes as no surprise that the Elijah-Elisha section of DH deepens the
compromise: even non-Davidic monarchy (in the north) is good if it is
Yahwistic (Jehu), bad if it is Baalistic (Ahab and Jezebel). Some of the

---

[6] See Gottwald (130), with some older references. The most important work is in
the volume edited by Robert Coote. Todd (3–11) provides a useful picture. She
helpfully notes that the struggle "had its roots in the institution of kingship itself"
(3), and makes the link between the religious and the socioeconomic dimension (9–
10). Rentería (1992: esp. 87–95) offers a more complicated political analysis, but
one compatible with the same general picture.

stories of Elijah and Elisha, as the Deuteronomists inherited them, surely projected monarchy as a fall from Israel's ancient ideal. Yet in its total presentation of these prophets DH cannot hold onto this perspective. Its further compromise is no more capable than the earlier one of providing a stable ideology to defend.

I shall test my thesis by using the "historical scenario" as a heuristic device for rereading the Shunammite's story.

2 Kgs 4:8–10 might stand alone as a felicitous vignette, perhaps the very best, of the "historical scenario." Elisha is clearly itinerant. The Shunammite woman is not said to be attached to "the sons of the prophets," but she could be. The hospitality she extends is just what the prophet would need and could expect from his partisans. Her being wealthy need not negate the scenario; there is no reason why the resistance movement could not have had the support of relatively well off people (see Todd: 9, for the woman as an "example of status inconsistency").

The woman assumes that she and Elisha are comrades in a cause.[7] All the tension and competition in the story develops because Elisha does not share this assumption. The woman's assumption becomes her presumption, the fundamental offense for which she must be chastised. What she offered "in the spirit of the revolution" Elisha turns into a personal obligation. He must not be beholden to her. He must reward her for her hospitality. For her part, the woman's indignant responses to his offers are a sharp denial that any obligation exists, as if to say, "You are not beholden to me, and it does you no credit and the cause no service if you think you are!"

Insult is added to injury by the form that Elisha's first offer takes: "Would you have a word spoken on your behalf to the king or to the commander of the army?" (4:13). "How," the woman implies, "can you make *that particular* suggestion? We have no truck with kings and generals!" This, I suggest, is the point of "I live among my own

---

[7] Rentería, who generally accepts the "historical scenario," tackles the problem of a prophet's relation to his partisans in an interesting way: "The prophet acknowledges he needs them as followers by responding to their petition, and he does not elevate himself above them by performing miracles *for* them, but rather helps them to perform the miracles themselves. . . . This is not to say that the prophet offered a relationship of total equality" (1992:117).

people." Her people are the people of the resistance movement. How can the leader of the resistance be so cozy with the king?[8]

How, the reader may add, can he keep a personal servant? Is it really possible to reconcile the resistance prophet who travels light, making do with the basic amenities, with the prophet who commands the services of a such an attendant? Elisha has not previously needed a servant, no more did Elijah before him.

Our use of the "historical scenario" to reread the story has highlighted, then, the fundamental ideological contradiction in DH, and given added power to the feminist-literary reading.

The Futility of Elisha the Prophet

In addition to Shields's feminist reading, and to the development of the "historical scenario" especially in the Coote volume, this essay has a third important root in recent scholarship. In his recent book, *Elisha and the End of Prophetism*, Wesley Bergen shows how the career of Elisha, at least as it is depicted up to 2 Kgs 8:6, lacks any coherent purpose and descends into futility.

From his first appearance, Elisha appears to have his life's script written for him. According to 1 Kgs 19:15–17, Elijah was to anoint Elisha his successor (see 2 Kgs 2:1–14), and to anoint Hazael as king of Syria and Jehu as king of Israel. The latter two tasks remaining undone by Elijah, Elisha inherits them. He turns to these tasks immediately after 2 Kgs 8:6: he anoints Jehu (9:6) and is involved in the rise of Hazael (though he doesn't anoint him; 8:7–15).

Elisha's script implicitly includes continuing the conflict with King Ahab, with his sons Ahaziah and Jehoram, who both become king, and especially with Queen Jezebel. Ahab and Ahaziah die before Elisha's career really begins. Jezebel and J(eh)oram do indeed die, in accordance with the script, as the direct result of Elisha's anointing Jehu (9:14–37). Jehoram is presumably the king with whom Elisha interacts in some of the stories in 2 Kgs 3:4–8:6.

Others have noted how Elisha's actual career diverges from the script written for him, but Bergen is the first to investigate the matter

---

[8] With a little imagination we might go on to connect also the woman's rejection of a child with the "historical scenario." Perhaps she is practising revolutionary abstinence, avoiding having children in order better to serve the cause of resistance.

using a sophisticated narratology and with a specific focus on Elisha as a character. Literary-feminist reading of the Shunammite and the sociopolitical study of the ninth century BCE have not been in close touch with each other, and Bergen's is in fact the only work really in touch with both camps.[9] Although his interests do not lead him to attend very closely to the social science dimension, he writes with a general sense of the "historical scenario." In the following summary I stress the scenario more than Bergen does, but without adding anything in principle to his work.

From the point where Elisha takes up Elijah's mantle (2:13) there is little indication that he is following his prescribed mission until it suddenly resumes at 8:7 and then moves swiftly to its conclusion. Before 2 Kgs 8:7 there is no reference to Baal worship as a problem, and only oblique reference to Jezebel (Bergen, 1999:175). When Elisha interacts with the king of Israel, the king is given no name, so we are not directly reminded of the conflict with the house of Ahab.

Lacking the purpose for which he was chosen, claims Bergen, Elisha's story up to 2 Kgs 8:7 loses *any* sense of purpose. He has no prophetic mission, merely an "ability to do unnecessary miracles" (104). His itineracy becomes an aimless wandering about (90). Bergen notes the absence of Yahweh from these stories (175).

Elisha's wonder-working becomes bifurcated. His "miracles are alternately set within the world of the kings . . . or the people of Israel . . . or a combination of the two worlds. . ." (175). He helps the needy and the sons of the prophets (4:1–7, 38–44; 6:1–7), but these miracles alternate in a purposeless way with others that happen in the world of kings and officials (3:4–27; 5:1–27; 6:8–7:20). Bergen tellingly says of 2 Kgs 8:4–5 that Elisha has become merely an "object of entertaining stories" to titillate the king of Israel (153).

These observations can easily be recast in terms of the "historical scenario." The miracles that benefit the needy fall within the scenario, while those performed for kings contradict it. Bergen provides the necessary exegetical underpinning to my sense that DH loses its way in these chapters. He himself concludes (177–78) that the Elisha stories shut off an option which they (along with the Elijah stories) appear to open up. Prophetic power might have become the

---

[9] In fact he first sketched his thesis in the Coote volume (Bergen, 1992). Rentería keeps feminism very much to the fore, but it is of a kind quite different from Shields's literary approach.

foundation of an alternative polity, but in fact Elisha ends up merely as more powerful than the king *within* the monarchical polity, and hence available for the service of kings.

In the terms of my earlier discussion, once monarchy is accepted in principle, it becomes too dangerous to present prophets as fundamentally opposed to it even in its most degenerate form. The Deuteronomists still glimpse, through the layers of their ideological compromise, the fact that to oppose *any* monarchy is to oppose *every* monarchy, and they draw back from the implication. If Elisha's sole purpose is to carry out a textual program which the text itself has lost its ability to sustain, how can his career *not* become futile?

Elisha's drift away from his script comes to an end exactly at 2 Kgs 8:6, the end of the Shunammite's story. Can we say with equal precision where the drift begins? Bergen traces it all the way back to 2 Kings 2. To my mind, however, chap. 3 must be treated differently. In this chapter Jezebel, though not a character, is at least alluded to, and in the most negative terms (vv. 2, 13). The king of Israel is sometimes given a name (3:1, 6, 8), emphasizing his connection to the house of Ahab, as he is not again until 8:16. Elisha attacks the king bitterly for the crimes of his parents (3:13–14). A comment by Long on 8:4 suggests a humorous extension of this last point. Long remarks that Gehazi's recital of Elijah's "great deeds" invites us to look back on "all of chs. 3–7" (1991b:98). But I surmise that Gehazi discreetly omitted chap. 3 from his recital, since it reflects so poorly on the very king to whom he is speaking![10]

Nothing up to 2 Kgs 4:12 is incompatible with the "historical scenario." Elisha may not have been following his script with any great precision, but nothing obliges us to think that he has abandoned it.[11] It is 4:12–13, where Elisha all at once keeps a servant and has influence with the king, that marks the decisive break with the script.

---

[10] It is true that Elisha expresses regard for the King of *Judah* (3:14), which does not square with the theoretical antimonarchism of the "historical scenario." This exemplifies the first level of the Deuteronomic compromise, judging kingship not by its merits as a system, but by whether it is Davidic.

[11] This analysis leaves out of consideration 2:19–25 and 4:1–7. There is no problem with 2:19–22 and 4:1–7, which fit the "historical scenario" (4:1–7 will in fact help my case at a later stage). 2:23–25, though it is exhibit A in the case for the pointlessness of some of Elisha's miracles, is at worst neutral in regard to the scenario.

The Narrative Necessity of the Female Character

Though the issues are a bit fuzzier at the beginning than at the end, I believe I have established that the space in which Elisha completely loses track of his mission is the exact narrative space of the Shunammite's story. When the story begins, the "historical scenario" is still intact; when it ends—just at the point where Elisha's mission ostensibly gets back on track—the scenario is in tatters. The collapse of the scenario happens in and through the defeat and diminishment of a powerful woman.

The woman's defeat is linked in the most obvious way with the issue of class. Her first appearance coincides with the raising of the class issue through the simultaneous appearance of the servant and the king (4:8–13; see my earlier summary). The corresponding final six verses (8:1–6) feature the selfsame characters. The servant and the king, in a wonderful levelling of class distinction, share a yarning session whose object and whose victim is the woman.

Why is the gender dynamic essential to the narrative process, and how is it linked to the class dynamic? We can answer this at a variety of levels. One kind of answer is unashamedly modernistic: to bracket gender equity in the quest for other kinds of equity is to lose any chance of achieving the other kinds. This answer is informed by such recent experience as the failures of socialism over gender issues. I make no apology for starting at this level; such modernistic statements function heuristically as a way into old texts, a way that was not open before the rise of feminist criticism.

Another sort of answer can be developed out of the literature of the "historical scenario." Rentería, who reads the Elijah-Elisha stories with reference to what we know of gender relations in societies like Israel, makes the following statement: "The Jehu military faction . . . headed up by male warriors, was unlikely to have been sympathetic to women in non-traditional roles and probably eager to restore members of that sex to their proper Yahwistic roles" (123–24). In this view, whatever equity the prophetic movement sought did not include gender equity. This casts severe doubt on the movement's revolutionary credentials: when it came to the crunch, keeping women down would be more important than raising the peasantry up!

I am sympathetic, for political reasons, to this line of inquiry, but am troubled by its overestimate, as it seems to me, of how much we really know about the ninth century. So I am interested in testing in this essay (and in my other work) the extent to which we may do an equally political reading of the Bible using different, narratological methods. I find it encouraging that my conclusion in this instance is quite compatible with Rentería's, though arrived at very differently.

The logic of the Shunammite's story, writ large, is the logic of the whole Elijah-Elisha cycle. Its message—as we have read it first by itself and then in relation to the larger narrative space which it defines—is as follows. When a strong woman appears, her diminishment takes precedence over other textual programs, including those related to class struggle. The men in the text, wherever they may stand in relation to class struggle, join forces to put down the woman. This exactly mirrors what happened at the outset of the Elijah-Elisha cycle, when the mission of the prophets—the fight for true religion and the fight for social justice—was turned into a crusade against the strong woman Jezebel. The battle *for* relief from the Omride kings lost its way as soon as it was conceived as a battle *against* a woman. The cycle falls to pieces over the gender issue *later* because it was misconceived in gender terms *from the beginning*. It should in no way surprise us that in Jezebel's narrative absence (between 2 Kgs 3:13 and 9:7) the character who comes most to the fore is a woman, a powerful woman. Utterly different as she is, the Shunammite is Jezebel's alias, for in the *real* battle being waged, the battle at a deeper level than the class struggle, *any* strong woman is *every* strong woman.

Once this alias is recognized, we can see other connections. The Shunammite's domination over her husband unmistakably reflects Jezebel's domination over Ahab. Even the emphasis on the woman as "mother" (4:19, 20, 30) plays off on Jezebel as "mother" (3:2, 13; 9:22). Another important connection is the theme of fertility. The "bad" religion for which Jezebel stands is "fertility" religion. The wonderful birth, death and resurrection of the Shunammite's son implies a counter-claim, on behalf of Elisha and Yahweh, to control human fertility. This last connection provides an approach to 2 Kgs 4:1–7 (whose status was left unclear by my discussion of chap. 3). This is another story about Elisha and a woman, a woman who is specifically said to be attached to "the sons of the prophets" (v. 1), and it also deals with fertility—this time vegetable fertility, the multiplication of the oil. Placed right before the Shunammite's story, it is a warm-up for the main event.[12]

Bibliography

Bergen, Wesley J.
    1992   "The Prophetic Alternative: Elisha and the Israelite Monarchy." Pp. 127–37 in *Elijah and Elisha in Socioliterary Perspective*. Ed. Robert B. Coote. Semeia Studies. Atlanta: Scholars Press.
    1999   *Elisha and the End of Prophetism*. JSOTSup 286. Sheffield: Sheffield Academic Press.

Coote, Robert B., ed.
    1992   *Elijah and Elisha in Socioliterary Perspective*. Semeia Studies. Atlanta: Scholars Press.

Culley, Robert C.
    1976   *Studies in the Structure of Hebrew Narrative*. Semeia Supplements. Philadelphia: Fortress Press; Missoula: Scholars Press.
    1992   *Themes and Variations*. Semeia Studies. Atlanta: Scholars Press.

Gottwald, Norman K.
    1993   "The Plot Structure of Marvel or Problem Resolution Stories in the Elijah-Elisha Narratives and Some Musings on *Sitz im Leben*." Pp. 119–30 in *The Hebrew Bible in Its Social World and Ours*. Semeia Studies. Atlanta: Scholars Press.

Jobling, David
    1986   *The Sense of Biblical Narrative: Structural Studies in the Hebrew Bible*. Vol. I. 2nd ed. Sheffield: Sheffield Academic Press.
    1998   *1 Samuel. Berit Olam*: Studies in Hebrew Narrative and Poetry. Collegeville, MN: Liturgical Press.

Long, Burke O.
    1991a   "The Shunammite Woman: In the Shadow of the Prophet?" *Bible Review* 7: 12–19, 42.
    1991b   *2 Kings*. FOTL 10. Grand Rapids: Eerdmans.

---

[12] I regret my failure, through inadvertence, to take account in this essay of another major contribution to the literary-feminist reading of my text: Fokkelien van Dijk-Hemmes, "The Great Women of Shunem and the Man of God: A Dual Interpretation of 2 Kings 4:8–37," pp. 218–30 in *A Feminist Companion to Samuel and Kings*, ed. Athalya Brenner (Sheffied: Sheffield Academic Press, 1994).

Rentería, Tamis Hoover
1992   "The Elijah/Elisha Stories: A Socio-cultural Analysis of Prophets and People in Ninth-Century B.C.E. Israel." Pp. 75–126 in *Elijah and Elisha in Socioliterary Perspective.* Ed. Robert B. Coote. Semeia Studies. Atlanta: Scholars Press.

Shields, Mary
1993   "Subverting a Man of God, Elevating a Woman: Role and Power Reversals in 2 Kings 4." *JSOT* 58:59–69.

Todd, Judith A.
1992   "The Pre-Deuteronomistic Elijah Cycle." Pp. 1–35 in *Elijah and Elisha in Socioliterary Perspective.* Ed. Robert B. Coote. Semeia Studies. Atlanta: Scholars Press.

READING STORY IN JUDGES 1

Susan Niditch

Introduction

The careful and creative work of Robert Culley always reminds me of Shakespeare's line, "The play's the thing." Sensitive to methodological issues, critically aware of new and old trends in the study of biblical literature, Culley urges us to engage with the story first, its language, content, patterning, and theme. In this regard, Culley walks in the footsteps of the influential Russian formalist Vladimir Propp. In analyzing tales, Propp was interested in their sociological setting, historical provenance, and implicit worldviews, but wrote that such matters cannot be addressed until a tale's "functions"—its plot or pattern of content—are understood (1968:15–16; 1984:11, 50, 110, 115). Too often, however, scholarship on Judges 1 has not begun with questions about the story but with questions about the history behind it, questions about purpose, polemic, setting, and world-views.

Previous Scholarship

Approaches to Judges 1, of course, relate to and run in tandem with questions about the book as a whole. Joshua and Judges have frequently been considered quintessential contrasting portrayals of the way in which Israel established itself in the land. It is suggested that Joshua presents a sweeping, linear, totalistic conquest that rids the land of unfit enemies, emptying it out for the allotment of tribal portions, but Judges portrays Israelite progress as more halting and patchy, a series of gains and losses as Israelites vie with others for control. A cursory reading of Judges 1 might seem to match it with the latter model. The question then follows as to which of these models has greater historical validity, with many suggesting that Judges 1 is of some value in this regard. Wright finds reliability in traditions about the cities at 1:27–33 and concerning Bethel (107–8), though his main interest is in the historical value of Joshua 10. Soggin writes, "it is clear that the fragmentary account is the one closest to the events, though that does not mean we should fall into a false sense of security and think that we have a text which is ancient and homogenous in all its parts" (26; see also Gurewicz: 38; Gray: 188–89, 194).

Some still looking for history in the "story" of Judges and Joshua (without reading story as a story or asking what the story really is) see Judges 1 as following Joshua in a historically or chronologically sequential fashion. First comes initial military success, then difficulty at keeping control of lands.

> The problem of the conquest is not solved, therefore, by the mere denial of the historicity of Josh 10:20ff on the ground of its assumed conflict with Judges 1. On the contrary, there is much to be said for the essential accuracy of the Deuteronomic tradition concerning the conquest: namely, that there was a campaign by Joshua which achieved an amazing success in attacking certain key Canaanite royal cities but that there was also a long period of struggle for possession which continued after Joshua's death. (Wright: 114)

While Lawson Younger separates himself from judgments concerning historical reliability, he suggests that Joshua and Judges are portraying such a typical war pattern (227).

In the work of such scholars concerned less with historicity than with historiographic orientation, additional emphases emerge. However, in this case as well, scholars tend to leap too quickly to conclusions about the ancient author's purpose, setting, and worldview without close enough attention to the story. Noting that Judah seems more successful than the other tribes in Judges 1, Brettler finds a pro-Judean orientation (see also Sweeney: 526–27; O'Connell: 3, 7). The view in Judges 1 is often matched with the pro-monarchic or pro-Davidic orientation that scholars claim to find in the book as whole. Some find a "late" (Auld: 285), Deuteronomic or priestly (Van Seters: 338–42) orientation governing the chapter as a whole, often with appropriate theological implications about moral decline.[1] Sweeney points in particular to a polemic against northern Ephraim in the chapter and against Bethel in the Book of Judges as a whole (527–28).

But what is the story? First, is Judges 1 a whole, a single story in some sense? Is it a set of little stories or a collection of allusions to stories, a series of tags or annal entries? Auld, for example, treats the chapter as a collection of derivative snippets or commentaries based upon similar material in Joshua joined with the more self-standing stories about Adoni-bezek, Achsah, and the founding of Luz (276, 266), while Van Seters (338) and Sweeney (521) treat it as a whole with a particular polemical *tendenz*. Is Judges 1 to be regarded as the introduction to the book of Judges and part of that story? Is it rather a bridge between Joshua and Judges and to be regarded as part of this more extended narrative? However one draws the boundaries of Judges 1, one has a somewhat different story. Such questions matter. There is, for example, a big difference in the story if it ends with the boundary of the Amorites at 1:36 or with the scene at Bochim in chap. 2 (2:1–6).

For heuristic purposes, like Van Seters (338) and Sweeney (521) we will begin by exploring the composition in 1:1–36. It certainly works as a whole on one level, opening with Israelite conquests, closing with the boundaries of the Amorites that demarcate the extent of that conquest. The disposition of each of the Israelite tribes has been accounted for in between. We recognize that the chapter functions in various narrative trajectories as the Bible now stands and that its many pieces can, in fact, be viewed as separable wholes, matters to which we will return. Taking our cue from Robert Culley, however, first we look at Judges 1 itself, its language, content, and pattern.

Language

Judg 1:1–36 is dominated by the recurring traditional language of military engagement and victory, found throughout Israelite war accounts: עלה, נכה, לכד, לחם םם. Explicit reference to the ban is found at 1:17, while formulaic phrases evocative of the ban are found at vv. 8 and 25 (cf. Josh 10:28; 11:11; Deut 13:16). Formulas indicating divine assistance are found at vv. 4, 19, and 22, "And the Lord gave . . . into

---

[1] See Klein: 29–30, who does not attach the supposed decline to questions of authorship.

their hands" (cf. Num 21:2, 3 and 22; Judg 11:21, 30); "And the Lord Judah with them," (cf. Gen 21:22, Exod 18:19, אלהים עמך; Deut 20:1, כי יהוה אלהיך עמך; see also Gen 26:3; Josh 1:9, 17; Judg 6:12; 1 Sam 20:13; 2 Sam 14:17, etc.). Terminology of dispossessing begins at v. 19, while a formulaic description of not dispossessing dominates vv. 27–35: "[Israelite tribe] did not dispossess [name of certain cities/ groups] and [the group] dwelled in their midst and became forced labor." The catalogue of victories and incomplete victories is punctuated in three places by an interesting vignette or cameo scene within the more annalistic frame (1:5–7 [Adoni-bezek]; 1:12–15 [Caleb and Achsah]; 1:23–26 [happy turncoat]). The story of the reconnaissance and the happy turncoat in vv. 23–26 has parallels in the traditional war lore of the Hebrew Bible, the tales of Rahab (Josh 2:1– 24; 6:22–25) and of David (1 Sam 30:11–15). In the story about Rahab and the brief report about the Egyptian informant, Israelite troops obtain the cooperation of a member of the enemy camp. This assistance, of course, furthers the warrior heroes' military aims but also as a literary device, formulaically marks the positive plans of the deity for Israel, approval and success in the offing. The tale of Achsah is found also in Joshua. The essential pattern of the warrior's wife- getting is found all over the world and in the Israelite tradition in the tale of David, Saul, and Michal (see 1 Sam 17:25; 18:17–27). These tales and the story of a captive Adoni-bezek exhibit the use of proverbial or formulaic language and internal repetition typical of the traditional literature of the Israelites. Note, for example, in 1:5–7 the repetition of the grizzly and dehumanizing portrait of the conquered king, his toes and thumbs cut off. As Adoni-bezek is treated, so he had treated his human conquests. Adoni-bezek's rhythmic lament in v. 7, literally, "As I did, so God has repaid me," underscores the theme of just desserts emphasized by the repetition. A comparable English proverb might be, "As you sow, so shall you reap."

Does the language suggest sources and or borrowings, for example, a victory source, a catalogue of incomplete victories, a tale source? Auld suggests that the author of Judges 1 may have quoted or reworked material now housed in Joshua 13–19 (276, 284) while Moore suggests a source shared by the two (5–6).

To be sure, Judges 1 contains traditional material that may have circulated in various settings and in variant forms: briefer or longer or differently nuanced versions of separable portions of content (e.g.

versions of tales of the founder of Luz or various stories about the exploits of the brother tribes Judah and Simeon); various combinations of the content now found in Judges 1 (e.g. a separately circulating catalogue of peoples set at forced labor by Israelite/Josephite tribes with or without tales of their exploits; versions leaving out the nice narrative vignettes about Adoni-bezek, Achsah's field, and the founder of Luz).

One need not merely speculate about some of the variants that existed in the tradition. Judges 1 and the wider biblical tradition give evidence of the variation, a variation we might add that is embraced and not harmonized away. Judges 1 itself contains three differing notices about the disposition of Jerusalem (1:7, 8, 21) and two different implied versions of the conquest of Hebron, one involving a leadership role for Judah at 1:10 and another for Caleb at 1:20. Caleb plays the role at Josh 15:13–14 and Joshua the role at Josh 11:21. The story of the conquest and disposition of Debir, involving Othniel, Caleb, and Achsah is found with slight variations at 1:11–15 and Josh 15:15–19. The biblical tradition also includes variants about the disposition of Hormah (Judg 1:17 versus Num 21:3). We also note that Judah's complaint about success in the hills and failure in the plain is Ephraim's formulaically described problem in Josh 17:16. Language of not dispossessing, of remaining in Israel's midst, and of the Canaanites being made into forced labor is shared by Judges 1 and Josh 17:12–13; 16:10.

In the light of these many variants, the question for us is not what is "borrowed" from whom or adapted from which source. The answers to such questions are always hypothetical because we have in preserved written form only a small finite slice of what must have been a much richer tradition available to composers. Such questions, moreover, may betoken a scholarly orientation inappropriate to the oral world mentality of multiplicity and variation that lies behind the Israelite tradition. Israelite narration as set in the Hebrew Bible is frequently not neatly linear. The world is created twice, as are man and woman; Abraham and Moses each experience God's call more than once with certain differences. Israelite writers have gathered these stories and scenes and linked them together; surely they were as capable as we in noticing repetition and contradiction. The versions are preserved and told often more in the style of anthology than single-stranded narration. And together they achieve a message, a story, the pieces of which sometimes bounce and bump up against one another, admitting to tensions in world-view that characterize Israelite culture and self-identity, their understanding of themselves and history. Often tensions are not resolved or harmonized, but are expressed. What we wish to ask is what are these particular, traditionally expressed pieces of content as here joined together saying as story, and what are they not saying. Are the pieces being expressed and used a certain way here to serve a particular polemic? What is the governing myth? Does the myth in Judges 1 differ from that of Joshua or frame Judges in a certain way? To explore these questions one needs to take a closer look at possible polemics and sources in the story.

The Story: A Closer Look

The chapter begins with the death of Joshua, a piece of content that frequently worries source and redaction critics because he seems to pop up in 2:6 alive, to die again in 2:8, and be buried in 2:9. Such an apparent case of Homer's nodding is, however, a feature of the preserved written tradition of Israel. Who killed Goliath, David or Elḥanan (Gunn: 23)? Why does Samuel not die after his testament scene (1 Samuel 12); he dies chapters later after his cue (1 Sam 25:1). Bumpiness of this kind is generally attributed to an awkward combining of sources. One might suggest rather that such bumpiness is an integral characteristic of a particular episodic style in Hebrew Scriptures. Such a theory allows that many pieces of Scripture would have had a living context in some form apart from the current arrangement, and it respects the "plot" of each piece apart from the whole.

At the same time, we must be alert to the webs of meaning, expressiveness, and form which frame and connect slices of tradition, the pieces of Scripture, the Tradition with a capital "T." The death of the leader is an important recurring motif in Hebrew Scriptures that often marks a watershed, a new period, a new sort of leadership, or a new set of challenges. It is thus throughout the tradition, as formula and content mirror political realities.

The phrase, "And it was after the death of so and so," is found at Judg 1:1 in reference to Joshua and at Josh 1:1 concerning Moses, so that the beginning of the Book of Judges parallels that of Joshua, and the life story of Joshua parallels that of Moses (as so often in the biographies, e.g. the detail at Exod 3:5 and Josh 5:15). This formulaic marker is found also at Gen 25:11 (concerning Abraham), at Lev 16:1 (concerning the sons of Aaron), and at 2 Sam 1:1 (concerning Saul), (see also variants at Judg 8:33; Gen 50:15; Judg 9:55). At Judg 1:1 an author within the tradition employs the death of leader formula to signal that what follows is a significant phase in the life of the people.[2]

The narrative introduction at 1:1, the note of Joshua's passing, and the need to find replacement leadership, however, might well provide the opportunity for an author to endorse a particular variety of polity. The case that emerges from a close reading, however, again is more complicated than simple polemics allow. Verse 1 formulaically indicates request for a divine oracle (See 1 Sam 22:10; 23:2; 28:6; 30:8; 2 Sam 2:1; 5:19, 23; 1 Chr 14:10, 14; Judg 20:18, 23, 27; 1 Sam 10:22) and is often found in war contexts, for example, in Judges 20 (vv. 18, 23, 27), a telling of the civil war between Benjamin and Israel. The oracle responds that Judah is to go first. This indication of primacy is taken as significant by those in search of a pro-Judahite or pro-Davidic polemic, for God says he has given the land into his (Judah's) hand. In v. 3 comes the offer of cooperation from Judah to Simeon, suggesting that the ancient historiographer imagines a kind of league between tribes, tribes ethnically linked by tradition as sons of Leah.[3] This section of the annals thus cannot be used to see a negative moral assessment from a Deuteronomic or other writer. What of the cameo of Adoni-bezek (vv. 5–7)? The story here seems to say that power is ephemeral; kings come and kings go. Adoni-bezek acknowledges this ironically with a proverb about just desserts, one which also points to God's role as arbiter.

Verses 8–11 refer to Judah's victories and then concentrate on the story of the conquest of Debir by Othniel who wins a bride for his efforts (vv. 12–15), a plucky one at that in the MT tradition, a fully traditional tale found twice in Scripture (see also Josh 15:15–19). As

---

[2] The reference point of 2:7 within the book is simply different, an allowable reprise that is not an aesthetic affront, but well within the boundaries of biblical narrative style.

[3] L. Klein's suggestion that Judah here disobeys the letter of God's command at v. 2 (in asking for assistance rather than going alone) is belied by the clear indication of divine favor at v. 4, "and Yahweh gave the Canaanites and the Perrizites into their hands (23)."

noted above, the pattern of the story is found in the story of Saul/David as well, as David must defeat Philistines to earn his wife (1 Sam 17:25; 18:17–27). In the MT version, the tale, like that of Adoni-bezek, seems a comment on the serendipitousness and unexpected movability of power. In this case, the power is between men and women, fathers and daughters, daughters and husbands. Achsah demands the pools after having instructed her fiancé to demand land. Another tag or annal at v. 16 refers to the Kenites' relationship to Moses and their moving to the wilderness of Judah. Next comes the announcement of the brother tribes' victory over Hormah (see above on variants) and of Judah's victories over three Philistine cities.

All of this looks positive for Judah to be sure, but the story punctuated as it is by vignettes with larger thematic significance about the vagaries of power does not make for overt or triumphalist propaganda especially given alternate versions of v. 18 and what follows in v. 19. While the MT v. 18 can be seen as a fulfillment of God's promise at Josh 13:6 eventually to displace the five rulers of the Philistines listed as unconquered at Josh 13:3, Old Greek and Old Latin manuscripts of Judg 1:18 agree with the MT of Josh 13:3 and Judg 3:3 that these cities are not conquered. Clearly various ancient Israelite audiences received the textual tradition as preserved in the Old Greek and related traditions. For them, the pro-Judean theme would be quite tempered. Brettler notes that versions of certain victories mentioned in Joshua and Judges tend to highlight Judah's role here, for example, Judah in Hebron (Judg 1:10) versus Joshua (Josh 11:21), though Caleb is also featured at Judg 1:20; Judah bans Jerusalem (1:8) whereas in Josh 15:63, Judah does not drive out the Jebusites and in Judg 1:21, it is Benjamin who cannot drive out. Yet what is to be made of the fact that Joseph's failure in the valley in Josh 17:16, 18 is applied to Judah in Judges (1:19) with a variation on the same formulaic language involving the chariotry excuse! Surely, a Judean writer who purposefully makes the sort of changes suggested by Brettler would keep the failure in the valley applied to the North. Indeed, the larger tradition admits of a theme of Israelite victory in the hills and defeats in the plain. In describing Ahab's confrontation with the Aramaeans, the biblical report declares that the servants of the king of Aram regard the geopolitical and military situation as follows:

Gods of the hills are their gods. For this reason they are stronger
than we. But if we fight them on the plain, see if we don't turn out to
be stronger than they. (1 Kgs 20:23)

This is a vicious untrue rumor to be sure, as the Aramaeans soon
learn, but the formulaic declaration about the hills may hold more than
a little historical truth. Finkelstein and others read the archaeological
evidence to suggest that Israel's earliest settlement region actually was
in the central highlands, the hills of Ephraim and to a lesser extent
those of Benjamin and Judah (81; see also Mazar: 350–51).

The least we can suggest is that something much more
interesting and complex is going on in Judges 1 than a pro-Judean
polemic, be it a product of the southern monarchy in its heyday or of a
later writer pining for a Davidic ideal. Further proof is provided by the
tale of the founder of Luz. A block of material dealing with victory is
followed by some equivocation in 1:19–21, but references to inability
to win is followed by a tale of complete success by the sons of Joseph.
A formulaic marker of divine approval (1:22; see above) is followed
by the scene involving the founder of Luz. The helpful turncoat always
indicates a positive war result for those he encounters and so it is
inaccurate to suggest that all goes poorly for the North and that they
are somehow being put in their place by Southern writers. Indeed, in
its current use and setting the tale of the founder of Luz points to an
acknowledgment of the way in which power and control fluctuate. His
people are displaced by the sons of Joseph and he then goes off to
found a city in the land of the Hittites. One Luz is gone, another
established. The vision in Judges 1 in contrast to the outlying portion
of Joshua is of non-absolute human power, a theme reinforced by all
three vignettes. In this respect, as Moore and others have noted, Judges
and material in Joshua 13–17 contrast with threads that dominate in the
beginning and end of the book of Joshua such as 21:43–44 and 11:16–
23 with their absolute certainty about total successful conquest.

Chapter 1 of Judges follows waves in vv. 18–26 of more and
less success with uniformly framed indicators of incomplete success,
but even in these cases only Dan suffers, described as oppressed
(pressed) by the Amorites (1:34). Again they, like Judah earlier in the
chapter, are described as limited to the hills and unable to expand into
the plains. All of the other northern tribes do not eliminate their
enemies "who dwell among them," they do not disinherit them, but

they do subjugate them. Where is the consummate failure? Where is the theological indication of why they do not fully eliminate the enemy? It is simply not in the story of Judges 1.

Rather, a writer presents what is believed to be a history of Israel's take over of the land, one that may jibe in some respects with the actual archaeological record (early Israelite presence in hills) if not with any of the specific theories of the conquest, infiltration, revolution, or pioneer settlement models. The writer clearly believes there was an attempted conquest. He pays service to the ideology of the ban (1:17; see also vv. 8, 25). In this he shares a world-view with Joshua, but the author of Judges treats the coming into the land in a less totalistic fashion than the Joshua envelope, perhaps more realistically dealing with the fact of the existence of a large northern Canaanite population throughout the period of the monarchy and later. Indeed, Judges 1 reflects the disposition of the land's population without making value judgments concerning Israelites' worthiness to conquer. Power fluctuates; control of land is not permanent nor is political power. This is what the language and content reveal when one reads Judges 1 as story.

The Larger Tradition

How does this story fit in the larger Israelite tradition as preserved in Hebrew Bible? Its open endedness, its lack of overt polemic, allows it to be interpreted various ways. On one level the stories of incomplete success can be integrated into the recurring biblical and ancient Near Eastern theme linking military success with divine approval. Displeasure of the gods brings failure; displeasure is often caused by some sort of moral failing however that is defined, whether disloyalty to the god or inhumanity to humans. Witness the Moabite king's confessions concerning Kemosh:

> Omri was king of Israel, and he oppressed Moab for many days because Kemosh was angry with his country. (trans. Jackson: 97)

This theological frame helps to structure tales of the judges and dominates the book as a whole: Israel sins, is politically oppressed as punishment, and calls out to God who then raises a savior, the "judge." This theme is not found in the story of Judges 1 itself but such a theme may be seen to shine back upon chap. 1 from the larger book or be seen to reflect the covenantally rich speeches and scenes in Joshua. The theme linking divine approval or disapproval with military outcome is certainly emphasized in the Hebrew Bible as a whole and in the Book of Judges, beginning with the scene at Bochim in chap. 2. More interesting, however, are the contradictions and tensions that reside in Joshua-Judges, reflecting tensions in the tradition as a whole, in Israelite world-view and sense of self.

Conquest: Totalistic or Not

There are two views of an Israelite occupation of the land in Hebrew Scriptures, but as others have noted it is not a Joshua versus Judges picture. Rather the book of Joshua itself presents side by side views of a centrally led, Israel-wide, totalistic conquest and a more tribally concerned, halting process of occupation.

Josh 10:40 refers to Joshua's defeat of the whole land, hill country and the Southland and the lowland—all their kings, leaving nothing alive as God commanded. Joshua is the leader of all Israel, his success complete (see 11:10–12, 16–20, 21–23). In chap. 13, however, are references to unconquered lands (2–6), and 13:13 refers to Israel's inability to drive out certain groups "who dwell in Israel to this day." As allotments or inheritances of each tribe are described, the author moves to a tribe by tribe, rather than Israel-wide orientation, and one is made to see that the tribes or individuals within them such as Caleb or Othniel have to take control of what is theirs; total success in these central chapters of Joshua as in Judges is not complete. (See, for example, Josh 15:63; 16:9, 10; 17:12, 16.)

In chaps. 13–17, the references to less than total conquest, like those in Judges 1 with which these passages share content and language (cf. Judg 1:19 and Josh 17:16; Judg 1:27–28 and Josh 17:12–13; Judg 1:29 and Josh 16:10; Judg 1:21 and Josh 15:63) are without the theological value judgment found in the strongly covenantal passages of Joshua and Judges usually attributed to Deuteronomic writers. In these annals the author blames chariotry and not moral weakness for shortcomings when he assigns blame at all (see Judg 1:19 and Josh 17:16).

Like Joshua, Judges 1 mixes images of uniform conquest with those of incomplete disinheritance. The sweeping success of the first half of the chapter joins with stories of subjugation rather than annihilation. In the inherited tradition as a whole, such wavering indicates a fundamental tension in Israelite world-view. It is believed that God has promised Israel the land of milk and honey. The group's myth includes such promise of the land. If so, what are the Canaanites still doing there? The totalistic conquest that in Joshua is set beside the more halting version is a kind of exercise in wish-fulfillment. The book of Judges wrestles with the same problem, what Geertz describes as a contradiction between the way things ought to be and the way they are (100–102). Theological explanations that frame Judges dominate in the book's current form, as military or political setbacks are punishment for breaking covenant, but the excuses offered are several and varied as Israelites chew over this essential contradiction between the promise and reality, a contradiction that held one way or another for virtually all of Israel's history. Does Israel fail because of the better weaponry mentioned in chap. 1? Is the enemy left in the land to test Israel's covenant faithfulness (Judg 2:20–23; 3:4) or is it to give experience of war to those who had no previous experience (Judg 3:1–2)?

Political Models

A second contradiction dealt with in Judges 1 and found throughout that book and the larger tradition involves the clash between two concepts of polity, one centralized based on common ties to a leader or state, one decentralized based on perceived kinship bonds.

We have noted in Joshua the model of a unified Israel under Joshua interrupted by issues having to do with tribal claims. So too in Judges 1. Judah is shown as leader tribe having primacy at the opening, a role that is not found after v. 18. A Judah-led duo gives way to a tribe by tribe accounting. "House of Joseph" in vv. 22–26 gives way to a discussion of Manasseh, Ephraim and the rest of the tribes. In Judges as a whole, a polity of state versus a polity of tribes is a recurring concern and here is where the supposed pro-monarchic or pro-Davidic theme becomes so murky. Gideon, contrary to the views of Klein (63, 67–68) and Sweeney (524), is portrayed as an essentially good leader who like Moses, Aaron, and David suffers a lapse in covenant faithfulness (the ephod business). He is a humble lad called by God in a powerful theophany. He bravely overthrows the altar of Baal and continues to receive divinely sent signs of pre-ordained success. He triumphs in war against Israel's enemies giving Israel peace for forty years, dies at a ripe old age and is buried with his ancestors. Note the reference at the end of his biography (8:35) to "all the good he had done for Israel." It is shown to be a positive trait of this hero that he refuses kingship and dynasty. Speaking in the voice of the anti-monarchic *tendenz* in the tradition, he declares, "I will not rule you nor will my son rule you. Yahweh rules you (8:23)." Only his evil son Abimelech establishes a monarchy in a bloody coup. The gruesome tale of Abimelech who is defeated ignobly at the hands of a woman (9:43) and the parable of Jotham (9:7–15), a traditional tale type, subversive and anti-monarchic at its very root, can be read as extremely critical of kingship. The framer of the tales of Gideon and his son is aware of how easily this form of polity becomes oppression and treachery. To this composer, as to the authors of 1 Samuel 8, 12 and Deuteronomy 17, monarchy is at best a necessary evil. Where is the positive pro-monarchic polemic in Judges as a whole? The recurring refrain, "In those days there was no king in Israel; each person would do what was right in his eyes" (Judg 17:6; 18:1; 19:1; 21:25), does punctuate events that are considered to be troubling or clearly irregular, from a particular Yahwistic perspective, but the refrain is a thin reed upon which to rest a theory concerning a pro-monarchic (Lasine), pro-Judean (Brettler, O'Connell) or anti-Ephraimite (Sweeney) polemic. What if this formula marks not an implicitly pro-monarchic polemic but is a way of declaring events to belong to a long-ago past? This interesting set of myths is in fact used to wrestle with long-standing tensions in the tradition even while the tales are a bit unorthodox or embarrassing from a particular, strict Yahwistic perspective that we associate with Deuteronomic writers.

 And yet to suggest that the author(s) of Judges are critical of kingship rather than polemicizing for it and that the pro-Judean outlook is less apparent than others have asserted is not to suggest that the authors are fully supportive of more non-centralized modes of governance. Complications and disappointments emerge in attempts to call up tribes for group defense (e.g. Judges 5) and in disputes about participating in battles in order to win booty (Judges 8). Such scenes point to the problems inherent in a decentralized political system that relies on temporary charismatic leadership. The tale of murder, vengeance, and civil war in Judges 19–21 deals centrally with issues of loyalty. Does Benjamin join a pan-Israelite community to root out evil-doers or do they try to protect the men of Gibeah, their kin? Should Israel cut off Benjamin or help to preserve their name in Israel? All of these are issues concerning what constitutes unity or wholeness. Such questions are not answered neatly in Judges but ambiguously as authors waver back and forth or remain on the fence.

Judges 1 beautifully reflects and expresses these essential ambi-valences in Israelite identity through the use of vignettes and historio-graphic annal lines expressed in the traditional-style language of ancient Israelite tradition. The chapter is not simple propaganda, but a bridge between Joshua and Judges and a complex expression of Israelite historiography, a mythography admitting of tension and multiplicity, a window on its author's views of the past that relate to his own perception of reality.

The story of Judges 1 is complicated, a microcosm in many ways of the larger slice of Israelite tradition that surrounds it. A close, careful look at Judges 1 as story leads one to appreciate the multi-facetedness of the material and to try to understand its tensions and self-contradictions, for to understand and accept these is to begin to understand an Israelite's own view of his people's history and identity.

Bibliography

Auld, A. G.
 1975 "Judges and History: A Reconsideration." *BT* 25:261–85.

Boling, Robert
 1975 *Judges: Introduction, Translation, and Commentary.* AB 6A. Garden City, NY: Doubleday.

Brettler, Marc
 1989 "The Book of Judges: Literature as Politics." *JBL* 108:395–418.

Culley, Robert C.
 1976 *Studies in the Structure of Hebrew Narrative.* Semeia Studies 3. Missoula: Scholars Press.

Finkelstein, Israel
 1985 "Response." Pp. 80–83 in *Biblical Archaeology Today.* Ed. A. Biran. Jerusalem: Israel Exploration Society.

Geertz, Clifford
    1973   "Religion as a Cultural System." Pp. 87–125 in *The Interpretation of Cultures*. New York: Basic.

Gray, John
    1967   *Joshua, Judges and Ruth*. The Century Bible. London: Nelson.

Gunn, David
    1990   "Threading the Labyrinth: A Response to Albert B. Lord." Pp. 19–24 in *Text and Tradition. The Hebrew Bible and Folklore*. Ed. Susan Niditch. Atlanta: Scholars Press.

Gurewicz, S. B.
    1959   "The Bearing of Judges i-ii on the Authorship of the Book of Judges." *Australian Biblical Review* 7:37–40.

Jackson, Kent
    1989   "The Language of the Mesha Inscription." Pp. 96–130 in *Studies in the Mesha Inscription and Moab*. Ed. Andrew Dearman. Atlanta: Scholars Press.

Klein, Lillian
    1989   *The Triumph of Irony in the Book of Judges*. JSOTSup 68. Sheffield: Almond.

Lasine, Stuart
    1984   "Guest and Host in Judges 19: Lot's Hospitality in an Inverted World." *JSOT* 29:37–59.

Mazar, Amiliar
    1992   *Archaeology of the Land of Israel*. New York: Doubleday.

Michalowski, Piotr
    1983   "History As Charter: Some Observations on the Sumerian King List." *JAOS* 103:237–48.

Moore, George Foote
    1895   *Critical and Exegetical Commentary on Judges*. ICC. Edinburgh: T. & T. Clark.

O'Connell, Robert H.
    1996   *The Rhetoric of the Book of Judges*. Leiden: Brill.

Propp, Vladimir
    1968   *Morphology of the Folktale*. Austin: University of Texas Press.
    1984   *Theory and History of Folktales*. Trans. A. Martin and R. Martin. Ed. A. Liberman. Theory and History of Literature 5. Minneapolis: University of Minnesota Press.

Soggin, J. Alberto
    1981   *Judges: A Commentary*. Trans. Jolin Bowden. London: Westminster.

Sweeney, Marvin A.
    "Davidic Polemic in the Book of Judges." *VT* 47:517–29.

Van Seters, John
    1983   *In Search of History: Historiography in the Ancient World and the Origins of Biblical History.* New Haven: Yale University Press.

Wright, G. Ernest
    1946   "The Literary and Historical Problem of Joshua 10 and Judges 1." *JNES* 5: 105–14.

Younger, K. Lawson, Jr.
    1994   "Judges 1 in Its Near Eastern Context." Pp. 207–227 in *Faith, Tradition, and History. Old Testament Historiography in Its Near Eastern Context.* Eds. A. R. Millard *et al.* Winona Lake: Eisenbrauns.

ICELANDIC AND ISRAELITE BEGINNINGS
A COMPARATIVE PROBE

Norman K. Gottwald

The pertinence of aspects of Icelandic culture for understanding the literature and society of ancient Israel has long been cited in biblical studies, but only on a few limited points. Particular attention has been paid to the Icelandic prose genre of "saga," a term extensively borrowed to describe certain of the history-like narratives in the Torah and Former Prophets (Gunkel: xxvii-lvi; Westermann: 30–35; Coats: 3–7). Also, a presumed oral stage in the development of Israelite laws has been compared to the oral preservation and recitation of Icelandic law. The so-called minor judges of Judg 10:1–5 and 12:7–15 have been construed on analogy with the Icelandic "lawspeaker" who was responsible for enunciating the corpus of Icelandic law in a triennial cycle at the annual convocation of the governing Icelandic assembly (Alt: 102–3; Noth: 103 n.1).

So far as this writer can determine, what has not been examined in any depth or detail is the way in which these points of comparison are situated in the respective societies of Iceland and Israel. It is a truism of comparative social and cultural studies that all comparisons of particular cultural items across cultures must take into account how the compared items are lodged contextually within their larger societies. Thus, my interest in this brief essay is two-fold: first, to provide some basic information on early Icelandic society that seems largely beyond the knowledge and interest of most biblical scholars; and second, employing the Icelandic-Israelite nexus as an exemplary case, to indicate both the ways in which hypothetical comparisons of societies may be illuminative and the cautions and caveats necessary to bring such comparisons under disciplinary control. It is not my intent to offer any firm conclusions about ancient Israel derived from the Icelandic experience, but rather to suggest how the Icelandic venture poses imaginative possibilities and promising lines of inquiry for biblical studies.

Because comparative social and cultural studies arose prominently within anthropology when that discipline was largely devoted to synchronic studies that looked at self-contained societies "frozen in time," cross-cultural comparison in biblical studies has inherited the habit of treating the compared elements by dislodging them, not only from their larger cultural contexts, but also by disengaging them from their historical trajectories. In fact, in making comparative judgements, macro-historical studies as a whole have grossly neglected both the histories of the societies compared and their interactions with other societies (Mann: 27–32, 518–41).

In other words, in comparative biblical studies there has been a crippling neglect of the labour of reading other societies and their histories. The hard work of becoming critically aware not only of the histories of such societies but also of the significant problems of interpretation of available material, social formation, and major debates about historical reconstruction is often not done in biblical studies. The issue, then, is one of knowing how to read another society properly so that comparison may be carried out in a productive manner. To be sure, this enlargement of the comparative task mandates an inquiry far beyond what can only be suggested here. Since the various scenarios of Israelite beginnings will be known to readers, this essay will not recapitulate them. With a focus on the lesser known Icelandic history and literature, selected aspects of Israelite origins will be discussed in the light of the Icelandic experience.

My reading of Icelandic history takes shape within the context of "a third wave" of Icelandic historical studies: the first wave took traditions at near face value, the second wave doubted almost everything the traditions claimed, and the third wave judiciously affirms a plausible cultural and social history anchored by a sequence of chronologically secure events such as the settlement, the establishment of self-government, subsequent modifications in legislative and judicial mechanisms, the introduction of Christianity, the writing down of the lawcode, the compilations of Old Norse mythology, the escalation of the blood feud, and the eventual acceptance of Norwegian sovereignty. This third wave, and my own reading, has been greatly informed by the juncture of new historiography and reflexive anthropology.

Icelandic Beginnings

The origins of Icelandic society can be pinpointed to a single moment in time, and its development through more than two centuries of oral culture can be traced with considerable confidence due to the subsequent blossoming of multiple specimens of various literary genres that supplement one another in conjuring up the pre-literary past. While none of the documents adhere to the strictest canons of modernist historiography, they do provide a reliable historical outline and they richly attest to the ethos and the institutions of the early settlers. Building on the chronologies, lists of settlers and officials, settlement locations, and cited public events in *The Book of the Icelanders*, written by Ari Thorgilsson ca. 1122 CE (Hermannsson: 1–46), and in *The Book of Settlements*, composed shortly thereafter (Palsson and Edwards: 1–13), a network of cross-references to laws, sagas, and ecclesiastical writings allows a surprisingly full and coherent reconstruction. The dates for the main developments in Icelandic history, while not absolutely demonstrable, are widely taken to be accurate within a variation of a few years at most.

Apart from a handful of Irish monks, Iceland was an uninhabited island in the North Atlantic when, between 870 and 930 CE, it was settled by some thousands of Norwegians who, according to tradition, left their homeland to escape the hegemony of King Harald, the Fair Haired, who was striving to bring all Norway under his rule. This migration was part of the Viking age, but unlike other Scandinavians who specialized in pillage and trade, the settlers of Iceland subsisted primarily on limited agriculture and predominant stockbreeding, supplemented by fishing, although in time they fully participated in the network of North Atlantic seafaring commerce that facilitated informational and cultural exchanges. In 930 CE, the Icelanders developed a decentralized form of legislative and judicial self-rule, generally known as the Commonwealth or Freestate, that persisted until 1262 CE when they accepted a treaty of union with Norway, and even then the commonwealth retained a measure of autonomy within Norwegian sovereignty (Johannesson). Iceland fell under Danish rule in 1380, and underwent four centuries of social and economic decline, until a movement for independence led to its creation as a sovereign state in 1918, still under the Danish crown, and finally to its declaration as the Republic of Iceland in 1944 (Lacy: 166–249 *passim*; Hastrup, 1995:107–15).

The earliest Icelandic society was organized around aristocratic families with local "strong men," who as chieftain-priests balanced one another's power by building alliances of followers with fluctuating membership. Successful migration had required seaworthy vessels with sufficient crews, supplies, and livestock, so that the social organization of the migrants around chiefs with extended families, dependent clients, and slaves was established as the foundation of Icelandic corporate life from its inception. The migrants may have numbered as many as 20,000, and the populace may have grown to 60,000 within a hundred years or so, figures that incidentally are roughly comparable to estimates of the early Israelite population at the beginning and close of the period of the Judges (Finkelstein: 30–35). The Icelandic laws, brought from Norway and modified to meet the new conditions, existed in oral form for nearly two centuries, until 1118 CE when they underwent codification. The governing body, known as the Althing, was an annual assembly of 36, later 39, leading chiefs drawn from the four quarters into which the land was divided in 963 AD, followed eventually by the addition of a fifth quarter. The assembly met annually for legislative and judicial purposes, in particular to rehearse the laws and to decide disputed cases that were not resolved in local and regional jurisdictions. There was no executive branch in the Commonwealth. The sole chief officer was known as the Lawspeaker whose responsibility it was to recite the accepted body of laws *in toto* over a three-year cycle at the annual meeting of the Althing. He was backed up by a panel of "experts" with whom he consulted in the event of dispute over the terms of particular laws (Byock, 1988; Meulengracht Sorensen: 17–73).

Alongside the law, there developed sagas, genealogies, and myths, all of them initially oral, which only began to be written down after some two centuries, beginning about 1100 CE, stimulated by the introduction of a literate Christian culture into Iceland. With the emergence of writing, there was a remarkable florescence of literary activity. Icelandic literati, situated at a moment of transition between oral and written knowledge, developed a pronounced intellectual culture that not only preserved the old traditions but added poetry, genealogies, chronicles and histories of their own.

Because Iceland had no natural resources that invited pillage, the land was spared the turmoil of war from abroad, although its internal fortunes were far from idyllic or non-violent. It remained an economy shaped by the strictures of an austere natural environment. Dominated by glaciers and volcanos, as little as one-fifth of the island could be cultivated, and the birch forests were soon exhausted. Fortunately, edible marine life was plentiful, and the climate, tempered by the Gulf Stream, allowed livestock to be left in the open most of the year. More threatening to internal stability was the custom of the blood feud, requiring compensation by retaliatory killing or payment by blood-money (Byock, 1982). The national council and the oral law served to restrain the blood feuds within bounds that prevented civil war, no doubt abetted by the fierce sense of independence that was the pride of chiefs and their clients. Nevertheless, after three centuries or so, the rough balance of chieftainships gave way to greater inequality of wealth and power and more savage feuding than the existing social and political mechanisms were able to contain. It was due to this mounting internal dissension and violence that Iceland turned to its country of origin and accepted Norwegian sovereignty toward the end of the thirteenth century (Sveinsson).

Icelandic religion was at first overwhelmingly, if not exclusively, Old Norse religion. Saga traditions claim that a few of the original settlers had accepted Christianity, but, if so, the Christian profession declined after settlement. The Old Norse mythology of the Icelanders was eventually collected and written down in the Edda, in both poetic and prose versions (Turville-Petre: 1–34). Local chiefs were priests who presided over sacrifice at modest shrines, often in a structure attached to a chieftain's estate. Lacking a differentiated priesthood with hegemonic claims, the Old Norse religion was part of the warp and woof of the general society. It stressed the virtues of familial honor, the nobility of individual achievement and devotion to civic duty, promised the rewards of good health and prosperity, and was haunted by a keen sense of the power of fate (Toorn). Christianity came to Iceland in force about 1000 CE, but for some time was rather loosely controlled from Rome. Although there were appointed bishops, local chiefs practiced what amounted to a lay priesthood alongside other priests trained on the continent, pagan shrines were converted to churches, and the coexistence and mixture of Old Norse and Christian elements was pronounced (Byock, 1988:137–64; Hastrup, 1985:179–89).

An Inter-Reading of Icelandic and Israelite Beginnings

The above extremely condensed account of Icelandic history, society, culture and religion provides a provisional basis to attempt some systemic comparisons with ancient Israel. Admittedly, such comparison can initially be no more than "a probe" to explore features that may be worthy of further research and theorizing. At a minimum, however, such a probe constructs a network of social historical processes and structures in which particular comparisons can be contextualized and in which the overall trajectories of the two peoples can be traced with full allowance for their distinctiveness as well as the points where they exhibit similarities that may be mutually illuminating.

The proper starting point for a comparison is doubtless the nature and status of the sources of our information. Literary and historical criticism of the Icelandic documents has followed a broadly similar course to that of biblical criticism. After an initial abounding trust in Old Icelandic traditions as historically referential, scholars grew severely skeptical that any preliterate Icelandic history could be reconstructed (Einarsson: 3–68). In recent years, a moderating position, prompted in large measure by developments in historiography and anthropology (Hastrup, 1985; Andersson and Miller; Turner), finds a very large measure of reliability in what the traditions relate about the circumstances of settlement, demographic composition of the settlers and their descendants, and the social, political, and religious structures of the populace. Although two centuries and more separated the founding events from the commitment of traditions to writing, there is considerable scholarly confidence that the outline of events, processes and structures during the initial oral phase is substantially correct as reported, although many details are doubtless misplaced, exaggerated, or even invented, and a certain "idealization" of the early heroic age must be allowed for (Meulengracht Sorenson: esp. 133–55).

Why such confidence in the historical worth of these traditions? For one thing, the patriarchal family structure pyramided into chiefly rule was committed to cultivating genealogical records. Also, the eventually codified oral law of the Althing "rings true" to the conditions described in sagas and chronicles. Furthermore, the records of Icelandic beginnings were never submitted to a single overarching set of religious interpretations, either Old Norse or Christian. Diverse religious practices and meanings are recounted within what remains an essentially "secular" history. The anecdotal information about various settlers and their descendants are colorfully mundane, for these early figures are not burdened with symbolic religious identities to be emulated by later generations. As "freemen" who departed their Norwegian homeland at a cost, the settlers are honored for their individuality and their conflicting admixture of noble and base character and behavior. Above all, however, *The Book of the Icelanders* and *The Book of Settlements* provide the kind of historical benchmarks that are not found in the episodic, often dischronologized sagas of Iceland and which serve to provide a context and anchor points for the wealth of details about customs and daily life in the sagas.

By comparison, literary and historical critics of ancient Israelite traditions have encountered grave, some would say insurmountable, obstacles to confidence in the historical reliability of the origin traditions. The primary difficulty is that the origin traditions have undergone systematic revision and editing from a much later perspective than was the case in Iceland, namely, only after Israel had passed through monarchic statehood to a scattered and then reconstituted peoplehood within great empires. This contrasts decisively with the commitment of Icelandic origin traditions to writing while its original decentralized commonwealth was still operative. This "reading back" of later Israelite-Jewish experience into the origin traditions proceeds within a unifying frame of reference that makes it extremely diffiult to establish coherent settings for texts that claim to tell us about earlier phases of Israelite history and culture. The effort to separate out more or less trustworthy traditions from this anachronistic framework has not produced generally agreed results (see the discussion of issues in Gottwald, 1993; 1997).

In terms of the basic narrative flow of the Hebrew Bible, Israel is pictured as a twelve-tribe unity from the exodus onward. Nonetheless, standing in pronounced tension with this premised unity of all-Israel, the traditions provide anecdotal information about the actions of individual tribes, subgroups and personages, as well as lists, annals, and poems, which do not blend with the alleged unity and which in many instances flatly contradict it. Again, by contrast, the Icelandic origin stories never allege that there was a single coordinated migration, but resolutely recount the movements and settlements of particular leaders and groups, beginning with Ingolf in 870 CE. The settler stock was composed of refugee Norwegians who in time developed a "national" identity within an experimentally evolved decentralized polity that did not depend upon a master plan provided by religion or by a single great leader. Iceland has no Moses or Joshua, and it has no covenant with Thor, the chief Norse deity, and the "Torah" it does have is of its own arduous creation. In short, the Israelite origin stories present problems of revisionist literary, historical and religious homogenization of a magnitude simply not encountered in the Icelandic origin stories.

It is essential, therefore, to realize that as narrative the two origin stories operate on different temporal axes, the Icelandic taking a shorter range view within the founding era, and the Israelite taking a longer range view from well beyond the founding conditions. Nevertheless, there are intriguing parallels between the anecdotes, genealogies, and lists in the two sets of traditions. These correspondences suggest that the decentralized social and political structures of early Iceland and early Israel may have had a good deal in common, even if the early Israelite situation is more difficult to discern through the heavy veil of late editing. Whenever they provide more than the bare information about genealogy, migration, and settlement, both the Icelandic accounts and the Israelite accounts love to dwell upon the experiences and exploits of particular leaders, on their bravado and foibles, on their struggles in gaining and losing land, on their rivalries and feuds, on cameo details of their daily lives and of their religious practices. In all the so-called historical books of the Hebrew Bible, and most especially in the book of Judges, these fragmentary and idiosyncratic literary fragments are poorly coordinated with the premise of a unified Israelite religion and polity. It is just such uncoordinated glimpses into Israelite beginnings, closely correspondent to the Icelandic accounts, that are most likely to retain original memories not altogether eclipsed by the revisionist retrojections of a later age. The great challenge is to disengage these potentially early Israelite memories from the late redactional frameworks in which they are set and to recontextualize them in plausible premonarchic settings.

To this interpreter, it is striking that Icelandic and Israelite beginnings are both described in retrospect as highly reactive to centralized politics. The official ideology of both sets of traditions is that the original settlers were fleeing from political oppression. This is patent for Iceland, since the precisely dated initial migrations from Norway to Iceland were undertaken to escape the rule of King Harald. The migrations are claimed to have been driven not by economic hardship or greed, but by a political determination to be "free men." In the case of Israel, our sources are of course more disputed, since Israelite beginnings are overlaid with totalizing comprehensive religious judgments of the sort that are absent from accounts of the Icelandic beginnings. It is clear, however, that the Torah identifies a massive Israelite reaction to Egyptian domination, and Joshua-Judges gives abundant testimony to hostility toward kingship and a preference for decentralized self-rule. However, just as the growth of social hierarchy in Iceland led to its voluntary submission to the Norwegian monarchy, so the eventual growth of unequal wealth and power in Israel, coupled with the Philistine threat, led to Israel's voluntary adoption of monarchy.

The emphasis on flight from King Harald's hegemony, while generally treated as credible, probably does not do justice to all the factors motivating the Icelandic settlers. We do find anecdotes about settlers who had fallen on hard times in Norway or had been involved in actual or suspected crimes. On a larger scale, land scarcity and overpopulation in Norway has been argued as the prime motivation for emigration, but with little evidence. Enterpreneurial hunger for new economic opportunity has also been proposed. By and large, however, it is not likely that the Icelanders expected to gain any immediate economic advantage by leaving Norway. Rather, what they seem to have hoped for was to be free of the levies on their resources that Harald sought to impose. In effect, they appear to have been gambling a momentary economic risk in exchange for an eventual economic return on their labor that would at least be equal to their fortunes in Norway. This return on their labor would actually be greater because they would be politically free to allocate the surplus on their own terms. Also, during the time of Icelandic settlement, Viking conquests in Britain, Ireland, and on the continent had suffered setbacks, so that Icelandic colonists are suspected to have included migrants from those regions. As far as can be seen, no quest for religious freedom was involved since the migrants in the majority carried their Old Norse religion with them and displayed tolerance toward the few Christians among them.

Beyond the expressed will to escape Egyptian oppression, the Israelite traditions picture Canaan as a desirably productive land when compared to the wilderness that had to be traversed to get there, but Canaan could not compare with the fertility of the Nile Valley. The point at issue is that Israel by gaining Canaan would be able to control its own production as it could not in Egypt. If, however, we take the point of view, which this writer favors, that Israel was largely constituted of people already in Canaan, many of whom migrated from the lowlands into the hill country, it is evident that the productive potential of the hill country was far less than that of the plains. But, once we add the political motivation to be free of the domination and the disintegrative chaos of the city-states concentrated in the plains, the political economic frontier of the highlands was an understandable lure, provided it could be mastered (Gottwald, 1981:489–587, 650–63). This probe of the two beginnings serves to underscore that economics is not a solitary isolated motivation but co-exists with politics in the form of political economy as a critical factor in shaping the behaviors and choices of people under duress. The capacity of a general movement toward political self-determination to encompass many additional motivations, some highly self-serving, appears plausible both in early Iceland and early Israel.

As it turned out, whatever motley assortment of motivations and factors brought the colonists together, the Icelanders crafted a unique form of decentralized rule that offered a viable oligarchic alternative to monarchy for several centuries and provided an ordered society within which the striving for power was modulated by custom and law. Whether such was ever the case in premonarchic Israel remains of course a matter of heated dispute. Lacking the actual information about an ordered Israelite tribal league, or amphictyony, of the sort envisioned classically by Martin Noth, it can at least be said that the congeries of biblical traditions about premonarchic tribal life, which in many respects correspond to the traditions about early Iceland, are of the sort that an intertribal confederation might best account for. This is not to say that a putative Israelite confederation will have been closely analogous to the Icelandic commonwealth. It is rather to say that the range of judicial, customary, social organizational and quasi-political agreements that seem to be shared by the Israelite tribes argues for regularized intertribal cooperation of some sort. To be sure, it is difficult to say if any of the biblical laws, so extensively redacted, actually stem from earliest times. Certainly the content of many of the laws in the Covenant and Deuteronomic Codes accord well with prestate conditions of life. It is also clear that a blanket objection that laws could not be sustained in oral form over decades and centuries is effectively countered by the Icelandic cultivation of the oral law.

Nonetheless, if such an intertribal confederation existed in early Israel, why is its foundation and constitution not set forth in the traditions? In this writer's judgment, the probable reason is that information about the overarching social organization of early Israel had grown dim or obscure over time and any curiosity about what its constitution might have been was short-circuited by the entirely different social and religious agenda of later Israelite-Jewish communities. On this issue the Icelandic experience is highly instructive. The Icelandic commonwealth was very familiar to its literary traditionists because the commonwealth was still in force when they wrote, preserving a living tradition across more than two centuries, and, moreover, maintaining a sharp distinction between the Old Norse and more recent Christian components. The mechanisms of Israelite inter-tribal cooperation were apparently already "dead history" when literary traditionists living in monarchic and colonial conditions gathered together what was remembered of a past now well beyond their own clear comprehension. Even so, the later Israelite-Jewish traditionists have passed on a remarkable assortment of odd vignettes and fragments of that premonarchic past, of such a vivid and "unorthodox" nature, compared to the standards of their time, that it seems impossible to believe that they could have fabricated them or, indeed, that they would have had any reason to do so.

The objection that there could not have been any sort of ordered intertribal Israelite polity because of the dissension and bloodshed between the tribes and the irregular, even outrageous, moral and religious behavior of early Israelite leaders is far from decisive when we observe that the very people who developed the precise formal structure of the Icelandic commonwealth were in frequent conflict and given to bloodshed that the commonwealth moderated and regulated but did not preclude. This sort of conflict of opposed interests among "equals" who lack a sovereign head is precisely what requires some formal structure and process to keep it from destroying the society. It is this double-edged endorsement of blood feud and its containment in Iceland that has been illuminated by the anthropological concept of resolving communal crisis by means of "social drama" (Turner). May not the same be true of the conflicts and containments articulated in the traditions of Joshua and Judges?

Finally, the religious fortunes of the Icelandic settlers may also offer some suggestive insights into early Israelite religion. Icelandic religion in its Old Norse and Christian forms is sorted out rather clearly in the early documentation. The "Christianization" of Iceland that sparked the writing down of the old traditions did not seek to efface or blur the Old Norse religious affiliations that were dominant before 1000 CE and which continued to play a large part in Icelandic culture. We have explicit references to the pre-Christian temples, sacrifices, sacred mountains, and to the priestly functions of the chiefs. On occasion, anecdotes about particular settlers and their descendants clearly identify them as adherents of Old Norse or of Christian faith. Sometimes the reports denigrate the Old Norse religion, but often they are entirely neutral and sometimes especially pious pagan worshippers are praised as men of virtue. The procedures by which Old Norse temples were converted to Christian churches and the chieftain-priests of the old religion became Catholic priests are recounted in straightforward manner. There is a sense that the two faiths were in competition without ever resorting to holy war on one another, and that for some decades an Icelander might easily convert from one to the other, and even practice elements of both faiths simultaneously. The fact that the old mythology was written down in the Edda under Christian auspices indicates that the Catholicism entertained by Icelanders was not only more tolerant of the religion it displaced than was the case in other regions of Christendom, but that the Old Norse religion was recognized as an intrinsically valuable part of the Icelandic heritage.

Icelandic moderation and pragmatism in religious matters is well illustrated by a report of Ari in *The Book of the Icelanders* concerning the negotiation and compromise through which Christianity was endorsed in the Althing in 1000 CE and brought into an essentially cordial alliance with commonwealth law and the structures of a decentralized polity. Thorgeir, lawspeaker at the time, citing the destructive wars between the kings of Norway and Denmark, told the Althing "that the people would be in a sorry plight if men in this land were not all to have the same law; and he remonstrated with them in various ways that they should not let this come to pass, saying that it would lead to disturbance, and that certainly it was to be expected that there would occur such fights between men that the land would be laid waste thereby." Ari goes on to quote directly the conclusion of Thorgeir's speech, "And now it seems advisable to me that we do not let their will prevail who are most strongly opposed to one another [those who wanted separate laws for Old Norse and Christian adherents], but so compromise between them that each side may win part of its case, and let us all have one law and one faith. It will prove true that if we sunder the law we will also sunder the peace" (Hermannsson: 66; Hastrup, 1985:183–86).

This rather extensively documented interplay of two religions is suggestive of what may have occurred in the instance of early Israelite religion. The Hebrew Bible of course gives the dominant impression that the Israelites who settled in Canaan were a people religiously unified in covenant with the God Yahweh. It further indicates that the cult of Yahweh was utterly hostile to all other cults and that insofar as Israelites were faithful to their religion they were fanatically opposed to any indulgence in or compromise with non-Yahwistic cults. On the other hand, the same traditions attest to abundant instances of Israelites engaged in worship of other deities, but always with the open or implied stigma that they were apostate in doing so. This revisionist stigmatization of whole tracts of early Israelite religion as "apostate" does not jibe with the undercurrent of the text, but seems more amenable, as in Iceland, to interpretation as a relatively peaceful competition among cults rather than all-out warfare. These religious practices, highly irregular from a late biblical monotheistic perspective, are attested over centuries of Israelite history until they finally diminish or disappear in the reconstituted Jewish community. Worship of female deities is reported in the biblical text, and archaeological finds indicate that in some circles Yahweh had a female consort, Asherah. To complicate matters further, various alternate names for Yahweh, especially El(ohim) alone or in compounds such as

El Shaddai or El Elyon, were names derived from the presumably forbidden cults. In short, there is mounting evidence that Yahweh was not the sole deity of Israel from earliest times, but one of a number of competing deities. Although Yahweh apparently held the advantage of being the official state deity of both Israel and Judah, monotheistic exclusivity developed very slowly, and only with full force after the fall of both states.

In sum, the results of this limited probe suggest some broad similarities between Icelandic and Israelites origins with respect to their revulsion at political centralization, their mixed patterns of agrarian/pastoral subsistence, their relatively loose social organization, their production of a rich variety of oral traditions, and their diversity of religious cults and practices. What stands out as a primary rupture in the comparison are the very different junctures in the historical trajectories of the two peoples when the oral origin traditions were committed to writing. For Iceland this literary ingathering of the origin traditions was early on, at a time when the fundamental conditions of the Old Icelandic commonwealth still prevailed, whereas Israel's literary ingathering of the origin traditions occurred only after the founding conditions had passed away and Israel had moved on, first to statehood and eventually to reconstitution as stateless enclaves of colonially dependent people. Had Iceland garnered its origin traditions on the same historical scale as Israel did, the Icelandic literary florescence would have occurred under late Danish rule during the stirrings for independence in the eighteenth and nineteenth centuries, and the Christian reading of the past would have severely truncated and obscured the Old Norse religious data. Given this reality, two contrary conclusions are possible. On the one hand, the circumstances of Icelandic traditioning may simply confirm us in the belief that Israelite beginnings have been obscured beyond all hope of recovery in the course of their late revision. On the other hand, we may employ the outlines of better known Icelandic beginnings to explore the social, political and religious implications of the undigested traces of Israelite beginnings that have managed to survive in the anecdotal, annalistic, and poetic fragments later Israelite and Jewish traditionists have preserved for us, even as they innocently or deliberately misconstrued them.

Bibliography

Alt, Albrecht
1966 "The Origins of Israelite Law." Pp. 81–132 in *Essays in Old Testament History and Religion*. Oxford: Blackwell.

Andersson, Theodore M. and William I. Miller
1989 *Law and Literature in Medieval Iceland*. Stanford: Stanford University Press.

Byock, Jesse L.
1982 *Feud in the Icelandic Saga*. Berkeley: University of California Press.
1988 *Medieval Iceland: Society, Sagas, and Power*. Berkeley: University of California Press.

Coats, George W.
1983 *Genesis with an Introduction to Narrative Literature*. Grand Rapids: Eerdmans.

Einarsson, Stefan
1957 *A History of Icelandic Literature*. Baltimore: Johns Hopkins.

Finkelstein, Israel
1988 *The Archaeology of the Israelite Settlement*. Jerusalem: Israel Exploration Society.

Gottwald, Norman K.
1981 *The Tribes of Yahweh: A Sociology of the Religion of Liberated Israel, 1250–1050 B.C.E.*. 2nd ed. Maryknoll: Orbis.
1993 "Recent Studies of the Social World of Premonarchic Israel." *Currents in Research: Biblical Studies* 1:163–89.
1997 "Triumphalist vs. Anti-Triumphalist Versions of Early Israel: A Response to Articles by Lemche and Dever in Volume 4 (1996)." *Currents in Research: Biblical Studies* 5:15–42.

Gunkel, Hermann
1917 *Genesis*. 4th Auflage. Göttingen: Vandenhoeck & Ruprecht.

Hastrup, Kirsten
1985 *Culture and History in Medieval Iceland: An Anthropological Analysis of Structure and Change*. Oxford: Clarendon.
1995 *A Passage to Anthropology: Between Experience and Theory*. London and New York: Routledge.

Hermannsson, Halldor, ed. and trans.
1930 *The Book of the Icelanders by Ari Thorgilsson*. Islandica 20. Ithaca: Cornell University Library.

Johannesson, Jon
1974 *A History of the Old Icelandic Commonwealth*. Winnipeg: University of Manitoba Press.

Lacy, Terry G.
1998 *Ring of Seasons: Iceland—Its Culture and History*. Ann Arbor: University of Michigan Press.

Mann, Michael
1986   *A History of Power from the Beginning to A.D. 1760*. Vol. 1.
        The Sources of Social Power. Cambridge: Cambridge
        University Press.

Meulengracht Sorensen, Preben
1993   *Saga and Society: An Introduction to Old Norse Literature*.
        Odense: Odense University Press.

Noth, Martin
1960   *The History of Israel*. 2nd ed. New York: Harper & Brothers.

Palsson, Hermann and Paul Edwards, trans.
1972   *The Book of Settlements: Landnamabok*. Winnipeg: University
        of Manitoba Press.

Sveinsson, Einar O.
1953   *The Age of the Sturlungs: Icelandic Civilization in the
        Thirteenth Century*. Islandica 36. Ithaca: Cornell University
        Press.

Toorn, M. C. van der
1955   *Ethics and Moral in Icelandic Saga Literature*. Assen: Van
        Gorcum.

Turner, Victor W.
1971   "An Anthropological Approach to the Icelandic Saga." Pp.
        349–74 in *The Translation of Culture: Essays to E. E. Evans-
        Pritchard*. Ed. T. O. Beidelmann. London: Tavistock.

Turville-Petre, E. O. G.
1964   *Myth and Religion of the North: The Religion of Ancient
        Scandinavia*. New York: Holt, Rinehart and Winston.

Westermann, Claus
1980   *The Promises to the Fathers: Studies in the Patriarchal
        Narratives*. Philadelphia: Fortress Press.

ON READING THE STORY OF THE MAN OF GOD FROM JUDAH IN 1 KINGS 13

John Van Seters

One of the most difficult stories in biblical prose narrative to read and interpret is this strange story of the man of God from Judah. The great diversity of readings of this tale, often contradicting each other, is testimony to this difficulty. My purpose in this piece is not to add one more such effort nor to review the many previous attempts,[1] but to suggest some reasons for the difficulties in reading this text and draw out some implications for the labour of reading in other parts of the Old Testament.

It seems to me rather obvious that the initial task in interpretation is to establish the limits of the story and the relationship that it has with its larger narrative context. Many studies limit the interpretation of the story to whatever lies within 1 Kgs 13:1–32 and assume that it was originally independent or that the redactional connections before and after are of little significance to its meaning. Yet it is clear that the story assumes the religious innovations by Jeroboam in the previous chapter (12:26–33) and was composed with these in mind. Furthermore, the fulfillment of the prophecy of the man of God and the reference to his grave in the region of Bethel (2 Kgs 23:15–20) is also a vital part of the story. This leads to a discussion of its relationship to the DH which has so much invested in both the "apostasy" of Jeroboam and the reforms of Josiah. I will not repeat here the

---

[1] For a review of earlier studies with bibliography see especially Eynikel (227–28) and Knoppers (47–64). Some more recent studies may be found in my bibliography.

discussion of these issues that I have presented in another place (forth-coming), but will merely summarize my conclusions. (1) The story is a post-Dtr addition that was composed for this specific context and was fitted in between 12:30 and 13:34. (2) The story also includes 2 Kgs 23:15–20 with the remark in 23:4b, as well as 2 Kgs 17:24–34.

There have been many attempts to recover an early pre-Dtr story by eliminating from it all the connections with 1 Kgs 12:26–33 and 2 Kgs 23:15–20 as the work of redactors, and by also attributing to these same redactors all the problematic features of the story that are otherwise unmotivated by the ideological concerns of a Dtr redactor.[2] Against this has been advanced the position that the language throughout is uniform and uniformly late and the whole is built with a simple structure which resists such fragmentation. Furthermore, the strategy of appealing to redactors does not actually offer a solution to the presence of problematic features of the text; it only relegates them to another level where they are just as difficult to explain.

The problematic nature of invoking a redactor to explain the story's connection with its context may be illustrated by the recent suggestion of Simon (130–54, esp. 131–36). He proposes the original limits of the pre-Dtr story as containing 1 Kgs 13:1–32a with its conclusion in 2 Kgs 23:16–18, but he recognizes that such a story must have had an exposition in the prior "sins of Jeroboam" and its conclusion must have been part of an account of the reform of Josiah. The present exposition in 1 Kgs 12:26–33 and its further link in 13:32b–34 are the work of the Dtr redactor, as is the context in 2 Kings 23. So Simon proposes that an original version of Jeroboam's cultic innovations, which stood before 1 Kgs 13:1, and an original account of Josiah's reform activity, which linked 1 Kgs 13:32a with 2 Kgs 23:16–18, has been supplanted by a rather clumsy and repetitive Dtr redactor. Such a scenario of redactional activity is highly speculative and fails to reckon with the problems in both 1 Kgs 12:26–33 and 2 Kgs 23:15–20 as well as the great unlikelihood that there ever was a pre-Dtr account of either Jeroboam's apostasy or Josiah's reform.[3]

I will therefore proceed to look at the story as defined by its broader limits and list some of its problematic aspects. This list does

---

[2] For a review of previous attempts and yet another multi-redactional proposal see Herr.

[3] See Knoppers: 25–44; Eynikel; Van Seters, 1983:313–14; forthcoming.

not claim to be all-inclusive but only to contain enough examples to illustrate the point. The following are some of the problems in the story of the man of God in 1 Kings 13, most of which have been observed by previous scholars:

1. The story has clear connections with, and is built into, the prior account of Jeroboam's apostasy, but the man of God does not address any of these nor does he censure Jeroboam. He only utters this curious prediction against the altar that Jeroboam has built. This is totally uncharacteristic of Dtr in his presentation of prophetic confrontation of evil rulers as the account in the next story in 1 Kings 14 makes clear.

2. Jeroboam is said to have mounted the altar and be standing on the top of it to offer incense (hiphil, קטר). There seems to be a confusion here between offering incense on a small altar or stand and the large altars for animal sacrifice which one would expect on the occasion of a festival and which is also suggested by the "ashes" (דשן) of animal victims in vv. 3, 5.[4]

3. The prediction about the "sacrifice of all the priests of the high places upon the altar" is linked to the installation of such priests in 12:31, 32 and the fulfillment in 2 Kgs 23:20 (where it includes the altars of all the high places). Yet the human "sacrifice" of all of the illegitimate priests is an action so completely inappropriate for the righteous Josiah that scholars have sought other explanations for the "plain reading" of the text (Marcus: 68 n. 5). By contrast there is no suggestion that the idolatrous priests in Judah were treated in this way. Such a reform portrayal is grotesque.[5]

4. The nature of the prediction within the story of 1 Kings 13 is quite meaningless, especially in the precise naming of Josiah (Marcus: 73–76). This is so obvious that scholars have been quick to attribute it to a redactor. Yet such a prediction is entirely unique and not the least in the style of a Dtr editor. The announcements of judgment in Dtr are

---

[4] The language here reflects late liturgical usage. It is true that the verb קטר in the hiphil can mean to sacrifice in a more general sense with the type of sacrifice in the accusative. But when used in the absolute sense without object it refers to burning incense (see BDB, 882–83).

[5] Is it influenced by the story of Elijah's slaughter (שחט) of the prophets of Baal in 1 Kgs 18:40? The latter episode could have been construed by the author of 1 Kings 13 as a sacrifice.

invariably related to the king and his household, about which nothing is said here.

5. The sign of the splitting of the altar and the spilling of the ashes seems totally pointless in relation to the prediction. Its only function seems to be as a miracle to prove that the one who speaks is indeed a man of God. But then the king seems to react even before the miracle can take effect and so set the stage for a second miracle that clearly makes the first superfluous. The narration of the two miracles is certainly muddled.

6. The reaction of the king to the events, *viz.* the total lack of concern about the altar and the extension of friendship to the man of God, seems entirely inappropriate.

7. The report by the man of God concerning the divine instructions not to eat or drink in Bethel and not to return by the way that he came, which is repeated three times, seems clear enough, if it means that the man of God is to refrain completely from association with the people of Bethel. This obvious sense, however, seems to be confused by the remark in v. 10 that he returned to Judah by a different route. This has given rise to all manner of ingenious explanations and is even used as the clue for interpreting the whole (see Rofé: 174–75).

8. The distinction between the man of God for the prophet from Judah and the old prophet (נביא) for his northern counterpart seems to be a convenient literary device to distinguish these two anonymous figures. But the author seems not content with this and repeats additional qualifying clauses for each which makes the reading rather tedious. Indeed, there is so much tiresome repetition, which some regard as literary artistry (Marcus: 90), that one might judge the author to have very limited narrative skills.

9. Does the man of God travel to Bethel and return on his own ass? There is only one ass mentioned at any one time, which is rendered with the definite article "the ass" and which clearly belongs to the old prophet. Yet when the man of God finally leaves Bethel for the second time on "the ass that belongs to the prophet," the prophet is still able to go out to recover his body on "the ass" which the sons have saddled for him. This is another case where repetition of stereotyped phrases (as with the divine prohibition of eating and drinking and returning to Bethel) creates serious contradictions in the text.

10. The fact that this miracle-working man of God loses all power of discernment so that he can be deceived by a lying prophet

seems unprecedented in the prophetic stories. The very next story demonstrates that true prophets are not deceived. The man of God is not disobedient; he is merely stupid.

11. Why is it that the word of Yahweh does not come directly to the man of God? Lying prophets who do so for their own benefit do not receive oracles from Yahweh. The story indicates from the sequel that the prophet spoke the truth the second time. This makes a total mockery of any distinction between true and false, or obedient and disobedient, prophets. The author contradicts all of the norms of prophecy but still wants us to take the prophetic oracles seriously. How the story can teach any "lessons" about true and false prophets or obedience to the word of God is hard to imagine.

12. The attack by the lion who does not eat either the prophet's corpse or attack the ass is truly a miracle and proves the word of God given by both prophets. But nothing is said about the second miracle, for when the second prophet arrives to find the lion guarding the body, it does not attack him or his ass while he removes the body for burial.

13. The presentation of the sequel in 2 Kgs 23:15–20 is also full of problems. The way in which the destruction of Bethel and its altar is described is confused (v. 15) and if the altar is destroyed then how can it be used to burn human bones (v. 16). The usual way to treat the latter problem is to assign them to different redactional levels, but both texts relate to the story in 1 Kgs 12:31–13:33.

14. The remarks about the grave of the man of God in 2 Kgs 23:16–18 do not make any sense. We are asked to believe that there was a specially marked grave by which the local inhabitants could identify a Judean prophet who had precisely predicted the destruction of their sanctuary. If they preserved his memory and his prophecy then why did they maintain the sanctuary as a place of worship? It is like suggesting that Amaziah of Bethel (Amos 7:10–14) was the one responsible for preserving the oracles of Amos.

15. The same contradiction about the destruction of the high places (v. 19) and the slaughter of the priests on the altars (v. 20) occurs at the end of the account as between vv. 15 and 16. Again, the details of both verses rest upon the earlier story of the man of God.

16. The curious remark in 2 Kgs 23:4 that the king "carried their ashes to Bethel" makes no sense in its context and seems entirely motivated by the presentation in vv. 15–20.

The above list of examples clearly demonstrates that the story of the man of God from Judah is incoherent throughout. Since the general assumption of literary analysis is that the work as originally composed would have been coherent and consistent, there is a marked tendency to attribute the inconsistency and incoherence to redactors. But why a redactor would deliberately create confusion when it does not seem to contribute to any clear editorial purpose, as most of the above examples would suggest, is no less problematic and therefore inexplicable. Simon (139–40) gives an example of this kind of reading when he relegates 13:3 and 5 to a later redactor. This is particularly curious in that Simon spends considerable space on the discussion of "sign" and "portent" in this story and their distinction, but these are the only texts in which either are specifically identified as such.

A second strategy is to attribute some special significance to the problems. The contradictions and incoherence is intentional to create a parody of prophecy, or certain types of it, as in the similar case of Balaam and his donkey or the book of Jonah. This is David Marcus's reading and it is very attractive because the parallels in the other stories do seem to have this quality about them. Yet it is hard to see how the various strategies that he reviews solve the kinds of problems that arise in this text and few are actually addressed by him. If the types of prophecy represented by the two prophets are satirized then it is hard to see why so much of the story is taken up with the confirmation of their oracles and presented as "historical" fact within the larger narrative. The satire of Jonah makes absolutely clear the disobedience of the prophet as the point of departure for the unfolding of the story. Likewise, Balaam is parodied in the episode of the she-ass (Num 22:22–35) in order to discredit him as a true and obedient prophet as he is presented in the larger story. However, there is no such clarity in the man of God from Judah story.

A third strategy of reading is to employ the method of intertextuality. This can mean different things to different readers. On the one hand, it can mean that the account may be enriched in its meaning by association with other texts with similar terminology and allusions to other stories. In this way also what is confusing and problematic may be clarified by the comparison. On the other hand, intertextuality can mean that the author had before him a body of material that he used as a resource for motifs and elements in the composition of his account and if the borrowing was not done skillfully, the result may have given rise to the incoherence observed in the text. Let us examine a few examples of intertextuality.

The miracles performed by the man of God in 1 Kgs 13:3–6 have some similarity with the plagues of Exodus. The motif of performing a miracle (verb נתן with מופת) in accordance with divine instruction is closely paralleled in language by P's presentation of a miracle by Moses and Aaron in their encounter with Pharaoh in Exod 7:8–9. The affliction of the king with the withering of his hand and its subsequent restoration as it was before is like the second "sign" given to Moses in his call (Exod 4:6–8), whereas the request of the king for the man of God to intercede on his behalf for healing is like Pharaoh's frequent requests of Moses during the plagues. Yet the combination of these motifs in this story is very clumsy because both miracles happen at the same time and yet there is no record of their producing either belief or obstinacy. The scene seems to be pointless. Unlike the plagues story, nothing is directly demanded of Jeroboam so there is no result. Only in v. 33 does the account suggest that Jeroboam persisted in his evil ways, referring to the earlier apostasy, so that in some vague way the episode at the altar was intended as a warning.

There is another parallel in 2 Chr 26:16–23 that may shed some light on this episode. The Chronicler tells the story of how King Uzziah of Judah presumed to enter the temple and offer incense (hiphil קטר) on the incense altar. When he was confronted by the chief priest Azariah and his fellow priests for doing only what consecrated priests can do according to the law (= P code), the king became angry. At that moment he was struck with leprosy on his forehead and was expelled from the temple. This story suggests that the author of the man of God story may have borrowed the motifs of the king offering incense contrary to the law for which he is punished when he becomes angry at the man of God. However, so many other elements have become mixed with these that the whole scene is very confused. He receives no reprimand for his cultic activity and unlike Uzziah, he is healed upon request.[6]

---

[6] One cannot argue, as some do (see Simon: 133), that merely offering sacrifices of any kind would make the king culpable. There are other examples of kings, such as David and Solomon, who offer sacrifices without blame (2 Sam 6:17–18; 1 Kgs 3:4; 8:62–64). Even Ahaz, who builds a new altar and then mounts it to sacrifice on it (2 Kgs 16:10–16), is not blamed for this particular action (contra Simon). In fact, it is the Ahaz of the Chronicler (2 Chr 28:25) who builds high places in Jerusalem

Furthermore, it is not clear how we are to understand the invitation of Jeroboam to the man of God in v. 7 to dine and to receive a gift. This would be similar to the offer of a gift to Elisha by Na'aman for healing which is then simply refused by the prophet (2 Kgs 5:15–17). But the answer of the man of God turns the king's remarks into a bribe to eat and drink in Bethel which he declares is contrary to a divine command (about which the king could have known nothing). This in turn is similar to the attempt of Balak's servants to persuade Balaam to come with them to Moab, which Balaam rejects in the same way.[7] In the Balaam story, however, the funds from Balak were intended to influence the oracles before they were given. That was no longer possible in the man of God story. The two quite distinct motifs, the offer of a gift after healing and the offer of a bribe to influence the prophet's behavior have become muddled.

Much has also been made of the similarities between the man of God from Judah and Amos. The latter is a Judean who prophesied in the north particularly against the sanctuary of Bethel and even against its altars (Amos 3:14; 5:5; 7:10–14). He is told by Amaziah the priest to return to Judah and eat bread there and to never again prophesy at Bethel "for it is the king's sanctuary." In his response, Amos suggests that he is not a "prophet" (נביא). Here are again a number of motifs that could explain various features in the story of 1 Kings 13. Nevertheless, there is scarcely any basic similarity between the two prophets and a "historical" connection can hardly be taken seriously. At most, the book of Amos is part of a body of literature that could have been used as a source for useful motifs in ways quite different from the original prophecy.

The other prophetic book whose language and style it resembles is the book of Jonah. In both Jonah and the man of God story, the act of delivering the oracle of judgment against Nineveh or the altar of Bethel is described by the expression "to proclaim against," קרא with על (1 Kgs 13:2, 4, 32; Jonah 1:2; cf. 3:2, 4). Other shared features, such as the use of the miraculous including the divinely directed animals and the disobedience of the prophet, have suggested that the two stories belong to the same genre of parable or parody (Rofé; Marcus).

---

and the cities of Judah and offers incense to other gods that is the model for Jeroboam in the 1 Kings 13 account.

[7] I see no reason to impugn the unequivocal rejection of either Balaam or the man of God in this story as Reis does (379).

But these apparent similarities are offset by contrasts. The deity in the Jonah story is patient with the wayward prophet, saves him by means of the great fish and shows mercy towards the foreign population under judgment. In the man of God story, the judgment against Bethel is final and the prophet who is duped into disobedience is killed by the divinely appointed lion. In Jonah the parody on nationalistic prophecy succeeds by narrative skill and design. If the man of God story is read as parody, it is so only by accident.

This leads me to the conclusion that the difficulties in reading this text cannot be blamed on incompetent editors or redactors; nor can they be solved by intertextuality. They are the result of a lack of literary skill by the author. The incoherence resides in the original text and even the translators of the Septuagint and other versions, while improving it slightly in places, could not save the whole. The mode of composition seems to have been the gleaning of motifs and elements from a body of earlier literature which included such late pieces as Jonah, the P Code and Chronicles. Such a collage of materials has created a very confusing text. It is also the author of the story that is responsible for fitting it into its present context in the DH. There is no need to posit a redactor for this purpose or for any of the compositional mistakes that we have observed. If the text is not coherent and consistent then perhaps one should be very cautious about trying to discover what it is about and especially from drawing theological and moral lessons from it.

Nevertheless, I have argued elsewhere (forthcoming) that the story is a vilification of the Bethel temple, which was still in use for some time in the exilic and post-exilic periods, and the Samaritan community. Taking all of the parts of the story together this general attitude seems obvious, especially if no part of the Josiah reform had anything to do with Bethel and the cities of Samaria. The repeated prohibitions against eating and drinking, even with Yahweh worshippers in Bethel, and against traveling to the region, except as Josiah did to destroy its places of worship and slaughter its priests, seem to make the point clearly. It is a fairly crass piece of anti-Samaritan religious propaganda constructed with little narrative skill or sensitivity to religious and moral issues. If the text is read as parody (so Marcus), it is unintentional, and the object of the parody has become the deity of the author. It seems to me that it is precisely the religious perspective reflected in 1 Kings 13 that is being intentionally satirized in Jonah so that both pieces should be read together.

Bibliography

Eynikel, Erik
1990   "Prophecy and Fulfillment in the Deuteronomistic History: 1 Kgs 13; 2 Kgs 23, 16–18." Pp. 227–37 in *Pentateuchal and Deuteronomistic Studies: Papers Read at the XIIIth IOSOT Congress, Leuven 1989*. Ed. Chris Brekelmans and Johan Lust. Leuven: Peeters.

Herr, Bertram
1997   "Der wahre Prophet bezeugt seine Botschaft mit dem Tod. Ein Versuch zu 1 Kön 13." *BZ* 41:69–78.

Jepsen, Alfred
1971   "Gottesmann und Prophet: Anmerkungen zum Kapitel 1 Könige 13." Pp. 171–82 in *Probleme biblischer Theologie: Festschrift für Gerhard von Rad*. Ed. Hans W. Wolff. Munich: Kaiser.

Knoppers, Gary N.
1994   *Two Nations Under God: The Deuteronomistic History of Solomon and the Dual Monarchies*. Vol. 2. HSM 53. Atlanta: Scholars Press.

Marcus, David
1995   *From Balaam to Jonah: Anti-prophetic Satire in the Hebrew Bible*. BJS 301. Atlanta: Scholars Press.

McKenzie, Steven L.
1991   *The Trouble with Kings: The Composition of the Book of Kings in the Deuteronomistic History*. VTSup 42. Leiden: Brill.

Reis, Pamela T.
1994   "Vindicating God: another look at 1 Kings xiii." *VT* 44:376–86.

Rofé, Alexander
1988   *The Prophetical Stories*. Jerusalem: Magnes.

Simon, Uriel
1997   *Reading Prophetic Narratives*. Trans. Lenn J. Schramm. Bloomington: Indiana University Press.

Van Seters, John
1983   *In Search of History*. New Haven: Yale University Press.
Forthcoming "The Deuteronomistic History: Can It Avoid Death by Redaction?" in *The Future of the "Deuteronomistic History."* Leuven: Peeters.

THE LABOUR OF SHARING

John Dominic Crossan

My purpose here is to read certain texts as closely and comparatively as I can. It is in their interaction and combination that labour is hardest and meaning most elusive. It is also there that the deepest challenge lies. One set of texts is from the *Q Gospel* and the *Didache*. The other is from the *Didache* and *Shepherd of Hermas*. They are linked together not only by specific subject but also by their sequential position in the *Didache* itself. In reading the *Q Gospel* (from Matthew and Luke) and the *Didache* (1.2–5) I will focus on a closely related cluster of sayings that has generated controversy over their relationship. Despite arguments in favor of the dependence of the latter on the former, I will argue for their independence. In the next step, I will consider a second relationship, this time between the *Didache* (1.5–6) and the *Shepherd of Hermas* (2.4c–7), moving then to the linkage between the three texts—*Q*, *Didache* and *Shepherd of Hermas*—via the command to give. Finally, I will consider how the six-fold cluster with which I began might have come together in the first place by a comparison with *De Doctrina Apostolorum*. All this leads to a theological radicalism that has its roots in the Jewish God.

The *Q Gospel* and The *Didache*

Towards the start of the *Q Gospel* and the *Didache* there is a cluster of sayings so similar in content and structure that the question of their relationship becomes immediately pressing. Does either derive from the other? Do both derive from a common source? Is that source oral or written? If they are mutually independent versions, why was their *clustered* combination so important?

The Content of the Clusters

The common cluster has certainly four (*The Other Cheek, Give without Return, Love Your Enemies, Better than Sinners*), probably five (with *The Golden Rule*), and possibly six (with *As Your Father*) sayings. Here are the three clusters given in their respective sequences:

Matt 5:39–48 & 7:12 Sequence	Luke 6:27–36 Sequence	*Did.* 1.2–5 Sequence
The Other Cheek (5:39b–41)	*Love Your Enemies*	*The Golden Rule* (2b)
Give without Return (5:42)	(27–28,35a)	*Love Your Enemies* (3a, 3c)
Love Your Enemies (5:44)	*The Other Cheek* (29)	*Better than Sinners* (3b)
Better than Sinners (5:46–47)	*Give without Return* (30,	*The Other Cheek* (4a)
As Your Father (5:45, 48)	35b)	*Give without Return* (4b–5a)
The Golden Rule (7:12)	*The Golden Rule* (31)	*As Your Father* (5b)
	Better than Sinners (32–34)	
	As Your Father (35b–36)	

First, there is no common sequence within those three clusters, not between the *Q Gospel* and the *Didache* and not even between the present Matthean and Lukan versions of their Q source. Second, the International Q Project accepts the original *Q Gospel* sequence as Luke 6:27–29 (Matt 5:41), 30–36, with the presence of Matt 5:41 (go two miles) given a certitude-grade no better than D (Robinson, 1994:496–97). Third, there is a very striking difference across all three sets in that the Greek second person singular ("you") appears in *The Other Cheek* and *Give without Return* but the second person plural ("ye") appears in *Love Your Enemies* and *Better than Sinners*. Fourth, that grammatical divergence, obvious in Greek but lost in English translation, draws attention to those four sayings as constituting two blocks:

Block A, with singular "you," contains *The Other Cheek* and *Give without Return*.

Block B, with plural "ye," contains *Love Your Enemies* and *Better than Sinners*.

Viewed like that, the structural similarity between all three clusters becomes much more evident. Matthew has a sequence of Block A followed by Block B. Luke has a sequence of Block A inserted into the middle of Block B. The *Didache* has a sequence of

Block B followed by Block A. *The Golden Rule* can appear with those linked blocks either at the start in the *Didache*, at the middle in Q/Luke, or at the end and far outside in Matthew. It is also, by the way, singular ("you") and negative ("do not do") in the *Didache* but plural ("ye") and positive ("do") in the *Q Gospel*. *As Your Father*, that is, the general assertion of God as model, appears after the combined blocks in all three cases.

I presume, therefore, three points as I proceed. One is that the parallels between Matthew and Luke derive from their common *Q Gospel* source. Another is that Luke has conserved the original *Q Gospel* sequence more closely than has Matthew. A final one, therefore, is that the insertion of Block A into Block B in Luke was already present in the *Q Gospel*, as Kloppenborg has observed: "vv. 27–28, 32–33, 35a, c form a coherently structured piece of rhetoric, which was later supplemented by vv. 29–31, 34 and 35b" (177). But, granted all that, how are we to explain the relationship between the clusters of six sayings in the *Q Gospel* and in the *Didache*?

The Relationship between the Clusters

After more than a century of research scholars are still deeply divided on the *Didache*'s relationship to the canonical gospels (Crossan: 117–18). Is it dependent on them or completely independent of them? More specifically, what about the so-called "evangelical section" in *Did.* 2.3b–5a: is that cluster of sayings dependent or independent on Matthew and Luke?

First, with regard to the document as a whole. *The Didache in Modern Research*, a 1996 reprint of selected articles on the *Didache* from 1952 through 1992 either in their original English or translated from French, German, Italian, and Hebrew, has flatly contradictory back-to-back articles by Jonathan Draper and Christopher Tuckett. Draper concluded in 1985, after a Cambridge University doctoral dissertation in 1983, that

> the Jesus tradition in the Didache . . . suggests, firstly, an independence over against the Synoptic Gospels' context, order and wording of the sayings is independent and cannot be derived from either [Matthew and/or Luke]. The material Didache has in common with Matthew and Luke *never* includes material these evangelists have drawn from Mark. It coincides with what is normally described

> as the 'Q' source in these Gospels, and seems to confirm the
> hypothesis that sayings of Jesus were collected and circulated in a
> more or less fixed form, whether oral or written, before the
> collection was incorporated into the Gospels as we have them.
> (1985:283; 1996:90)

Tuckett, however, concluded in 1989, after a meticulous study of the
parallel texts, that

> the parallels between material in different parts of the Didache and
> material in the synoptic gospels . . . can be best explained if the
> Didache presupposes the finished gospels of Matthew and Luke. . . .
> Precisely how the gospels were available to the author of the
> Didache is impossible to say: they may have been available as
> separate texts; they may have been already combined to form a
> harmonized text. However, the evidence of the Didache seems to
> show that the text is primarily a witness to the post-redactional
> history of the synoptic tradition. It is not a witness to any pre-
> redactional developments. (1989:230; Draper, 1996:128)

The basic methodological principle for determining such
dependency is explicitly clear in Tuckett: "If material which owes it
origin to the redactional activity of a synoptic evangelist reappears in
another work, then the latter presupposes the finished work of that
evangelist" (1998:199; 1996:95). But that principle works best when
we have Matthew and Luke using Mark as a source since we ourselves
still have all three texts in front of us. We can then determine, by
comparison with Mark, what exactly is redactional in those other texts:
when Matthew agrees with Mark against Luke, we have redactional
Luke; when Luke agrees with Mark against Matthew, we have
redactional Matthew. We can see with relative clarity how each redacts
its Markan source. The principle works worst, however, when we have
Matthew and Luke using the *Q Gospel* as a source. We know the *Q
Gospel* itself for sure only when Matthew and Luke agree exactly in
their separate presentations of it, when, in other words, they fail to
redact it at all. If either redacts it or even if both redact it differently,
we lose any secure base text for comparison and cannot really tell what
was there in the *Q Gospel* and what was done to it by either or both
evangelists. We may be quite certain that a saying was in the *Q Gospel*
because we have redacted versions of it in both Matthew and Luke.
But we may also be unable to determine the exact wording of it in the
Q Gospel itself. That may be adequate for general purposes but it is

inadequate if one needs to compare a precise word or phrase from the *Q Gospel* with some other text. And that is exactly the situation we are in with *Did*. 1.2b–5b. The parallels from that section of the *Didache* appear in the *Q Gospel* as Matt 5:39b–48=Luke 6:27–36 but those verses are so different that it is already notoriously difficult to decide for sure the sequence and content of that *Q Gospel* section.

Second, with regard to *Did*. 1.3b–5a, the section that concerns me in this article. Helmut Koester in 1957 and, with much greater detail, Bentley Layton in 1968 argued that the *Didache* is totally independent of the synoptic gospels except for *Did*. 1.3b–2.1 which is a later insertion into the completed text. That later insertion derived from harmonizing together the different versions of certain sayings in Matthew and Luke. In *The Historical Jesus*, I accepted that position. In terms of purpose, Layton concluded that,

> The concern of the author, or rather, compositor, of the *Didache* passage—his choice of material once having been made—seems to have been primarily stylistic, to the exclusion of any overriding theological or scholarly interests—a fact which perhaps sets him apart from his colleagues. It is such concern for style and form that appear to control the relationship between the *Didache* verses and their postulated sources. (351)

In terms of date, he concluded that the insertion was made "after A.D. 150 ca. into a form of the *Didache already published* some fifty or a hundred years earlier" because, "within the circles in which the first edition of the *Didache* circulated, only by the time of the interpolation had Christianity felt itself to be clearly differentiated from the matrix of Jewish teaching within which it arose" (381–82). The debate, of course, is not whether *Did*. 1.3b–2.1 is a redactional insertion but whether it is a redactional insertion derived from canonical harmonization. As we see below, it certainly is a redactional insertion but within the *Didache*'s own compositional development.

Layton's article showed, and showed rather brilliantly, *how* such a harmonization of the Matthean and Lukan versions of the sayings in *Did*. 1.3b–2.1 *could* have been done. But *if* it was done and *why* it was done are even more preliminary problems. I now see four basic objections to his interpretation. First, it is necessary to postulate a Christian-Jewish community's written constitution operating for fifty to a hundred years without any such Jesus-tradition in its official training program. That might be possible: one could respond, in the light of 11.8, that it was the "ways" (*tropoi*) and not the "words" (*logoi*) of the Lord Jesus that were normative for this community. But then, second, somebody who knows Matthew and Luke changes the *Didache* only by adding in these few sayings in 1.3b–2:1. Nothing is added to change its eucharistic ritual nor its apocalyptic expectation to agree with those gospels. Next, by the time of that postulated insertion, those gospels were taking on normative status, yet the inserter harmonizes them rather freely. The result, in effect, is a third version rather than a simple harmonization and, as Layton notes, style seems to be foremost in this individual's mind. Finally, there is no indication that those inserted sayings come from Jesus or from the gospel of Jesus. They are never cited as such. As Rordorf put it: "A harmony of the Gospels presupposes that the basic text has canonical authority. But with a canonical text it is impossible to chop and change as the *Didache* does; it is not permissible to complete it by glosses and commentaries." And so he concluded "that the *Didache* certainly did not put together its material from the completed versions of the Synoptic Gospels, more exactly from Matthew and Luke" so that "the *Didache* [1.3–6] has preserved a Jesus tradition independently of the Synoptic Gospels" (411).

My present working hypothesis is, therefore, that the *Didache*, and especially 1.2b–5b with which I am primarily concerned, are totally independent from any of the synoptic gospels or any harmonized versions of Matthew and Luke. If one looks in isolation at those *Didache* passages with synoptic parallels, one can probably argue to a draw on dependence or independence. But if one looks at those passages in total *Didache* context, as Milavec or Henderson does, for example, it is extremely difficult to see synoptic dependence. And that creates a very big problem.

The Meaning of the Clusters

As long as the sixfold cluster of sayings in *Did.* 1.2b–5b was judged dependent on a harmonization of Matt 5:39b–48 and Luke 6:27–36, it was of little wider interest. But if they are independent clusters, they raise some important questions.

First, are we dealing with an oral cluster of five sayings? Tradition, let us say, holds those five together, but oral performance and eventually scribal transmission invests the exact content and specific sequence quite divergently. Maybe, therefore, we have at least one example of what Barry Henaut failed to find in his recent study on oral tradition and the gospels. "It has not," he said, "been possible to establish even one instance where a chain of oral sayings has reached two literary authors independently" (299). Could a sixfold oral chain of sayings have reached the *Q Gospel* and the *Didache* texts independently of one another? That is not impossible in theory but most unlikely in the present case because of that discrepancy between the Greek second person singular ("you") in *The Other Cheek* and *Give without Return* but the second person plural ("ye") in *Love Your Enemies* and *Better than Sinners*. I cannot imagine that divergence between those two blocks being maintained in an oral transmission. I conclude, therefore, that a written source for that sixfold cluster lies behind both the *Q Gospel* and the *Didache*.

Second, could the *Q Gospel* (in best reconstruction) and the *Didache* come out as divergently as they do from a common written source. Of course, because, for example, the differences between Matthew and Luke, each working with the written *Q Gospel*, are as great or greater than those between the *Q Gospel* (in best reconstruction) and the *Didache* itself. If, in other words, both were using a common written source for that sixfold cluster, it could still come out as divergent as it is now.

Third, then, comes the most difficult question: what else can be said about this written source? It is an extremely radical mini-catechism of Christian life in which *The Golden Rule* receives a commentary defining it not just offensively but defensively, not just actively but passively. Do not do, in other words, what you would not want done to you *even or especially in self-defense*. If you do not want to be struck, do not strike, *even back*. Furthermore, the commentary is based, not just on the word of Jesus but on the nature of God. That is clear within the cluster in the *Q Gospel* but is half in it and half after it in the *Didache*. These are the parallels:

Matt 5:45 & 5:48	Luke 6:35b–36	*Did.* 1.5 & 1.4 (parts)
so that you may be children of your Father in heaven; for he makes his sun rise on the evil and on the good, and sends rain on the righteous and on	you will be children of the Most High; for he is kind to the ungrateful and the wicked.	for the Father's will is that we give to all from the gifts we have received.

the unrighteous. . . .		
Be perfect, therefore, as your heavenly Father is perfect.	Be merciful, just as your Father is merciful.	. . . and you will be perfect . . .

In the case of the *Didache*, only the now enigmatic "and you will be perfect" is still inside the cluster. The Father is now outside it as part of the following complex and it is divine will and divine command that is emphasized rather than divine character and divine nature. That extra-cluster position draws attention to the second set of parallel texts.

The *Didache* and The *Shepherd of Hermas*

This first part of the *Didache* has not only that striking parallel with the *Q Gospel* but another and equally striking one with the *Shepherd of Hermas*. It is again a case of twin clusters too similar for coincidence although a common written source is not as certain in this instance. The parallels here are in *Did.* 1.5–6 and *Herm. Man.* 2.4c–7.

The Command to Give

Both texts speak of "the commandment" (ἐντολή) and define it as "giving to all" or "giving to each." Both base that commandment on the distributive will of God with almost verbatim the same phrase. Both agree that, no matter the situation, "the giver . . . is innocent" in both *Did.* 1.5b (ὁ διδοὺς . . . ἀθῷος ἐστιν) and *Herm. Man.* 2.6 (ὁ . . . διδοὺς ἀθῷος ἐστιν). But both mention sanctions for the receiver: no penalties if the need was true, penalties if the need was false. The receiver must be sure "why he took and for what" or else a "penalty" is inevitable in both *Did.* 1.5c (δώσει δίκην, ἱνατί ἔλαβε καὶ εἰς τί) and *Herm. Man.* 2.5 (διατί ἔλαβον καὶ εἰς τί . . . τίσουσιν δίκην). And, finally, both texts emphasize that givers should not use suspicions about the motivations of receivers as an excuse for not giving. *Did.* 1.6 demands: "let your alms sweat into your hands until you know to whom you are giving." *Herm. Man.* 2.4 demands: "give in simplicity to all who need, not doubting to whom you shall give and to whom not."

I focus here on the commandment to give because that is where the two sets, *Q Gospel* and *Didache* on the one hand, *Didache* and

Shepherd of Hermas on the other, overlap on a single saying, *Give without Return*. Here are the parallel texts given in Greek so that you can see similarities and differences and also in deliberately wooden translation:

Matt 5:42	Luke 6:30	*Did.* 1.4–5	*Herm. Man.* 2.4c
To one asking from you give,	Give to everyone who begs from you;	If anyone takes from you yours [sing.], do not ask back, for you are not able.	Give in simplicity to all who need. . . .
and the one wanting to borrow from you do not turn away.	and if anyone takes away yours [pl.], do not ask back.	To everyone asking you give and do not ask back, for to all the Father wills it be given from his own gifts.	give to all, for to all God wills it be given from his own bounties.
[a] τῷ αἰτοῦντί σε δός,	[a] παντὶ αἰτοῦντί σε δίδου	[b] ἐὰν λάβῃ τις ἀπὸ σοῦ τὸ σόν, μὴ ἀπαίτει, οὐδὲ γὰρ δύνασαι	πᾶσιν ὑστερουμένοις δίδου ἁπλῶς . . .
[b] καὶ τὸν θέλοντα ἀπὸ σοῦ δανίυασθαι μὴ ἀποστραφῇς	[b] καὶ ἀπὸ τοῦ αἴροντος τὰ σὰ μὴ ἀπαίτει.	[a] παντὶ τῷ αἰτοῦντί σε δίδου καὶ μὴ ἀπαίτει πᾶσι γὰρ θέλει δίδοσθαι ὁ πατὴρ ἐκ τῶν ἰδίων χαρισμάτων	πᾶσιν δίδου. πᾶσιν γάρ ὁ θεὸς δίδοσθαι θέλει ἐκ τῶν ἰδίων δωρημάτων

All of those five versions have a double formulation: positive and negative in the *Q Gospel*, double negative with intermediate positive in the *Didache*, and double positive in the *Shepherd of Hermas*. By positive I mean a command like "give," by negative I mean a command like "do not ask back." There is also a parallel to that saying in the *Gospel of Thomas* 95: "[Jesus said], If you [pl.] have money, do not lend it at interest. Rather, give [it] to someone from whom you will not get it back." That is another double formulation, now negative followed by positive. To give means not to ask back.

That double formulation allowed Matthew to mute the more radical articulation with a more normal interpretation. Matt 5:42a is the unqualified radical formulation of the command but 5:42b interprets "giving" as "lending (δανίσασθαι)," then enjoins "not turning away (beforehand)" rather than "not expecting back (afterward)," and uses the aorist rather than the indicative possibly to emphasize a special occasion rather than regular procedure. That muting does not seem to have happened in Luke or in the *Q Gospel* despite the fact that "giving" is equated with "lending" not only in Luke but also in the *Q Gospel* itself. Luke 6:30 itself has equally radical commands: 6:30b is simply the negative equivalent of the positive formulation in 6:30a. In other words, despite its parallelism with Matt 5:42, Luke 6:30 has nothing at all about "lending." But that equation of "giving" and "lending" appears a few verses later in Luke 6:34 and 35b, which have no Matthean parallels: "If you lend (δανίσητε) to those from whom you hope to receive, what credit is that to you? Even sinners lend (δανίζουσιν)to sinners, to receive as much again. But . . . lend (δανίζετε), expecting nothing in return." That is a comparison of "sinners" lending to get the same back and of "you" lending without expecting to get anything back. In that case, "giving" and "lending" mean the same thing: *give/lend without any return*.

Whatever the scope of Matthean and Lukan redaction in these verses, "giving" interpreted as "lending" must have been in the *Q Gospel*, since it appears, however differently, in both redactions. I conclude that both the *Q Gospel* and Luke, even with "giving" equated to "lending," do not intend to mute the saying's radicality but to insist that giving/lending should expect no return. The same seems true of *Gospel of Thomas* 95. The first or negative half is not too radical: its simply forbids interest. But the second half does not say, "give to someone without interest" but, "give to someone from whom you will not get it back." That is the same command as in the *Q Gospel*.

The Model of God

It is well known that the Two Ways doctrine, the dichotomy of a way of good and a way of evil, came from earlier purely Jewish tradition into later Christian Jewish usage (Suggs). Second, a Christian Jewish version of the Two Ways in a Latin document entitled *De Doctrina Apostolorum* gives the best idea of what the Two Ways in *Didache* 1–6 would have looked like before the redactional insertion of 1.3–2.1 during the *Didache*'s initial composition. With that comparison you can see, for example, how *The Golden Rule*, already present in *Did.* 1.2b, facilitated the insertion of that sixfold cluster of sayings interpreting *The Golden Rule* as in the *Q Gospel*. But there is an even more interesting comparison between *De Doctrina Apostolorum* and the *Didache* (Goodspeed: 6, 304):

De Doctrina Apostolorum 4.8–9 (Latin)	*Did.* 4.8–9 (Greek)
You shall not turn away from the needy, but shall share everything with your brethren, and you shall not say it is your own. For if we are partners in what is immortal, how much more ought we to consecrate from it! For the Lord wishes to give of his gifts to all [*Omnibus enim Dominis dare vult de donis suis*].	You shall not turn away the needy, but shall share all things with your brother, and you shall not say they are your own. For if we are sharers in what is immortal, how much more in mortal things?
You shall not withhold your hand from your sons, but from their youth up you shall teach them the fear of the Lord.	You shall not withhold your hand from your son or your daughter, but from their youth up you shall teach them the fear of the Lord.

That Latin phrase is almost verbatim the same as those Greek ones seen above: "to all the Lord/God wills to give from his gifts." The omission of that sentence here in *Did.* 4.8b is not surprising as it had appeared earlier in 1.5b and the author may not have wanted a repetition. But its presence in *De Doctrina Apostolorum* 4.8 indicates the pre-*Didache* status of the radical idea that all gifts belonged to God who gives to some only for sharing with all. I emphasize, in other words, that this is not a new Christian radicalism but an older Jewish and, thence, Christian Jewish radicalism and based on the radicalism of the Jewish God.

One postscript. There is a saying attributed to Jesus in Acts 20:35 and placed by Luke on Paul's lips as he says farewell to the leaders of Asia at Miletus. "In all this I have given you an example that by such work we must support the weak, remembering the words of the Lord Jesus, for he himself said, 'It is more blessed to give than to receive.'" In his earlier study of that saying William Stroker judged that it "was a proverbial maxim of very widespread currency in the Graeco-Roman world" which "was secondarily attributed to Jesus" (1970:121–22). But in a more recent survey he associated it with this context in *Did.* 1.5 and *Herm. Man.* 2.4–5. He also gives an example of their combination in the *Apostolic Constitutions* 4.2–3: "For truly blessed is he who is able to support himself and does not take up the place of the orphan, the stranger, and the widow, since the Lord said that he giver is more blessed than the receiver. For again it is said by him: Woe to those who have and receive in hypocrisy, or who are able to support themselves and wish to receive from others. For each shall render an account to the Lord God on the day of judgment" (1989:227). I think that is a better conclusion. The saying in Acts 20:35 is an aphoristic condensation of texts such as those in *Did.* 1.5–6 and *Herm. Man.* 2.4–5.

Conclusion

The labour here is to read all of those texts together and to glimpse lives and communities appearing through their lenses. First, if we only had that first set of parallel texts, we might judge it all idealistic rhetoric with no actual, practical implications. But the second set proves that some people were trying to live with and by those prescriptions. You do not have to worry about a freeloader, about what *Did.* 12.5 terms a "Christ-hustler" (χριστέμπορος), unless those admonitions to share possessions are being put into actual practice. Second, both complexes insist that God stands behind those commands. In the second set it is the will and commandment of God that is emphasized. But in the first set it is the character and nature of God that is underlined. This is how God acts to friends and foes alike, therefore, so also should you. It is a human radicalism based on a divine radicalism or, better, on a divine normalcy. Third, this seems less about compassionate almsgiving than about distributive justice. We are, in other words, distributors rather than owners of goods, channels rather than recipients of bounty. "You shall not say it is your own. For the Lord wishes to give of his gifts to all."

Bibliography

Crossan, John Dominic
    1996   "Itinerants and Householders in the Earliest Kingdom Movement." Pp. 113–29 in *Reimagining Christian Origins: A Colloquium Honoring Burton L. Mack*. Ed. Elizabeth A. Castelli and Hal Taussig. Valley Forge, PA: Trinity.
Draper, Jonathan A.
    1985   "The Jesus Tradition in the Didache." Pp. 269–87 in *Gospel Perspectives*. Ed. David Wenham. *The Jesus Tradition outside the Gospels 5*. Sheffield: JSOT.

Draper, Jonathan A., ed.
1996   *The* Didache *in Modern Research.* AGJU 37. Leiden: Brill.

Goodspeed, Edgar J.
1950   *The Apostolic Fathers: An American Translation.* New York: Harper.

Henaut, Barry W.
1993   *Oral Tradition and the Gospels: The Problem of Mark 4.* JSNTSup 82. Sheffield: JSOT.

Henderson, Ian H.
1992   "*Didache* and Orality in Synoptic Comparison." *JBL* 111:283–306.
1995   "Style-Switching in the Didache: Fingerprint or Argument." Pp. 177–209 in *The Didache in Context: Essays on Its Text, History and Transmission.* Ed. Clayton N. Jefford. NovTSup 77. Leiden: Brill.

Jefford, Clayton N.
1989   *The Sayings of Jesus in the Teaching of the Twelve Apostles.* Supplements to *Vigiliae Christianae.* Texts and Studies of Early Christian Life and Language 11. Leiden: Brill.

Jefford, Clayton N., ed.
1995   *The Didache in Context: Essays on Its Text, History and Transmission.* NovTSup 77. Leiden: Brill.

Kloppenborg, John S.
1987   *The Formation of Q: Trajectories in Ancient Wisdom Collections.* Studies in Antiquity and Christianity. Philadelphia: Fortress Press.

Köster, Helmut
1957   *Synoptische Überlieferung bei den apostolischen Vätern.* TU 65. Berlin: Akademie.

Layton, Bentley
1968   "The Sources, Date and Transmission of *Didache* 1.3b–2.1." *HTR* 61:343–83.

Milavec, Aaron
1989   "The Pastoral Genius of the Didache: An Analytical Translation and Commentary." Pp. 89–125 in *Religious Writings and Religious Systems. Systemic Analysis of Holy Books in Christianity, Islam, Buddhism, Greco-Roman Religions, Ancient Israel, and Judaism.* Vol. 2. *Christianity.* Ed. Jacob Neusner, Ernest S. Frerichs, and A. J. Levine. Brown Studies in Religion 2. Atlanta: Scholars Press.

Robinson, James M., *et al*
1990–97   "The International Q Project." *JBL* 109:449–501; 110:494–498; 111:500–508; 112:500–506; 113:495–500; 114:475–485; 116:521–25.

Rordorf, Willy
    1991   "Does the Didache Contain Jesus Tradition Independently of the Synoptic Gospels?" Pp. 394–423 in *Jesus and the Oral Gospel Tradition*. Ed. Henry Wansbrough. JSNTSup 64. Sheffield: Sheffield Academic Press.

Stroker, William Dettwiller
    1970   *The Formation of Secondary Sayings of Jesus*. Ann Arbor, MI: University Microfilms International.
    1989   *Extracanonical Sayings of Jesus*. SBLRBS 18. Atlanta: Scholars Press.

Suggs, M. Jack
    1972   "The Christian Two Ways Tradition: Its Antiquity, Form, and Function." Pp. 60–74 in *Studies on New Testament and Early Christian Literature: Essays in Honor of Allen P. Wikgren*. Ed. David Aune. NovTSup 33. Leiden: Brill.

Tuckett, Christopher M.
    1989   "Synoptic Tradition in the Didache." Pp. 197–230 in *The New Testament in Early Christianity: La Réception des écrits néotestamentaires dans le christianisme primitif*. Ed. Jean-Marie Sevrin. Leuven: Leuven University Press.

THE KILLING FIELDS OF MATTHEW'S GOSPEL[1]

Gary A. Phillips

"No statement, theological or otherwise, should be made that would not be credible
in the presence of the burning children."
Irving Greenberg

"The Holocaust-world touched *none but* the innocent. What is innocent if not birth?
Who is innocent if not children?"
Emil Fackenheim

Murder of the innocents. Readers of the Bible find this an all too familiar and unsettling occurrence in Jewish narrative and Christian gospel: Pharaoh tosses new-born Jewish males into the Nile (Exod 1:22); Herod slaughters all the Jewish children of Bethlehem and its neighborhood (Matt 2:16). God is complicitous in the violence, slaughtering every Egyptian first-born human being and animal left unprotected by the blood sign (Exod 11:12). And indiscriminate as well: Job's ten children, Haman's ten sons, and countless Canaanite children in the wrong place at the wrong time. Israelite, Egyptian, Persian, Canaanite innocents, all subjects of narrative violence.[2] Stories of incredible violence provoke the question of credible reading.

---

[1] This essay is dedicated to Robert Culley in honor of the quality of intellect and gentle integrity he brings to the field of biblical studies and, more importantly, for the respect and support he gives to his students and colleagues. I also would like to acknowledge the invaluable help of two other dear friends, Fred Burnett and Danna Nolan Fewell, who, too, insist upon asking about the children.

[2] On the issue of the ethics of reading and children see Danna Nolan Fewell's anticipated *Children of Israel: Reading the Bible for the Sake of Our Children.*

Narratives of violence exercise a powerful hold upon readers' imaginations, and they can incite violence. The Matthean story of Herod's slaughter of the innocents and the associated guilt for Jesus' death falling upon Jews and their children is a case in point (see Cohen, 1983, 1993; Roth). The blood-libel in Matthew 27, aimed squarely at the "Jews," and given theological legitimacy by no less than Augustine and Luther, echoes today in religious and ethnic triumphalist rhetoric and action: a scriptural text about violence becomes a scriptive pretext for anti-Semitic attitudes and ethnic cleansing. Whether serving as justification or inducement or both, Matthew's narrative crosses over from gospel to genocide, from story to history.

Matthew's Jews are mythically and indelibly marked. Vilified as the killers of children and the Christ, the Jews (i.e. the Scribes and Pharisees) are the sons of those who murdered the prophets (23:31), "serpents, brood of vipers" (23:33), "hypocrites" (23:13, 23, 25, 27), the people from whom the promise of the future has been decisively withdrawn (23:37–38). The differences are absolute: the old and the new, Moses and Jesus, "us" and "them," those who are in and those out, the blessed and the cursed, the apocalyptically rewarded and punished. Matthew's narrative fosters the construction of a "Judaism" and "Jews" as a persistent historical and religious problem awaiting and inviting in the minds of some a final solution.[3] The biblical narrative is a mine field of potential anti-Semitic violence (cf. Burnett). It is a literary and literal killing field.

Matthean narrative violence and the Holocaust have become inextricably linked in the literature, theological and philosophical reflection, and cultural imagination of the West. The identification of Matthew 2 and 27 with the deaths of twentieth-century Jews is not fanciful, but an unfortunate fact, a fateful connection seared permanently into cultural memory. What are we to make of this connection? Some readers dismiss the notion of an anti-Semitic Matthew; other readers say Matthew's text leads right up to the gates of the *Lager* and into the crematoria. This link between Matthew's text and the murder of Jewish innocents points to the complex role of biblical narrative and culture: Matthew 2 "lives on" interpretatively as

---

[3] It is a toss-up which gospel narrative is finally the most anti-Jewish and gets used for anti-Semitic purposes. See Sanders on Luke-Acts (115).

an intertext and gloss upon a mad moment in twentieth-century life; it serves programmatically as an inducement to the killing itself. Both. Gospel fiction turned lethal, Crossan might say (xi).

The close tie between Matthean narrative violence and Holocaust murder of the innocent poses a double challenge to the credibility of readers of the Bible. The first challenge is a critical one: to understand the complex connection between biblical literature and *Lager* and the role Matthew's narrative plays in expressions of cultural violence against the innocent. The second is ethical: to act responsibly when confronted by texts with a history of lethal associations, namely to interrupt the killing work. The critical task and the ethical task are likewise inextricably connected. Credible reading after Auschwitz, Greenberg says, must face the test of the children.

"After Auschwitz Everything Brings Us back to Auschwitz"

There is little doubt that the Bible is a text that cultivates the best in readers; it is equally true that the Bible amplifies the worst side of our humanity (Phillips and Fewell: 3). Biblical narratives have a robust cultural life of their own, independent of authors and original audiences. These narratives are generative of other narratives, of mythologies, and in important ways of forms of culture itself. In giving contour and texture to the way people live and die in the world, narratives are not merely forms of cultural expression; they condition historical existence. Narratives are foundational to experience. In the words of Stephen Crites, "the formal quality of experience through time is inherently narrative" (291). This means that *story* makes all the difference not only in the ways readers live but, to put it starkly, who gets to live and to die. What gospel scholars often under appreciate is the autonomy and imaginative power of biblical narratives to alter the lives of real readers.

Luke Timothy Johnson and John Dominic Crossan present contrasting views on the issue of the anti-Semitism of Matthew's text and the broader ethical questions facing credible biblical scholarship. Johnson seeks to recast the anti-Semitic charge against Matthew by appeal to polemical rhetorical practices of late antiquity: everyone spoke, and sometimes acted, violently against their opponents, Jew and Gentile alike. He doesn't "worry about what to do with this language so much as about what the language was doing" (419).[4] In short, "grasping the conventional nature of the polemic can rob such language of its mythic force and thereby its capacity for mischief." Johnson, however, effectively underestimates the power of language, narrative and myth, and overestimates the capacity of historical analysis to correct for the imaginative potential of texts to create worlds of meaning and mayhem.

John Dominic Crossan, by contrast, challenges biblical scholars to do a far better job of identifying the latent anti-Semitism in early Christian gospels and the Christian triumphalism of critical scholarship. For example, Raymond Brown's description of Matthew 27 as "the most effective theatre among the Synoptics" is more than a misleading statement. The effect is to excuse, or, worse, be implicated in the violence enacted with a text by a costly downplaying of this as so much cultural "mischief." Scholars must become better analysts and interpreters of present culture, attentive to the ways the biblical narrative is foundational to current lived experience for better or worse. The biblical tie to the Holocaust has given this critical task new urgency.

In short, for post-Holocaust readers of the Bible, to paraphrase Irving Greenberg, all commentary, critical or otherwise, must meet a higher standard to be credible: the presence of the burning children. In Wiesel's words, "After Auschwitz everything brings us back to Auschwitz" (205). To say that historical and literary critical statements are accountable to the innocents themselves is then to ask: How does the Matthean story of the murder of the innocents and the defamation of Jewish children live on in contemporary culture shaping attitudes, imaginations and actions? How does the text give warrant to the exclusion, even killing, of Jews and their children? And what are we to do with such texts and readings?

Fraternal Interruption/Unseamly Reading

Recently Emil Fackenheim has taken special note of the textual killing potential of the biblical text. He focuses upon the responsibility

---

[4] By recasting the issue as a matter of rhetorical convention, Johnson diverts attention away from what readers actually do with these texts. He averts his eyes from the faces of the specific children who live out the Matthean narrative action.

Christian readers have to Jewish texts and to Jewish and non-Jewish children. "Through the centuries," Fackenheim argues, "Christians have imagined that Jews spend their days rejecting the Christ, or to put it into worse words, killing him all over again, as they are said to have done originally" (102). Christians must do better than this. But how is one to be a credible reader of the Jewish Bible after Auschwitz? Commenting on Matt 2:16–19 and the identity of Rachel's children he observes: "Without the New Testament passage, the children of Rachel, evidently, are Jews and they alone. With it . . . they are Christians and they alone, for in them Jeremiah's prophecy is 'fulfilled.' A fraternal Jewish-Christian reading of the Rachel-text, then, seems impossible both with Matthew and without it" (81). Fackenheim points to a paradoxical double bind: after the Holocaust the Matthean text makes it impossible for Christians to read with Jews and impossible to live without them. Yet, in spite of Auschwitz there remains some slight chance of success. But that possibility demands a rupture in what he labels "seamless" Christian reading.

"Seamless" reading is the sort that proceeds past the events of 1933–45 without radical disruption. Seamless reading is what one hears in this assessment of the Matthean passion account: "The most effective theatre among the Synoptics, outclassed in that respect only by the Johannine masterpiece" and "a Matthean composition on the basis of a popular tradition reflecting on the theme of Jesus' innocent blood and the responsibility it created" (Crossan: xi, quoting Brown: 832–33). "Capacity for mischief," Johnson's words, belongs to the same genre. A grotesque mis-statement. Whether theologically, exegetically or historically inspired, seamless reading invites a careless complicity in the events that breathes death into the "naked text" as Fackenheim calls it. Seamless reading is one way Christian readers enable Matthew's text to murder the children all over again.

Instead, Fackenheim calls for an interruption or shock (*Erschütterung*) in the Christian soul that is not mediated through theological categories but by the event of the Holocaust itself. This is comparable to what the Jewish philosopher and Talmudic reader Emmanuel Levinas calls a "shaken conscience" in which consciousness is profoundly disturbed by conscience through the breaking through of the face of the other. The interruptive moment of ethical encounter is the coming face-to-face with the suffering innocents. For Levinas the face is the place where the infinite breaks through the finite, where the good in all of its height is encountered, where responsibility for the other is met. In a meditation on Amos 5:19, Levinas says, "the death of the starving children thrusts us into the snake pit, into places that are no longer places, into places one cannot forget, but that do not succeed in placing themselves in memory, in organizing themselves in the form of memories. We have known such pits in this century" (85). Credible reading stands in that pit with the children and remembers.

Auschwitz has ruptured the Bible and along with it seamless critical scholarship. Nothing is the same again because there is a *novum* in history, namely the conjunction for the first time of *birth* and *crime* (Fackenheim: 87). Knowing this, readers of the Bible must read differently, deferentially, deliberately for the children, lest they contribute to the formation of a culture that makes the murder of the innocents natural, inevitable, biblical.

How does one read Matthew 2 "interruptively?" The first step is to determine the ways the Matthean story and the Jewish Holocaust live on together. How do they reinforce each other intertextually, participating in the formation of mythic consciousness, particularly of national and cultural self-expressions, though contemporary literature and cinema, as well as other forms of modern culture? By noting examples of the way the biblical text glosses and underwrites literary and aesthetic expressions, biblical scholars may learn something about the capacity of texts to live on in complex ways. The second step is to read for the children by refusing to take Matthew as a violent template. In other words to allow the face of the children to interrupt our ways of reading and making sense. This is the beginning of credible reading.

Culture of Violence

It is spring 1999 in Kosovo and a genocide of ethnic Albanian men, women and children is underway. Even as NATO bombs fall on downtown Belgrade, the Serbian ethnic cleansing of Kosovo Albanians accelerates. Matthew's text is a powerful accelerant to the genocide. In a cruel twist, the Matthean narrative and the experience of the Nazi genocide of Jews and Gypsies shape Serbian ethnic identity and action. The celebrated 1389 Battle for Kosovo, dramatized poetically in *The Mountain Wreath,* serves as a mythologized moment in Serbian self-understanding that directly shaped nineteenth-century Serbian christological self-expression. "Christoslavism" is the argument that Slavs are by essence Christians, and conversion to any other religion constitutes a betrayal of race and religion; massacre or sacred cleansing is therefore one's religious duty (Sells, 1996:51). In this legend Lazar is betrayed and subsequently put to death by turncoat Muslim Slavs. In this Slavic "passion play," the brutal slaughter of Slav "Christ-killers"—Muslim children, women and men—is celebrated during Advent season. The Matthean slaughter of innocents works as a subtext scripting Serbian mythic consciousness and providing justification for subsequent cleansing actions.

Matthew's mythic power in shaping Serbian nationalism is public and real. Michael Sells reports that a 1989 dramatization of *The Mountain Wreath* played to more than a million people in Kosovo (1997). On that occasion Slobodan Milosevic renounced Kosovan autonomy and initiated a violent military repression. With Serbian memories of their own World War II experience at the hands of the Nazis refreshed, the dramatized Matthean murder-of-the-innocents narrative helped inflame a new genocidal spirit directed now against the ethnic Albanians. Victims become victimizers; past and present converge; subtexts become pretexts; narrative events mythologize ethnic history. German atrocities, mediated by the Matthean narrative itself, ironically scripts a fresh wave of violence whose effects are currently realized in brutal relocation and repression. Matthew's story of the killing of the innocents freely crosses cultural boundaries, religious identities and historical epochs. The Matthean narrative is hard at work shaping Serbian mythic time as killing time.

In the Russian novel *Life and Fate*, the link between Matthean narrative and the Holocaust becomes a vehicle for probing basic ethical questions. The setting for Vasily Grossman's fictional history is the battle for Stalingrad. An eyewitness to the Holocaust, Grossman was the first journalist to publish an account of a German death camp. Grossman wrestles with the central questions: Were the deaths of 350,000 souls in any sense a justifiable price to pay to defeat evil? On what grounds does one justify the cost of the lives of innocent women and children? Is there any reason to be confident that Western political and religious institutions, linked to the biblical tradition, provide a basis for knowing and doing the good? Grossman turns to the

Matthean story and its Hebrew Bible intertexts to gloss the character Mostovsky's struggle to give an accounting:

> Many books have been written about the nature of good and evil and the struggle between them. There is a deep and undeniable sadness in all this: whenever we see the dawn of an eternal good that will never be overcome by evil . . . the blood of old people and children is always shed. Not only men, but even God himself is powerless to lessen this evil.
>
>> "In Rama was there a voice heard, lamentation, and weeping, and great mourning, Rachel weeping for her children, and would not be comforted, because they were not."
>
> What does a woman who has lost her children care about a philosopher's definition of good and evil? (406)

Grossman laments the fact that "prophets, religious leaders, reformers, social and political leaders are impotent" in the face of evil, indeed that lofty goals and sacred texts make matters worse. In spite of, indeed ironically on account of, Western political and religious institutions, the words of Jer 31:15 are fulfilled. The inevitability of human and divine complicity with Evil is affirmed, and always the innocent bear the consequence when Good and Evil contest one another. As in Bethlehem so also in Stalingrad: innocent children perish for the sake of some theological good or ideological cause. But Grossman finds such cost and its supporting logic unbearable: "I do not believe in the good, I believe in kindness. . . . Not even Herod shed blood in the name of evil; he shed it for his version of the good. Herod's good" (405).

At one point a German officer attempts to persuade Mostovskoy that Russians and Germans really have much in common, and that Russians have something to learn from German hatred of the Jews and, above all, their experience of liquidating them by the millions. Stalin's true genius, Liss suggests, is a definitional one: he had "seen the hidden brotherhood between Fascism and the Pharisees" (401). Liss says, "You and I both know that it's not on battlefields that the future is decided" (402). The decisive battle is waged with those mythic narratives and logical arguments that link arms to justify the deaths of the innocents as acceptable cost.

In short, the credible response to such gospel complicity is not to offer a counter-myth and counter-argument (for example a better "historical" or "literary" case) equally grounded in the same Western cultural traditions, but recognition of a goodness that Levinas says is "a goodness without witnesses, a little goodness without ideology. It could be called goodness without thought. The goodness of men outside the religious or social good" (91). A goodness that interrupts ideology, Bible and its application.

The third release in the highly successful *Planet of the Apes* film series reveals the degree to which the deep cultural association of Matthew's narrative with the Holocaust has become natural. *Escape From the Planet of the Apes* plays upon a reversal of Matthew's murder-of-the-innocents plot: innocent chimpanzee adults and child, rather than human beings, are targeted for elimination. In this film biblical violence is shaded with humor and a thinly veiled political message. Under pressure to produce a winning script, one that would retain a predominately teenage following and in order to capitalize on the growing youth opposition to the Vietnam War, the producers tap the all-too-familiar biblical plot. Entertainment, political opposition to the Vietnam War, biblical violence, xenophobic mythology and the profit incentive combine to produce "effective theatre."

Three chimpanzees return from the future to the Great Consternation of American Leaders. Prompted by the birth of a child to the speaking chimpanzee couple, the military seeks to kill them all. The last-second switch of the speaking chimpanzee child Milo for a "dumb" chimpanzee child serves to disparage an unpopular American military who look ever so much like the bumbling Germans of "Hogan's Heroes": the captives outsmart their captors at every turn. Importantly, the plot reversal protects the option of another sequel. Lost, in the rush to celebrate the survival of the intelligent chimpanzee and the series, is that "dumb" chimpanzee whose bullet-riddled body is unceremoniously dumped into the water in a manner that calls to mind Pharaoh's dispatch of male Hebrew children into the Nile. The parents hardly fare better. Like Matthew's Jesus, Milo lives for a future apocalyptic conflict, which becomes the theme of the final installment in the series; and like the dead children of Bethlehem, the death of the unnamed chimpanzee child is put in service to the human-like child whose survival is assured.

The allusions to Jewish Holocaust are transparent: the President's scientific adviser is a German Otto Hasslein, a scientist whose goal is to ensure racial and species purity; a Commission that makes a "final" recommendation; an internment camp where Mengele- type scientific experimentation (involuntary interrogation and abortion) takes place; and of course "transport cars" in the form of circus wagons used to move apes and other animals about. Himmler's *Lager*, Herod's Bethlehem and technoculture converge. The imaginative link is underscored in the following exchange in which the American President responds to Hasslein's proffered advice:

> "Now what do you expect me . . . to do about it? Alter what you believe to be the course of the future by slaughtering two innocents, or rather three now that one of them is pregnant? Herod tried that and Christ survived."
>
> "Mr. President, Herod lacked our facilities."

Narrative roles undergo reversal: Americans for Germans, chimpanzees for humans, and chimpanzees for Jews. Already identified with Nazis in the popular press after the Calley-led massacre at MyLai, American soldiers are portrayed as German killers of the innocent. From the point of view of anti-Vietnam war ideology operating at the surface of the film, Americans are cast in a decidedly negative moral light, but in relation to the "species" ecological war which evokes deeper religious and techno-scientific macro-narratives and experiences, the moral status of the Americans' actions is more ambiguous, conflictual. Hasslein raises the question of moral duty:

> "How many futures are there? And which future has God, if there is a god, chosen for man's destiny. If I urge the destruction of these two apes am I defying God's will or obeying it? Am I his enemy or his instrument?"
>
> "An assassin would say the latter. Do you approve of assassination?"
>
> "Well, Mr. President, we condoned the attempted suicide of Hitler because he was evil."
>
> "Yes, but would we have approved of killing him in babyhood when he was still innocent, or killing his mother when he was still in her womb, or slaughtering his remote ancestors. We have no proof, Hasslein, that these apes are evil."

. . . .

"Mr. President, the people must be told that the killers of today
could become the mass murderers of tomorrow."

The Matthean narrative script is at work in Hasslein's struggle to
discern the right moral action. The xenophobic response of killing the
baby chimpanzee is given biblical legs to stand on. With the human
species and its destiny at stake, the murder of the innocents is
rationalized in a way that the movie does not seriously challenge.
Grossman's worry is confirmed again: the killing of innocents is
legitimated when a basic cultural, theological or philosophical
principle needs defending.

Even if we grant that the film has purposefully conflated
narrative elements in order to expose the ambiguity of moral action,
other cultural texts have slipped in to reinforce a deadly message about
the non-humans. There is a more onerous twist in that the innocent
chimpanzee becomes victimized twice. Not only does Matthew 2
forecast the present (1973 CE) death of the chimp, Matthew 27
anticipates a future (3955 CE) that has already happened, a future
where Apes have committed atrocities against humans. While being
interrogated, the mother Chimpanzee confesses that she has dissected
human beings, a gruesome image championed in the original movie
release. The identification of chimpanzee actions with Nazi practices
turns victim into victimizer. And evoked is the medieval charge that
Jews ritually murdered and cannibalized Christian babies, which fueled
pogroms since the Middle Ages, and the Christoserbian legitimation of
the murder of ethnic Albanian children. The murder of innocent Milo
is doubly legitimized as an efficient Herodian-like past action and a
just response for a future atrocity that will already have been
committed in the future. The past is the future, the future past. Killing
them for the past, killing them for the future. Both victims and
victimizers, the chimpanzees can't win for dying. The Matthean
narrative with its Holocaust intertext crosses national, temporal, ethnic,
and now species boundaries in order to neutralize the enemy.

Neutralizing the Hebrew Text

The cinematic portrayal of the Matthean story/Holocaust
connection brings us full circle back to the point where we began,

namely the Matthean text and biblical violence. How does the way the Matthean narrative visually scripts the elision of past and future, victim and victimizer, in *Escape from the Planet of the Apes* offer a clue about the way Matthew uses story to neutralize the Jewish Exodus narrative as a Jewish foundation myth? How do we interrupt Matthew's reading of the Hebrew text thereby interrupting Matthean violence at its source?

Matthew makes much of Hebrew scripture in the construction of the Jesus narrative. Traditional biblical scholarship typically explains the intertextual[5] relationship of one text to another as a process of "influence": one text evokes another in the form of a direct citation or as an allusion. Matthean commentators have long centered on Matthew's "use" of the Old Testament in terms of the explicit citation of Hosea, Jeremiah and Micah texts. Critics have also sought to pinpoint the "allusions" in Matt 2:13–23 to the beginning of Exodus (usually 4:19–20). Luz has noted the parallels between this Matthean text and a second story, namely the rescue of the Moses child and the murder of Israelite boys by Pharaoh in Exodus 1 and 2 (cf. Luz: 144). The parallels between Moses and Jesus are thick and conflictual, and they are routinely accounted for in terms of the "influence" of the Old Testament text upon Matthew.

But doesn't the "influence" also flow in the opposite direction? In terms of the lived nature of this intertextual relationship, as Fackenheim shows, Matthew's text is the one with a far greater "influence." Matthew and Exodus follow a common narrative course, one that extends beyond the boundaries of the killing stories themselves where critics traditionally draw the citational limits when charting Matthew's relationship to his Hebrew intertexts. Against Brown and others who suggest that Matthew's text repeats or augments that structure by "inserting" into it prophetic citations, I suggest a more basic deformation of narrative structure and meaning is underway, one that has profound effects on the way Matthew's readers henceforth will understand the foundation story that shapes Jewish life and faith. The Matthean narrative takes the Mosaic infancy and adult death stories, which form *in nuncio* the body of the Jews' Exodus and

---

[5] Julia Kristeva defines intertextuality as a "permutation of texts. . . . [I]n the space of a text several utterances drawn from *other texts intersect and neutralize one another* (113; translation and emphasis mine).

Conquest foundation myths, and interpretively trump them with the Jews' very own prophetic texts. Matthew "kills" the Jews' foundation narrative with the aid of prophetic discursive material.[6]

Matt 2:15   Exod 4:22 (calls son out of Egypt)
   Hos 11:1 citation
Matt 2:16   Exod 4:23 (killing of male children)
Matt 2:18   Exod 4:23/24; Gen 35:16–20 (allusion to Rachel's death),
            Gen 32 (Jacob's struggle with "Angel of God")
   Jer 31.15 citation
Matt 2:20   Exod 4:19 (mother and child to safety)
Matt 2:23   Exod 4:13–15 (naming Jesus/God) (naming Jacob,
            Gen 32:28)
   Isa 11:1 citation(?)
Matt 3:1   Exod 4:27 (exit to wilderness, ἐρήμω)
Matt 3:6   Exod 4:31 (people repent/believe, λάος)
Matt 3:7   Exod 5:1 (Φαρισαίων/Φαράω)

When presented as an intersection of stories, Matthew's neutralizing effect is severe. Matthew's text employs Hebrew prophetic texts to subvert the original Mosaic mythic story and to kill it off by radically distorting its characters and action just as the Serbian myth of Lazar recasts Kosovo Muslims as the enemy and Hasslein makes chimpanzees the victimizers. The intertextual effect of recalling the Exodus stories and then prophetically attacking them, by trumping Moses with Jesus (especially in chaps. 5–7), is painful enough. But Matthew's text does even greater damage to the Jews. This, I suggest, is Matthew's hidden source of power for imaginative and real-life damage. In the process of beginning afresh with the wilderness narrative (Matt 3:1–4:1) in which Jesus and John the Baptist now displace Moses and Aaron in their lead roles, Matthew fashions one more deadly narrative insult that turns the text figuratively and literally against the Jews. The larger matrix distortion invites readers to identify the Pharisees and Scribes as the opponents of Jesus who first make their appearance on the Gospel scene in 3:7 as structurally and homophonically identified with Pharaoh's appearance in Exod 5:1. With the identification of Pharisees and Pharaoh (Φαρισαίων/Φαράω) the meaning of the narrative of the killing of the Jewish innocent is now shockingly turned on its head: Egyptian political and religious leaders

---

[6] The aspect of *neutralization* is pivotal for Kristeva because it underscores intertextuality's ideological and cultural-critical edge.

are identified narratively within the matrix of texts with Jewish political and religious leaders. The *Jews* under Herod's leadership become responsible for the death of their own children just as the narrator will later identify the Pharisees as responsible for the killing of their own prophets (23:37). This is analogous to the reversal pattern found in *Escape from the Planet of the Apes*. Future "non-humans" ultimately responsible for their own past innocents' death.

In the Jewish associative identification with Pharaoh, a vile portrait of a people wicked enough to kill their own children emerges, ironically and pitifully reinforced and condemned by their own narratives and foundation stories. An old foundational narrative in which Jewish children are murdered by Egyptians now becomes a new foundation story for Christian readers in which the Jews are murderers and are to be murdered. It is the acceptance of responsibility for infanticide associated with Jews which is reiterated in that most horrific of statements in Matt 27:25: "And all the people answered, 'His blood be on us and on our children.'"[7] Out of their own mouths and narratives the Jews condemn themselves and their children. We do not have far to go to arrive at the killing of Jews as legitimated by their very own "rewritten" Scriptures. We are at the borders of Kosovo, the gates of Auschwitz.

By identifying the Jews with Pharaoh, with their own bondage and their own complicity in the death of their children, Matthew invites readers to read past, present and future culture in terms of anti-Jewish violence. Through the juxtaposition not just of individual texts but a matrix of textual and narrative roles and actions, the Matthean text encourages its readers to join in constructing "the Jews" as vile perpetrators of one of the most horrendous crimes imaginable, a charge that Christians have kept alive for centuries. Thus Matthew encourages a narrative and theological triumphalism by shaping the reader to be a "scribe fit for the Kingdom" and to pull from the treasure room what is new and old (13:52). In other words, readers are invited to appropriate for their own purposes those living texts and narratives and turn them back in an aggressive, murderous way against their very authors. It is

---

[7] Johnson concludes his essay by saying that knowing the polemical patterns of antiquity enables us to "relativize our party's version." I suggest Johnson "relativizes" not only the reality of the Matthean text's power but the ethical responsibility the historian has to take that deadly power and its victims seriously. See Wyschogrod.

precisely what *Escape from the Planet of the Apes* does. It is a double homicide: of infants and of foundation stories.

Interrupting the Text and the Killing

Matthew's intertextual reading of Exodus and the Gospel's close association with the Holocaust event challenge us as critical, post-Holocaust readers to seek an alternative to seamless reading of biblical narratives. We come face-to-face with the ethical challenge and responsibility as Grossman says, to say "No" to Matthew's use of Hebrew scripture, "No" to the commentary tradition that averts the eyes or relativizes the problem, "No" to a critical interpretive practice that resists recognizing its own cultural implicature in readings that kill. Seamless and unseemly readings must be aggressively interrupted. How? By attention to the capacity of texts, especially narratives of violence, to live on and off of others.

How and why the Matthean survives literarily and aesthetically as a textual killing field at the same time as the children it speaks of are silenced is a deeply disturbing irony. But irony is no stranger to Matthew's Gospel. At the same time, irony opens the door to fundamental textual, interpretive and ethical questions about the subtle and not-so-subtle role of the Bible in shaping a culture of violence, and about critical reading that understands itself first and foremost as a moral activity that sets out deliberately to interrupt such violence. Levinas reminds us that the death of the innocents "thrusts us into the snake pit, into places that are no longer places, into places one cannot forget, but that do not succeed in placing themselves in memory, in organizing themselves in the form of memories. We have known such pits in this century" (85). Pits are being dug in Kosovo today as I write.

Becoming better, more critically imaginative readers of contemporary culture is one thing that is needed. Credible scholarship interrogates and, like ethics, interrupts easy identifications: fascist with Pharisee, Pharaoh with Pharisee, chimpanzee with Jew. Moreover, with certain notable exceptions, biblical critics have not adequately come to grips with the event of the Holocaust nor broken the grip of a certain disciplinary thinking that regards the ethical as subordinate to professional duty. We can do better as Crossan says.

Interruption occurs when particular innocent children disrupt the power biblical texts exercise in shaping our perceptions and informing our world. By attending to these children's faces and other innocents whose deaths rupture our critical strategies and our memory, we open ourselves to the possibility of saying "No" to all texts, biblical or otherwise, that kill children, biblical or otherwise. Short of a shaken conscience nothing is credible.

Fackenheim, Wiesel and Levinas demand of credible readers of the Bible that we recognize the relationship of history to text. Our responsibility to the Children of the Book is to interrupt the murder, interpretively, if necessary, with violence itself. Short of action, even a shaken conscience is not credible.

Bibliography

Brown, Raymond
    1994   *The Death of the Messiah: From Gethsemane to the Grave. A Commentary on the Passion Narratives in the Four Gospels.* 2 vols. Anchor Bible Reference Library. New York: Doubleday.

Burnett, Fred
    1992   "Exposing the Anti-Jewish Ideology of Matthew's Implied Author: The Characterization of God as Father." *Semeia* 59:155–91.

Cohen, Jeremy
    1992   *The Friars and the Jews: The Evolution of Medieval Anti-Judaism.* Ithaca: Cornell University Press.
    1993   "The Jews as Killer of Christ in the Latin Tradition, from Augustine to the Friars." *Traditio* 29:1–28.

Crites, Stephen
    1971   "The Narrative Quality of Existence." *JAAR* 39:291–311.

Crossan, John Dominic
    1991   *Who Killed Jesus? Exposing the Roots of Anti-Semitism in the Gospel Story of the Death of Jesus.* San Francisco: HarperSanFrancisco.

Eaglestone, Robert
    1997   *Ethical Criticism. Reading After Levinas.* Edinburgh: Edinburgh University Press.

Escape From the Planet of the Apes
    1971   Twentieth Century Fox Home Entertainment. Beverly Hills.

Fackenheim, Emil
    1990   *The Jewish Bible after the Holocaust: A Rereading.* Bloomington: Indiana University Press.

Fewell, Danna Nolan and Gary Phillips
    1997   "Drawn to Excess, or Reading beyond Betrothal." *Semeia* 77:22–47.

Greenberg, Irving.
    1976.   "Cloud of Smoke, Pillar of Fire: Judaism, Christianity, and Modernity after the Holocaust." Pp. 9–54 in *Auschwitz: Beginning or a New Era? Reflections on the Holocaust.* Ed. Eva Fleischner. New York: KTAV.

Grossman, Vasily
    1985   *Life and Fate.* London: Harvill.

Johnson, Luke Timothy
    1989   "The New Testament's Anti-Jewish Slander and the Conventions of Ancient Polemic." *JBL* 108:419–41.

Kristeva, Julia
    1969   *Semeiotiké. Recherches pour une sémanalyse.* Collections Tel Quel. Paris: Seuil.

Levinas, Emmanuel
    1994   "Beyond Memory. From the Tractate *Berakhot, 12b–13a.*" Pp. 76–91 in *In the Time of the Nations.* Indianapolis: Indiana University Press.

Luz, Ulrich
    1985   *Matthew 1–7: A Commentary.* Trans. Wilhelm Linss. Minneapolis: Augsburg Fortress.

Phillips, Gary and Danna Nolan Fewell
    1997   "Ethics, Bible, Reading As If." *Semeia* 77:1–21.

Roth, Cecil
    1993   "The Mediaeval Conception of the Jew." Pp. 171–90 in *Essays and Studies in Memory of Linda R. Miller.* Ed. Israel Davidson. New York: Jewish Theological Seminary of America Press.

Sanders, J.T.
    1984   "The Salvation of the Jews in Luke-Acts." Pp. 104–28 in *Luke-Acts: New Perspectives from the Society of Biblical Literature Seminar.* Ed. C. H. Talbert. New York: Crossroad.

Sells, Michael
    1996   *The Bridge Betrayed: Religion and Genocide in Bosnia.* Berkeley: University of California Press.
    1997   "'Christ Killer' Mythology and the Tragedy in the Balkans." *Explorations* 11:5.

Wyschogrod, Edith
    1998   *An Ethics of Remembering: History, Heterology and the Nameless Others.* Religion and Postmodernism. Chicago: University of Chicago Press.

LABOURING WITH ABUSIVE BIBLICAL TEXTS
TRACING TRAJECTORIES OF MISOGYNY

Pamela J. Milne

The labour of reading, the theme around which this volume in honour of Robert Culley is structured, will have a different meaning for every contributor. The theme is an apt one since it captures the sense of care and detail, the work of meticulous scholarship that has characterized the many contributions made by Culley to contemporary Hebrew bible scholarship in general and to the academic study of the bible in Canada in particular.

For me, the labour of reading biblical texts has changed significantly from the late 70s and early 80s, when I was a graduate student trying to become the first to produce a doctoral dissertation under Culley's supervision, to the present, when I am changing career directions after the disbanding of the religious studies department[1]

---

[1] The department at the University of Windsor was disbanded in 1996 after a Senate investigation into a formal complaint made by all the women faculty and two women student representatives from the departmental council concerning serious violations of Senate bylaws by the department head. These violations had the effect of excluding and/or limiting the participation of women members of the council. The senior administrators appointed by Senate to investigate the complaint concluded that the violations had occurred. Had these been the only gender-related problems to emerge from the religious studies department, they would not likely have resulted in the decision to disband. Two previous investigations of gender harassment complaints had not produced significant changes in the academic environment for women, and it seemed that closure was the next step. While this

within which I used to teach courses on Hebrew bible. There are two senses in which reading the bible has been a labour that I wish to discuss in what follows. The first sense is the struggle to do any academic work at all as a woman in a traditionally male discipline. The second sense is the struggle to read, as a feminist, texts that present increasingly more vexing problems of sexism.

The major task of my graduate years was to make a transition from the historical focus I had pursued as a student at the University of Michigan to a literary focus so that I could complete doctoral studies with Culley at McGill. Although difficult at the time, that change in focus was fortuitous insofar as literary approaches not only have been predominant in biblical scholarship in the last quarter of the twentieth century, but they have been particularly important to the feminist biblical scholarship that has grown so rapidly during my own career.

My studies up to and including the doctoral dissertation were not feminist,[2] but I was keenly interested in the efforts of biblical scholars such as Phyllis Trible and Phyllis Bird whose writings marked the emergence of what I would later discover was actually the second stage of feminist biblical criticism in North America.[3] I had come to biblical studies through an interest in archaeology that seemed, at the time, less alienating than the philosophy I studied as an undergraduate. Eventually, the novelty of situating ancient texts in their ancient Near Eastern contexts was overshadowed by a growing awareness that biblical material was no less androcentric than the Greek, mediaeval or modern philosophy I had tried to abandon.

---

decision alleviated the immediate problem for women faculty, it did not address the larger concerns of how to prevent or stop such situations in the future.

[2] My doctoral dissertation used the theory and an analytical tool of a dead, white, male, Russian folklorist, Vladimir Propp, to analyze the stories of Daniel 1–6 in which the main characters are all male (Milne, 1988a). The task of the dissertation was simply to assess the usefulness of Propp's model of the narrative surface structure of the heroic fairy tale as a tool for describing narratives in the Hebrew bible.

[3] The first stage is generally identified as emerging in connection with the women's rights movement in the eighteenth and nineteenth centuries in the United States in response to the habitual use of the bible to justify the secondary and subordinate status of women in American society (De Swarte Gifford; Milne, 1995). There is, of course, evidence of women in Europe engaged in biblical interpretation for centuries before this time (Gössmann).

Pursuing feminist interests proved impossible during the first several years of post-Ph.D. employment for two reasons. The first was the relative absence of feminist biblical scholarship in Canada, a result no doubt of the low numbers and percentage of women scholars employed in this or any area of religious studies.[4] In the Society of Biblical Literature, a section on "Women in the Biblical World" was initiated in the early 1980s, but there was no comparable space for feminist scholarship within the Canadian Society of Biblical Studies. In this sense, the labour of doing feminist readings was not dissimilar to the labour of women who attempted woman-centred critical readings of the bible for the past thousand years. Gerda Lerner (139) makes the point that from the middle ages to the nineteenth century in Europe and North America, there are examples of women thinkers confronting the patriarchy of both biblical texts and its male interpreters. But those women lacked an intellectual community and there was no collective memory of their ideas. Each worked in isolation, unaware of the feminist-critical work that had been done before. Though I had the luxury of access to published feminist criticism, there was no local intellectual community of support within which I could function.

The second impediment to pursuing feminist academic interests was an academic work environment that was supportive neither of feminist research nor of women academics. Nothing in my student experience had prepared me for the alienation I experienced as a tenure-track assistant professor at the University of Windsor. It did not take me long to realize that feminist research would make the tenure process extremely difficult, if not impossible.[5] My experience in these

---

[4] Studies would show that compared to other humanities disciplines, religious studies had a disproportionately low percentage of women in graduate studies and in full-time faculty positions in Canada (Remus *et al*: 147–49). This situation persists to the present and is worsened by the fact that just as women were beginning to make inroads in the discipline, universities began closing or downsizing religion departments across the country.

[5] As a result of my experience, I worked with other women academics to develop and implement university-wide equity procedures. Senate bylaws now mandate that feminist and other non-traditional forms of scholarship must be evaluated in an equitable way. Moreover, we now have equity provisions built into our faculty union's collective agreement with the University. All hiring and promotion/tenure decisions now must take place in the presence of an equity assessor appointed by the administration.

years, along with my observations of the difficulties experienced by other women faculty, radicalized me. It made me understand more fully than ever before the feminist insight that the personal is political.

Only once I had secured the protection of tenure, did I begin to undertake feminist research both in biblical studies and in gender equity studies. No longer was the desire to do feminist research just an intellectual curiosity. Now it became a necessity to try to understand how and why sexist attitudes persist so strongly even in places like universities where I had expected to find more enlightened views. Most feminist scholarship today largely ignores the subject of religion and especially the bible, thinking that religion is somewhat peripheral to the central problems women must address. It seemed to me, however, that the cultural influence of the biblical tradition on western society has been profound. Understanding what images and views of women are promoted by that tradition seemed to me to be an important component to understanding contemporary attitudes. One of the major insights of eighteenth- and nineteenth-century American feminists was that the issues of racial and sex discrimination were linked insofar as those determined to deny equal rights to Blacks and to women regularly appealed to the bible to justify their position. As a result of the success of the anti-slavery movement and the ongoing struggles of African Americans in the United States, one rarely now finds the bible being appealed to as a justification of racism. In other parts of the world too, such as South Africa, the bible is no longer seen by very many as a source that can be used to justify apartheid.

The same cannot be said, however, with respect to sexism. Sexist attitudes are still deeply ingrained in our own and many other cultures influenced by the biblical tradition. And it is still not at all uncommon to find the bible being used to promote the notion that women are, by divine design, secondary and inferior to men.[6] Histori-

---

[6] It is, of course, obvious that not all men hold sexist views, nor do all women hold non-sexist views. It is the case, nonetheless, that the powerful in patriarchal culture have made and continue to make use of the biblical tradition in profoundly sexist ways. In the early 1980s, Krister Stendahl was already deeply aware of the cultural problem of which I speak here. He wrote: ". . . that the male community has found aid and comfort in its chauvinism in the name of the Bible is relatively easy to document in western culture" (204–5). Unfortunately, not much has changed despite his efforts to address what he called the "public health" issues of biblical studies.

cally, Christian theologies of women have been built primarily on interpretations of the Adam-Eve story of Genesis 2–3. For this reason, this text has been the centre of feminist interest for centuries. Like so many before me, I felt compelled initially to examine this text and feminist efforts to analyze it (Milne, 1988b, 1989).

The overwhelming feminist consensus on this story, arrived at by confessionally committed scholars led by Phyllis Trible (1978), was that the biblical text itself was not the source of the problem for women. Rather, the problem was centuries of misinterpretation by male scholars. Though Trible made this argument in a much more sophisticated way using the strategies of rhetorical criticism, it was essentially the same argument advanced by many of the women who had tackled this text in earlier centuries.

My initial enthusiasm for Trible's analysis had wavered as I wondered how so many men for so many years could have been so obtuse with respect to the meaning of this text. More distressing than past interpretation was the contemporary interpretive work that gave no indication of being familiar with feminist studies, much less of incorporating any of them.[7] Others were having similar doubts about the nature and locus of the problem with respect to the Adam-Eve story (Clines, Lanser, Jobling). One of the most telling questions was posed by David Jobling, who challenged Trible's thesis that the Adam-Eve story was actually a liberating one promoting gender equality by asking who, in such a patriarchal society as ancient Israel, could have composed a feminist talc (Jobling: 42). In my work, I argued that the underlying structure of Genesis 2–3 was thoroughly patriarchal and that the woman-denigrating male interpretations of the past and present represented not simply the sexism of the interpreter but a substantially well-founded representation of the sexism of the text itself.

Despite the fact that several of us were reaching similar conclusions about the deeply rooted patriarchal nature of Genesis 2–3, such views have been largely marginalized or ignored in the feminist theological circles that dominate feminist biblical criticism. Recently, however, support for the view that Genesis 2–3 is structured in a way

---

[7] At that time I cited a doctoral dissertation produced at Harvard (Wallace) and an article in the *Journal of Biblical Literature* (Walsh) as examples of this blindness to feminist work (Milne, 1988b:19).

that promotes a gender hierarchy privileging the male has come from a new direction, a sociological analysis by Stuart Charmé.

Charmé examined how a group of boys and girls, aged four to eleven, understood and interpreted the Adam-Eve story. Specifically, he wanted to study the impact of gender on interpretation: did girls respond differently to this story than did boys? By studying young children, Charmé hoped to minimize the extent to which hermeneutic or theological background would shape their responses. Children's responses, he argued, could give us "valuable insight into how this story is initially being absorbed and incorporated without the more complicated theological overlay of various religious authorities and traditions" (28).

Charmé concluded that the explanations provided by the children reveal the powerful force of traditional views of the gender of god and the gender roles for men and women that are legitimized by god (28). Moreover, gender appears to have a great impact on how children interpret and evaluate the behaviour of Adam and Eve (33). Charmé (36) suggests that the parallels between the responses of the boys and traditional interpretations of the text are probably not coincidental: "Hermeneutical consistency between centuries of Western theology and young boys today probably indicates not that the boys interviewed were theologically precocious, but rather that traditional interpreters were very much boys at heart" (37).

Whereas the boys saw Adam as the innocent victim and placed blame on Eve, the girls rarely saw Adam as completely innocent. For many girls, responsibility was seen as shared. Girls were also more likely to offer motives other than disobedience or gullibility to explain Eve's actions (38). Not surprisingly, then, boys judged Eve more harshly and suggested more punitive and violent punishment for her than did girls (39).

As a result of his study, Charmé notes that "[n]ot only is religion a powerful force contributing to children's gender role socialization, but children's gender identity is a powerful lens through which they will view religion."

I find Charmé's work helpful, not only because it explicitly lent support to my argument about the structure of Genesis 2–3, but also because it has provided me with a new framework within which to reflect on my subsequent study of the book of Judith (Milne, 1993) as well as on an awareness that I have come to about the biblical tradition as a whole. The awareness is that the level of misogyny and gyno-phobia in biblical texts increases over time. This is quite easily seen in New Testament material where feminists have often argued that texts that most likely go back to the time of the Jesus movement or the historical Jesus are more egalitarian than those, such as the household codes, that emerge from a later time when the early church is forming its institutional structure. In my view, there is a similar kind of negative development through the Hebrew bible and Apocrypha.

Unlike many feminist scholars, I do not think there is comfort to be taken from demonstrating that the older the tradition, the more woman-friendly it might be. Rather, I think feminist scholars need to ask why and how misogyny and gynophobia seem to increase over time. There must be a process at work here and, until we can understand it, we are not likely to be able to disrupt its momentum. This is where Charmé's work seems to provide some useful insight. If male creators of the tradition read (or heard) their sources with the same kind of gender lens (ear) as did the boys who interpreted Genesis 2–3, then it may be virtually inevitable that the tradition they create becomes progressively more woman-hostile. His work suggests that there may be significant differences between the way men and women interpret texts.

With this idea in mind, I want to examine some late texts to trace elements from earlier traditions that have developed the trajectory of misogyny and gynophobia and, in doing so, I want to attempt to identify aspects of the tradition that were magnified by being read through the lens of male gender. The Apocryphal book of Judith will serve as a starting point because it is a very late text, generally dated to the last third of the second century BCE, and one which many analysts have argued is one of the few strongly woman-positive biblical texts. Judith has been widely, though not exclusively, seen as a positive female character. She was described by some as a feminist heroine and by others as a feminist's heroine because she bravely delivered her people from destruction at the hands of a powerful enemy army by decapitating the enemy general. If it actually does offer a feminist heroine, this book would appear to stand as a counter-voice to many other texts from this same period.

To examine this issue, I undertook a narrative surface structure analysis for the purpose of determining what kind of tale this is and what role Judith plays within it (Milne, 1993). Of the narrative models

I tested on the book, the epic-struggle model appeared to account for its structure best. Within this tale type, however, Judith played the role not of heroine but of the hero's (god's) helper. Even though she was central to the story, her narrative role was a secondary one. So, on the narrative structural level, there seemed to be a problem in looking to Judith as a heroine, feminist or not.

Beyond this, there were aspects of the character, Judith, that I, as a feminist, did not find acceptable in a feminist model. Judith is, ultimately, a wholly male construct who is fully subservient to the patriarchal parameters of the story.[8] Though she may be seen to act bravely and to endanger herself for the sake of her people, the way in which she acts sends other messages as well. The image of Judith is a very dangerous one, because it so promotes the classic *femme fatale* motif and in doing so problematizes women's bodies, particularly their physical appearance and their sexuality. Here may be an example of how different messages are taken from a text. A feminist or pro-feminist analyst of this story does not tend to read the *femme fatale* motif as central or significant. For the traditional male reader, however, it may well be the most important message of the text.

The Judith story is also an interesting place to observe the development of the woman-negative trajectory. As a literary construct, Judith takes up and develops the character, Jael, found in the much earlier texts of Judges 5 and 4.[9] In Judg 5:24–27, Jael is an unsuspecting tent wife who finds her space invaded by a male stranger asking for a drink. Jael provides him both drink and food, then kills him by using a mallet to drive a tent peg into his head. This text provides no motivation for her action nor any explanation of how she accomplished it. From the verses preceding this section of the text, the

---

[8] Margarita Stocker, in her recent extensive study of the Judith story in western culture, argues that "the Book of Judith has a feminist premise . . ." but that "despite its own thematics, [it] cannot afford to be feminist." Judith, "was merely an instrument of the true patriarchal power. . . ." However, Stocker finds "a feminist implication" in Judith's action that she thinks is "not repressible." (Stocker: 6, 8–10). Jobling's question to Trible might be just as relevant here because it would be difficult to imagine who in such a patriarchal culture would have been able to construct a feminist premise or write a story with feminist implications.

[9] While it is not my intention to enter into the debate about the date of this material, I am accepting the notion that the poetic version in Judges 5 is much older than the prose version in Judges 4 (Freedman, Boling).

reader can construct a scenario of a relatively vulnerable woman who is being confronted by a potentially very dangerous military man. He is standing up when she delivers the blow to his head. The poetry of the text emphasizes that the blow is forceful enough to shatter and crush his head, causing his body to sink to the ground at her feet. No words are spoken by Jael. And though there is no explanation of how she did what she did, neither is there any hint that she seduced or tricked this man to his death.

In Judg 4:17–22, however, the author of the prose version of the story feels compelled to explain what is not explained in the earlier poetic version. The explanations provided introduce motifs of female deceitfulness and weakness and the ridicule that accompanies the destruction of a powerful man by a woman. Here, Jael goes out of her tent to meet Sisera. This time, she is armed with the words given her by the narrator/author to lure the commander into her tent and to deceive him into thinking he has found safety. According to this version, she sneaks up to and kills him while he lies defenseless under cover and asleep.

In Judith, this motif gets further elaboration. When her community is being threatened with annihilation at the hands of the forces of Holofernes, Judith volunteers herself to deal with the problem that the men cannot handle. She develops a strategy of seduction in which she bathes herself with ointments to give her body an attractive perfume, dresses herself in attractive clothing, styles her hair and decorates herself with jewelry. She deliberately prepares her body to be enticing to men. Then using her body as her main weapon, she journeys from her town to the enemy camp and actively seduces Holofernes. She tricks him into a drunken stupor, and rather than just crushing his head to kill him, she severs his head from his body and takes it with her as booty back to her own town. Here is a character who gives expression to the deepest male fears about women: she is literally out of male control, she teases but frustrates a male's sexual appetite, and she kills a man when he is completely helpless. Judith shows how very dangerous a woman can be for all her perceived weakness. Because she is a literary creation, however, she can be tamed and rendered less threatening by having her, as a character, willingly return to her proper role within patriarchal society. Good girl that she is, she embraces the patriarchal system and deflects all credit to the male deity at the end of the story.

In some ways, the Judith story can be seen as a development of the Esther story as well as the Jael story. Like Judith, Esther uses her bodily beauty to gain access to power structures in a foreign context and, having done so, provides the impetus that leads to the death of an important and powerful male character who threatens the safety of her people. Unlike Judith, however, Esther remains a character fully within male control: the control of her uncle who directs her life and the control of her husband to whose power she is carefully deferential. Moreover, the obedience and subservience to men displayed by Esther is set in stark contrast with the rebellion of Vashti. The message could hardly be clearer, even if it were not so explicitly stated as it is in Esth 1:16–22: challenging male authority will bring you ruin, if you are a woman, while submission will bring you success.

Another example of the trajectory can be seen in a comparison of the comments about women in Proverbs and Sirach. Neither book shows us individual women characters but rather the metaphorical images of woman wisdom and the strange/loose woman and categories or types of women like the adulteress and the good wife. Both books exhibit a strongly dualistic mentality in which the opposition of good woman/bad woman is basic. "Good" and "bad" are evaluative terms defined completely from the male perspective. The good woman is one who most fully meets the needs and serves the interests of a man. The bad woman is the polar opposite. Recent feminist work has moved away from the earlier tendency to isolate and romanticize the woman wisdom imagery and has shown the extent to which this polarizing functions to render women suspect (Yee). Discerning the difference between the good woman, woman wisdom, and the bad woman, the loose woman, is presented in Proverbs as a life-and-death matter for men. A strong suspicion and fear of women appears to be the prudent stance for the wise man in light of this ideology.

Sirach's discussion of woman adopts the same "good woman/ bad woman" framework used in Proverbs. The two most distinguishing features of the discussion of women in this book are the extent of the focus on women (seven percent of the whole) and the predominance of negativity in the comments. Warren Trenchard has noted that Ben Sira reconstructs earlier sources that might have been read as positive or neutral, like parts of Proverbs, in such a way as to render them negative. The most vitriolic comments are reserved for daughters as daughters (169–70). Claudia Camp agrees that nowhere else is there such a virulent attack on women, except perhaps in Ezekiel (1991:5). The fear of women that may have been generated by the comments in Proverbs is expressed in Sirach as profound hatred of women. The depth of Ben Sira's contempt for women is perhaps nowhere better expressed than in Sir 42:17: "Better the wickedness of a man than a woman who does good."

Trenchard and Camp go in different directions, however, in their assessment of Ben Sira's negativity toward women. For Trenchard, it represents merely the personal views of the author and does not correspond to attitudes in wider society. He bases this conclusion on the fact that Sirach extends, rather than merely repeats, the views found in Proverbs (2, 167–73). The logic of such an argument escapes me. Camp concludes just the opposite. She argues that Ben Sira was embedded in his own cultural context, most importantly, the honour/shame system, and this context is both elucidated by and elucidates his writings. Whereas for Trenchard, Ben Sira is merely a misogynist voice crying in the wilderness, for Camp, he is the roar of a society in which money and women are the over-determined symbols of male honour (1991:28, 38).

Why the biblical tradition seems to develop to this level of misogyny and gynophobia is a critical question. The influence of dualistic Greek philosophical traditions in the post-exilic period may be one explanation for the intensity of the negativity expressed toward femaleness in the late texts.

One might also speculate that the status of women in post-exilic Jewish society was very low. Such an assumption, however, is challenged by Tamara Eskenazi who posits just the opposite social scenario (25). She suggests that references in Ezra-Nehemiah condemning marriages to foreign women should be understood in the light of textual evidence from Elephantine in which Jewish women could divorce husbands and both inherit and hold property (27–31). If women in Judah had similar rights at this time, then the underlying issue here is the loss of land through inheritance in mixed marriages. Eskenazi draws upon the work of Camp (1985:233–54) and Meyers to argue that in the post-exilic period, when Judah was kingless, the family reemerged as the central authoritative unit, as it had been in pre-monarchical times. Along with it, came the more equitable distribution of power between men and women that Meyers sees in the pre-monarchical community (31–36). Eskenazi (41) takes special note of the fact that, in Ezra-Nehemiah, women are specifically included in public gatherings of the community (Ezra 10:1; Neh 8:2–4).

Eskenazi's evidence seems modest to me, and even if we could concede that women in the post-exilic period were less oppressed than during the monarchical period, we are hardly talking about equity here. However, it is tempting to see the growing rhetoric of misogyny in the biblical tradition as somewhat parallel to our own situation in which the rhetoric of neo-sexism (usually called "backlash") is an effort to stall and roll back the significant but not sufficient gains of women during the last half of the twentieth century. Indeed, much of the contemporary neo-sexist rhetoric appeals to the biblical tradition for its authority and status and many of the social movements dedicated to returning women to a "properly inferior place," groups such as the Promise Keepers, are strongly anchored in the biblical tradition.

Perhaps Charmé's work offers another possibility for under-standing how this negativity develops through the very process of male reading and interpretation of earlier material. It may not be at all coincidental that it is precisely from the last 2 centuries BCE onward when interpretive interest in the Adam/Eve story arises. Prior to this time, there is virtually no reuse of this text in the biblical tradition, unlike the exodus tradition that is frequently utilized. When Genesis 2–3 does begin to be interpreted (along with Gen 6:1–4), it is typically for the purpose of explaining the evilness of women (Prusak: 89–91). From this time onward, woman and evil are virtually synonymous. The theme of Eve as seductive, a theme most feminist analysts insist is not in the original text, became a central component of the interpretive tradition. In other words, Jewish and early Christian writings, when interpreting earlier traditions such as Genesis 2–3, did so through the lens of a male-constructed gender ideology steeped in the misogyny of the post-exilic period, an ideology that understands woman as wholly Other and dangerous. When ideas about women such as those expressed by Ben Sira are understood as a context in which texts such as Genesis 2–3 were being read, the kind of interpretation that emerges should not be surprising.

The work of some feminists has already begun to illustrate how male gender ideology renders problematic aspects of femaleness and woman that are not, in themselves, problematic. Gale Yee has shown how the voice of women becomes suspect and dangerous when the speech of lady wisdom and the loose woman are presented as difficult to distinguish one from the other. Esther Fuchs has demonstrated how the powerlessness of women in a male-dominated society is masked by presenting deceitfulness as a defining characteristic of women. In a similar way, post-exilic texts also problematize the physical beauty of women. The father in Proverbs warns his son not to desire the beauty of an adulterous woman or be captured by her eyelashes (Prov 6:25), while a beautiful woman without sense is compared to a gold ring in a pig's snout (Prov 11:22). In discussing the good wife, the author notes that a woman's charm is deceitful and her beauty vain (31:30).

In Sirach, the danger of a woman's physical beauty is further developed, yet the benefits of having a beautiful good wife are acknowledged. On the one hand, Ben Sira advises his male readers not to look at a shapely woman because many have been seduced and ensnared by a woman's beauty (Sir 9:8; 25:21). On the other hand, a good wife has a beautiful face, a stately figure and shapely legs (Sir 26:17–18) Ben Sira concedes that a woman's beauty lights up a man's face and there is nothing he desires more (Sir 36:27). A woman's beauty, therefore, is desired and sought after, but is potentially very dangerous.

Such thinking renders characters like Esther and Judith very conflicted. While they each accomplish something very positive for their people, they do so using their physical beauty in ways that highlight the very warnings in Proverbs and Sirach. Esther, having gained access to power through her beauty, is instrumental in the destruction of a man. Judith's seductive use of her beauty is even more obvious. Even "good" women ensnare and seduce men with their beauty. Hardly surprising then that Ben Sira prefers the wickedness of a man to a woman who does good!

The reading of texts like the bible is not done in a strictly linear way, as Susan Lanser has shown. The problem with the misogyny of the later material is that it comes to be read back through earlier material and this, in turn, helps the trajectory to continue, as it so obviously does in early Christian tradition.

While Trible's feminist interpretive strategy was to appeal to divine "intentionality" to save the bible from sexism, different strategies have been employed by feminists more recently. A central one has been to employ reader-response theory to argue that meaning does not reside in the text itself but is produced when a reader reads a text. Feminist critics such as Cheryl Exum attempt to disrupt some of the cultural and ideological codes in biblical narratives in order to expose the difficulty patriarchy has in justifying the subjugation of women and, thereby, to undermine the text's patriarchy by constructing feminist (sub)versions (11–12).

But this very strategy begs the question of the possible differences produced by male and female readers of the same text, differences to which Charmé's study lends support. I am not optimistic that individual reading efforts by a few feminist scholars, even ones widely published, will result in a significant change in the way the majority of readers read these texts. Even if patriarchy has difficulty justifying the subjugation of women as Exum suggests, it appears that most male interpreters past and present do not.

The bible is certainly not as important in our society as it once was. As a feminist, I may take some comfort in that reality, but for the fact that its trajectory of misogyny and gynophobia continues to spiral though our new cultural scriptures: television, movies, video games and the web. The labour of reading biblical texts has not lessened with time for me. It has intensified as the nature of the problem appears more complex than it once did. Ben Sira and the boys in Charmé's study may not be very different for all their temporal separation. There is much feminist labour yet to be done and perhaps none as urgent as that of exploring the gender lens through which male readers of the bible have so often seen, and continue to see, women as the dangerous Other.

Bibliography

Bird, Phyllis
    1974   "Images of Women in the Old Testament." Pp. 41–88 in *Religion and Sexism: Images of Women in Jewish and Christian Traditions*. Ed. Rosemary R. Ruether. New York: Simon and Schuster.

Boling, Robert G.
    1975   *Judges*. New York: Doubleday.

Brenner, Athalya, ed.
    1994   *A Feminist Companion to Exodus and Deuteronomy*. Sheffield: Sheffield Academic Press.
    1995   *A Feminist Companion to the Latter Prophets*. Sheffield: Sheffield Academic Press.

Camp, Claudia
1991 "Understanding Patriarchy: Women in Second Century Jerusalem through the Eyes of Ben Sira." Pp. 1–39 in *"Women Like This": New Perspectives on Jewish Women in the Greco-Roman World*. Ed. A. J. Levine. Atlanta: Scholars Press.
1985 *Wisdom and the Feminine in the Book of Proverbs*. Bible and Literature Series 11. Sheffield: Almond.

Charmé, Stuart Z.
1997 "Children's Gendered Responses to the Story of Adam and Eve." *JFSR* 13:27–44.

Clines, David
1990 "What Does Eve Do to Help? And Other Irredeemably Androcentric Orientations in Genesis 1–3." Pp. 25–48 in *What Does Eve Do to Help and Other Readerly Questions to the Old Testament*. JSOTSup 94. Sheffield: JSOT.

De Swarte Gifford, Carolyn
1985 "American Women and the Bible: The Nature of Woman as a Hermeneutical Issue." Pp. 11–33 in *Feminist Perspectives on Biblical Scholarship*. Ed. Adela Y. Collins. Chico: Scholars Press.

Eskenazi, Tamara
1992 "Out of the Shadows: Biblical Women in the Postexilic Era." *JSOT* 54:25–43.

Exum, J. Cheryl
1993 *Fragmented Women: Feminist (Sub)versions of Biblical Narratives*. Pennsylvania: Trinity Press International.

Freedman, David Noel
1980 "Divine Names and Titles in Early Hebrew Poetry." Pp. 77–129 in *Pottery, Poetry and Prophecy: Collected Essays on Hebrew Poetry*. Winona Lake: Eisenbrauns.

Fuchs, Esther
1985 "Who is Hiding the Truth? Deceptive Women and Biblical Androcentrism." Pp. 137–44 in *Feminist Perspectives on Biblical Scholarship*. Ed. Adela. Y. Collins. Chico: Scholars Press.

Gössmann, Elisabeth
1993 "History of Biblical Interpretation by European Women." Pp. 27–40 in *Searching the Scriptures: A Feminist Introduction*. Ed. Elisabeth Schüssler Fiorenza. New York: Crossroad.

Jobling, David
1986 "Myth and Its Limits in Genesis 2:4b–3:24." Pp. 17–43 in *The Sense of Biblical Narrative: Structural Analyses in the Hebrew Bible II*. Sheffield: JSOT.

Lanser, Susan
1988   "(Feminist) Criticism in the Garden of Eden: Inferring Genesis 2–3." *Semeia* 41:67–84.

Lerner, Gerda
1993   "One Thousand Years of Feminist Bible Criticism." Pp. 138–66 in *The Creation of Feminist Consciousness: From the Middle Ages to Eighteen-Seventy.* New York: Oxford University Press.

Meyers, Carol
1988   *Discovering Eve: Ancient Israelite Women in Context.* Oxford: Oxford University Press.

Milne, Pamela
1988a   *Vladimir Propp and the Study of Structure in Hebrew Biblical Narrative.* Sheffield: Sheffield Academic Press.
1988b   "Eve and Adam: Is a Feminist Reading Possible?" *Bible Review* June:12–21, 39.
1989   "The Patriarchal Stamp of Scripture: The Implications of Structuralist Analysis for Feminist Hermeneutics." *JFSR* 5:17–34.
1993   "What Shall We Do with Judith? A Feminist Reassessment of a Biblical 'Heroine.'" *Semeia* 62:37–58.
1995   "No Promised Land: Rejecting the Authority of the Bible." Pp. 47–73 in *Feminist Approaches to the Bible: Symposium at the Smithsonian.* Ed. Hershel Shanks. Washington, DC: Biblical Archaeology Society.

Newsom, Carol
1989   "Woman and the Discourse of Patriarchal Wisdom." Pp. 142–60 in *Gender and Difference in Ancient Israel.* Ed. Peggy L. Day. Minneapolis: Fortress Press.

Prusak, Bernard
1974   "Woman: Seductive Siren and Source of Sin? Pseudepigraphal Myth and Christian Origins." Pp. 89–116 in *Religion and Sexism.* Ed. Rosemary Radford Ruether. New York: Simon and Schuster.

Remus, Harold, W. C. C. James and Daniel Fraikin
1992   *Religious Studies in Ontario: A State-of-the-Art Review.* Waterloo: Wilfrid Laurier Press.

Stocker, Margarita
1998   *Judith: Sexual Warrior.* New Haven and London: Yale University Press.

Stendahl, Krister
1982   "Ancient Scripture in the Modern World." Pp. 202–14 in *Scripture in the Jewish and Christian Traditions: Authority, Interpretation, Relevance.* Ed. Frederick E. Greenspahn. Nashville: Abingdon.

Trenchard, Warren
　　1982　　　*Ben Sira's View of Women: A Literary Analysis.* Chico:
　　　　　　　Scholars Press.

Trible, Phyllis
　　1978　　　*God and the Rhetoric of Sexuality.* Philadelphia: Fortress
　　　　　　　Press.
　　1984　　　*Texts of Terror: Literary-Feminist Readings of Biblical
　　　　　　　Narratives.* Philadelphia: Fortress Press.

Wallace, Howard
　　1985　　　*The Eden Narrative.* HSM 32. Atlanta: Scholars Press.

Walsh, Jerome T.
　　1977　　　"Genesis 2:4b–3:24: A Synchronic Approach." *JBL* 96:161–
　　　　　　　77.

Yee, Gale
　　1989　　　"'I Have Perfumed My Bed with Myrrh': The Foreign Woman
　　　　　　　(*'issa zara*) in Proverbs 1–9." *JSOT* 43:53–68.

PLAYING IT AGAIN
UTOPIA, CONTRADICTION, HYBRID SPACE
AND THE BRIGHT FUTURE IN MICAH

Erin Runions

Utopic Interventions?

The book of Micah has always intrigued scholars with its abrupt shifts from descriptions of punishment and desolation to descriptions of victory and a bright future. These more hopeful scenes occur in 2:12–13, 4:1–8, 5:1–8, and 7:8–20, and are most often interpreted by scholars as later additions to the original corpus, though there are a few who argue that they are the words of Micah with respect to specific situations.[1] Quite apart from considerations of their original historical situation is the question of how these more "positive" elements might function persuasively. When I first began thinking about these passages, I wondered if they might be utopic interventions in the text, operating as Fredric Jameson puts it, "to confront us with our incapacity to imagine Utopia" (Jameson, 1982:156); or perhaps as Enrique Dussel says, "to guide our reflection even though it be only to see the alienation in which we live and [to] realize the need for liberation at diverse levels" (139). Yet when read carefully, these texts reveal ambiguities which might in fact call into question their utopic

---

[1] The details of dating for each passages differ from scholar to scholar, but in general those who opt for a later dating include Wolff, Mays, Renaud, Lescow (1972a), while those who consider these to be the words of Micah include Waltke, Shaw. Allen straddles the two views, considering 2:12–13, 4:5 and 5:1–8 to be authentic and 4:1–4, 6–8, 7:8–20 to be from other periods (251).

and liberatory potential; it seems that many of them extol the virtues of domination and servitude.

I will center my reading on Mic 4:1–8; however, as I develop my argument, I will read the other "hopeful"[2] texts intertextually alongside this passage. It is my contention that Mic 4:1–8, in conjunction with 2:12–13, 5:1–8, and 7:8–20, does indeed operate as a sort of utopic space, but one, after the fashion of Louis Marin, which lets contradictory elements play. I will take this one step further, building on Homi Bhabha's notion of hybridity, to argue that this play of contradictory elements creates what might be called a hybrid space between text and reader: that is, a space that both disrupts the text's colonizing drive and challenges the reader's ideological position.

Two qualifications: First, I am not trying to give a "right reading" of this passage, but rather to play with the possibilities for reading it. Second, Bhabha in particular may seem a strange conversation partner, given that he looks at cultural signification in modernity; however, because he proposes ways to "revision" situations of oppression produced through colonization, his work provides interesting ways to think about texts that seem to hold oppressive or colonizing elements. Using a Bhabhian trick of rhetoric, I will say that in applying him to the biblical text, I will neither be taking him fully at his word, nor me fully at mine (1994:188). Indeed this is *a reading*— which Robert Culley reminds me is all I can do—of this text using a particular theorist. As such I hope it reflects my appreciation for Culley's careful supervision of my doctoral dissertation, for working through Micah and Bhabha with me, and at the same time for being open to the political directions I have taken in my work (and my extra-curricular involvements), as are reflected in this paper.

Micah 4:1–8

At first glance, Mic 4:1–8[3] does fit the most conventional definition of a utopia: it is a fictional place, a non-place, full of ideals. Indeed, the house of Yahweh is an exalted mountain to which nations

---

[2] "Hope" seems to be the word that scholars generally use to describe these passages.

[3] Since Mic 4:1–4 appears almost identically in Isa 2:1–4, a number of scholars have split Mic 4:1–8 up into a number of different oracles. Because I am not so interested in the origins of the oracles, I am reading the section together.

stream. Yahweh judges between many peoples and rebukes great nations, who subsequently beat their swords and spears into plow-shares and pruning knives. In this time war is not practiced nor learned; fear is banished; everyone lives happily under "his"[4] own vine and walks with "his" own God; the lame are gathered as a remnant; Yahweh is king; and Zion is a fortified tower. Given this contrast to the war and destruction featured in the rest of the book, the passage even seems to meet a slightly more nuanced definition of utopia, that is, a vision of the future which is formulated in opposition to the existing order (Moylan: 163).[5] Perhaps after all, this is the kind of textual intervention intended to reflect back to readers their own alienation and violence, and their distance from this idyllic scene.

But as I looked at the text again, questions began to crowd in, blocking my view of utopia. What is the real nature of the relationship between Yahweh and the nations? What does it mean that Yahweh judges between the nations and rebukes them (4:3)? Why must the mountain of Yahweh be raised up *more* than the other mountains and hills (4:1)? Who are the lame to whom Yahweh has done evil, and why has he now gathered them together to be their King (4:6–7)? And if war is over, why is Zion likened to a "tower of the flock" (מגדל עדר) and some kind of fortified space (עפל) (4:8)?[6] Who is this tower towering over? Is Zion fortified because it is excluding someone or something, or because it is holding something in, perhaps the nations, perhaps the lame remnant? Following this line of thinking, more questions arise. Do the nations beat their swords and spears into

---

[4] The text uses masculine singular forms.

[5] This view of utopia is linked to utopia as text. There are others who feel that literary description can only diminish utopia. Marx, Bloch and Mannheim would be of this school (see Moylan: 160–61). For these thinkers utopia is revolutionary practice. For instance, Mannheim considers a vision of the future utopian only if it "breaks the bonds of the existing order" (192). He adds, "For the sociologist, 'existence' is that which is 'concretely effective,' i.e. a functioning social order which does not exist only in the imagination of certain individuals but according to which people really act" (193–94).

[6] It is not exactly clear what is meant by Ophel (עפל) here, but the references to Ophel in Chronicles and Nehemiah seem to imply some kind of fortified hill in Jerusalem. It should also be noted that the references to עפל in 2 Chr (27:3; 33:14) are in the context of the fortification project of Jotham and Manasseh, respectively. Also, מגדל tends to imply fortification: it seems to signify watchtower in 2 Kgs 17:9, 18:8, 2 Chr 26:9; strong tower (מגדל עז) in Judg 9:51, Ps 61:4, Prov 18:10; towers along the wall in 2 Chr 14:6, 32:5.

gardening utensils because they want to, or because they must, to make the land yield produce? Is war not taught out of concern for people, or to ensure that the domination of Yahweh's mount will never be challenged?

In view of all these questions, this text seems also to have the capacity to reflect to me the things I find most alienating. Many of the images might be considered figures for oppressive societal or global problems: the mountain of Yahweh, a figure for domination of one nation over others; Yahweh's judgment, a figure for racial discrimination; his kingship, a figure for authority and hierarchy; the beaten weapons, a figure for expropriation of cultural resources; the untaught war, a figure for the regulation of resistance through educational state apparatuses (for instance universities);[7] and the lame enclosed in the fortified Zion, a figure for incarceration as an attack on those already disadvantaged. Seen in this light, I might call this passage ideological, rather than utopian, after Karl Mannheim's discussion of these two terms, that is, an ideological discourse that is "effective in the realization and the maintenance of the existing order of things," rather than breaking "the bonds of the existing order" (192).

Perhaps, by reading my own political frustrations onto this passage, I have distorted needlessly one of the more hopeful passages in scripture,. In truth, I have wondered if I should stick to developing the liberatory aspects of this text. But two things stop me. First, I am not alone in wondering about the liberatory nature of this text. In *Biblical Hermeneutics and Black Theology in South Africa* (1989), Itumeleng Mosala uses Micah as an example of the kinds of contradictions between "oppression and oppressors, exploitation and exploiters" that are inherent in the production and presentation of biblical text (33). In his discussion of this particular passage (126–34, 150), Mosala separates out the various redactional strata, analyzing them for their class and ideological affiliations, and for their ability to provide "a positive hermeneutical connection with the struggles of" black working class people in South Africa (153). He considers most of 4:1–8, with the exceptions of vv. 2–3, to be representative of an imperialist theology developed by the "formerly powerful class, whose

---

[7] See Althusser's "Ideological State Apparatuses" (1984) where he describes the educational state apparatus.

pride has been hurt by exile" (134). For Mosala, the imperialist *tendenz* in most of this passage makes it unusable as a liberatory text.

The second thing that stops me from accepting the liberatory aspects of this passage, *de facto*, is the intertextual links to the other "hopeful" passages in the book. Whether or not all these passages should be grouped together is another question, but I do so partly because others have, and partly because these passages do repeat key words and themes. I would like to take up three of these themes here. They are: the nations, the remnant, and Yahweh as king.

Nations, Remnant, Kings

As mentioned, the nations appear in 4:1–8 as docile guests on the mount of Yahweh. They appear somewhat differently in 5:1–8 and 7:8–20, as threats which are conquered. Assyria appears in 5:4 as a threat walking in "our" land and on "our" citadels. This menace is soon vanquished, though, by leaders raised up for the purpose of ruling the lands of Assyria and Nimrod with the sword. The theme of Israel's counterattack is continued in 5:7–8 where the remnant of Jacob is figured as a ravaging lion among the nations, destroying everything in its path without mercy. Likewise in chap. 7, the nations might be read as a threat which is overcome. In 7:12 Assyria and the cities of Egypt come to Jerusalem from afar, which is arguably reminiscent of the nations streaming to the utopic mountain of Yahweh in 4:1–2. The difference here is that their arrival is followed in 7:13 by a promise of devastated land, causing me to wonder if 7:12–13 is an image of the attack by the nations. This is followed by the image of Israel's counter attack in 7:17, where the nations appear humiliated: ashamed, licking the dust, and trembling in their fortresses.[8] When all of these verses from chaps. 5 and 7 are read along with the passage in chap. 4, the landscape changes: it does not seem that the nations are streaming to this utopic mountain of their own will, or if they are, perhaps they are only to be held captive in retaliation for their prior attacks.

Likewise, there seems to be some dispute about the nature of the remnant. The aggressive nature of the remnant in chap. 5 stands in stark contrast to the remnant in 4:7, that is, the collection of the lame,

---

[8] For other examples of domination of the nations in Micah see 4:11–13; Mic 6:5 contains an allusion to the conquest of Canaan.

gathered to become a mighty nation and ruled by Yahweh. In 2:12–13, the language is remarkably similar, Yahweh will gather the remnant like a flock murmuring in its pen. As their king, he will break out of the gate, and they will follow him. In 7:18, the remnant is the remnant of El's inheritance, like an embarrassed leftover, whose sins El passes over. What exactly then is the position of the remnant in these passages? Is it a favoured grouping, or is it sinful remains of former glory? Is it a ravaging lion, or a wounded flock ruled by Yahweh? Are they enclosed in the fortified Zion, or have they burst out of their enclosure?

Finally, what kind of king is Yahweh? All four of the so-called positive passages in Micah refer to him in some way or another as the shepherding ruler. In our "utopic" passage, it is explicit that Yahweh is king, and implied that he is shepherd through the use of the verbs אסף and קבץ. In 2:12–13 the connection between shepherd and ruler is clear: Yahweh is the shepherd who gathers his flock (again with the verbs אסף and קבץ) and then breaks out of their pen before them. In 5:1–3, the ruler appears to be a human substitute, coming from Bethlehem, "to stand and shepherd in the strength of Yahweh, in the majesty (גאון) of the name of Yahweh." Finally, in 7:14 there is an appeal to a 2nd person masculine figure to "shepherd your people, with your staff, the flock of your inheritance." Yet each of these references raises questions about the nature of the shepherd. For instance, might the גאון of Yahweh's name connote arrogance as it does so often elsewhere in the Hebrew Bible?[9] Or, why does the shepherd carry a staff, if his sheep are loyal? And could אסף and קבץ really imply, as Willis suggests, "the king gathering his army for battle" (1966:198)?[10] Indeed we might question whether the shepherd-king is really an image of caring, as is so commonly asserted, or is it an image of controlling sheep so that they can be made useful, or led to the

---

[9] גאון seems most often to be a negative term, signifying arrogance or a pride that needs to be brought down, see: Lev 26:19; Job 35:12; Ps 59:13; Prov 8:13; 16:18; Isa 13:11, 19; 14:11; 16:6; 23:9; Hos 5:5; 7:10; Jer 13:9; 48:29 (= Isa 16:6); 50:44; Ezek 7:20, 24; 16:49, 56; 30:6, 18; 32:12; 33:28; Amos 6:8; Zeph 2:10; Zech 9:6; 10:11. Sometimes it is a positive term signifying majesty, splendour, or pride in a positive sense, see: Exod 15:7; Job 37:4; 40:10; Ps 47:5; Isa 2:10, 19, 21; 4:2; 24:14; 60:15; Nah 2:3.

[10] See 1966:198 n. 1, 199 n. 2 for long lists of references for these verbs in connection to preparation for battle.

slaughter? Or, does the shepherd in fact lead the people of Israel out of oppression, into the promised land, as is implied in 7:15, with a reference to the exodus (implicitly linking the staff of 7:14 to the staff of Moses). But if the promised land is gained through conquest and violence, is Israel then the oppressor, with Yahweh leading the way? (cf. Warrior).

Not only do nations stream in and out of the mountain of the lord then, but it seems that texts do too, leaving their imprint, their questions, their contradictions behind. In all of these examples—nations, remnant, and Yahweh as king—the utopic elements of 4:1–8 seem to be put into question at one moment, only to be reinforced in the next, and then to be destabilized once again. By the end of these intertextual readings I must admit, I am less and less certain about what is depicted. Are the nations welcome on the mount of Yahweh, or are they there because they are conquered and captured in revenge for their attempted conquests? Is the remnant a special, rescued, and cared for grouping, or a wounded and submissive flock, waiting for the whim of its owner? Is their shepherd a despot, or a liberator leading them out of their pen, breaking down whatever gets in their way, teaching them to do the same, like a lion among its prey?

Utopiques

The ambivalence of this compilation of images brings to mind Louis Marin's discussion of utopia.[11] In his *Utopiques: Jeux d'espaces* (1973), Marin gives a reading of the original *Utopia*, written by Thomas More in the 16th century (1516). Here he makes a number of suggestions about the literary functioning of utopia, arguing that it is an "organization of space as a text" (24) which plays with time, signification, ideological discourses, and understandings of "historical reality" (25, 249–50). As this kind of playful textual space (24–25), utopia operates as a neutral and supplementary third term (21) between contradictions within material conditions of existence, ideology, and representations of reality. That is, utopia, as a textual production, is able to hold distance between contradictions, without synthesizing them, operating as a "double figure, an ambiguous representation, the

---

[11] For a longer discussion and application of Marin, see Boer, whose work put me on to Marin.

equivocal site of possible synthesis and productive differentiation" (22). Utopia is a supplementary space that allows for limitless contradiction to play infinitely (21). Utopia is also, according to Marin, an ideological critique of dominant ideology, in that as a fictional construct, it displaces the structures and discourses in which it was formed by putting them at a distance (249) and allowing them to play. As fiction, it both hides and reveals the contradictions in its own societal conditions of production.

Mic 4:1–8, especially once read intertextually with these other passages in Micah, certainly seems to be an ambiguous space, one that holds together contradictions, allowing them to play. Perhaps then, it is in this way a critique of its own conditions of production. Perhaps in allowing the contradictory themes of liberation and domination to play, the text displaces and critiques the very power structures in which it was formed.[12] Perhaps this is, after all, the prophetic way of using utopia to reflect the problems with expansionist politics and to point out the need for liberation. But because I would not like my reading to depend on speculations of historical context or conditions of production, I am going to push the exploration of utopia as a third term one step further, by looking at how it might critique both the images within the text, and my own ideology in approaching the text.

In order to do this, I turn to Bhabha's notions of Third Space and hybridity, which resonate with Marin's conception of utopia as a neutral third term. Bhabha's notion of a hybrid, Third Space between colonized and colonizing cultures, that is neither one (Self/colonizer) nor the Other (colonized), but somewhere "in-between" sounds remarkably like Marin's neutral term appearing "between one and the other, neither one nor the other, as the missing third term" (32).[13] For Bhabha the Third Space is a space of hybridity, the space produced by the interaction between colonized and colonizer; it is an supplemen-

---

[12] Marin, however, argues that utopia as a literary genre could only develop with the rise of capitalism. According to Marin, it is only the moment when the conflict between the social conditions and forces of production generates the economic conditions for its solution that ideological critique and theory (as operative in utopic discourse) can come to the fore (253–56).

[13] Marin and Bhabha do not necessarily ground their theories the same way philosophically. Marin is specifically Husserlian (45–46), and Bhabha bases his notion of Third Space and hybridity in large part on Lacan and a Derridian critique of Lacan, but they both come out in favour of a dialectic that does not privilege negation (Bhabha, 1994:173; 1996:202; Marin: 128).

tary, indeterminate, undecideable space, as is Marin's utopia (152). Both envision a dialectic space which does not sublate or synthesize difference (Bhabha, 1994:173; Marin: 21). More importantly for thinking about how utopic spaces in Micah might critique ideology, hybridity puts the logic of colonization at a distance, displaces it, and thus allows it to undermine the authority of that colonization.

Hybridity

Hybridity is for Bhabha a means for reversing domination in colonial contexts. Colonial domination is, according to Bhabha, "constructed through disavowal (that is, the production of discriminatory identities that secure the 'pure' and original identity of authority)" (1994:112). In other words, in colonial (and postcolonial) contexts the fear of cultural difference is contained, disavowed by, "the fantasy of origin and identity" (1994:67); the resulting categorization of difference is what produces and justifies discrimination (*those people, not from our origin, not like us*).[14] However, Bhabha argues, in a colonial context,[15] the mimicry which is demanded of colonized peoples by colonizers, "the desire for a reformed, recognizable Other, as a subject . . . that is almost the same, but not quite" (1994:87) produces something new, something hybrid. The very demand for imitation which tries to establish one culture as "superior" and "original" produces hybridity. Thus, the discrimination produced by the strategy of disavowal, becomes a "discrimination between the mother culture and its bastards, the self and its doubles, where the trace of what is disavowed is not repressed but *repeated* as something different—a mutation, a hybrid" (1994:111, emphasis mine).

The repetition of cultural signs, but differently, is a key concept for Bhabha's work, and for the possibility of revisioning situations of oppression. Static repetition is for Bhabha a symbol of enforced western control. Bhabha writes:

---

[14] For a much more complex explanation of the roles of disavowal and recognition in the production of stereotype and discrimination, see Bhabha's essay "The Other Question" in *The Location of Culture* (1994).

[15] This continues, though differently, in a postcolonial context: cultures are transformed by transnational "migration, diaspora, displacement, relocation" (1994: 172) and consequently translational relations. With the advent of these new cultural negotiations, cultures are increasingly hybrid.

> In Casablanca [a symbol of colonial rule] the passage of time
> preserves the identity of language. . . . 'Play it again, Sam', which is
> perhaps the Western world's most celebrated demand for repetition,
> is still an invocation to similitude, a return to the eternal verities. In
> Tangiers [a symbol of colonized space, by way of contrast, where
> signs repeat sporadically, discontinuously, differently], as time goes
> by it produces an iterative temporality that erases the occidental
> spaces of language—inside/outside, past/present, those foundational-
> ist epistemological positions of Western empiricism and historicism.
> (1994:182)

For Bhabha, language and signs of culture circulate within colonial
contexts in a way that produces a sort of non–sense, a hybridity that
disturbs western notions of "sense." The re-presentation of signs in this
hybrid space of colonized "non-sense" disturbs typical Western
language which fortifies "linear time consciousness" (1984:96). It also
disturbs colonial recognition of "objects" (other races, cultural icons,
texts, etc.) as distinct from the colonizing subject (1984:99–100, 113–
14). Thus hybridity is the re-playing and re-marking of difference,
which undermines both the temporal (linear time) and spatial (subject/
object distinctions), on which Western empiricism rests.

Hybridity therefore puts authority, which depends on the ability
to discern difference (different "objects") and simultaneously to disa-
vow it, into question. "Hybridity is the revaluation of the assumption
of colonial identity through the repetition of discriminatory identity
effects. It displays the necessary deformation and displacement of all
sites of discrimination and domination" (1994:112). Said another way,
in displaying the colonial culture, but doing so differently, hybridity
reveals the constructed nature of colonial rule, putting its originality,
the "myth of origins," into question. In this way, hybridity displaces
the dominant culture's own notions about self-identity. The repetition
of the "original culture" through mimicry has the subversive effect of
unsettling the "mimetic or narcissistic demands of colonial power" by
turning the "gaze of the discriminated back upon the eye of power"
(1994:112). Thus, hybridity can be used to reread and reorder
dominant discourses, allowing for subaltern voices, suppressed in the
stifling of difference, to emerge.

Reading Hybrid Space

To return to Mic 4:1–8, I might say that this passage, standing alone, exhibits a number of the colonial traits that Bhabha mentions. The fantasy of origin, identity, and superiority appears in the mount of Yahweh, established in the tops of mountains, above hills. Yahweh's power is established in his ability to gather and shepherd the lame, to *make them* a remnant and rule them (4:7). Yahweh's authority is confirmed by his ability to discern difference, to know the nations enough to categorize them, to judge between them, to discriminate against some. The desire for reform and mimesis is evidenced in the dream of the nations learning to walk in the ways of Yahweh. Yet even so, the nations, it seems, are permitted to follow their own gods (4:5)—they can be different, but not too different—but the fact that they learn the ways of Yahweh establishes Yahweh as superior.

Yet when these themes are *repeated* in the intertextual reading of this passage, they begin to deform and displace the sites of discrimination and domination in the text. Eternal verities mutate, contradictions come to the fore, and facile readings which know and categorize the text are disturbed. The idyllic Mount of Yahweh, becomes a place of captivity and control. But then Yahweh the judge becomes Yahweh the shepherd, and then Yahweh the one needing to liberate his people (perhaps from his own rule?). The nations "needing to be reformed" are those in power before they are humiliated. The remnant, lame because of something done to it by Yahweh, and enclosed under surveillance in the fortified Zion, is liberated, becoming a roaring lion. In short, the text and the images within it become hybrid, losing their capacity to discriminate, or to be contained and controlled. With the introduction of different textual times and spaces, the gaze of the discriminated (in this case, the remnant and the nations) is turned back upon the eye of power (Yahweh). This unsettles the narcissistic demand of Yahweh for the nations to obey and imitate passively, and for the remnant to be gathered passively. The nations and the remnant are acknowledged as active and aggressive, "subjects of their own history and experience" (Bhabha, 1994:178), rather than as the submissively controlled objects of Yahweh.

The story does not end here though; hybridity operates in another, quite different way in the process of reading. Hybridity is also formed in the third space of interpretation; that is the space where I encounter the text, where my ideology, my expectation that I know what is best for the world, meets the text. Let me elaborate with an example (and the details of this were not foreseen before I started writing). I have always been a pacifist. I have believed in non-violent resistance, for me and for the rest of the world, and I have defended this position hotly in debate. Mic 4:1–8 then, seems like a perfect text to extol, with its abolition of weapons and regime of peaceful instruction. Yet when I see this apology for non-violence set next to the scene of the lame, enclosed and ruled remnant, I wonder about the sudden need for a peaceful domain in the midst of an otherwise fairly violent book (cf. 4:13; 5:7–8). I am beginning to consider the *possibility* at least that the call to lay down weapons might be a way of controlling resistance, of keeping down the already oppressed. Whether or not I adopt this as my final reading of the passage, the very possibility of such biblical manufacture of consent has prompted me to interrogate my own commitment to non-violence. Given that I live in an economy largely stimulated by the industry of war—an industry sustained by attack on, or exploitation of, other nations—am I in any position to be spouting non-violent ideals? Perhaps it is only through violence that oppressed peoples can break out of their situations of oppression, and I am thinking here of the Zapatistas in Mexico, the IRA in Ireland, or the Tamil resistance in Sri Lanka. Thus, in the third space of interpretation, the text repeats my own prohibition on violence, but in repeating it, hybridity is formed between my understanding of non-violence, and the possibility of coercion suggested by the text. This has the effect of displacing my commitment to non-violence with my desire to try to stand in solidarity with the oppressed. In this way, my knowledge of the "best way to live," is displaced and the authority of my non-violent ideological stance challenged.

Letting the Contradictions Play

I have tried to show that in the hybrid space of intertext and interpretation, this text opens up new possibilities for critique of authoritative imagery, and for reconsideration of ideological commitments. By way of conclusion, I'd like to think of this reading as one embodying a Jamesonian turn. In the last chapter of *The Political*

Unconscious (1981), entitled "The Dialectic of Utopia and Ideology," Jameson argues that all ideologies are utopian in that they are based in class consciousness. Because class consciousness necessarily entails some form of collectivity, some "sense of solidarity with other members of a particular group or class" (1981:290), it is therefore utopian; it embodies a collectivity which "figures for the ultimate concrete collective life of an achieved Utopian or classless society" (1981:291). He makes another move then to say that any Marxist analysis should not only "unmask and demonstrate the ways in which a cultural artifact fulfills a specific ideological mission, in legitimating a given power structure," but it must also seek "to project its simultaneously Utopian power as the symbolic affirmation of a specific historical and class form of collective unity" (1981:291). Along these lines, though with less attention to historical moments, this reading has tried not only to point out the ideological commit-ments of the text, but also its utopian potential in playing the contradictions within my own material conditions of existence and political discourse. Interrogation and reevaluation of eternal truths, ideological commitments, hidden oppressions: this is the stuff of a more just world.

Bibliography

Allen, Leslie C.
    1976   *The Books of Joel, Obadiah, Jonah, and Micah.* Grand Rapids:
                Eerdmans.

Althusser, Louis
    1984   "Ideological State Apparatuses (Notes toward an Investiga-
                tion)." Pp. 1–60 in *Essays on Ideology.* London: Verso.

Barthes, Roland
    1975   *The Pleasure of the Text.* Trans. R. Miller. New York: Hill.

Bhabha, Homi K.
    1984   "Representation and the Colonial Text: A Critical Exploration
                of Some Forms of Mimeticism." Pp. 93–122 in *The Theory of
                Reading.* Ed. Frank Gloversmith. Sussex: Harvester Press.
    1990   "Introduction: Narrating the Nation." Pp. 1–7 in *Nation and
                Narration.* Ed. Homi K. Bhabha. London: Routledge.
    1993   Interview by Maria Koundoura and Amit Rai. *Stanford
                Humanities Review* 3(1):1–6.
    1994   *The Location of Culture.* London: Routledge.

1996   "Unsatisfied: Notes on Vernacular Cosmopolitanism." Pp.
            191–207 in *Text and Nation: Cross-Disciplinary Essays in
            Cultural and National Identities.* Ed. Laura Garcia-Moreno
            and Peter C. Pfeiffer. Columbia, SC: Camden House.
1997   "Halfway House: Homi K. Bhabha on Hybridity." *Artforum*
            May 11–12:125.

Boer, Roland
1997   *Novel Histories: The Fiction of Biblical Criticism.* Playing the
            Texts 2. Sheffield: Sheffield Academic Press.

Craigie, Peter C.
1985   *The Twelve Prophets, Volume Two: Micah, Nahum, Habakkuk,
            Zephaniah, Haggai, Zechariah, and Malachi.* Daily Study
            Bible. Philadelphia: Westminster.

Derrida, Jacques
1974   *Of Grammatology.* Trans. Gayatri Chakrovorty Spivak.
            Baltimore: Johns Hopkins.

Dussel, Enrique
1985   *Philosophy of Liberation.* Trans. Aquilina Martinez and
            Christine Morkovsky. Maryknoll: Orbis.

Hagstrom, David Gerald
1988   *The Coherence of the Book of Micah: A Literary Analysis.*
            SBLDS 89. Atlanta: Scholars Press.

Hill, Eugene D.
1982   "The Place of the Future: Louis Marin and His *Utopiques.*"
            Science Fiction Studies 9:167–79.

Hillers, Delbert R.
1983   "Imperial Dream: Text and Sense of Mic 5:4b–5." Pp. 137–58
            in *The Quest for the Kingdom of God: Studies in Honor of
            George E. Mendenhall.* Ed. H. B. Huffmon, F. A. Spina and A.
            R. W. Green. Winona Lake: Eisenbrauns.
1984   *Micah: A Commentary on the Book of the Prophet Micah.*
            Hermeneia. Philadelphia: Fortress Press.

Huntington, John
1982   "Utopian and Anti-Utopian Logic: H. G. Wells and His
            Successors." *Science Fiction Studies* 9:122–46.

Jameson, Fredric
1981   *The Political Unconscious: Narrative as a Socially Symbolic
            Act.* Ithaca: Cornell University Press.
1982   "Progress Versus Utopia; or, Can We Imagine the Future?"
            Science Fiction Studies 9:147–58.

Kaiser, Walter C. Jr.
1992   *The Communicator's Commentary: Micah-Malachi.* Dallas:
            Word Books.

Lescow, Theodor
 1972a "Redaktionsgeschichtliche Analyse von Micha 1–5." *ZAW* 84:46–85.
 1972b "Redaktionsgeschichtliche Analyse von Micha 6–7." *ZAW* 84:182–212.

Luker, Lamontte M.
 1987 "Beyond Form Criticism: The Relation of Doom and Hope Oracles in Micah 2–6." *HAR* 11:285–301.

Mannheim, Karl
 1970 [1929] *Ideology and Utopia: An Introduction to the Sociology of Knowledge.* Trans. Louis Wirth and Edward Shils. New York: Harcourt, Brace and World.

Marin, Louis
 1973 *Utopiques: Jeux d'espaces.* Paris: Les Éditions de minuit.

Mason, Rex
 1991 *Micah, Nahum, Obadiah.* Old Testament Guides. Sheffield: JSOT Press.

Mays, James Luther
 1976 *Micah: A Commentary.* OTL. Philadelphia: Westminster.

McKane, William
 1995b "Micah 2:12–13." *JNSL* 21(2):83–91.

More, Thomas
 1964 [1516] *Utopia.* Ed. Edward Surtz, S.J. New Haven: Yale University Press.

Mosala, Itumeleng
 1989 *Biblical Hermeneutics and Black Theology in South Africa.* Grand Rapids: Eerdmans.

Moylan, Tom
 1982 "The Locus of Hope: Utopia Versus Ideology." *Science Fiction Studies* 9:159–66.

Pixley, George V.
 1991 "Micah—A Revolutionary." Pp. 53–60 in *The Bible and the Politics of Exegesis: Essays in Honor of Norman K. Gottwald on His Sixty-fifth Birthday.* Ed. David Jobling, Peggy L. Day, and Gerald T. Sheppard. Cleveland: Pilgrim.

Renaud, B.
 1977 *La Formation du livre de Michée.* Paris: Gabalda.

Ricoeur, Paul
 1986 *Lectures on Ideology and Utopia.* Ed. George H. Taylor. New York: Columbia University Press.

Shaw, Charles S.
 1993 *The Speeches of Micah: A Rhetorical-Historical Analysis.* JSOTSup 45. Sheffield: Sheffield Academic Press.

Waltke, Bruce
    1988   "Micah." Pp. 137–207 in *Obadiah, Jonah, and Micah.* Ed. D. J.Wiseman. TOTC 23a. Downers Grove, IL: Inter-Varsity.

Warrior, Robert Allen
    1989   "Canaanites, Cowboys and Indians: Deliverance, Conquest and Liberation Theology Today." *Christianity and Crisis* 49:261–65.

Willis, John T.
    1966   "The Structure, Settings, and Interrelationships of the Pericopes in the Book of Micah." Ph.D. diss., Vanderbilt University.
    1969a   "The Structure of Micah 3–5 and the Function of Micah 5, 9–14 in the Book." *ZAW* 81:191–214.
    1969b   "The Authenticity and Meaning of Micah 5, 9–14." *ZAW* 81:353–68.

Wolff, Hans Walter
    1990   *Micah: A Commentary.* Trans. Gary Stansell. Minneapolis: Ausburg.

IN JOB'S FACE/FACING JOB

Edward L. Greenstein

"Our notion of text governs how we read, what we look for, what we notice, and what we ignore...."—Robert C. Culley (23)

Commentators tend to admit that in God's speeches to Job from the whirlwind, there is no explicit answer to the challenging questions Job had raised throughout the poetic discourses. Job had sought to know the justification for his suffering, under the assumption that he was being punished for sins and transgressions that were known to God but not to him (e.g. Job 13:23). He wants to hear an explanation in God's own words (e.g. 23:5). When YHWH appears to him in the whirlwind, Job receives a response, but it is not the sort of answer Job had asked for. Is it an answer at all? My teacher H. L. Ginsberg suggested in class that having God speak past Job was

Readers of God's speech from the whirlwind tend to identify with God. They understand God's discourse as a proper—or at the least a necessary—defense of God's cosmic governance and even as the only response the Deity can give to a presumptuous Job. "When man cannot maintain his own righteousness, then he must not think that it is lawlessness which prevails in the world. He must subject himself to the mighty will of God, trusting to the *fact* [emphasis added] that man has *his* righteousness and God *his*; and when they do not harmonize, then it is not that God's justice goes against that of man and suspends it, but that it transcends it and goes deeper the poet's way of indicating that God had no answer (cf. e.g. Williams, 1971, 1978; Robertson; Whedbee; Hoffman). If there is an answer, in what way is it an answer? What kind of a response does Job receive?

Commentators have answered these questions variously. There would seem to be no limit to readers' responses. The whirlwind speeches, more than any other section of the book, appear in the diverse literature written about them like a readerly Rorschach test. Were we to seek to limit the range of possible readings of the whirlwind speeches, we might at least set down one rule, which those less readerly oriented than I call a textual constraint: our interpretation should not attribute to God any assessment that contradicts the one direct comment on Job's personal behavior and speech that YHWH makes: that Job has spoken correctly and that his companions have not (42:7; cf. e.g. Wilcox: 206).[1] We may not want to go as far as Williams (1971:236) and conclude that God is there condemning Godself, but it is clear that God is approving what Job has said. We are not bound to share God's view of Job—we may choose to condemn Job for mis-speaking—but it will be hard to find irony in this pronounce-

than man is able to penetrate" (Pedersen, 1926:373). While many critics do not assume that righteousness has anything to do with the Deity's response, they do tend to view God and God's appearance in a positive light. The following excerpt from the admirable commentary of Habel is fairly typical: "Yahweh appears to Job as he did to heroic figures like Noah and Abraham. The God of the heroic past is not an otiose high god who has returned into oblivion. . . . Job's heroic faith has provoked the *deus absconditus* into becoming the *deus revelatus*, even before Sinai" (Habel, 1985:527–28), and so on. In the revealed presence of God it is assumed that Job finds consolation for his sufferings (e.g. Brenner, 1981:137).

Thus, YHWH of the whirlwind discourse is for Habel, and many others (cf. most recently Whybray: 157–58), the God of the historic and "heroic" covenant and of revelation, as he is for many the God of creation and its mysteries (e.g. von Rad, 1972: 225; Habel, 1992). For Janzen (esp. 254–59), Job comes to "agree" with God that the human must take an active role in balancing the "dialectic" between "freedom" and "order" that is inherent in biblical creation. To justify God and to find Job to be ment by God.

It is by now fairly common-place to regard the divine speeches as ambiguous and enig-matic (e.g. Williams, 1978: 64; Brenner: 129). Two things have become clear to many: God almost entirely avoids or evades the question of justice, but at the same time demonstrates his own knowledge of nature's intricacies. Jung discerns the thrust of the God speeches, from the "grot-esque" challenge of the puny and afflicted Job by mighty YHWH— as though Job were a commen-surate rival—to his display of control, of power, over the forces of nature. God does not point to the morality of nature but precisely to its immorality. God as creator points not to his justice but to his power. Such an under-standing jibes with the fairly widespread assessment today, that God's rhetoric, in the form of questions that Job is not in a position to answer, does not have the effect merely of demonstra-ting to Job that his knowledge is small while God's knowledge is great. God's rhetoric beats Job down, making him feel, in a way, that the dungheap on which he sits is precisely where he belongs.

Yet, even readers who appreciate the ambiguities of the divine discourses, like Habel, seek a moral meaning to the fact

finally in agreement with God is, in the end, to take God's side. To take God's side is to favor the divine perspective over the one Job espoused throughout the dia-logues. Readers of the divine speeches, then, tend to identify with God, and for some, like Janzen, so does Job.

It is not enough that during the earlier chapters of the book, in the poetic dialogues with the friends, readers came to identify with Job, the paragon of integrity and courage, even though, as Clines points out, such identifi-cation is pure self-flattery. The reader is not in Job's league, neither in righteousness nor in courage. Nevertheless, readers deign to see themselves in Job.

In reading the speeches of God, as we have seen, people tend to step up their self-aggran-dizement and identify more with God's views than with those of Job, who is here presented not as a daring fighter with words but as a humiliated victim, who has, with God's blessing, suffered the worst forms of tragedy and on top of that ceaseless physical pain, and now severe disappoint-ment and demoralization. At the very best Job appears as a poor slob who can, thank God, be rehabilitated once he comes to see things God's way. In the all too common reading, Job is that God takes care of the wild animals: "The motif of providence for wild animals has its implied counterpart in Yahweh's concern for human life" (Habel, 1985:544; cf. e.g. LaCocque, 1996:139).[2] Notice the commentator's oblique acknowledgement of his own role in providing the logic of the inference: YHWH's "concern for human life" is "implied." It is an explicit product of the reader's will. In a more subtle line of argumentation, readers like Gordis have drawn an analogy between the "order and harmony in the natural world" and the presence of "order and meaning in the moral sphere, though often incomprehensible to man" (Gordis: 133). The analogy is the product of the interpreter's search for a moral message. This message may come, however, in the face of a relatively direct message from the Deity: that the world is morally neutral, that it contravenes the ethical expectations of Job and his friends, that it testifies to God's powers as creator and to his knowledge of its arcane curiosities.

Let us, with some of the critics, take another look at God's exhibits. The biblical doctrine of retribution finds one of its quintessential expressions in Deut 11:13–17. We read there that those who obey God's com-

brought to "repent" of his words, to undergo "self-humiliation," and to mortify" himself (Dhorme: 647).

Job has been sitting on the dungheap so long he is now treated as though he were a part of it. Ah, the power of metonymy. Now when I say, Job has been treated like dung, I do not mean only by God. God, after all, is only a character in the sad story. Everything about God is a product of what the poet has written (which we understand, I ought to add, only as we understand it) and what the reader has chosen to interpret. If Job is treated like dung, it is not really by God that Job is treated this way, it is by the reader that Job is treated like 'a piece of the dungheap.

Why would the reader want to treat Job that way? What could make a reader turn against Job? What might turn the reader from a champion of Job to a collaborator of Job's companions, who, like phony physicians, as Job says (מְפְלֵי שָׁקֶר; Job 13:4), offer only failed remedies that are meant to be efficacious because they are thought to be God's?

Does the reader who takes God's side in the face-off with Job succumb to a self-righteous impulse to see it God's way and assimilate to God? Is the mandments will enjoy "the rain of your land in its time" so that they can successfully grow their crops, feeding themselves and their animals. If the people stray from the divine instructions, God will shut down the sky in anger, holding back the life-sustaining rain.

The Deuteronomic formulation of the doctrine of retribution has a close echo in the divine speeches to Job (cf. LaCocque, 1981:37; Zemach: 16). In Job 38:25–26, God asks Job (shows Job how little he knows) about the rain: "Who splits open a channel for the downpour? A path for the thunderstorm? Bringing down rain on a land of no man—the desert without a human in it?" The Deity makes a point of the fact that God produces rain not as a reward to people for their good behavior but precisely in a place where no one lives. The rain is depicted not as a moral instrument of reward and punishment but precisely as a phenomenon that has nothing to do with human conduct. Many (e.g. Habel, 1985:542; Janzen: 238; LaCocque, 1996:140) read the passage positively: see how God cares about the uninhabited region! But there is no word here exuding care or providence. Control perhaps, power certainly, but not providence. One could make

adoption of the divine perspective a will to power, to perch oneself in the position of advantage *vis-à-vis* other humans, be they characters or real persons?

Or does the reader come to acknowledge one's own limits and begin to regard oneself as lowly, as Job is generally taken to do? Does the reader succumb to an impulse to be humiliated?[3] Does the reader exploit the act of reading for the sake of self-mortification, out of masochism? Or has the reader turned toward God because one has turned against Job?

Does Job's genuine righteousness unsettle the reader—intimidate, breed resentment? Do readers come to envy Job, who during the chapters of dialogues with the friends held fast to his integrity and won our admiration? Does our admiration need to sour and spoil, turning into contempt? Are we, following the dialogues and the bombast of Job's most junior colleague, Elihu, whose very name means "God is he," who does not hesitate to speak for God, who identifies with God, who, it turns out, even anticipates God in many points—are we just waiting for an opportunity to turn on Job, to participate in his humiliation, to show our contempt for someone who would dare to be better

a case for the positive interpretation were there an accompanying point about God providing rain for people. But that point
is not made. A different theological point is made: God rains
where people can receive no
benefit from it. Doesn't the
divine speaker turn the Torah's
doctrine of retribution on its
head? What prevents some
readers from seeing it? Perhaps
the other divine exhibits convey
the sense of a moral structure in
the world.

Let us examine another exhibit.[4] Eliphaz in his first response to Job presents a number of
images that reflect the ultimate
justice that, to his mind, characterizes reality. In one of them, the
lion, which violently lives off the
lives of less powerful animals,
ends up in old age with broken
teeth; as a result, he "perishes for
lack of prey, and the young lions
[i.e. the whelps who depend on
their parents for food], are
destroyed" (Job 4:10–11). Job, in
his speeches, relates to the cruel
violence of the lion as one of his
images of God. God hunts him
down (10:16), grabs him by his
nape, and mangles him (16:12; cf.
Williams, 1978:65). Which of
these two views of the lion will
the Lord adopt in the whirlwind
speech—that of Eliphaz, which
lays emphasis on the pathetic fate

than we will ever be?

Some recent commentators
claim that, no, readers of the
whirlwind speeches actually sym-
pathize with the much harrassed
Job. Robertson (1977: 48–49)
and Penchansky (1990: 52–53),
for example, acknowledge the
common perception that the Lord
in the addresses to Job seeks to
justify to this man this God's
behavior, but they find the effect
ironic: "Because Job has said he
would ask unanswerable questions, Job comes off as the wise
one and God seems wise only in
the sense of being evasively
cunning" (Robertson: 49). Readers, writes Penchansky (53),
"feel the depths of Job's sadness
and fear." What, then, is the
source, for these readers, of their
sympathy with Job? Is it because
he has proved his case that God's
treatment of him, and anyone else
who might be like him, was
unjustified and wrong? Is it
because he has stood his ground
before the Deity, thereby demonstrating again his integrity and
courage?

For Robertson (51–53), it is
because Job had been right about
God all along. Between the two
of them, God (who, we know
from the Prologue, is operating
altogether outside the realm of
good and evil, but out of selfish,
or personal, interests only, to

of the lion, or that of Job, in which God empathizes with the king of beasts?

In Job 38:39 God asks Job: "Is it you who goes on the hunt for prey for the lion, satisfying the appetite of lions?" The clear implication is: It is I who go hunting for food for the lion. Job had characterized God as a lion-like hunter, and this is precisely the image that God projects here. Habel (1985:544) observes the apparent contradiction between "Yahweh's concern for lions" and "the principle of retribution which Eliphaz found operating in the destruction of the lioness and her whelps." And yet, Habel in his very next sentence suggests the analogy between God's explicit care for animals and a putatively implicit care for humans.

Habel, like Job's friends, wants to speak for God, supplying the expression of divine providence for people that is so sorely lacking in the whirlwind speeches. The lack becomes even more evident when one compares a text like Psalm 104, another, but very different, inventory of God's providence in creation. There, too, God is said to provide food for "the lions who roar out for prey" (Ps 104:21). But in the psalm, a sensitive balance is struck between God's care for the

prove a point to one of his agents, the satan) and Job (who, we know from the Prologue, is "innocent and upright, one who fears God and turns away from evil," as the narrator says [1:1] and as God says [1:8]), only one can, as in a lawsuit, be in the right. Thus, Job, who, honest to a fault, could find nothing wrong in himself, attributed corruption to God, for example: "If I were in the right, his mouth [reading פיו for פי with many commentators; e.g. Fohrer: 199] would condemn me; Though I were innocent, he would aggrieve me. . . . If I were to wash with soap-plant, Cleanse my hands with lye, He would plunge me in the mud—Even my clothes would despise me!" (9:20, 30). And God claims to interpret Job's accusations as nothing but recrimination: "Do you deny my justice and condemn me so that you may appear in the right?" (40:8).

For Penchansky (53), the reader's sympathy stems from pity: "The reader mourns with Job as he cowers before a superior power." Penchansky assumes, as do nearly all translators and commentators, that in his responses to God after the first and second parts of the whirlwind speeches, Job capitulates, "cowers," as Penchansky says. Robertson adopts the same literal earth and its animals and God's concern for human beings. We read there, for example, of how God "makes grass grow for the cattle, herbage for human use, bringing food out of the ground; and wine to gladden a person's heart, brightening his face more even than oil, and food for a person to dine" (vv. 14–15).

God's relations to nature in the whirlwind discourse represent control, not care; they are amoral (cf. in general Tsevat). Compare the features of some of the other animals God adduces. God feeds the young of the raven, which is known for preying on other wildlife (38:41). God heeds their cry (שׁוע) for food, but not Job's cry (שׁוע) for justice (19:7; cf. Habel, 1985:544). The wild ass is set free (חפשׁי) by God (39:5), whereas, as Job has pointed out (cf. Habel, 1985:545–46), the human slave is free (חפשׁי) of his master only in the grave (3:19b). This wild ass lives in the steppe (39:6), where "he need never hear the shouts of a driver (נגשׂ)" (39:7). How much more miserable the fate of a human prisoner, bound in fetters, who only in death "will no longer hear the voice of the taskmaster (נגשׂ)" (3:18).

Or consider the ostrich, which abandons its young and ruthlessly leaves them to the menaces of understanding of Job's words as Penchansky and the others do (51), but he hears in them an ironic tone (52); Job capitulates "tongue-in-cheek" "in order to calm God's whirlwinds." Robertson's detection of Job's irony is, of course, inconclusive, and Penchansky speaks for many, in fact nearly everyone, in observing that the meaning of Job's words is "ambiguous," bedeviled by "linguistic usages inaccessible to modern interpreters" (53). If so, then why does Penchansky, along with everyone else, choose to read Job's words as the expression of resignation rather than resistance? Why interpret Job's reply one way when the text is at least "ambiguous," meaning there is another way to do it?

The crucial passage, as commentators indicate, is Job's second response, in 42:2–6, and the final verse in that brief pericope in particular: על כן אמאס ונחמתי על עפר ואפר.

This is the problematic text. For a summary of philological interpretations, see Curtis, Morrow, Dailey (127–29), and van Wolde (242–50). The first major difficulty relates to the verb אמאס which virtually all commentators insist is transitive and "must have an object" (Good, 1990:376; cf. e.g. Driver and Gray: 2.348; Habel, 1985:576). Under this nature (39:13–16; cf. Lam 4:3). Why does she behave in this manifestly callous manner? "Because God has taken her mind off wisdom, given her no share of understanding" (v. 17). She is the way she is because God has made her that way. And that is the very point of the God speeches. The world is the way it is because that is how God wants it. It is part of the divine plan that the young of the ostrich will be left for larger animals to trample underfoot (39:15). What is the message in that for Job?

For Habel (1985:547), the ostrich's behavior "is the exception which tests and interprets the rule." But is the ostrich different from the rest of creation, or a representative instance of it? Is the ostrich, perhaps, a reflection of its creator? That possibility will seem not at all unlikely when one moves to the next divine discourse and considers, with Job, the nature of the Behemoth and the Leviathan.

The second of YHWH's addresses to Job dilates primarily on descriptions of the two great, primordial (40:19) beasts. These beasts are not characterized by goodness but by their terrifying power (cf. e.g. Good, 1990:369). At the beginning of this discourse, God bellows: "Do you dare challenge my justice, con-

assumption, commentators go hunting for the supposedly missing object. Some find the object in the following words, such as "dust and ashes" (e.g. Patrick; Good, 1992:67–68; Dailey: 137–38), but most find the object in the reader's imagination, feeling that Job must have rejected his own words (e.g. Kuyper; Pope: 289–90; Tur-Sinai: 578)[5]—or despised himself (e.g. Gordis: 120; Humphreys: 115). Readers have Job taking back his words in spite of the unambiguous assertion of the Deity that Job has spoken correctly (42:7). Although some stalwart adherents of the view that Job has recanted interpret God's statement to refer only to the last thing Job said, that is, that he was sorry for mis-speaking (so most recently Whybray: 172), that interpretation does not sit well with the fact that it is incorporated into an address to Eliphaz and Job's other interlocutors. The contrast between their mis-speaking and Job's on-the-mark discourse must refer to what Job said in the dialogues, which is the only context in which such a contrast would make sense.

Job's words in 42:6 should therefore accord with Job's theological views in the dialogues (cf. Miles: 324). After all, nothing God has said or shown him in the demning me so that you seem in the right?" (40:8). But it is not to testify to God's justice that the Behemoth is displayed. It is brought forth in an obvious though indirect answer to God's very next question to Job (40:9): "Have you an arm as powerful as God's? Can you thunder as loud as he?"

The Behemoth is the very quintessence of brute strength: "See how its power is in its loins, its strength in the muscles of its torso!" (40:16). Its limbs are made of iron and bronze (v. 18). The only one who can approach and control it is God, and even he must do it with a weapon (v. 19). The image appears calculated to intimidate a man like Job. Why, he could not even pierce its nose with a hook, much less ensnare and tug on it (v. 24). This image provides a transition to the Leviathan, another creature Job could not even put a hook into (vv. 25–26).

The terrifying nature of the Behemoth is only implied. The dread surrounding the Leviathan, whose body is a veritable suit of impregnable armor (41:5ff.), is spelled out: "Who can take position before him?" (41:2). "His teeth are surrounded by terror!" (v. 6). Even "the gods are in dread when he rears, in dismay when he thrashes" (41:17). YHWH

whirlwind discourses has contradicted the essential claims that Job has made (see the parallel discussion). Good would seem much closer to the mark in interpreting Job in 42:6 to say that his "repenting of dust and ashes" means that he has abandoned his belief or expectation that the world is governed by a principle of moral retribution (1992:68). I find, however, no independent basis for taking "dust and ashes" to be a biblical metonym for "the entire religious structure of guilt and repentance."

It is my philological conviction that words, phrases, and figures should, wherever possible, be interpreted according to established meanings or in the light of known references. Biblical literature, like ancient Near Eastern literature in general, even in highly poetic texts like Job, operates within known conventions and not through idiosyncratic inventions. Words and phrases may be used differently, but their new meanings will then result from new synthesis or through transformation of the conventional.

"Dust and ashes" will then mean what it does in Job 30:19: "I have become like dust and ashes." It is a figure for the debased human condition, just as it is in its apparent literary source, asks Job if he can "play with it (התשחק בו) like a bird" (40:29). The question is not innocent. Its language is a plain allusion to Ps 104:26, where God is said to have "fashioned the Leviathan so as to play with it (לשחק בו)" (cf. e.g. Habel, 1985: 573). For Job the Leviathan is unapproachable. For God it is a plaything.

In Genesis 1, God creates the "great sea-monsters" (התנינם הגדלים; v. 21), but only the human beings are made in God's own image (vv. 26–27). In the whirlwind speeches, God describes the Leviathan as a partial reflex of himself. The Leviathan is described, among other things, with "torches running out of his mouth, fiery flames flaring out; smoke coming out of his nostrils . . . his throat burns with coals, a flame flashing out of his mouth" (41:11–13). The description is familiar not from characterizations of the Leviathan but from the famous image of YHWH in Ps 18:9 (cf. 2 Sam 22:9): "Smoke rises in his nostrils, consuming fire from his mouth, coals burning forth from him." The Leviathan is in part an image of God.

Williams (1971:246) and Robertson (1977:50–51) have already concluded that the Behemoth and the Leviathan, as well as the other creatures made by God, are reflexes, symbols, of

Gen 18:27, where Abraham says: "Here, I have deigned to speak to My Lord, though I am dust and ashes," that is, human (cf. Curtis: 501). Job is "sorry about" (נחמתי על) the way it is for humans (see Curtis; cf. Miles: 324–25).

It remains for us to interpret the verb אמאס which, as was said, is generally parsed as transitive (or emended; see Morrow). In Job, the verb מאס in the Qal conjugation is, contrary to the oft-repeated claims, sometimes intransitive (elsewhere in 7:16; 34:33; 36:5), and it sometimes has the meaning it ordinarily does in the Nif'al, *viz.*, "to be fed up" (Givati: 138). Cf. 7:16: מאסתי לא לעלם אחיה חדל ממני כי הבל ימי, which we may tentatively render: "I've had it! I won't live forever. Let me alone for my days are only a breath!"

Job then in this reading does not capitulate at all, but continues to express the same despair he has been expressing all along. Yes, Job had heard about God with his ears and has now been privileged to see God with his own eyes (42:5). But what he has learned is what he has already known: "I know that you can do anything, that you cannot be stopped from any scheme" (42:2). That this acknowledgement is not a token of admiration their creator. Their brute power and terrifying nature are, then, the qualities that stand out in the whirlwind theology.

And it is precisely these divine qualities that were already discerned by Job. Job had nearly from the outset described God as "Wise in heart and sturdy in strength . . . Who moves mountains without their knowing, who overturns them in his rage; who shakes the earth from its setting, so that its pillars fall apart; who orders the sun not to shine, puts a seal over the stars; spreads the sky all alone, and tramples the back of god-Sea . . ." (9:4–8). In addition to being impressed with God's sheer, morally irrelevant power, Job is impressed with God's terror: "(Would there were a magistrate) who would remove (God's punishing) rod from upon me, (remove) his dread that it would not terrify me; then I could speak and not fear him" (9:33–34).

By showing Job the vast extent of God's power and terror in the whirlwind discourses, in addition to brow-beating Job with "impossible questions" (Humphreys: 112), God has indeed succeeded in shutting Job up: "I am so lightweight! How can I answer you? I place my hand over my mouth. I've spoken once—I'll speak up no more;

(so, e.g. Andersen: 291) but one of contempt is clear, or ought to be, from the fact that the latter clause in this statement is a parody of what God himself had said in Gen 11:6b concerning the builders of Babel (see Greenstein: 254).

It is true that in 42:3 Job admits that he "spoke of things without really understanding, of wondrous things without really knowing." But nowhere in this admission does he indicate that what he said was wrong, that he had mis-spoken. He rather corrects his earlier claim that he had "seen all" and gained real "understanding" through his hearing (Job 13:1–2). Job's evidence was more limited than he had thought; but nothing God has told or shown him has required a revision of his theological claims. God has finally answered Job, but the answer has only confirmed what he had feared to be the case all along, exactly what he did not want to hear.

The implication of our analysis of Job's final reply, according to which Job may resign himself to the way things are but cannot come to a different understanding of things, is clear. If readers wish to see Job as the same man of integrity and courage that they had found him to be in the dialogues, they have spoken twice—I'll say no more" (40:4–5).

The result is to silence Job, but not to tell him anything he did not know (cf. e.g. Polzin: 105). It has been argued that God points to Behemoth and Leviathan in order to teach Job a lesson (Kinnier Wilson; cf. Habel, 1985:574; Good 1990: 365–68): that Job cannot subordinate the great monsters. But Job had never contended that he could control such a power as the Leviathan. That he always knew. Why would any reader want to suggest that Job needed to learn that? The answer seems obvious. One has assumed God's point of view. One has, like many readers, begun to take God's questions at face value, as though they were truly meant to elicit information. But they do not elicit new knowledge, for God knows what Job knows about God. God only has more evidence, and he flaunts it in Job's face. In the end he can only confirm what Job had said.

a basis for doing so. Job's words need hardly be taken as surrender. But translators and commentators who have been in a position to find Job to stand his ground, to acknowledge that the text's ambiguity could be read in line with Job's views rather than God's, have not done so. Thus, one of the most recent and sophisticated discussants of our passage, van Wolde, begins by pointing to the ambiguities in Job 42:1–6 and concludes by having Job "recognize [. . .] YHWH's way of looking." She chooses to interpret such that Job sees things God's way when all along he has been maintaining an independent critical stance. One can only wonder why one would want to have Job surrender his autonomy when one is free to do otherwise.

Notes

[1]　The Lord's remark in 42:7 is often reconciled with a critique of Job by reading it as if it were from a conflicting textual source; cf. recently Newsom (133). Job, in this view, spoke properly in the frame-tale, not in the dialogues.

[2]　Whybray (161) sees in God's "loving care" for wild animals a message to humanity that it should not overestimate its own importance to God. Whybray does not reckon with the tension between this view of God and the covenantal view in the Torah.

[3]　I am not interested here in discussing the Christian perspective (e.g. Williams, 1992:226–28, relating to R. Girard) wherein Job is a prefiguration of the victimized Jesus and God is the God of the victims; such a God is hardly the one who appears in the whirlwind speeches in Job.

[4]　My discussion here has benefited from a fine paper by my former student David Booth, written at the Jewish Theological Seminary of America, Spring 1996.

[5]　Whybray (171) suggests a variation on this interpretation: Job "rejects" "his earlier apprehension about God that had led him to challenge him."

Bibliography

Andersen, Francis I.
1975　　　　*Job: An Introduction and Commentary.* Tyndale Bible Commentary. Leicester: Inter-Varsity.

Brenner, Athalya
1981　　　　"God's Answer to Job." *VT* 31:129–37.

Clines, David J. A.
1990　　　　"Deconstructing the Book of Job." Pp. 106–23 in *What Does Eve Do to Help? And Other Readerly Questions to the Old Testament.* JSOTSup 94. Sheffield: Sheffield Academic Press.

Culley, Robert C.
1993　　　　"Psalm 102: A Complaint with a Difference." *Semeia* 62:19–35.

Curtis, John B.
　　　　　　"On Job's Response to Yahweh." *JBL* 98:497–511.

Dailey, Thomas F.
1994　　　　*The Repentant Job: A Ricoeurian Icon for Biblical Theology.* Lanham: University Press of America.

Dhorme, Eduard.
1967　　　　*A Commentary on the Book of Job.* Trans. Harold Knight. London: Thomas Nelson.

Driver, Samuel R., and George B. Gray
1921　　　　*A Critical and Exegetical Commentary on the Book of Job.* 2 vols. ICC. New York: Scribner's Sons.

Fohrer, Georg
1963　　　　*Das Buch Hiob.* KAT. Gütersloh.

Givati, Meir
    1979   "Explicit and Implicit Irony in the Speeches of Job." Pp. 130–
                39 in *The Ben-Zion Luria Volume*. The Israel Society for
                Biblical Research. Jerusalem: Kiriath Sepher [in Hebrew].

Good, Edwin M.
    1990   *In Turns of Tempest: A Reading of Job with a Translation*.
                Stanford: Stanford University Press.
    1992   "The Problem of Evil in the Book of Job." Pp. 50–69 in *The
                Voice from the Whirlwind: Interpreting the Book of Job*. Ed.
                Leo G. Perdue and W. Clark Gilprin. Nashville: Abingdon.

Gordis, Robert
    1965   *The Book of God and Man: A Study of Job*. Chicago: Univer-
                sity of Chicago Press.

Greenstein, Edward L.
    1996   "A Forensic Understanding of the Speech from the
                Whirlwind." Pp. 241–58 in *Texts, Temples, and Traditions: A
                Tribute to Menahem Haran*. Ed. Michael V. Fox *et al*. Winona
                Lake: Eisenbrauns.

Habel, Norman C.
    1985   *The Book of Job*. OTL. Philadelphia: Westminster
    1992   "In Defense of God the Sage." Pp. 21–38 in *The Voice from
                the Whirlwind: Interpreting the Book of Job*. Ed. Leo G.
                Perdue and W. Clark Gilprin. Nashville: Abingdon.

Hoffman, Yair
    1982   "Irony as a Central Means of Expression in the Book of Job."
                Pp. 157–74 in *Bible Studies: Y. M. Grintz in Memoriam*. Ed
                Benjamin Uffenheimer (= *Te'uda* 2) [in Hebrew].

Humphreys, W. Lee
    1985   *The Tragic Vision and the Hebrew Tradition*. Philadelphia:
                Fortress Press.

Janzen, J. Gerald
    1985   *Job*. Interpretation. Atlanta: John Knox.

Jung, C. G.
    1969   *Answer to Job*. Trans. R. F. C. Hull. Princeton: Princeton
                University Press.

Kinnier Wilson, John
    1975   "A Return to the Problem of Behemoth and Leviathan." *VT*
                25:1–14.

Kuyper, Lester J.
    1959   "The Repentance of Job." *VT* 9:91–94.

LaCocque, André
    1981   "Job or the Impotence of Religion and Philosophy." *Semeia*
                19:33–52.
    1996   "Job and Religion at Its Best." *BibInt* 4:131–53.

Miles, Jack
    1995   *God: A Biography*. New York: Alfred A. Knopf.

Morrow, William
    1986   "Consolation, Rejection, and Repentance in Job 42:6." *JBL* 105:211–25.

Newsom, Carol A.
    1993   "Cultural Politics and the Reading of Job." *BibInt* 1:119–38.

Patrick, Dale
    1976   "The Translation of Job XLII 6." *VT* 26:369–71.

Pedersen, Johannes
    1926   *Israel: Its Life and Culture I-II*. Oxford: Oxford University Press.

Penchansky, David
    1990   *The Betrayal of God: Ideological Conflict in Job*. Louisville: Westminster/John Knox.

Polzin, Robert M.
    1977   *Biblical Structuralism: Method and Subjectivity in the Study of Ancient Texts*. Philadelphia: Fortress Press; Missoula: Scholars Press.

Pope, Marvin H.
    1965   *Job*. Anchor Bible. Garden City: Doubleday.

Rad, Gerhard von
    1972   *Wisdom in Israel*. Trans. James D. Martin. London: SCM.

Robertson, David
    1977   *The Old Testament and the Literary Critic*. Philadelphia: Fortress Press.

Tsevat, Matitiahu
    1980   "The Meaning of the Book of Job." Pp. 1–37 in *The Meaning of the Book of Job and Other Biblical Studies*. New York and Dallas: Ktav/Institute for Jewish Studies.

Tur-Sinai, N. H.
    1967   *The Book of Job: A New Commentary*. Rev. Ed. Jerusalem: Kiryath Sepher.

Whedbee, William
    1977   "The Comedy of Job." *Semeia* 7:1–39.

Whybray, Norman
    1998   *Job*. Readings. Sheffield: Sheffield Academic Press.

Wilcox, John T.
    1989   *The Bitterness of Job*. Ann Arbor: University of Michigan Press.

Williams, James G.
    1971   "'You Have Not Spoken Truth of Me': Mystery and Irony in Job." *ZAW* 83:231–55.

1978   "Deciphering the Unspoken: The Theophany of Job." *HUCA*
              49:59–72.
1992   "Job and the God of Victims." Pp. 208–31 in *The Voice from
              the Whirlwind: Interpreting the Book of Job*. Ed. Leo G.
              Perdue and W. Clark Gilprin. Nashville: Abingdon.

Wolde, E. J. van
1994   "Job 42, 1–6: The Reversal of Job." Pp. 223–50 in *The Book of
              Job*. Ed. W. A. M. Beuken. Leuven: Leuven University Press
              and Uitgevereij Peeters.

Zemach, Eddy
1989   "What Did God Answer Job?" *Moznayim* 61/9:14–17 [in
              Hebrew].